THE FACSIMILE LIBRARY

Other titles in preparation

THE LITERARY HISTORY

OF THE

AMERICAN REVOLUTION

1763—1783

BY

MOSES COIT TYLER

Sometime Professor at the University of Michigan
and at Cornell University

With an Introduction by
RANDOLPH GREENFIELD ADAMS
Director of William L. Clements Library
Ann Arbor, Michigan

———

VOLUME I
1763—1776

———

Published for
FACSIMILE LIBRARY, INC.
BARNES & NOBLE, Inc., NEW YORK

TO

JEANNETTE GILBERT TYLER

THIS BOOK

IS

LOVINGLY DEDICATED

BY

HER HUSBAND

PREFACE

THERE would, perhaps, be no injustice in describing this book as the product of a new method, at least of a method never before so fully applied, in the critical treatment of the American Revolution. The outward history of that famous procedure has been many times written, and is now, by a new breed of American scholars, being freshly rewritten in the light of larger evidence, and under the direction of a more disinterested and a more judicial spirit. In the present work, for the first time in a systematic and a fairly complete way, is set forth the inward history of our Revolution—the history of its ideas, its spiritual moods, its motives, its passions, even of its sportive caprices and its whims, as these uttered themselves at the time, whether consciously or not, in the various writings of the two parties of Americans who promoted or resisted that great movement.

The plan of the author has been to let both parties in the controversy—the Whigs and the Tories, the Revolutionists and the Loyalists—tell their own story freely in their own way, and without either of them being liable, at our hands, to posthumous outrage in the shape of partisan imputations on their sincerity, their magnanimity, their patriotism, or their courage. Moreover, for the purpose of historic interpretation, the author has recognized the value of the lighter, as well as of the graver, forms of literature, and consequently has here given full room to the lyrical, the humorous, and the satirical aspects of our Revolutionary record—its songs, ballads, sarcasms, its literary facetiæ. The entire body of American writings, from 1763 to 1783, whether serious or mirthful, in prose or in verse, is here delineated in its most characteristic examples, for the purpose of exhibiting the several stages of thought and emotion through which the American people passed during the two decades of the struggle which resulted in our national Independence.

By comparison, then, with the usual way of dealing with the subject, this study of the American Revolution brings about a somewhat different adjustment of its causal forces, of its instruments, its sequences, its acts, and its actors. The proceedings of legislative bodies, the doings of cabinet ministers and of colonial politicians, the movements of armies, are not here altogether disregarded, but they are here subordinated: they are mentioned, when mentioned at all, as mere external incidents in connection with the ideas and the emotions which lay back of them or in front of them, which caused them or were caused by them. One result of this method, also, is an entirely new distribution of the tokens of historic prominence—of what is called fame—among the various participants in that very considerable business. Instead of fixing our eyes almost exclusively, as is commonly done, upon statesmen and generals, upon party leaders, upon armies and navies, upon Congress, upon parliament, upon the ministerial agents of a brain-sick king, or even upon that brain-sick king himself, and instead of viewing all these people as the sole or the principal movers and doers of the things that made the American Revolution, we here for the most part turn our eyes away toward certain persons hitherto much neglected, in many cases wholly forgotten—toward persons who, as mere writers, and whether otherwise prominent or not, nourished the springs of great historic events by creating and shaping and directing public opinion during all that robust time; who, so far as we here regard them, wielded only spiritual weapons; who still illustrate, for us and for all who choose to see, the majestic operation of ideas, the creative and decisive play of spiritual forces, in the development of history, in the rise and fall of nations, in the aggregation and the division of races. Accordingly, in this particular history of the American Revolution, our heroes are such, not because they were mighty ministers of state, or mighty politicians and law-makers, or mighty generals; our heroes are such, chiefly, because they were mere penmen—only essayists, pamphleteers, sermon writers, song writers, tale tellers, or satirists, the study of whose work, it is believed, may open to us a view of the more delicate and elusive, but not less profound or less real, forces which made that period so great, and still so worthy of being truly understood by us. Finally, as we have here to do, not so much with the old, official, and conspicuous actors in the Revolution as, in many cases, with its unseen, its unofficial, and its almost unremembered ones,—as we here concern ourselves less frequently with the political and military chiefs of that stormy transaction, and more frequently with its literary chiefs,—so, also, are we here brought into a rather direct and familiar acquaintance with the American people themselves, on both sides of the dispute, as, sitting at their firesides or walking in their streets, they were actually stirred to thought and passion by the arrival of the daily budget of news touching an affair of incomparable moment to themselves. Just what this book aims to be, then, is a presentation of the soul, rather than of the body, of the American Revolution; a careful, independent, and, if possible, an unbiased register of the very brain and heart of the sorely divided people of the land, as these wrought, and rejoiced, and suffered, in the progress of those tremendous political and military events which constitute the exterior and visible framework of our heroic age.

Often, while engaged in the studies upon which this book is founded, and now, still more deeply, as I pass in final review their formulated results, have I been impressed by the tragedy and the pathos of the period between 1763 and 1783, as the birth time of a most bitter race feud—a race feud implacable, perhaps, and endless, but altogether needless; of a fatal disagreement between the two great branches of a race which, at this moment, holds an historic position in the world and an historic opportunity, not only the most extensive and the most splendid, but the most benignant, that was ever attained by any similar group of human beings upon this planet. To show that this race feud need not, after all, be an endless one, that already its fierceness has had expression enough, and that its wrath has now too long outlasted the going down of the sun; in short, to bring together once more into sincere friendship, into a rational and a sympathetic moral unity, these divided members of a family capable, if in substantial harmony, of leading the whole human race upward to all the higher planes of culture and happiness,—this is an object which, in our time, draws into its service the impassioned desires, the hopes, the prayers, the labors, of many of the noblest men and women in Great Britain and in America. I must confess that, in the book now offered to the public, I have written a new history of the origin and growth and culmination of this race feud, so far as I am able to do so, in the simple service of historic truth, and without permitting myself to be turned this way or that by any consideration touching the practical consequences that might result either from fidelity or from infidelity to my duty as an historian. At the same time, I now greatly mistake the case, if one practical consequence of this history, so far as it may find readers at all, shall not be eirenic, rather than polemic,—namely, the promotion of a better understanding, of a deeper respect, of a kindlier mood, on both sides of the ocean, among the descendants of those determined men who so bitterly differed in opinion, so fiercely fought, and, in their anger, so widely parted company, a century and a quarter ago.

In the researches which the present work has required—researches that have been in progress, though with many interruptions, for more than twenty years—I have been aided directly and indirectly by many persons, whose kindness, gratefully recognized at the time, I here publicly commemorate in this general acknowledgment; but, for special help, particularly in the discovery or in the use of rare literary materials, I desire to express my deep obligations to Mr. F. D. Stone, of the library of the Pennsylvania Historical Society; to Mr. Paul Leicester Ford, of Brooklyn; to Mr. Franklin Burdge, of New York; to Mr. Wilberforce Eames, of the Lenox Library; to Mr. William Kelby, of the library of the New York Historical Society; to Professor Franklin B. Dexter, of Yale University; to Mr. John Nicholas Brown, of Providence; to Mr. William E. Foster, of the Providence Public Library; to Mr. Edmund M. Barton, of the library of the American Antiquarian Society; to Mr. Charles A. Cutter, formerly librarian of the Boston Athenæum, and to Mr. William C. Lane, the present librarian of that institution; to Dr. Justin Winsor, the librarian of Harvard University; to Mr. F. L. Kiernan, superintendent of circulation in the Harvard library; and to Dr. Samuel Abbot Green, of the library of the Massachusetts Historical Society. Of course, during many years, I have had innumerable occasions, in the prosecution of my work, to tax the unfailing courtesy and helpfulness of Mr. George William Harris, the librarian of the University with which I am connected. To its assistant librarian, also, Mr. Willard Austin, I am greatly indebted for his patient and expert assistance in revising the proof-sheets of this book.

M. C. T.

CORNELL UNIVERSITY,
24 January, 1897.

CONTENTS.

THE FIRST VOLUME: 1763-1776.

CHAPTER I.

LITERARY ASPECTS OF THE PERIOD OF THE REVOLUTION.

CHAPTER II.

THE PRELUDE OF POLITICAL DEBATE: 1761–1764.

CHAPTER III.

UNDER THE MENACE OF THE STAMP ACT: NOVEMBER, 1774–APRIL, 1765.

CHAPTER IV.

THE AMERICAN DEBATE AS ENLIVENED BY A BRITISH PAMPHLETEER : 1765.

CHAPTER V.

THE STAMP ACT AS A STIMULANT TO POLITICAL DISCUSSION : AUGUST, 1765–JANUARY, 1766.

CHAPTER VI.

AN EARLY PULPIT-CHAMPION OF COLONIAL RIGHTS: 1766.

CHAPTER VII.

DESCRIPTIONS OF NATURE AND MAN IN THE AMERICAN WILDERNESS: 1763–1775.

CHAPTER VIII.

BEGINNINGS OF NEW LIFE IN VERSE AND PROSE: PHILADELPHIA, PRINCETON, AND NEW YORK: 1763-1775.

CHAPTER IX.

BEGINNINGS OF NEW LIFE IN VERSE AND PROSE: NEW ENGLAND.
1763-1775.

CHAPTER X.

THE REKINDLING OF THE GREAT DISPUTE: 1766-1769.

CHAPTER XI.

BRITISH TEA AS A POLITICAL INTOXICANT IN AMERICA : 1770–1774.

CHAPTER XII.

THE SUMMONS FOR A GREAT AMERICAN COUNCIL: MAY–SEPTEMBER, 1774.

CHAPTER XIII.

THE PARTY OF THE LOYALISTS AND THEIR LITERATURE.

CHAPTER XIV.

LOYALIST SERMON WRITERS: JONATHAN BOUCHER.

CHAPTER XV.

THE LOYALISTS IN ARGUMENT AGAINST THE MEASURES OF THE FIRST CONGRESS—THE "WESTCHESTER FARMER": NOVEMBER, 1774– APRIL, 1775.

CHAPTER XVI.

THE LOYALISTS IN ARGUMENT AGAINST THE MEASURES OF THE FIRST CONGRESS : " MASSACHUSETTENSIS."

CHAPTER XVII.

THE LOYALISTS IN ARGUMENT AGAINST THE MEASURES OF THE FIRST CONGRESS : JOSEPH GALLOWAY.

CHAPTER XIX.

THE ENTRANCE OF SATIRE INTO THE REVOLUTIONARY CONTROVERSY: PHILIP FRENEAU, 1775.

CHAPTER XX.

THE SATIRICAL MASTERPIECE OF JOHN TRUMBULL: 1775.

CHAPTER XXI.

THOMAS PAINE AND THE OUTBREAK OF THE DOCTRINE OF INDEPENDENCE: JANUARY–JUNE, 1776.

CHAPTER XXII.

THE POPULAR DEBATE OVER THE PROPOSAL OF INDEPENDENCE : JANUARY–JUNE, 1776.

CHAPTER XXIII.

THOMAS JEFFERSON AND THE GREAT DECLARATION.

ERRATA

p. 31 (II), l. 7—*read:* Charles the Second

p. 80, l. 3—*read:* engendure

p. 175, l. 7—*read:* decks

p. 328 (Footnote 2), l. 18—*read:* Mr. Locker-Lampson

p. 363 (IV), l. 1—*read:* groundlessness

p. 393, l. 33—*read:* hands

p. 499, ¶1, l. 6—*read:* original

INTRODUCTION

It is appropriate that an introduction to a new edition of one of Moses Coit Tyler's histories of American literature should be written in Ann Arbor, for he enrolled as a student at the University of Michigan in 1852, after a boyhood spent in and around Detroit. Moreover, it was during the years he taught at the University, 1867-1873, 1874-1881, that he delivered the lectures which form the basis for his monumental work. The first two volumes relating to American literature in colonial times appeared while he was a professor of English literature at the University of Michigan; the two volumes on the literature of the American Revolution were published after he had moved on to Cornell University.

In Tyler's day, such a thing as a "professor of American literature" was unheard of. Even today American literature is taught in "departments of English." But today at least we do have that for which Tyler worked—professorships and courses in American literature. At Michigan, Tyler taught English *and* American history *and* literature. Today in Ann Arbor, there are two members of the faculty of professorial rank in the department of English, who are teaching American literature alone, and there are five of professorial rank in the history department who are teaching American history alone. Such has been the growth of our appreciation of the subjects in which Tyler was a pioneer. This growth, of course, can be matched at any of our leading universities.

It is interesting to observe that even before Tyler became a profound student of his subject in this country, he had already been a successful lecturer in England on the subject of American culture. We used to hear the fatuous question, "Who reads an American book?" The answer was then, and always had been "Englishmen."

It was in London in 1865 that Tyler wrote in his commonplace book,

"It strikes me as a capital plan to write six or eight elaborate lectures on 'The History of American Literature' — for a purely literary audience and with a view to publication."

The "six or eight lectures" grew until they became four volumes, the latter two of which are now reprinted.

As his biographers have said, Tyler yearned "to use literature as an instrument whereby students might be led to an understanding of the national culture." He certainly became one of the greatest teachers of the history of American culture. When he came to Ann Arbor, as James Barrill Angell said,

"He was already master of that attractive style which lent such a charm to everything that he wrote and inspired his classes with a love for the best in literature . . . In his private study he was already showing that deep interest in American History and the early American authors which gave shape and colour to his later works. He had a fine sense of humour which enlivened his instruction and made him a most agreeable companion."

It is always a question as to how much good a teacher really does, and whether students are really inspired by brilliant teachers. Both teachers and students disagree on this point. However, Tyler found one disciple in a young junior in the engineering school, who deliberately elected courses in literature and history. The student's name was William L. Clements. He had been born on the campus of the University, and had lived his boyhood in Ann Arbor while Tyler was making his name and reputation in the same town. The student went on to a successful career in business, but like many another American business man, he found his greatest pleasure in life in the reading and contemplation of books. He began to collect the books of which Tyler had talked, and from his book-collecting grew the library of Americana at the University of Michigan from which these lines are being written.

Nearly a quarter century after Professor Tyler's death, Mr. Clements gave his library to his University. Sitting one day in the Rare Book Room, he selected from the shelves a worn but precious book, a classic of early American literature, "that blazing and sulphurous poem," *The Day of Doom,* by Michael Wigglesworth. So popular was that book that today no perfect copy of either the first or second edition is known to exist. It was from a copy of the so-called sixth edition (Boston, 1715) that Mr. Clements began to read. He called in the members of the library staff and insisted that they gather around him and listen to his reading. Of course he selected that well known passage where the infant damned appear before the throne of the Almighty on Judgment Day and plead that it was not their fault that they had gone "from the womb unto the tomb" before they had a chance to redeem themselves from Original Sin. The Almighty, in this case, was evidently so impressed with the justice of the children's cause that he almost relented, but then recovered himself and boomed forth,

> "You sinners are, and such a share
>   as sinners may expect,
> Such you shall have; for I do save
>   none but my own Elect.
> Yet to compare your sin with their
>   who liv'd a longer time,
> I do confess yours is much less,
>   though every sin's a crime.
> A Crime it is, therefore in bliss
>   you may not hope to dwell;
> But unto you I shall allow
>   the easiest room in Hell."

"But," concluded Mr. Clements, "you ought to have heard Professor Tyler read that." To the day of Mr. Clements' death, a picture of Tyler hung on the wall of his study.

Much has been discovered and many new interpretations have been made in the field of American colonial literature since Tyler's first volumes appeared in 1878, yet it is not without significance that as late as 1930, Samuel Eliot Morison, in his *Builders of the Bay Colony* remarked, "The best general survey of the literature of seventeenth century New England is Moses Coit Tyler's *History of American Literature . . .*"

Tyler's daughter, Mrs. Jessica Austen, wrote a biography of her father in 1911, but it was not until the 1920s that a young student at the University of Michigan, Thomas Edgar Casady, undertook a thorough-going study of this pioneer historian. Tragically, Mr. Casady died just after his study had been accepted as a doctoral dissertation at the University and before he had had a chance to get it into shape for publication. In 1930, Professor Howard Mumford Jones revised Mr. Casady's volume, and it appeared in 1933 as *The Life of Moses Coit Tyler* under the joint authorship of Jones and Casady. In that volume Tyler appears as a many-sided man, whose interests and contact with life induced him to write authoritatively in other fields than that of American literature. The man was an indefatigable worker. Besides fourteen books, Jones and Casady were able to identify at least one hundred fifty-seven articles which he contributed to periodicals. At the time of his death, he had four books planned and partly composed.

Tyler was among the first to recognize that America was much more than a transplanted or expanded Europe, that America had, in and of itself, produced civilization in spite of, rather than on account of, its European background. In his introduction to his volumes on colonial literature, he wrote,

"There is but one thing more interesting than the intellectual history of a man, and that is the intellectual history of a nation. The American people, starting into life in the early part of the seventeenth century, have been busy ever since in recording their intellectual history in laws, manners, institutions, in battles with man and beast and nature, in highways, excavations, edifices, in pictures, in statues, in written words. It is in written words that this people, from the very beginning, have made the most confidential and explicit record of their minds. It is in these written words, therefore, that we shall now search for that record."

There is merit in Professor Jones' characterization of Tyler as "the first great historian of the national mind expressed in literature," as also in his summing up of this book: *"The Literary History of the American Revolution,* the product of some twenty years of reflection, study, and research, is, it needs scarcely to be said, a monument to American scholarship."

RANDOLPH G. ADAMS

Ann Arbor
November, 1940

CHAPTER I.

LITERARY ASPECTS OF THE PERIOD OF THE REVOLUTION.

I.—Three stages of intellectual development during the Revolution, with respect to the issues therein involved.

II.—The entire period characterized with reference to the promise of any literary outcome from it.

III.—The note of American literature during this period is its concern with the problems of American society, and of American society in a state of extraordinary alarm, upheaval, and combat.

IV.—The surprising amount of this literature considered as the product of a disturbed time—The peculiar quickening of the intellectual and emotional energies of man in times of Revolutionary excitement—The American Revolution to an unusual degree the result of ideal causes operating on a people keenly sensitive to such causes and to their possible ultimate effects.

V.—The need of distinguishing between those writings which were the result of general intellectual tendencies and interests apart from the Revolution, and those writings which resulted directly from it—The former to be found near the beginning and the end of the period—They represent the spiritual side of man's nature, his delight in the visible framework of the New World, or his curiosity respecting its primitive races ; also, the historic interest applied to the origin and development of English civilization in America— For literature in its higher sense, there were during the first decade of the Revolution two new centres of activity—The New England centre had its chief representative in John Trumbull—That of the Middle Colonies, in Philip Freneau—All these several forms of literature to be dealt with as apart from the characteristic life of the period, which is expressed in nine principal classes of writings.

VI.—The first class consists of the correspondence of the time—Special reasons for its development—Some of the best letter-writers of the period—This class of writings has but an incidental relation to the purpose of the present work.

VII.—The second class is made up of formal and official statements of political thought, called State Papers—The extraordinary service then rendered by these writings—They were the first authoritative and conspicuous presentation to the Old World of the intellectual condition of the New.

VIII.—The third class consists of oral addresses, secular and sacred—Their traits.

I

IX.—The fourth class consists of political essays, either in the form of brief letters communicated by eminent men to the newspapers, or in the form of pamphlets—The subordinate place of the newspaper in England and America in the seventeenth and eighteenth centuries—Explanation of the uncommon merit of the political essays then contributed to the newspapers —The English pamphlet as the immediate ancestor of the newspaper—The seventeenth and eighteenth centuries the classic period of the pamphlet in England—Our Revolution was wrought out in the last stage of this period, and was on its literary side chiefly a pamphlet war—The power of the political essay during the period of our Revolution as described by Sir Erskine May and John Richard Green—The predominance of the political essay in French literature just before and during the French Revolution— The interpretative value of such writings as set forth by Bishop White Kennet—Sir Edward Creasy's estimate of American pamphlets written in opposition to the Stamp Act.

X.—The fifth class consists of regular political satires in verse—The prominence of this form of literature during the Revolution due to conditions which no longer exist—Dryden as the founder of political satire in verse in modern English literature—Pope's relation to social and literary satire— Their influence on American writers re-enforced during the Revolution by the influence of Churchill—Churchill's career—His example a stimulus to American satirists, especially Trumbull, Freneau, and Odell.

XI.—The sixth class consists of the popular lyric poetry of the period—The frankness and variety of these folk-songs—The seventh class consists of the minor literary facetiæ of the controversy—The eighth class, of its dramatic compositions—To the ninth class belong the prose narratives of actual experience in the Revolution, whether individual or collective.

XII.—The dividing lines between these several classes of writings—The historic method in the treatment of these writings—Their chief importance as genuine and direct interpretations of the American Revolution, and of the American people who took part in it—Literature as the expression of society, and as the best witness to the character of a people —The humanistic and historic interest attaching to this period of American literature.

I.

IN the intellectual process of the American Revolution, are to be observed three well defined stages of development on the part of the men who began and carried through that notable enterprise. The first stage—extending from the spring of 1763 to the spring of 1775—represents the noble anxiety which brave men must feel when their political safety is imperilled, this anxiety, however, being deepened in their case by a sincere and even a passionate desire, while roughly resisting an offensive ministerial policy, to keep within the bounds of constitutional opposition, and neither to forsake nor to forfeit that connection with the Mother Country which they then held to be among the most precious of their earthly possessions. The second stage—extending from the spring of 1775 to the early summer of 1776—represents a rapidly spreading doubt, and yet at first no more than a doubt, as to the possibility of their continuing to be free men without ceasing to be English colonists. This doubt, of course, had been felt by not a few of them long before the day of the Lexington and Concord fights; but under the appalling logic of that day of brutality, it became suddenly weaponed with a power which mere words never had,—the power to undo swiftly, in the hearts of a multitude of liegemen, the tie of race, the charm of an antique national tradition, the loyalty, the love, and the pride of centuries. The third stage—extending from the early summer of 1776 to the very close of the whole struggle—represents a final conviction, at least on the part of a working majority of the American people, that it would be impossible for them to preserve their political rights and at the same time to remain inside the British empire,—this conviction being also accompanied by the resolve to preserve those rights whether or no, and at whatsoever cost of time, or effort, or pain.

Of course, the intellectual attitude of the Loyalists of the Revolution—always during that period an immense and a very conscientious minority—correlated to that of the Revolutionists in each one of these three stages of development: in the first stage, by a position of qualified dissent as to the gravity of the danger and as to the proper method of dealing with it; in the second and the third stages, by a position of unqualified dissent, and of implacable hostility, as regards the object and motive and method of the opposition which was then conducted by their more masterful fellow-countrymen.

II.

Taking our stand, therefore, near the beginning of what proved to be a Revolutionary period, and casting our eyes forward across that entire tract of time as now spread out before us under the light with which history shines upon it, let us interpret to ourselves its peculiar character, particularly with reference to the promise, or even the possibility, of a literary outcome from it.

Not a period of repose, civic or domestic or personal, as we see at the first glance; not a period of quiet respiration for man, or woman, or society; no normal social movement; the forces of heart and of brain not left free to assert themselves in undisturbed or spontaneous action; a time, rather, of exceptional upheaval, perturbation, tumult, in which the English race in America appears to be in desperate struggle for self-preservation against fatal assault from without and from within; hence, a time in which violent political action, and subsidiary to that, long, painful, and costly military action, absorbs nearly all possible energies locked up in that population of Americans. Moreover, it is to be noted that the deepest impulse to all this enormous social upheaval and effort is derived from the need, only gradually making itself manifest, and even then to only a portion of the community, of a complete and final detachment of America from all external authority whatsoever, whether resident in England or elsewhere on this planet. "But, in reality," so pleaded, with pathetic seriousness, many of the best Americans of that time, "in reality, is there such need of our detachment from external authority, especially from the authority of the Mother Country?" And to this question, the very people who asked it never failed to make answer, firmly and sternly,— "No!" And they were sincere; but on the issue thus framed, came that final and dreadful divergence among the Americans themselves, which led to a mutual animosity more rancorous, more inappeasable, than even the animosity of the Revolutionary party toward their British assailants. This most bitter discord, within a population that needed all its force united and massed against the common danger from without, only added intellectual complication and a sort of exquisite ferocity to a period already sufficiently enmeshed in confusion and hate.

Such is the epoch into which we now presume to look in search of literature: an epoch, as it appears, uptorn by moral earthquakes, and swept by hurricanes of passion; a fatal time, sorrowful, grim, pitiless ; a time of immense hope, of immense wrath, of immense despair; a time when, even among ancient friends, even among kinsmen once most dear, were flashing eyes and clenched fists, whole families being broken asunder forever in death, or in a hatred worse than death; a time of battle-fields, and prison-ships, and scaffolds, of cities sacked and burned, of rich provinces laid waste and left bleeding and desolate ; weeks and months dragging themselves out into years during which, for two or three millions of men and women, life and all that life is worth living for, were in suspense. In such an epoch, why look for literature ? Can it be supposed that, at such a time, any literary thing was, or could have been, done in this land, which it would be worth our while now to shake from the dust of a hundred years, and to inspect even for a single moment ?

It has fallen to my lot to turn over and to look through very many pages, in manuscript and in print, produced during that period; and I must bear witness that I have not found many pages, whether serious or sportive, amid the lines of which did not seem to be audible the reverberation of that old civic rancor,—reluctant but at last determined revolution, eager and fierce resistance to revolution. This, indeed, is the one best note of sincerity, of authenticity, in these writings. And since the authentic and sincere literature of any period is the recorded utterance of the uppermost and the undermost thought of that period,—its thought and emotion both,—there would be room for distrust or for disdain should we find proof that many Americans, between 1763 and 1783, had written altogether disinterested or passionless pages, or had dealt with tranquil literary themes, in song or story or philosophy, wholly apart from those themes that were then rushing to mortal combat in the brains and on the battle-fields of that time.

III.

The chief trait, therefore, of American literature during the period now under view is this: its concern with the problems of American society, and of American society in a peculiar condition—aroused, inflammable, in a state of alarm for its own existence, but also in a state of resolute combat for it. The literature which we are thus to inspect is not, then, a literature of tranquillity, but chiefly a literature of strife, or, as the Greeks would have said, of agony; and, of course, it must take those forms in which intellectual and impassioned debate can be most effectually carried on. The literature of our Revolution has almost everywhere the combative note; its habitual method is argumentative, persuasive, appealing, rasping, retaliatory; the very brain of man seems to be in armor; his wit is in the gladiator's attitude of offense and defense. It is a literature indulging itself in grimaces, in mockery, in scowls : a literature accented by earnest gestures meant to convince people, or by fierce blows meant to smite them down. In this literature we must not expect to find art used for art's sake. Nay, art itself, so far as it is here at all, is swept into the universal conscription, and enrolled for the service of the one party or of the other in the imperilled young Republic. No man is likely to be in the mood for æsthetics who has an assassin's pistol at his head. Even the passion for the beautiful has been known to yield to the instinct for self-preservation.

IV.

Looking, then, into this period of great civic trouble, and being content that the authentic literary product of it should also have a troubled look—a look of anxiety and wrath and combat—our next discovery is the rather notable one that such a period actually had a literary product very considerable in amount. Even in those perturbed years between 1763 and 1783, there was a large mass of literature produced in America. This fact will perhaps bring to us a surprise, almost a perplexity. Is it credible ? How can this be ? Certainly, great deeds were done in those years, and great words spoken—words that had the quality of great deeds; and yet, as we shall be tempted to say, that was a time for fighting, not for writing: it was a time for a game of politics astute, robust, unrelenting; for the courage of a creative statesmanship ; for a diplomacy with wit enough to confront and conciliate a world; for a generalship that could make an army look military, though dressed in rags, that could make that army march though it had no shoes, that could make it formidable though destitute of gunpowder; for a daily and a nightly warfare, on the part of two or three millions of people, against starvation, and rags, and bankruptcy; and it may well seem incredible that, under such circumstances, any people could produce writings which should have any quality that now entitles them to literary remembrance, or which it would not be a barbarous ingratitude for us to subject to criticism.

This is the first view of the situation. Let us now look a little deeper, and we shall see that, within the range of those literary forms capable of articulating the moods of a period of civil and military conflict, large literary production is the very result to be expected. For on what does any sort of literary production depend ? Of course, it depends on the quickening of man's nature, especially of his intellect and his emotions. And what is a period of war, and especially of civil war, and more especially of revolutionary civil war, but an extraordinary quickening of the intellectual and emotional energies of man ?

The turbulence of the time may, indeed, become so great as to drive out from the human spirit all sense of security; but in that case, the only certain result on literature will be to drive out the tranquil forms of literary expression, leaving all the forces of the quickened life of the people free to concentrate themselves upon those forms of literary expression which are not tranquil, that is, which are combative.

Moreover, in the case of the American Revolution, literary production within the special range thus indicated, was likely to be the greater for the reason that that Revolution was pre-eminently a revolution caused by ideas, and pivoted on ideas.   Of course, all revolutions are in some sense caused by ideas and pivoted on them; but in the case of most revolutions, the ideal causes of them are not generally perceived, and therefore are not generally acted upon until those ideal causes become fully interpreted through real evils, generally through a long experience of real evils. This was the case, for example, with the French Revolution.   But in the case of the American Revolution, the people did not wait until ideal evils had become real evils. With a political intelligence so alert and so sensitive as to discern those evils while still afar off, they made their stand, not against tyranny inflicted, but only against tyranny anticipated.   They produced the Revolution, not because they were as yet actual sufferers, but because they were good logicians, and were able to prove that, without resistance, they or their children would some day become actual sufferers.   As was said of them by a great contemporary statesman in England, they judged " of the pressure of the grievance by the badness of the principle."   They augured " misgovernment at a distance."   They snuffed " the approach of tyranny in every tainted breeze." [1]   Hence, more than with most other epochs of revolutionary strife,

---

[1] Edmund Burke, " Speech on Moving his Resolutions for Conciliation with the Colonies," March 22, 1775.   " Works," ii. 125.

our epoch of revolutionary strife was a strife of ideas: a long warfare of political logic; a succession of annual campaigns in which the marshalling of arguments not only preceded the marshalling of armies, but often exceeded them in impression upon the final result.

An epoch like this, therefore,—an epoch in which nearly all that is great and dear in man's life on earth has to be argued for, as well as to be fought for, and in which ideas have a work to do quite as pertinent and quite as effective as that of bullets,—can hardly fail to be an epoch teeming with literature, with literature, of course, in the particular forms suited to the purposes of political co-operation and conflict.

V.

In preparing ourselves to deal properly with the Literary History of the American Revolution, we shall be much helped by keeping in mind the distinction between two classes of writings then produced among us: first, those writings which were the result of certain general intellectual interests and activities apart from the Revolutionary movement, and, secondly, those writings which were the result of intellectual interests and activities directly awakened and sustained by that movement.

The presence of the first class we discover chiefly in the earlier years of this period, before the Revolutionary idea had become fully developed and fully predominant ; and, again, in the later years of the period, when, with the success of the Revolution assured, the Revolutionary idea had begun to recede, and men's minds were free to swing again toward the usual subjects of human concern, particularly toward those which were to occupy them after the attainment of Independence and of peace.

There, to begin with, are those writings which stand for the spiritual side of man's nature,—his thought respecting the Divine and the human and the relations between the two, respecting the mystery of existence, respecting the law of life here and hereafter. Even amid all the uproar and anguish of a harsh political and military conflict, this sovereign interest of the soul could never be stifled; nay, in the prevailing instability of all earthly good, men were driven more than ever to find sustenance and repose in the consideration of a form of good that should outlast the world. Thus, it was in 1769 that Joseph Bellamy published his "Four Dialogues between a Minister and his Parishioner concerning the Half-Way Covenant" [1]; it was in 1770 that John Woolman published his "Considerations on the True Harmony of Mankind" [2]; it was in 1773 that Samuel Hopkins published his "Inquiry into the Nature of True Holiness." [3]

There, also, are those writings which stand for the delight of man in the visible framework of nature in the New World, and for his curiosity to pierce into the secrets of that New World as hidden in plant, and mineral, and animal: descriptions of the American wilderness, narratives of travel among the native peoples, with sketches of their characters and ways. Most prominent in this group are the "Historical Account of Bouquet's Expedition against the Ohio Indians," the "Journals" of Major Robert Rogers, together with his "Concise Account of North America," William Stork's "Description of East Florida," Carver's "Travels through the Interior Parts of North America," and James Adair's "History of the American Indians."

There, likewise, are the writings which stand for the interest of the American people in their own past, testifying in this case, also, to a noble impulse surviving from the colonial time; such as the fragments of local history by Stephen Hopkins, by Amos Adams, by Nathan Fiske; the ponderous historical monograph of Robert Proud on the origin of Pennsylvania; the ecclesiastical histories of Morgan Edwards and of Isaac Backus; and, above all, the two

---

[1] The Works of Bellamy, ii. 665–711.
[2] The Works of Woolman, 350–381.
[3] The Works of Hopkins, iii. 3–141.

noble volumes of Thomas Hutchinson on the history of Massachusetts down to within fifteen years of the Stamp Act.

Even for literature in the higher sense of that word,—literature as an expression of the æsthetic mood, literature apart from mere instruction, apart, also, from the aims of any debate,—we shall find, within the first decade of this period and before its culmination into the final violence of the Revolutionary controversy, the beginnings of a new and a truer life in America. Of this new literary life there were, in general, two chief centres, one in the New England, one in the Middle Colonies. The New England literary centre was at New Haven, and was dominated by the influence of Yale College, within which, especially between 1767 and 1773, was a group of brilliant young men passionately devoted to the Greek and Roman classics, and brought into contact with the spirit of modern letters through their sympathetic study of the later masters of English prose and verse. The foremost man in this group was John Trumbull. The new literary life of the Middle Colonies had its seat in the neighborhood of New York and Philadelphia, and was keenly stimulated by the influence of their two colleges, and also by that of the College of New Jersey under the strong man who came to its presidency in 1768. The foremost representative of this new literary tendency was Philip Freneau, a true man of genius, the one poet of unquestionable originality granted to America prior to the nineteenth century. Of him and of his brother poet in New England, it is to be said that both began to do their work while still in youth; both seemed to have a vocation for disinterested literature in prose as well as in verse; both were reluctantly driven from that vocation by the intolerable political storm that then burst over the land; both were swept into the Revolutionary movement, and, thenceforward, the chief literary work of both was as political satirists. From about the year 1774, little trace of an æsthetic purpose in American letters is to be discovered until after the close of the Revolution.

While, therefore, these several forms of literature, as produced among us at any time between 1763 and 1783, have their value as enabling us to ascertain and to feel certain minor phases of the life of that period, it is not into them that we are to look for an expression of its most characteristic life—the life that made that period so great in its effects upon the development of the American people, and still so interesting to all students of the later history of mankind.   The characteristic life of the period we now have in view was political, and not political only, but polemic, and fiercely polemic, and at last revolutionary; and its true literary expression is to be recognized in those writings, whether in prose or in verse, which gave utterance to that life.   Such writings seem naturally to fall into nine principal classes.

VI.

First, may here be named the correspondence of the time; especially, the letters touching on public affairs which passed between persons in different portions of America, and in which men of kindred opinions found one another out, informed one another, stimulated, guided, aided one another, in the common struggle.   Indeed, the correspondence of our Revolution, both official and unofficial, constitutes a vast, a fascinating, and a significant branch of its literature.   Very strange would it have been had it been otherwise.   An immense peril was, or seemed to be, approaching those kindred but sundered communities.   In all those communities the men who meant even by force to resist that peril, or to resist those who thought there was a peril to be so resisted, needed to ascertain one another's existence, to interchange opinions, to come into united measures.   This they could not do, in those days of arduous and snail-paced travel, by personal interviews; and therefore far more than can ever again be the case, communication by writing was then the only means of bringing about any general concert of thought or action.   Moreover, at that

time, the art of letter-writing for ordinary personal uses had
not yet been overtaken by the fatal boon of cheap postage,
and perhaps the still more fatal boon of stenographic dicta-
tion; and consequently it had not lost consciousness of its
own fine function, nor become content that its missives
should, in personal quality at least, be worth as little as
they now cost. In those days men and women still took time
to write letters, and to write them with their own hands,
and to put ideas into what they wrote, and the individual
touch, deliberate and deft expression, playfulness, and
grace, and force.

Undoubtedly, the best of all the letter-writers of the time
was Franklin; and next to him, perhaps, were John Adams,
and Abigail Adams, his wife. Indeed the letters of Mrs.
Adams, mostly to her husband, and covering this entire
period, are among the most delightful specimens of such work
as done by any American: they are alive with the very moods
and scenes of the Revolution; they reveal, also, the strong
intelligence, the high faith, the splendid courage of that
noble matron, and the secret of her life-long power as the
intellectual companion of her husband, his one and only
confidante, and the inspirer of all that was greatest and
best in his career. Not far behind these first three letter-
writers, if indeed they were behind them, must be mentioned Jefferson and John Dickinson; and, for shrewdness
of observation, for humor, for lightness of touch, for the
gracious negligée of cultivated speech, not far behind any of
them, was a letter-writer now almost unknown, Richard
Peters of Philadelphia. Of course, no one goes to the letters
of Washington, in the expectation of finding there sprightliness of thought, flexibility, or ease of movement; yet, in
point of diligence and productiveness, he was one of the
great letter-writers of that age, while all that he ever wrote
has the incommunicable worth of his powerful and noble
character—sincerity, purity, robustness, freedom from all
morbid vapors, soundness of judgment ripened under vast
responsibility. Who can hope ever to know the mind and

conscience of our Revolution, its motive, its conduct, its stern and patient purpose, or its cost, without studying Washington's letters ?

It does not belong to the purpose of the present work, to make any other than an incidental mention of this immense class of writings,—writings which, in fact, scarcely came to the public eye during that period, and which seem to require, as they would well reward, a separate treatise for their full presentation. Considerable portions of all this Revolutionary correspondence have now passed into print; very large portions of it still remain in manuscript; already much has perished by fire, by mildew, by neglect. As a whole, however, the epistolary record of the Revolution, could we now look upon it, would set forth for us, in vivid contemporary colors, every passing phase of that time of mighty commotion; and would embody for us naïve examples of narrative, of character-painting, of earnest and high-spirited discussion, and many a passage of genuine pathos, and satire, and wit.

VII.

The second form of literature embodying the characteristic life of our Revolutionary era, is made up of those writings which were put forth at nearly every critical stage of the long contest, either by the local legislatures, or by the General Congress, or by prominent men in public office, and which may now be described comprehensively as State Papers.

It is probable that we have never yet sufficiently considered the extraordinary intellectual merits of this great group of writings, or the prodigious practical service which, by means of those merits, they rendered to the struggling cause of American self-government, particularly in procuring for the insurrectionary colonists, first, the respectful recognition, and then the moral confidence, of the civilized world. The writers of these State Papers were the representatives of

the great party of discontent. They were among the ablest
and most cultivated men in the several colonies to which
they belonged. Prior to the occasion which first brought
them together into an intercolonial assemblage, they were
in person scarcely known to one another, while to the world
at large they were of course quite unknown. Indeed, the
world at large then knew but little of the American people
in any way, and cared still less for them. In spite of this,
however, the members of these intercolonial assemblages,
obscure provincial politicians though they then were,
began to send forth, first in the year 1765 and again in the
year 1774, their elaborate and stately appeals to the reason
and the justice of mankind. At the time when these
papers were issued, the people of Europe were becoming
dimly aware of some sort of political disturbance in America, and with that condescension which still sits so gracefully
upon them in their occasional allusions to us, were beginning to ask, what sort of people these Americans might be
like. Whether they were white, or red, or black, was not
then generally known in Europe, if indeed the mind of
Europe can be said even yet to be altogether clear upon
that difficult question; but were the Americans even a civilized people ? Evidently, whatever they were, they were
not disposed to an abject submission to their parent state;
but, in what spirit, according to what method, were they
asserting their supposed claims ? Was it in a spirit of
sheer lawlessness, of wild, fierce, and truculent insubordination ? And if the Americans were indeed sufficiently
advanced in culture to have acquired the art of writing,
what sort of announcements of themselves would they be
capable of putting forth ? Very naturally, their writings
would be crude in thought, inconclusive in reasoning, destitute of the great precedents and traditions of political literature as cherished in the older portions of the world, and
expressed of course in the fervor and rant of gasconading
patriotism and of revolutionary rhapsody. It was under
precisely these circumstances that the State Papers, for

example, of the Stamp Act Congress and of the Congress
of 1774, were borne across the Atlantic, and distributed
among the publicists of Europe. These constituted,
indeed, the first conspicuous and authoritative presentation
to the Old World of the intellectual and political condition
of the New. It is now known with what surprise many
enlightened men in Europe, who had imagined that the
Americans were a rabble of illiterate backwoodsmen, of
headstrong, blustering and law-defying revolutionists, then
read these political documents,—finding in them nearly
every quality indicative of personal, and national greatness,
—reverence, sobriety, conservatism, familiarity with history,
exact and extensive legal learning, the most lucid exposition
of constitutional principles, urbanity of tone, and a literary
execution at once graceful and forceful,—showing, indeed,
that somehow, out into that American wilderness had been
carried the very accent of cosmopolitan thought and
speech.

VIII.

The third class of writings directly expressive of the spirit
and life of the Revolution, consists of oral addresses, either
secular or sacred,—that is, of speeches, formal orations, and
political sermons. The interest now to be found in the
reading of these productions must be derived almost wholly
from one's perception of their value as authentic interpretations of the thought and passion of their time. Undoubtedly, the best words actually spoken during the Revolution
were the words that did not survive the occasions which
called them forth,—namely, the speeches that leaped from
the lips of a few great statesmen and orators in the strenuous passages of those debates which, in the provincial
assemblies or in the great congresses, decided the course of
American policy in opposition to the measures of the ministry. Spoken, as these speeches were, behind closed doors,
heard by no official reporters, they have lived since then
only in the historic effects they wrought, in vague tradition,

or in the fragmentary jottings of some ear-witness who happened to be a letter-writer or a diarist. As to the formal oratory of this period, much of which went into print, it must be described as having very little of the sparkle and flavor of Revolutionary life, being to a degree passing all modern endurance, verbose, stilted, and jejune. Unquestionably, the most vital of the survivals of the spoken eloquence of the Revolution are in the form of political discourses from a few chiefs of the Revolutionary pulpit.

IX.

The three classes of writings just mentioned, have their undoubted value in enabling us to trace the Literary History of the American Revolution; and yet their value for this purpose is somewhat less than that of the fourth class of writings now to be mentioned, namely, the political essays of the period. More than in all other publications, it was in these political essays that the American people, on both sides of the great controversy, gave utterance to their real thoughts, their real purposes, their fears, their hopes, their hatreds, touching the bitter questions which then divided them,—doing so under almost every form of expression, from serious argument and earnest persuasion, to mere invective, vituperation, and banter.

Respecting these political essays, however, a somewhat mechanical distinction has to be noted,—a distinction arising from the fact that some of them were written for publication in their newspapers, while the others were written for publication as separate tracts. This distinction, slight as it may seem, is worth considering, since it develops two rather important peculiarities attaching to all popular discussion in the eighteenth century, on both sides of the Atlantic,—the subordinate place then occupied by the newspaper, the supreme place then occupied by the pamphlet.

In our own time, the imperial function of journalism, as an instrument of immediate influence, in almost every

2

sphere of thought and action, is fully developed and fully recognized. The analogy can hardly deserve to be called a forced one, if modern journalism, for its instantaneous and enormous power, be compared to ancient oratory, as oratory was, for example, at Athens in her great days. Indeed, journalism has now grown to be the universal silent oratory of the human race: it is oratory dispensing with a vocal rendering, for the reason that it has found in the printed sheet a mightier elocution than that of the human voice.

Of course, at the period of the American Revolution, journalism had nowhere reached this advanced stage of effectiveness. In America, especially, the newspapers were petty, dingy, languid, inadequate affairs; and the department of the newspaper now devoted to editorial writing, then scarcely existed at all. Nevertheless, while the editor of those days was only the printer, and merely arranged and put into type what went into his paper, instead of himself writing any part of what went into it, he had, especially in times of excitement, the active assistance of a magnificent staff of unpaid contributors,—the foremost men in the land, politicians, lawyers, clergymen, scholars, and other men of cultivated thought and leadership,—who found the columns of these journals a convenient medium for the instant diffusion of their opinions, and who, accordingly, wrote for these dull-looking, ill-printed, little sheets, some of the most finished and most forceful specimens of literary work done among us in those days. In this particular, also, the newspapers then published in America differed but little from the newspapers then published in England. In the latter, says· the English editor of a recent edition of " Junius," " there existed none of those leading articles or elaborate commentaries on public questions, which now occupy so prominent a place in our daily papers. The correspondents of the press were then the only writers of political communications which bore the character of leaders ; and, as reports of the debates were not permitted, members of either house suffered equally with the people in possessing no common channel by which the one could learn, and the other convey, their sentiments. In consequence of this restrictive system, the correspondence of newspapers formed the most talented portion of their contents, influential men of all parties adopting this medium as the best for giving publicity to their opinions." [1]

We have but a slight step to take in passing from these brief political essays written for our Revolutionary newspapers, to those longer and more elaborate political essays which first saw the light in the form of pamphlets. In taking this step, however, it is well for us to recall the great part played by this form of literature in the two centuries preceding our own,—a form of literature now almost extinct. The pamphlet is the immediate ancestor of the newspaper ; and, like a good ancestor, it first carefully reared its colossal child, and then promptly got out of the way, leaving to its offspring the inheritance of the whole estate—which was, in fact, the entire world of readers. The maturity of journalism really meant the old age and death of pamphleteering. For the first three hundred years, however, after the introduction of printing, journalism was either unborn or in its infancy and during the most of that time, the pamphlet had perhaps the highest place among the instruments of immediate popular influence. The seventeenth and the eighteenth centuries may be called the classic era of the English pamphlet. No reader of English literature can forget how John Milton, just on the threshold of his manhood, and with all his powers of poetic utterance in fresh and jubilant action, turned away from the starry call of poetry, abandoned his dream of a great national epic on King Arthur, and of a dramatic poem on the Fall of Man, and gave up his health, his eyesight, and the vigor of the best twenty years of his life, in order to devote himself to this tremendous function of writing pamphlets on English politics. The chief significance of John Dryden in his non-dramatic and non-lyric poetry, may almost be said to be

---

[1] John Wade, in "Junius," ii. Preface, iii.-iv.

that which attaches to a writer of political pamphlets in verse. The power which centred in Dean Swift, and on account of which even great statesmen and noblemen paid court to a rough and plebeian priest in the Irish Establishment, was, in no inconsiderable part, derived from the fear and the hope he inspired as a writer of pamphlets. And when, shortly before our Revolution, Samuel Johnson, having in his Dictionary defined the word pension as " an allowance made to any one without an equivalent," and as being in England " generally understood to mean pay given to a state-hireling for treason to his country," himself submitted to receive a pension, doubtless many people in England felt that the pamphlets which he afterwards wrote in defense of the colonial policy of the ministry and in disparagement of the American claim, were so splendid an equivalent for this bounty of the government, as to protect him from the backward stroke of at least the first part of his own sarcasm.

It was in such a period, therefore,—the later stage of the classic pamphleteering period,—that our Revolution was wrought out. The great part performed in that conflict by pamphlets written by Americans on both sides of the question, was, therefore, fully in accord with the literary method then prevalent in all political discussion; and it has bequeathed to us the most abundant and the most important of all existing materials for our Literary History during that period. Indeed, to so marked a degree was this form of literature the chief weapon in the intellectual warfare of the American Revolution, that even its approach might have been challenged in the very words with which the approach of Gloster is challenged by Winchester, in the play:

> " Com'st thou with deep premeditated lines,
> With written pamphlets studiously devised ? " [1]

The political essay, then, whether in the shape of the newspaper article or in that of the pamphlet, gives us the

---

[1] King Henry VI. Part I. Act iii. Sc. 1.

most characteristic type of American literature for that portion of the eighteenth century. It is this form of writing, also, which is chiefly meant, when historians now speak of what they are apt to call the political press, in America or in England. Thus, the power of the political essay in America during the Revolution is perfectly, even if unconsciously, described by Sir Erskine May when, of the political press in England during the same period, he says, that, having first proved " its influence as an auxiliary in party warfare " it began " to rise above party, and to become a great popular power,—the representative of public opinion."[1] Another and a still later English historian has likewise called attention to the striking fact that even in England itself, " the political power of the press, and the struggle with America " began at the same time, that is, with the ministry of George Grenville.[2] In this respect, moreover, the literature of the American Revolution seems to correspond to that of France during the closing years of the eighteenth century,—" une littérature devenue toute politique, et, pour dernier œuvre, faisant naître la tribune."[3] Furthermore, the worth of just these literary memorials of political controversy, for interpreting the life of any people to whom such methods of political controversy are permitted, was recognised long before the American Revolution by a famous English prelate who was also a learned political philosopher. " The bent and genius of the age," said Bishop Kennet, " is best known in a free country, by the pamphlets and papers that daily come out as the sense of the parties and sometimes as the voice of the nation."[4]

Finally, as to the great body of those political essays

---

[1] May, " Const. Hist. Eng.," ii. 247.

[2] J. R. Green, " Short Hist. English People," 733.

[3] Villemain, " Tableau de la Littérature au XVIIIᵉ Siècle," iii. 195.

[4] Cited by Sir Walter Scott as a motto on the title-page of his great " Collection of Scarce and Valuable Tracts," somewhat improperly lettered on the back as " Lord Somers's Tracts." The sentence is taken from Bishop White Kennet's " Register and Chronicle, Ecclesiastical and Civil."

which were produced among us between 1763 and 1783, and through which may now be traced in unbroken sequence the development of the thought and passion of the American people during that period, it may justly be said that we ourselves have been slower to recognize their merits, than have been some of our kinsmen in England. Doubtless, among these writings are to be found not a few examples of crudity of thought and slovenliness of style, of partisan malice, of provincial pettiness, and of a dulness quite too dense for penetration by any faculties now possessed by us. Nevertheless, when Sir Edward Creasy said of the American pamphlets written in opposition to the Stamp Act, that " some of them are very able," and " for clearness of argument and boldness of political views, may be ranked with the splendid orations afterward pronounced on the same side in the British Senate," [1] he delivered a critical judgment which may be applied with equal truth to the American pamphlets written in the later stages of the same controversy.

X.

Closely associated with the political essay as the most powerful form of prose in the literature of the American Revolution, should be mentioned the political satire, as being likewise the most powerful form of verse during the same period, and as constituting the fifth class of writings directly expressive of its thought and passion.

With the political satire, also, as with the political essay, we have to note how its extraordinary prominence during the Revolution was derived from literary conditions which existed then, but which exist no longer. In the poetic literature of modern England, satire was first made a notable weapon in political controversy by John Dryden, even as social and literary satire was brought into fresh vogue by Pope, from whom, also, it descended along the line of his poetic disciples until it found its last great masters in Gif-

---

[1] " British Empire," 151.

ford and Byron. Accordingly, at about the middle of the eighteenth century, these thirteen communities of Englishmen in America, so far as they were under any literary tutelage, were in poetry under the tutelage chiefly of Dryden and Pope; and in their own experiments at satiric verse, dealing with phases of social and political life in their several neighborhoods, they reflect the influences which, in all the English-speaking world, had then given such splendor and favor to this not very noble species of poetry. Certainly, the best examples of satire to be met with among us before the Revolutionary dispute had reached its culmination, may be seen in the earlier and non-political verse of Freneau and John Trumbull. As a token, also, of the intellectual habits of that age, the fact should not be overlooked that the arrival of this rather flippant literary mode was not accepted without a shock of alarm and disapproval, especially in the more sedate communities; as was discovered, for example, by the most brilliant master of satire in New England, where, as he complained,

> "—— priests drive poets to the lurch
> By fulminations of the church ;
> Mark in our title-page our crimes,
> Find heresies in double rhymes,
> Charge tropes with damnable opinion,
> And prove a metaphor Arminian,
> Peep for our doctrines, as at windows,
> And pick out creeds of innuendoes." [1]

It happened, moreover, that just at the beginning of our Revolutionary era, an enormous impulse was given to the use of political satire in England, and consequently in America, through the tumultuous and dazzling success of Charles Churchill. Having in 1761, acquired sudden notoriety by his three non-political satires, " The Rosciad," " The Apology," and " Night," it was in 1762 and by his " Prophecy of Famine "—a tremendous onslaught on the

---

[1] Trumbull, " Poetical Works," ii. 75.

Scottish and other political enemies of Wilkes—that this brilliant but disorderly genius burst into the field of English politics.   Though his profligate life came to a sudden end only two years afterward, yet in that brief interval, and through a rapid succession of satirical poems, such as " The Duellist," " Gotham," " The Candidate," and " The Ghost," he had astonished the English and the American public by the energy and variety of his resources in the literary expression of political hate and scorn, and had given thereby a fresh revelation of the effectiveness of satire in political warfare.   No one can fail to see, also, that upon all his work, hasty and vindictive as much of it is, may be found, as John Forster has declared, " the coarse broad mark of sincerity." [1]   It is true that the impulse thus given by Churchill to the employment of political satire in verse was, as it deserved to be, almost as brief as it was violent; yet the greatness of his temporary influence is shown, not only in the fear of him and in the flattery of him on the part of some of the most powerful politicians in England, but in the admiration or the enmity with which he was regarded by the greatest of his literary contemporaries. Goldsmith described him as a mere partisan versifier " dignified with the name of poet," whose " tawdry lampoons are called satires," whose " turbulence is said to be force, and his phrensy fire." [2]   " I called the fellow a blockhead at first," said Dr. Johnson in 1763, " and I call him a blockhead still "; the " temporary currency " of Churchill's poetry being due, as the same critic thought, only to " its audacity of abuse," and to its " being filled with living names." [3]   Cowper, on the other hand, declared that Churchill was a great poet; that Churchill's merits were above those of " any other contemporary writer "; indeed, that for the technique of his art he made Churchill his

---

[1] " Edinburgh Review," lxxxi. 69.

[2] This was in the dedication to " The Traveller," published in December, 1764, only a month after Churchill's death.   Goldsmith's " Works," i. 4.

[3] Boswell, " Life of Johnson," i. 419, 418.

model.[1] At the sudden death of this poet militant many
an eminent man in England seems to have breathed a sigh
of relief; and the curious mixture of admiration and alarm
with which some of them had regarded him, is well conveyed in the comment made by Horace Walpole on the
news of Churchill's abrupt disappearance from the scene:
" The meteor blazed scarce four years."[2]

Of course, it is not without some effort of the imagination
that we shall now bring ourselves to understand the greatness of this satirist's influence on the literary method of
political controversy, especially in America. Much of that
oblivion which Johnson then so confidently predicted for
Churchill's poetry, has long since befallen it. That his very
name has now become indistinct to the mass of readers, and
that the sort of writing he did has lost its hold upon the
public respect, are abundantly implied in the question lately
asked by a clever English critic—" Where is the great, the
terrific, the cloud-compelling Churchill ?"[3] This is a question, indeed, which no one in America could have asked
during the two decades of American literature which we are
about to survey. Certainly, second only to the political
essay, among the literary forces of the American Revolution,
was the political satire, and the political satire as stimulated
by the success and shaped by the method of Churchill; and
without a clear recognition of Churchill's influence upon our
writers, will it be impossible to understand this extremely
important phase of the Revolutionary controversy.

It is true that in that controversy no great place was
given to satire until about the year 1775—that is, until the
debate had nearly passed beyond the stage of argument.
From that time, however, and until very near to the close
of the Revolution, this form of literature rivalled, and at

---

[1] Southey, "Life and Works of Cowper," i. 61.

[2] Cited in an article on Churchill in "Edinburgh Review," lxxxi. 86.
This article, which was by John Forster, is perhaps the best critical account of
Churchill yet made. In Southey's "Life of Cowper" is an interesting and
helpful chapter on Churchill.

[3] Edmund Gosse, "Questions at Issue," 105.

times almost set aside, the political essay as an instrument
of impassioned political strife.   On the Revolutionist side,
the chief masters of political satire were Francis Hopkinson,
John Trumbull, and Philip Freneau.   On the side of the
Loyalists, the satirical poet who in art and in power surpassed all his fellows, was Jonathan Odell.

XI.

It would be a mistake for us to forget that the development of political thought and emotion during the American
Revolution may be traced in other forms of verse than in
the form of regular satire,—in forms of verse, also, less artificial than such satire, nearer to the primary modes and
impulses of human nature, more spontaneous, more direct,
more universal.   For the sixth class of writings, then, characteristic of the period, we may take the popular lyric
poetry of the Revolution,—the numberless verses, commonly quite inelaborate and unadorned, that were written
to be sung at the hearth-stone, by the camp-fire, on the
march, on the battle-field, in all places of solemn worship,—
songs for the new fatherland, for home, for liberty,—party-
songs, army-songs, ballads, and hymns of patriotic thank-
fulness and trust.   Indeed, we shall find the path of that
tremendous conflict, especially the latter half of it, to be
strown with verses that seem to have sprung up like wild
flowers almost from the very ground over which angry men
were trampling, and that still seem to breathe forth what
was then in the hearts of the sorely divided people of this
land.   Without doubt, these folk-songs of the American
Revolution should now be of uncommon use to us, as
embodying, often roughly, always frankly, the sincere aspirations and antipathies of both parties in the war, or as
portraying those incidents of the long struggle, heroic,
pathetic, tragic, or mirthful, which at the time appealed to
the admiration, or sympathy of the people, to their hope,
or fear, or hatred, and, in many cases, to their mere delight

in the drolleries which always abound in the midst of happenings the most serious.

Our seventh class of Revolutionary writings will gather up the numerous literary memorials of the long struggle as a mere wit-combat, a vast miscellany of humorous productions in verse and prose which, trivial as they may seem, are yet too characteristic of the spirit and method of a great historic conflict to be here justly left out of the account. In these writings, we shall note the actual play of popular humor disporting itself amid all the ferocities of the conflict, the very jokes and jibes of the contestants, their frolicsome moods, even while in the act of fighting, their interpolations of loud laughter into the text of a composition that was in the main sufficiently serious, their literary burlesques, parodies, hoaxes, all the slight and casual reliques of the war as a war of ridicule and sarcastic repartee.

For the eighth class of Revolutionary writings, partly in prose, chiefly in verse, we shall bring together the dramatic compositions of the period,—a class not inconsiderable in number, in variety, in vigor, and thoroughly representative both of the humor and of the tragic sentiment of the period.

Finally, to the ninth class belong those prose narratives that sprang out of the actual experiences of the Revolution, and that have embodied such experiences in the several forms of personal diaries, military journals, tales of adventure on land or sea, and especially records of suffering in the military prisons. Besides these, there are several elaborate contemporary histories of the Revolution, as the third volume of Hutchinson's "History of Massachusetts," the four volumes of Gordon's "History of the Rise, Progress, and Establishment of the Independence of the United States of America," and the three volumes of Mercy Warren's "History of the Rise, Progress, and Termination of the American Revolution."

XII.

The classification we have thus made of the somewhat diversified mass of writings handed down to us from the American Revolution, should help us to form in advance a sufficiently clear general view of the range and nature of those writings, without imposing upon us any needless mechanical restraints as we try to come into direct contact with them.   In the further prosecution of our studies, it will be best for us to deal with the various writings included in these several groups, chiefly according to their historic sequence,—in the very order of time wherein they severally came into life and wrought their work in the world,—thus permitting the principal members of these different groups of literature to appear upon these pages, and to unfold their message to us, somewhat as they actually made their first appearance in the successive scenes of that great transaction in which they bore so significant a part.

This, of course, is not the place in which to express a critical judgment upon these writings, either as separate productions in literature, or as forming a collective body of literature associated with a great period in our national history.   Moreover, the chief purpose of the present work is to call attention to these writings, not so much for their independent artistic value as for their humanistic and historic value, interpreting, as they do, with direct and undisguised speech, the very spirit and life and inward process of the American Revolution, nay, the very spirit and life and character, the motives, the secret moods and experiences, of that race of Americans who were concerned in bringing about the Revolution, or in trying to stay its progress. Even the French people—a nation of artists almost from their birth, to whom, especially, literary art appeals with a delicate force seldom known among us—do not fail to recognize the legitimacy and the high worth of this purely representative aspect of literature.   " La littérature," they are accustomed to say, " est l'expression de la société." [1]   It is

[1] J. Demogeot, " Histoire de la Littérature Française," 565.

precisely this aspect of literature which we have chiefly before us, as we here study the writings of the American people in the period now under consideration,—viewing American literature, then, chiefly as the expression of American society, stirred, and at last convulsed, by the pangs and throes of Revolution. Respecting the soundness of our method, we scarcely need to be troubled by any doubt: we are but trying to come to an immediate and somewhat intimate knowledge of the American people in their most heroic age, by means of that through which, in any age, according to Matthew Arnold, "a people best express themselves—their literature." [1] Whatever, therefore, may be our final conclusion as to the purely artistic value of this portion of American literature, it must continue to have a deep interest for us, and in some degree for all other students of the history of human nature, as containing a perfectly sincere revelation of themselves on the part of a high-spirited people in a supreme crisis of their development. For, as has been nobly said, in our own time, by a most exacting master and critic of literary art, "nothing which has ever interested living men and women can wholly lose its vitality—no language they have spoken, nor oracle by which they have hushed their voices, no dream which has once been entertained by actual human minds, nothing about which they have ever been passionate, or expended time and zeal." [2]

---

[1] "On the Study of Celtic Literature," 24.
[2] Walter H. Pater, "Studies in the History of the Renaissance," 38.

CHAPTER II.

THE PRELUDE OF POLITICAL DEBATE: 1761–1764.

I.—The part of James Otis in the early development of the American Revolution.

II.—The argument on the petition for writs of assistance in the Superior Court of Massachusetts, 1761—The character and effects of Otis's speech—Contemporary testimony of John Adams.

III.—Otis's early career—His interest in classical studies—His " Rudiments of Latin Prosody"—His " Rudiments of Greek Prosody"—His sound taste in modern literature—His traits as a controversial writer.

IV.—Otis takes the lead of political opinion in New England—In the Massachusetts house of representatives, he calls to account the royal governor.

V.—Otis publishes " The Vindication of the House of Representatives," 1762 —Its importance in the development of constitutional ideas in America— Its leading propositions—Its relation to the subsequent literature of Revolutionary controversy.

VI.—Otis recognizes the new and stronger spirit of British colonial policy, beginning with the Peace of Paris, in 1763—The act of Parliament for raising an imperial revenue from the colonies, April, 1764—Official notification of the Stamp Act.

VII.—Otis arraigns this new policy in " The Rights of the British Colonies Asserted and Proved," July, 1764—Outline of this pamphlet—Its character and power.

VIII.—Otis's object was to find a constitutional basis for the permanent connection of the colonies with the British empire.

IX.—The debate carried on by Oxenbridge Thacher, in " The Sentiments of a British American," September, 1764—Thacher's personal history—The rational and conciliatory spirit of his argument for the recognition of American rights within the empire.

X.—Two other pamphlets for the same object, but from the industrial and commercial point of view—"An Essay on the Trade of the Northern Colonies," Philadelphia, 1764—" Some Thoughts on the Method of Improving and Securing the Advantages which accrue to Great Britain from the Northern Colonies," New York, 1764.

I.

No student of the American Revolution can have failed to notice how, from beginning to end, its several stages unfolded themselves and succeeded one another with something of the logical sequence, the proportion, and the unity of a well-ordered plot. It is quite other than a rhetorical commonplace to speak of the Revolution as a drama. And in this drama, James Otis was a very great actor. His mighty part, however, was played and completed in the earlier Acts. At the outset, no one is so prominent and so predominant. He even speaks the prologue. It is he who rushes upon the front of the stage in the first Scene, in the second, in the third. As the play goes on, he is still in the foreground,—his flashing eyes, his passionate words, his gestures of anger or of supplication, his imperious personality, seeming to direct the course of events, and to mark him as the hero of the whole plot. But, suddenly, long before the climax is reached, he disappears from the stage altogether: he no longer has any relation to the play, except as one of the motley crowd that are watching its progress, —a breathing effigy of James Otis, a man of disordered intellect and unsteady will, being occasionally seen moving mournfully through the lobbies of the theatre, and even gazing as a bewildered spectator upon the culmination of a plot which had once seemed to derive its chief force and direction from him. James Otis has no real part in the Revolution after 1769.

II.

In February, of the year 1761, the council-chamber of the Old Town House, in Boston, was the scene of a great legal debate. The room was a splendid and a stately one. The superior court of the colony was in session there. The five judges, including the chief-justice, presided in full wigs, bands, and robes of scarlet. From full-length portraits on the walls, Chares the Second and James the Second seemed to look down with mute indignation upon an assemblage of provincial politicians and lawyers, one of whom at least presumed on that occasion to discuss the spirit of their reigns and the limits of the royal prerogative, with an uncourtly frankness for which, had they been anything but painted kings, they would have sent him to the Tower. A great throng of people filled the place. The cause to be argued there might at first glance seem to be one of no great importance,—that of the legality of granting new writs of assistance to officers of the customs in the ports of Massachusetts,—the old writs, which had been freely granted in that colony under the reign of George the Second, being then about to expire in consequence of the death of that monarch.[1] Slight as the question may seem, it did in fact reach very far; it involved the property, the political standing, the liberties, the passions, of all the American colonists of England; and the trial of it, in the presence of that great and excited assemblage, may be said to have begun a new era in the history of the human race.[2]

The argument for the writ was made by Jeremy Gridley. The case in opposition was then argued, in the first instance, by Oxenbridge Thacher, a lawyer eminent for ability and probity, who, according to the testimony of one who heard him, spoke " with the softness of manners, the ingenuity and cool reasoning, which were remarkable in his amiable character."[3] Then Otis arose to speak upon the same side. Of the speech which he thus made, the historic importance, with reference to the American Revolution, has doubtless

---

[1] The account above given of the origin of this celebrated case differs in some important particulars from that usually given, e. g., in George Bancroft, " Hist. U. S.," last rev., ii. 531 ; in Tudor, " Life of Otis," 52–53 ; and in J. Adams, " Works," x. 246–247. This part of my narrative is founded on Quincy's " Reports of Cases Argued and Adjudged in the Superior Court of Judicature of the Province of Massachusetts Bay, between 1761 and 1772 "; especially its learned "Appendix I.," on Writs of Assistance, 395–540. The last is an important contribution to the early history of our Revolution, being the work of Horace Gray, formerly of the Suffolk bar, now one of the Justices of the Supreme Court of the United States.

[2] " This is the opening scene of American resistance," Bancroft, " Hist. U. S.," last rev., ii. 546.

[3] J. Adams, " Works," x. 247.

been overestimated by some writers. It is not an overesti-
mation of it to say, that it forms a notable landmark in the
history of our relations to the Mother Country: it is in itself
an authentic token of that sensitive and proud condition of
the American colonial mind out of which all the later acts
of Revolutionary resistance were born; while, among the
younger leaders of public opinion in the colony of Massachusetts, it gave a distinct addition both to that sensitiveness and to that pride. Only a few weeks before, Otis had
laid down the office of advocate-general, for the reason that
he could not support this very application for writs of
assistance,—these being a judicial precept which he proceeded
to describe as " the worst instrument of arbitrary power,
the most destructive of English liberty and the fundamental
principles of law, that ever was found in an English law-
book." " I must therefore," he continued, " beg your
honors' patience and attention to the whole range of an
argument that may perhaps appear uncommon in many
things, as well as to points of learning that are more remote
and unusual. . . . I shall not think much of my pains
in this cause, as I engaged in it from principle. I was solicited to argue this cause as advocate-general; and because I
would not, I have been charged with desertion from my
office. To this charge I can give a very sufficient answer.
I renounced that office, and I argue this cause, from the
same principle; and I argue it with the greater pleasure, as
it is in favor of British liberty, at a time when we hear the
greatest monarch upon earth declaring from his throne that
he glories in the name of Briton, and that the privileges of
his people are dearer to him than the most valuable prerogatives of his crown;[1] and as it is in opposition to a kind of

---

[1] " Born and educated in this country, I glory in the name of Briton. . . .
The civil and religious rights of my loving subjects are equally dear to me with
the most valuable prerogatives of my crown." From the speech of the young
king, George III., on opening the first parliament after his accession, 18 November, 1760. Hansard, " Parl. Hist. of Eng.," xv. 982. This allusion in
Otis's argument touched most expertly a royal utterance which was just then
not only a fresh topic of news in Boston, but a theme of prodigious interest

power, the exercise of which, in former periods of English history, cost one king of England his head, and another his throne. . . . The writ prayed for in this petition, being general, is illegal. It is a power that places the liberty of every man in the hands of every petty officer. . . . In the first place, the writ is universal, being directed . . . to every subject in the king's dominions. Every one, with this writ, may be a tyrant. If this commission be legal, a tyrant in a legal manner may control, imprison, or murder any one within the realm. In the next place, it is perpetual: there is no return. A man is accountable to no person for his doings. Every man may reign secure in his petty tyranny, and spread terror and desolation around him. In the third place, a person with this writ, in the day time, may enter all houses, shops, etc., at will, and command all to assist him. . . . Now, one of the most essential branches of English liberty is the freedom of one's house. . . . This writ, if it should be declared legal, would totally annihilate this privilege. Custom-house officers may enter our houses when they please. . . . Their menial servants may enter, may break locks, bars, and everything in their way; and whether they break, through malice or revenge, no man, no court, can enquire. . . . Thus, reason and the constitution are both against this writ. Let us see what authority there is for it. Not more than one instance can be found in all our law-books; and that was in the zenith of arbitrary power, namely, in the reign of Charles II., when star-chamber powers were pushed to extremity by some ignorant clerk of the exchequer. But had this writ been in any book whatever, it would have been illegal. All precedents are under the control of the princi-

---

throughout the whole British empire. The playfulness of Thackeray's comment, some fifty years ago, on the famous saying of young George III., should not keep us from seeing how shrewdly it penetrates into the inner truth of history: " Our chief troubles began when we got a king who gloried in the name of Briton, and being born in the country, proposed to rule it." " The Four Georges," 39.

ples of law. Lord Talbot says it is better to observe these
than any precedents. . . . No acts of parliament can
establish such a writ. . . . An act against the constitution is void.'' [1]

These sentences, being a part of some notes taken on the
spot by a young lawyer who was eagerly watching the
scene,[2] can give probably but a faint idea of the intellectual
range and force of an argument which occupied four or five
hours in the delivery, which exhibited great learning and
acuteness, and which constantly presented the subject as
having relations infinitely larger and more solemn than the
particular topic out of which it grew, showing, as its reporter
testifies, '' not only the illegality of the writ, its insidious
and mischievous tendency, but . . . the views and
designs of Great Britain, in taxing us, of destroying our
charters, and assuming the powers of our government, legislative, executive, and judicial, external and internal, civil
and ecclesiastical, temporal and spiritual; and all this
. . . with such a profusion of learning, such convincing
argument, and such a torrent of sublime and pathetic eloquence, that a great crowd of spectators and auditors went
away absolutely electrified.'' [3]

And the witness, to whose somewhat exuberant memoranda we are indebted for the only original description we
have of this great scene, and who was himself just entering
upon his own sturdy career in the service of his country,
seemed to the very end of his life to dwell with almost
equal enthusiasm upon the splendor and power of Otis's
oratory on that day, and upon the historic significance of
the wonderful speech in which Otis thus exhibited it.
'' James Otis was Isaiah and Ezekiel united.'' [4] His speech

---

[1] J. Adams, '' Works,'' ii. 523–525.

[2] Ibid. ii. 124 n. Also Horace Gray in App. to Quincy's '' Mass. Reports,''
479. The notes actually taken in the court room by John Adams seem to have
been written out with care shortly afterward ; and it is from these revised notes
that I have quoted.

[3] J. Adams, '' Works,'' x. 183.

[4] Ibid. 272.

was " in a style of oratory that I never heard equalled in this or any other country." [1]   " Otis's oration against writs of assistance breathed into this nation the breath of life." [2] " Otis was a flame of fire !   With a promptitude of classical allusions, a depth of research, a rapid summary of historical events and dates, a profusion of legal authorities, a prophetic glance of his eye into futurity, and a torrent of impetuous eloquence, he hurried away everything before him.   American Independence was then and there born ; the seeds of patriots and heroes were then and there sown. . . . Every man of a crowded audience appeared to me to go away, as I did, ready to take up arms against writs of assistance.   Then and there was the first scene of the first act of opposition to the arbitrary claims of Great Britain." [3]

III.

At the time of making that speech, James Otis was six-and-thirty years old.   After his graduation at Harvard, at the age of eighteen, he had spent a year and a half at home in the study of literature and philosophy ; then, devoting himself to the law, he had begun its practice at Plymouth in 1748 ; after two years of residence there, he had removed to Boston, and in spite of his youth, he had quickly risen to the highest rank in his profession.   In 1760, when he was five-and-thirty years old and had been for twelve years in the full tide of a laborious law-practice, he proved his continued devotion to fine literary studies by publishing without his name a book entitled " The Rudiments of Latin Prosody ; with a Dissertation on Letters and the Principles

---

[1] J. Adams, " Works," x. 362.

[2] Ibid. 276.

[3] Ibid. 247–248.   This characteristic bit of declamation by John Adams has perhaps been taken too literally and too seriously by some writers, as by W. V. Wells, who in his " Life of Samuel Adams," i. 44, has tried to show that Otis's speech " was not the prologue of the great drama." See, also, William Wirt Henry, " Life, Corr., and Speeches of Patrick Henry," i. 102.

of Harmony in Poetic and Prosaic Composition,''—a book of minute and precise textual scholarship,—a book which shows that its author's natural aptitude for eloquence, oral and written, had been developed in connection with the most careful technical study of details. No one would guess, in reading that book, that it was written by perhaps the busiest lawyer and politician in New England. It seems rather to be the production of some clever and painful classical professor, and to have been born of the cloistered leisure of a college. Indeed, so deep was the satisfaction of James Otis in these tranquil studies,—as a relief, doubtless, from the rough contentions of his public life,—that he wrote a similar treatise on '' The Rudiments of Greek Prosody,'' —which, however, was never printed, but perished in the general conflagration that, by his own hand, overtook all his papers near the close of his life.

Throughout his whole career, he held to his early love of the Roman and Greek classics, particularly of Homer; while in English his literary taste was equally robust and whole-some. At a time when some of his American and English contemporaries were surrendering themselves to the weak and imitative graces of that brood of small poets then chirp-ing in England,—as Shenstone, William Whitehead, Aken-side, Beattie,—this New England lawyer protested against the tendency, and pointed away to the true masters of English verse. To a young man, a kinsman and a name-sake of his own, in whose education he took a special inter-est, Otis wrote of certain Americans as being then '' very fond of talking about poetry, and repeating passages of it. The poets they quote I know nothing of; but do you take care, James, that you don't give in to this folly. If you want to read poetry, read Shakespeare, Milton, Dryden, and Pope, and throw all the rest in the fire. These are all that are worth reading.'' [1]

Yet with all Otis's soundness of taste as a student of lit-erature, he often seemed wholly lacking in taste when he

---

[1] Tudor, '' The Life of James Otis,'' 16–17.

himself came to the act of literary composition. He was a powerful writer, and he wrote much; but in the structure and form of what he wrote, there are few traces of that enthusiasm for classical literature which we know him to have possessed. Perhaps his nature was too harsh, too passionate and ill-balanced, to yield to the culture even of a literary perfection which he could fully recognize and enjoy in others. He was, above all things, an orator; and his oratory was of the tempestuous kind—bold, vehement, irregular, overpowering. When he took pen in hand, he was an orator still; and the habit of extemporaneous, impetuous, and reckless expression which he had long indulged in at the bar, controlled him at his desk. In writing upon any subject of controversy, he seemed to storm across his own pages in mighty rage, even as he had been accustomed to pace stormily up and down before a jury; to throw to the winds all the classic virtues in expression,—temperance, order, lucidity; to catch at bold allusions, flaming images, grotesque comparisons; and to leave unrevised upon the paper, and in all its original extravagance and inaccuracy, whatsoever in the fury of composition he had once flung down upon it. He seemed even to despise the correction of his own work, perhaps to be incapable of it. Thus, having on one occasion composed, on behalf of the house of representatives of Massachusetts, some very elaborate and very important state-papers, which had been afterward carefully revised and corrected by his political compeer, Samuel Adams, Otis said at the time, in his jocular fashion,—" I have drawn them all up, and given them to Sam to ' quieu-whew ' them," [1]—an indispensable literary process which, however it may be described, his own writings generally showed abundant proofs of lacking. And thus it came about, that the man whose taste in reading was so severely

---

[1] J. Adams, " Works," x. 367 ; Tudor, " Life of Otis," 316–317. It is not necessary to my present purpose to determine just what the papers were which Otis thus claimed to have written. See important note by W. V. Wells, in his " Life of Samuel Adams," i. 172–174.

classic, was often in his own writing an unrestrained barbarian. Disproportion, incoherence, exaggeration, coarseness, inaccuracy—these are faults not uncommon in his pages; and along with these, was a certain wildness of manner which early brought upon him, especially in England, the imputation of madness.

But great as are the literary blemishes upon Otis's work, that work is still full of power. Even its style, with all its Gothic irregularity and intemperance, is always vivid and significant,—at times, it is impressive to an extraordinary degree. His learning on many subjects was considerable, even if disorderly; and he had instant command over the resources of his own memory. He had, moreover, the ability to grasp quickly all the principles and facts of a given case, to pierce to the core of them, and to perceive the logic which controlled them; and even while pressing forward in his track along a zigzag path of his own choosing, and with many a wide and dangerous sweep of digression, he yet never lost sight of the logical goal which he had set out to reach. In his pamphlets, too, as in his speeches, he gave free rein to his enjoyment of humor, and to his uncommon faculty of sarcasm. A serious discomfiture of his opponent was never quite enough to appease his ambition in debate: he must also cover his antagonist with ridicule, and drive him from the field amid shouts of derision.

IV.

Otis's speech against writs of assistance made him at once a leader of public opinion in New England respecting the constitutional rights of the colonies, even as it vastly increased the public sensitiveness respecting official encroachments upon those rights. In the following year, 1762, occurred a series of events which still further intensified that sensitiveness, and gave to Otis the occasion for the first of those powerful controversial pamphlets, to which he owes his great place in the political literature of the Revolution.

It is interesting to note that, fully three years before the thirteen colonies were aroused by the Stamp-Act to an alarmed consideration of their constitutional rights in the matter of taxation, Otis was the hero of a little struggle in the single colony of Massachusetts, in which he had the opportunity of rehearsing in miniature the part he was to take in the larger subsequent struggle involving the whole continent; and to fix clearly in his own mind the logical formula under which, in protecting the rights of Massachusetts, the rights of all America were to be protected. " It shows in a strong light," as John Adams thought, " the heaves and throes of the burning mountain, three years at least before the explosion of the volcano in Massachusetts or Virginia." [1] In an emergency of considerable public danger, but at a time when the colonial legislature was not in session, Governor Bernard, with the advice of the council, had assumed authority to fit out an armed vessel, thereby incurring an expense not expressly provided for by the house of representatives. A few years before that time, such an act on the part of the governor would perhaps have been crowned with the public gratitude, or at any rate would have been passed over without disapproval. It denotes the alert and even the inflamed condition of the public mind respecting the barriers of prerogative, that at its next session the house of representatives, led on by Otis, boldly confronted the governor with its stern expostulation:— " Justice to ourselves and to our constituents obliges us to remonstrate against the method of making or increasing establishments by the governor and council. It is in effect taking from the house their most darling privilege, the right of originating all taxes. It is, in short, annihilating one branch of the legislature. And when once the representatives of a people give up this privilege, the government will soon become arbitrary. No necessity, therefore, can be sufficient to justify a house of representatives in giving up such a privilege; for it would be of little consequence to the

---

[1] " Works," x. 300.

people whether they were subject to George, or Louis, the king of Great Britain, or the French king, if both were arbitrary, as both would be, if both could levy taxes without parliament." [1]

On the very same day on which this bold address was sent to the governor, it was returned by him to the house, with a message earnestly entreating that body not to enter upon its minutes the words in which the " sacred and well-beloved name " of the king was " so disrespectfully brought into question." Upon the reading of this message, and in the midst of great excitement, and with cries of " raze them," " raze them," the house voted to expunge the " dreadful words under which his excellency " had " placed a black mark." But, as the governor still persisted in the claim that his course, in incurring expense not authorized by the legislature, was justifiable, the house appointed a committee to present to the public a more careful view of its own position. Of this committee, Otis was a member; and performing alone the work which had been assigned to the committee, he published, in the autumn of 1762, " A Vindication of the Conduct of the House of Representatives of the Province of the Massachusetts Bay: more particularly in the Last Session of the General Assembly."

V.

The importance of this pamphlet is very great, as illustrating both the intellectual traits of James Otis and the development in America of clear thought and of keen anxiety respecting the constitutional rights of the colonies. In the opinion of a critic inclined, certainly, to set its full value on any performance of Otis, this brochure " may be considered the original source, from which all subsequent arguments against taxation were derived." [2] The exas-

---

[1] The message of the house, from which these sentences are taken, was of course written by Otis. "A Vindication of the Conduct," etc., 15 ; also, Tudor, " Life of Otis," 119–120.

[2] Tudor, " Life of Otis," 122.

perating candor of the pamphlet, as well as the sting deftly
concealed in many an insinuation along its pages, is not
unfairly suggested even by the rhymed motto which confronts us on the title-page:

> " Let such, such only, tread this sacred floor,
>   Who dare to love their country and—be poor :
>   Or, good though rich, humane and wise though great,—
>   Jove give but these, we 've nought to fear from fate."

Passing over details which are of no permanent interest, we
find that Otis here bases his whole argument on certain
general propositions as to human rights, which it is perhaps
startling to see thus bluntly proclaimed in the colonies so
early as in 1762: " 1. God made all men naturally equal.
2. The ideas of earthly superiority, pre-eminence, and grandeur are educational ;—at least acquired, not innate. 3.
Kings were,—and plantation governors should be,—made
for the good of the people, and not the people for them.
4. No government has a right to make hobby-horses, asses,
and slaves of the subjects, nature having made sufficient of
the two former, . . . but none of the last,—which
infallibly proves they are unnecessary. 5. Though most governments are ' de facto ' arbitrary, and consequently the
curse and scandal of human nature, yet none are ' de jure '
arbitrary. 6. The British constitution of government as
now established in his majesty's person and family, is the
wisest and best in the world. 7. The king of Great Britain
is the best as well as most glorious monarch upon the globe,
and his subjects the happiest in the universe. 8. It is most
humbly presumed, the king would have all his plantation
governors follow his royal example, in a wise and strict
adherence to the principles of the British constitution, by
which, in conjunction with his other royal virtues, he is
enabled to reign in the hearts of a brave and generous, free
and loyal people. 9. This is the summit, the ' ne plus
ultra,' of human glory and felicity. 10. The French king

is a despotic arbitrary prince, and consequently his subjects are very miserable." [1]

Thus, even in the construction of a constitutional argument, James Otis reveals the habit of his mind, wherein gravity and frolic, logic and sarcasm, all rush together for expression. And the entire pamphlet is but an amplification of the ideas and the feelings which color these words, —an avowal of loyalty to the king so hyperbolical as to suggest its dangerous nearness to irony, a robust assertion of colonial rights under the British constitution, all blended with mirthful and contemptuous allusions to any man who should deny or qualify those rights. Everywhere he stands for the freeman's privilege of plain speech in the discussion of matters relating to the state: " The province can be in no danger from a house of representatives daring to speak plain English, when they are complaining of a grievance." [2] And he never lets his readers lose sight of the greatness of the principle at the bottom of all their petty altercations with provincial governors wanting to be despots; declaring, for instance, that if the doctrine then insisted on by Governor Bernard in Massachusetts had " prevailed in England, we should have heard nothing of the oppressions and misfortunes of the Charleses and the Jameses; the Revolution would never have taken place; the genius of William the Third would have languished in the fens of Holland, or evaporated in the plains of Flanders; the names of the three Georges would doubtless have been immortal,—but Great Britain, to this day, might have been in chains and darkness, unblessed with their influence." [3]

Certainly, the interest attaching to this pamphlet will not be diminished by a remembrance of its relation to the entire body of political literature produced in America during the subsequent twenty years. " How many volumes," exclaimed John Adams, with some characteristic exaggera-

---

[1] "A Vindication of the Conduct," etc., 17–21.
[2] Ibid. 25.
[3] Ibid. 44–45.

tion, " are concentrated in this little fugitive pamphlet, the production of a few hurried hours, amidst the continual solicitations of a crowd of clients !　.　.　.　Look over the declaration of rights and wrongs issued by congress in 1774. Look into the Declaration of Independence in 1776.　Look into the writings of Doctor Price and Doctor Priestley. Look into all the French constitutions of government; and, to cap the climax, look into Mister Thomas Paine's ' Common Sense,' ' Crisis,' and ' Rights of Man.'　What can you find that is not to be found, in solid substance, in this ' Vindication of the House of Representatives ' ? " [1]

VI.

Thus far in his career, this protagonist for colonial rights had grappled only with the subordinate and local agents of the English government,—with such small foemen as custom-house officers, provincial judges, and colonial governors, all of whom he was at liberty to treat as though they misrepresented the benignant and free spirit which he adroitly assumed as the commanding trait, not only of the British empire, but of its king and of its king's ministers. Behind this pleasant fiction, however, he was not long permitted to conduct the controversy.　The new zeal of English officers in America had been the result of a new and a sterner policy on the part of the government in England; and by the middle of the year 1764, Otis found it necessary to look beyond the petty colonial agents and consignees of the imperial authority, and to address his appeals directly to that authority itself.

For by that time, the evidence had become irresistible in the colonies that England had entered upon a new and a much more thorough system of colonial administration. Early in the previous year, she had concluded with France that proud treaty, whereby she received from her ancient enemy an enormous enlargement of her territorial posses-

---

[1] " Works," x. 310–311.

sions in America. Under all the circumstances, it was but
natural, it was but right, that England should think that at
last the time had come for an entire readjustment of her
somewhat loose, irregular, and unbusiness-like relations to
those American possessions, particularly with the view of
making them contribute some substantial help to the general cost of the empire, in the benefits of which they all
participated. For many years, acts of parliament had been
nominally in force in the colonies, imposing duties on the
importation of various articles of common use; but from all
these sources of revenue, and along with an outlay of more
than seven thousand pounds a year for its collection, the
treasury had received only an insignificant sum,—on an
average of thirty years, less than nineteen hundred pounds
sterling a year.[1] Up and down the entire coast of America,
the revenue laws had been notoriously evaded, with the
corrupt connivance, in many cases, of the very officers who
had been appointed to execute them.

This state of things was to continue no longer. A comprehensive scheme of colonial reconstruction was to be
drawn out. The laws of parliament for the procurement of
a revenue from America were to be strictly enforced; and
new laws were to be passed providing for a still larger revenue. All persons concerned in the collection of customs
were to be ordered to their posts; their numbers were to be
increased; more stringent instructions were to be given to
them; all who faltered in duty were to be dismissed. Moreover, the governors of colonies, and all other officers there,
civil, military, or naval, were to co-operate in the execution
of the new system, the efficiency of which, likewise, was to be
still further strengthened by the establishment of new courts
of admiralty.

All these tokens of a change in policy had been instantly
noted by Otis and by other sagacious American observers,
and had produced throughout the colonies no little uneasi-

---

[1] " The Regulations lately made concerning the Colonies," 57. This
pamphlet was inspired, if not actually written, by George Grenville.

ness, when, in the early summer of 1764, news arrived which seemed to justify their gloomiest apprehensions. An act had just passed,—so it was announced,—not only retaining but even enlarging, the old duties and restrictions on trade to and from America; for example, laying new and larger imposts on foreign wines, molasses, and sugar. But this was not the worst. In all former acts of this kind, the purpose of deriving a revenue from the colonies by authority of parliament, had been mercifully veiled under the pretext of simply regulating the trade of the empire. Now, all disguises were thrown off. For the first time in the history of English legislation, it was plainly mentioned in an act of parliament that the raising of a revenue from the colonies, by its direct authority, was the chief intent of the act.[1] And even this was not the worst. " These new taxes," wrote one of the secretaries of the treasury, " will certainly not be sufficient to defray that share of the American expense which America ought, and is able, to bear. Others must be added."[2] Among those others loomed, at that moment, the dark and sinister shape of the Stamp Act.

This latter measure, which proved to be of so mighty an import to America, to England, and to mankind, it had been the original purpose of the ministry to press upon the attention of the house of commons at its spring session in 1764; but in a spirit of politic forbearance, they had con-

---

[1] For the resolutions of the committee of ways and means, during the session from 8 December, 1763, to 19 April, 1764, embodying these plans for regulating and increasing taxes upon the colonies, see Hansard " Parl. Hist. of Eng.," xv. 1425–1434. The chief legal result of these resolutions was the act passed during that session, and containing in its preamble these epoch-making words : " Whereas it is expedient that new provisions and regulations should be established for improving the revenue of this kingdom, and for extending and securing the navigation and commerce between Great Britain and your majesty's dominions in America, which, by the peace, have been so happily enlarged ; and whereas it is just and necessary, that a revenue be raised, in your majesty's said dominions in America, for defraying the expenses of defending, protecting, and securing the same," etc., 4 George III. c. 15. " Statutes at Large," ix. 152–161.

[2] Quoted in Bancroft, " Hist. of U. S.," last rev., iii. 73.

tented themselves with giving notice of their intention to
bring in such a measure at the next session of parliament,
in the following year.[1]

VII.

The significance of all these acts of the home government, no man in America saw more clearly than did James
Otis; and it was in July, 1764, in the midst of the general
anxiety caused by the news of them, that he published his
gravest and most elaborate pamphlet, " The Rights of the
British Colonies Asserted and Proved." [2]

Of all his political writings, this is the most sedate. It
has even a tone of solemnity. It is as if he then realized
that the logical movement of the controversy in which he
had become involved, was rapidly sweeping him onward to
a position of appalling responsibility; from which soon
there would be no path of retreat; in which he would have
to deal no longer with local politicians and the subordinate
tools of power, but with the king of England himself, the
peers and commons of England, the whole illimitable might
of the British empire at that moment victorious beyond all
modern precedent. Thus, James Otis pauses in his career;
reviews the situation; reconsiders the grounds of his political faith; measures his own relation to the impending
contest; strengthens his fortitude by the renewed assurance
that the principles on which he had planted himself were
sound, and that the course of action which they demanded
of him, whether or not it should prove to be safe, was at
least right. Hence, it happens that this pamphlet has unwonted sobriety; few humorous or grotesque passages; few
bursts of passion; in many places a moderation of tone
almost judicial. Indeed, its moderation of tone, at the
time, gave considerable offense to some of his own asso-

---

[1] Hansard, " Parl. Hist. of Eng.," xv. 1427.

[2] Advertised in " The Boston Gazette " for 23 July, 1764, as published that
day.

ciates. The pamphlet was said to have satisfied nobody.
Yet it gave food for thought to everybody; and it is the
one work of Otis on which rests his reputation as a serious
political thinker.

It was impossible for him to find a basis for his theory of
immediate political duty, except in some clear system of
fundamental political thought. In trying to ascertain the
rights of the British colonies, he was driven back to a fresh
study of the primary rights of man; and thus his tract on
the relations between the British colonies and the British
parliament, becomes in some sense an institute of politics.
It may be said to fall into three portions: the origin of
government, the nature and rights of colonies in general,
and the nature and rights of the British colonies in particular.

In the first place, he holds that government is founded,
not on grace, nor on force, nor on compact, nor on property, but on the will of God as expressed in the necessities
of human nature; hence, that " an original, supreme, sovereign, absolute, and uncontrollable earthly power must exist
in and preside over every society, from whose final decisions
there can be no appeal but directly to heaven. It is, therefore, originally and ultimately in the people; . . . and
they never did in fact freely, nor can they rightfully, make
an absolute, unlimited renunciation of this divine right. It
is ever in the nature of the thing given in trust, and on a
condition the performance of which no mortal can dispense
with, namely, that the person or persons on whom the
sovereignty is conferred by the people, shall incessantly
consult their good. Tyranny of all kinds is to be abhorred,
whether it be in the hands of one, or of the few, or of the
many." [1]

In the second place, as regards the nature and rights of
colonies in general, he affirms that a colony is neither an
alien nor a menial member of the empire to which it belongs;
that it is " a settlement of subjects in a territory disjointed

---

[1] " The Rights of the British Colonies," etc., 12–13.

or remote from the mother country " '; that modern colonists " are the noble discoverers and settlers of a new world,
from whence, as from an endless source, wealth and plenty,
the means of power, grandeur, and glory, in a degree unknown to the hungry chiefs of former ages, have been
pouring into Europe for three hundred years past "; that
" those colonies have received from the several states of
Europe, except from Great Britain, . . . nothing but
ill-usage, slavery, and chains, as fast as the riches of their
own earning could furnish the means of forging them " ';
but that they " are entitled to as ample rights, liberties,
and privileges as the subjects of the mother country are,
and in some respects to more." '

When he comes, in the third place, to speak of the nature
and rights of the British colonies, he insists upon a distinction in their favor, founded on the august superiority of
the English constitution in its historic developments and
achievements on behalf of human liberty. Whatever may
be the case with the colonies of other nations, the colonies
of England, because they are the colonies of England, can
wear no badge of political servitude: the possession of full
political rights belongs to their lineage. " I think I have
heard it said, that when the Dutch are asked why they
enslave their colonies, their answer is, that the liberty of
Dutchmen is confined to Holland, and that it was never
intended for provincials in America, or anywhere else. A
sentiment this,—very worthy of modern Dutchmen; but if
their brave and worthy ancestors had entertained such narrow ideas of liberty, seven poor and distressed provinces
would never have asserted their rights against the whole
Spanish monarchy. . . . It is to be hoped none of our
fellow-subjects of Britain, great or small, have borrowed
this Dutch maxim of plantation politics. If they have,
they had better return it from whence it came; indeed they

---

¹ " The Rights of the British Colonies," 38.

² Ibid. 37.

³ Ibid. 38.

4

had.   Modern Dutch or French maxims of state never will
suit with a British constitution."[1]

Therefore, he insists that the rights of the British colonies
are based especially on the large and free principles of the
British constitution; that those principles were in force
before any charters for British colonies were given, and will
remain in force after all those charters shall have been
annulled; that in the latter case, the colonists would still
" be men, citizens, and British subjects "[2]; that every British subject, anywhere in the dominions of Great Britain,
" is by the law of God and nature, by the common law, and
by act of parliament . . .   entitled to all the natural,
essential, inherent, and inseparable rights of our fellow-
subjects in Great Britain "[3]; that all the colonies " are
subject to and dependent on Great Britain "[4]; that the
parliament of Great Britain, as the supreme legislature of
the empire, " has an undoubted power and lawful authority
to make acts for the general good, that, by naming them,
shall and ought to be equally binding as upon the subjects
of Great Britain within the realm "[5]; that no legislature,
" supreme or subordinate, has a right to make itself arbitrary "; that the supreme legislature " cannot take from
any man any part of his property without his consent in
person or by representation "[6]; " that no parts of his
majesty's dominions can be taxed without their consent;
that every part has a right to be represented in the supreme
or some subordinate legislature; that the refusal of this
would seem to be a contradiction in practice to the theory
of the constitution ; that the colonies are subordinate
dominions, and are now in such a state as to make it best,
for the good of the whole, that they should not only be
continued in the enjoyment of subordinate legislation, but
be also represented, in some proportion to their number and
estates, in the grand legislative of the nation; that this
would firmly unite all parts of the British empire in the

---

[1] " The Rights of the British Colonies," 58.
[2] Ibid. 50.   [3] Ibid. 52.   [4] Ibid. 49.   [5] Ibid.   [6] Ibid. 55.

greatest peace and prosperity, and render it invulnerable and perpetual.'' [1]

VIII.

Thus, the real object of Otis in this powerful pamphlet was not to bring about a revolution, but to avert one. There can be no doubt of the sincerity of his protestations of loyalty to England, on behalf of himself and of his fellow-colonists:—'' We all think ourselves happy under Great Britain. We love, esteem, and reverence our mother-country, and adore our king. And could the choice of independency be offered the colonies, or subjection to Great Britain upon any terms above absolute slavery, I am convinced they would accept the latter. The ministry, in all future generations, may rely on it, that British America will never prove undutiful, till driven to it, as the last fatal resort against ministerial oppression, which will make the wisest mad, and the weakest strong.'' [2]

To prevent so awful a catastrophe, therefore, Otis implores the government of England to recognize the colonies as in normal relations to the British constitution, and as entitled to some participation in that imperial council of the empire, by which the pecuniary burdens of the empire are distributed. Granting this, the disasters that now darken the horizon, and fill all hearts with dread, will forever sink out of sight.

But while the actual purpose of this pamphlet was to avert a revolution, its actual effect was to furnish the starting-point for the entire movement of revolutionary reasoning, by which some two millions of people were to justify themselves in the years to come, as they advanced along their rugged and stormy path toward Independence. It became for a time one of the legal text-books of the opponents of the ministry; it was a law-arsenal, from which other combatants, on that side, drew some of their best

---

[1] '' The Rights of the British Colonies,'' 99.   [2] Ibid. 77.

weapons. It expounded, with perfect clearness, even if
with some shrinking, the constitutional philosophy of the
whole subject; and it gave to the members of a conservative
and a law-respecting race, a conservative and a lawful pretext for resisting law, and for revolutionizing the government.[1]

IX.

Not far from the middle of the month of September, 1764,
—nearly two months, therefore, after Otis's blood-warm
pamphlet had set out on its journey into the world,—there
came from the press in Boston another and a quieter pamphlet, entitled " The Sentiments of a British American,"[2]
written by Oxenbridge Thacher, one of Otis's associates at
the Boston bar. Born about forty-four years before that
date, a graduate of Harvard in the class of 1738, he had
begun his career by taking up the hereditary vocation of
the family—that of the ministry; but lacking strength of
voice and a robust frame, he had failed to win in the pulpit
that success which, according to one of his ministerial contemporaries,[3] is often attained by those "who have only the
sounding brass to give them a reputation."

At the bar, to which he went with much reluctance, he
soon attained a distinguished position, on account of his
learning, acuteness, good sense, and the gravity and stain-
less probity of his character. Whatever quietness of manner

---

[1] In the same year in which this pamphlet of Otis's was published, there appeared in Boston a new edition of Wood's " New England Prospect," with a
somewhat remarkable preface in which were freely discussed the troubled relations between the colonies and the mother-country. This preface was declared
by James Bowdoin to have been written by Otis; and Robert C. Winthrop has
presented some considerations in support of that view. " Mass. Hist. Soc.
Proc.," vi. 250–251. From internal evidence, however, it seems to me altogether unlikely that Otis was the author of the preface, which, probably, was
the work of Nathaniel Rogers, A.M., of Harv., 1762. Pref. to Wood's " N. E.
Prosp.," ed. 1865, p. ix.

[2] Advertised in the " Boston Gazette " for September 17, 1764, as then just
published.

[3] J. Eliot, " Biog. Dict.," 454.

he may have had in act or speech was due to no lassitude of conviction on any subject; for within that fragile and invalided form there glowed a fiery spirit, intense in opinion, jealous and anxious for the right, and ready at any cost to contend against the arms or the arts of evil—or of what he took to be evil. Three or four years before the time at which he is here introduced to the reader, he had written for one of the newspapers a series of articles on an exciting matter of local interest; and these articles had been gathered up into a pamphlet, published in Boston in 1761 under the title of " Considerations on Lowering the Value of Gold Coins within the Province of Massachusetts Bay." That, apparently, had been his sole literary achievement prior to 1764.

A larger, a more difficult, a more impassioned subject he next took in hand, when, in that year, brooding over the approach of a mistaken and a disastrous parliamentary policy toward the colonies, he spread before readers both American and British " The Sentiments of a British American ": a calm, well-reasoned, manly, lawyer-like argument against the new measures of the imperial government; with no flourishes or tumults of speech; with not a touch of brilliance ; most sincere in tone, most conciliatory ; almost pathetic, likewise, in its tenderness of love and reverence for England. If we would now seize the very essence of the best American thought in its earliest stage of dissent from the new and firmer policy of the empire, we must at least glance at the outline of this argument by Oxenbridge Thacher.

A nation in great prosperity, thus his argument begins, should be on its guard against the special dangers which are apt to follow from great prosperity. Great Britain is now " arrived to a height of glory and wealth which no European nation hath ever reached since the decline of the Roman empire." This prosperity is in part due to its colonies, which, therefore, have a special claim to be taken into account in the development of imperial plans. No people on earth are more jealous of their rights than the British people. The American colonists are a part of the British people—not their " mere property." It is assumed that the British parliament intends to be just to the British colonies. The enquiry, therefore, is,—whether the British parliament, by its recent act " for granting certain duties in the British colonies . . . in America," has overstepped the line of justice toward those colonies.

To this act of parliament, there are five objections,—the first four affecting British subjects in America, the fifth affecting British subjects everywhere, particularly in Great Britain.

First, it is a tax,—a tax laid on the colonies without the consent of their representatives; and, in addition to that, a tax of peculiar hardship, because the colonies have already to bear a tax in support of their own subordinate governments. Nor is this objection removed by saying that the colonies, now enjoying the benefits accruing to them from the late war with France, ought also to share in the burdens which that war has entailed: for the war has been of no less benefit to Great Britain; while the war lasted, the colonies contributed to it their full proportion; by its territorial acquisitions, they are not particular gainers; Great Britain is a great gainer by them.

Secondly, the act gives an alarming extension to the courts of admiralty in America, subverting and abolishing many of the ancient rights of Englishmen under the common law.

Thirdly, the act gives to the commanders of the king's ships in American waters dangerous authority over the persons and the goods of British subjects there.

Fourthly, the act gives to all officers of the government in America, on land and sea, extraordinary powers, but without the usual checks of English law against the wanton and unjust exercise of those powers.

Fifthly, as this act imperils the interest of British subjects in America, so does it imperil the interests of British subjects in Great Britain. What spectacle is now produced before the eyes of men ? It is the spectacle of " a million and a half of British subjects disfranchised, or put under regulations alien from our happy constitution." And what pretense may not this " afford to after ministers to treat the inhabitants of the island itself after the same manner ! " [1] Nevertheless, upon this aspect of danger to England we do not now insist ; nor upon the ultimate damage which must fall upon England merely from the " alienation of the affec- tions " of her American children. This, however, we do insist upon : the immediate, material damage to the com- mercial interests of England through her retention and development of this new policy toward her colonies. For the greatest interest of England to-day is her colonial trade. But on what does her colonial trade depend ? Of course, it depends on the ability of the colonies to pay her for what they buy of her. The effect of this new legislation, how- ever, will be to force the colonies to stop buying of Eng- land, merely by taking from them the commercial facilities under which they have hitherto acquired the means of paying England. Henceforth, either they will manufacture their own goods, or they will go without them. In any case, England will have lost her best customers, and her chief trade will be ruined.

" These," says Oxenbridge Thacher, at last, as he brings his noble argument to a still nobler close, " are the senti- ments of a British American, which he ventures to expose to the public, with an honest, well-meant freedom. Born in one of the colonies, and descended from ancestors who were among the first planters of that colony, he is not ashamed to avow a love to the country that gave him birth ; yet he hath ever exulted in the name of Briton. He hath ever thought all the inhabitants in the remotest dominions of Great Britain interested in the wealth, the prosperity, and the glory of the capital. And he desireth ever to retain these filial sentiments. . . . He concludes all with his

---

[1] " The Sentiments," etc., 12.

most ardent wishes, that the happy island of Great Britain may grow in wealth, in power and glory, to yet greater degrees; that the conquests it makes over foreign enemies may serve the more to protect the internal liberties of its subjects ; that her colonies, now happily extended, may grow in filial affection and dutiful submission to her, their mother ; and that she, in return, may never forget her parental affections; that the whole English empire, united by the strongest bands of love and interest, formidable to the tyrants and oppressors of the earth, may retain its own virtue, and happily possess immortality." [1]

X.

These two pamphlets,—the one by Otis, the other by Thacher,—may fairly be said to give us the attitude of patriotic American lawyers and politicians in the year 1764, toward the new colonial policy of the British government, —a policy which, as was natural, they viewed chiefly in its political and legal aspects.　At about the time when these pamphlets were published in New England, in the Middle Colonies were published two other pamphlets, which should have great interest for us, as exhibiting the attitude of large-minded American merchants toward the same colonial policy, which, as was natural, they viewed chiefly in its industrial and commercial aspects.

The first of these pamphlets, entitled " An Essay on the Trade of the Northern Colonies of Great Britain in North America," was printed in Philadelphia in 1764, and was reprinted in London before the close of the year.[2]　Quiet and conversational in tone, pure in style, free from the pet-

<hr>

[1] " The Sentiments," etc., 16.

[2] I have used the London reprint, belonging to the library of Harvard University.　I do not remember to have met with the original Philadelphia edition, which is mentioned on the title-page of the London edition.　It appears to have been seen by Hildeburn : " Issues of the Pennsylvania Press," ii. 12.

tiness of provincial sentiment, and from every trace of asperity or harshness, it applies to British colonial policy the test of broad commercial considerations; and working out the argument with great practical knowledge, with ingenuity, candor, and force, it shows that the industrial interests of the whole British empire, and the prosperity of all British subjects, would be improved by taking off, rather than increasing, these tax-restrictions on the American colonial trade.

The second pamphlet, similar to the first in purpose and tone, but still stronger in execution, is entitled " Some Thoughts on the Method of Improving and Securing the Advantages which accrue to Great Britain from the Northern Colonies." [1] It was first published in a New York newspaper probably in August, 1764, whence it was republished in London in the following year. Containing no allusion to the proposal of a Stamp Act, with no mention even of the revenue law of April, 1764, with no denial of the right of parliament to tax the Americans, it deals only with the impolicy of all such measures,—their impolicy as affecting the practical interests of the whole empire and of every member of it.

The writer takes his stand at that point of time in the previous year, when, with inexpressible loyalty and delight, the American colonies heard of the Treaty of Paris whereby Great Britain had come into possession of all the vast American domain claimed by France east of the Mississippi River. In the presence of this stupendous success, two questions spring up:—first, how shall these American possessions, the old and the new, be secured to Great Britain ? —and, secondly, how shall they be improved to her greatest advantage ?

---

[1] I have used the London edition, also belonging to the Harvard library. The preface states that it is a reprint from the " New York Mercury." A pencilled inscription in the pamphlet states that George Bancroft considered it as the work of Mauduit. This must be a mistake ; since the doctrine of the pamphlet is the opposite of that held by Mauduit as regards parliamentary taxation.

The first question is easily answered.   From external attack, these colonies are secured by the fleet of Britain; and from the loss of them through internal revolt, she is secured by the fact, that she gives them no motive for such revolt: " History does not furnish an instance of a revolt begun by the people, which did not take its rise from oppression."   " As we are sure Britain will not oppress her colonies, and it is evident that nothing else can give them either power or inclination to rebel, we may safely conclude that they will remain steadfastly and firmly united to her, and by contributing to her wealth and power, continue to increase their own security, and that dependence which they esteem their happiness, and which carries with it so many real advantages." [1]

The answer to the second question is equally clear, although it involves considerations then less familiar.   The colonies can be made to yield the greatest commercial advantage to Great Britain, by being permitted to acquire the greatest commercial prosperity for themselves.   Not by taxing them, but by buying of them and selling to them, will the mother country make them most profitable to herself; and the more the colonies have to sell, the more will they have to buy, and the more will they have with which to pay for what they buy.   Of such commercial prosperity, what is the essential condition ?   It is freedom.   Why is it that the northern colonies, though under a stern climate and upon a hard soil, should already have yielded so immense a profit to the mother country ?   " This has no other cause, but that which made Rome the mistress of the world, gave grandeur, riches, and power to Venice, and at present constitutes the glory of Britain—liberty ! " [2]   " I will conclude all with this observation . . . that Britain, by being contented with all her colonies can yield— which may be obtained by a wise regulation of their trade— will found the greatest empire in the world, and such a one

---

[1] " Some Thoughts," etc., 9–10.

[2] Ibid., 15.

as her American subjects will ever find it their truest interest to support.'' [1]

Upon the whole, it may be said of this wise and most persuasive presentation, in 1764, of the American view as to British colonial policy, that had the brain of George Grenville and of George the Third been capable of absorbing it, there would have been no American Revolution.

---

[1] " Some Thoughts," etc., 23.

CHAPTER III.

UNDER THE MENACE OF THE STAMP ACT: NOVEMBER, 1774–APRIL, 1765.

I.

THE several writings thus far mentioned as products of the year 1764, are among the earliest manifestations, in literary form, of American disfavor toward the new taxing-policy of the government. A curious fact, however, attaches to all these writings. Though published weeks or even months after the official announcement of an intended Stamp Act, not one of them contains the slightest allusion to that measure; while, on the other hand, the actual passage, in April, 1764, of the act for deriving an imperial revenue from certain port-duties in the colonies, appears to be the one fact over which the American people are invited to take alarm. Thus, as it seems, the American people, bewildered in the thicket of passing events, did not at first perceive their true relations and proportions. But, at about the time of the appearance of Thacher's pamphlet, that is, in the early autumn of 1764, the appalling significance of the notice of the Stamp Act began to dawn upon them; and then, almost at once, the centre of gravity shifted from the immediate past to the immediate future,—from the measure that had become a law in the preceding March, to the measure that might become a law in the following March.

One of the earliest tokens of this change in the direction of the public solicitude, is to be seen in a bit of comic writing, the humor of which was already characteristic of the American mind, then, as since then, not unwilling to veil its serious and even its angry and uncompliant moods under droll anecdotes and grimly ironical terms of ultra-submissiveness. In the leading newspaper of Rhode Island there appeared, on the tenth of November, 1764, a communication [1] purporting to be from a rough and ready colonist in humble circumstances, a man without any knowledge of books, as he says, excepting the Bible and Pilgrim's Progress. Not long before, he had sat up one evening with a neighbor of his till eleven o'clock, trying to make out the bearings of this queer news about " a stamping law "; and, parting from his friend no wiser than before their talk began, he went to bed, and, straightway falling asleep, he had this dream:—" Methought the stamp law ended in one for stamping all our beasts of burthen, and for that end a ship had arrived with the branding-master and his company, who soon after sent order to our town to have all such beasts within a proper enclosure on a certain day. And, accordingly, in the morning of the day, I fancied that I saw all

---

[1] For a carefully authenticated manuscript copy of this " Dream," taken from the files of the " Providence Gazette," I am indebted to Mr. W. E. Foster of that city. I became aware of the existence of this curious piece, through an allusion to it in one of the pamphlets of " The Halifax Gentleman," who, perhaps from mere rumor, attributes it to Stephen Hopkins.

the horses of the town brought together in a pasture of my neighbor's, that was fenced better than ordinary—the pound being too small—and amongst them were about a half a dozen asses, being all we had.   Soon after, the brand-master with his retinue approached the pasture with great pomp, one carrying a large silver brand in the form of the letter S; and, upon entering the field, they began with the asses, and branded them without the least interruption. They then drew near to the horses, and would have laid hold on a stately bay horse; but, taking fright at the glittering of the brand, he snorted, kicked up his heels, and went off.   I was sorry to see him fling the dirt into the gentleman's face; and the whole drove being struck with the same panic, they leapt the fence, and ran off snorting and flinging up their heels, so that I saw them no more. And whilst the branding-company stared, and expressed some surprise at what had happened, a very ragged country-fellow said, with a facetious grin, that he ' always understood, till then, that the good people of England very well knew that none but asses would stand still to be branded.' " In the ominous silence which followed this rustic taunt, a gentlemanlike person who stood holding by the bridle a powerful horse, was approached by one of the branding-company, who requested the loan of the horse that he might ride it to head off the drove.   To this the gentleman politely assented, but at the same time advised the officer to remove his spurs—as the horse would not tolerate any rider so equipped; informing him at the same time, while he stooped down to unbuckle his spurs, that the drove of horses which he proposed to head off, would probably prove a little difficult to manage in that way,—since they " were all of the English breed, and the far greater part of them had for their sire and were descended from a very remarkable horse, known by the name of Old Noll, who, though he was not a showy beast, was firm and had courage, and might have been of great use but that his master fell in love with a huge pair of French spurs, and, contrary to all good advice, must needs mount Noll with them upon his heels; but, unhappily, the horse no sooner felt the spurs at his sides, but he gave his master such a fall as broke his neck; upon which the breed were out of credit for a while, and being sent hither, multiplied exceedingly.'' Upon this discouraging information, the officer concluded not to accept the loan of the gentleman's horse; and, after various other methods of procedure had been discussed without avail, the leading man of the town ventured to give to the branding-master this bit of gentle counsel:—'' ' Have you never heard that branding is a mark of property ? If the brand was once put on, I should not wonder if your next errand here was for the beasts—or their hides. Mutual confidence will give our master a better and more durable property in what we have, than any branding. But when distrust and diffidence comes in its stead, no good can ensue; opportunities will never be long wanting for masters to oppress their servants, or for servants to —— their masters.' Here, the whole of our company gave three huzzas, in approbation of our chief's discourse; in which I joined so heartily, that the good woman at my side gave me a hunch with her elbow, and asked me if I had the colic or gripes,—and so ended my Vision ! ''

II.

Not many weeks after the publication in Rhode Island of this droll and effective statement of the American case as against the mere proposal of a Stamp Act, there was published there a remarkable pamphlet dealing with the same subject but in a very different manner,—'' The Rights of Colonies Examined,''—a piece of political statement which should be of uncommon use to us in our effort to trace the earliest movements of cultivated and filial thought in America, over the issue which the imperial government seemed to be bent on forcing into prominence. This pamphlet was first issued from the press in Providence, on the twenty-second of December, 1764; it bore upon its front the dignified announcement, " published by authority "; and although the name of the author was not there given, the little book was at once known as the work of no less a person than Stephen Hopkins, then governor of the colony of Rhode Island.[1]

This man, scarcely known to Americans since those days, except for his tremulous autograph written beneath the Declaration of Independence, deserves remembrance also for services among the most precious that man can render to man,—for long and manifold services to American society in all its great interests of thrift, enlightenment, freedom, and order. A far-seeing and an accomplished statesman of the later colonial age, Stephen Hopkins, of the colony of Rhode Island, wrought a good work for all the colonies by helping them to see what were the safe limits of colonial submission; and with a heart that never trembled even when his hand shook, he stood by the side of the earliest and sturdiest statesmen of the Revolution, loyal and loving toward England, dreading with inexpressible dread a disruption of the colonial tie, but dreading still more any surrender to a doctrine of parliamentary authority which, to him, seemed to involve the decline and extinction of all manly civic life in this part of the world.

He was born one year after Benjamin Franklin; he died five years before Franklin; and as their long lives were thus nearly coincident in time, so was there a marked resemblance between the two men in intellectual traits, in studies,

---

[1] Under charters given by Charles II., both the governor of Rhode Island and the governor of Connecticut were elected by the people; and as the former now entered into public criticism of the policy of the home government, so the latter, who at that time was Thomas Fitch, did the same, in a pamphlet published at New Haven, October 11, 1764, and entitled " Reasons why the British Colonies in America should not be charged with Internal Taxes by Authority of Parliament,"—a serious presentation of the argument, not without sundry questionable statements both of fact and of law. He admits the necessity and propriety of external taxation by parliament, but denies that of internal taxation.

in practical successes, and in the systematic devotion of their great powers to the welfare of their fellow-men.[1]

The intention of Hopkins's pamphlet is happily conveyed to us by its motto:

> " 'Mid the low murmurs of submissive fear
> And mingled rage, my Hampden raised his voice,
> And to the Laws appeal'd." [2]

Like so many other political writers of this period, he comes to the problem of parliamentary authority, after an investigation into the origin of society, the nature of government, and the basis of the British constitution and of those political rights which under that constitution seemed to be the inheritance of all British subjects.

But are the American colonists entitled to all the rights of British subjects ? Hopkins contends that they are; and first, on general grounds. For, as he asserts, all colonies, in ancient and in modern times, " have always enjoyed as much freedom as the mother state from which they went out." [3] And, in the second place, if such be the fact respecting all other colonies than the British, " will any one suppose the British colonies in America are an exception to this general rule ?—colonies that came out from a kingdom

---

[1] Until within recent years, there has been no better account of Hopkins than is the sketch of him in Sanderson, " Biog. of the Signers," etc., vi. 223–260. This lack has now been admirably supplied by William Eaton Foster's monograph entitled " Stephen Hopkins, a Rhode Island Statesman. A Study in the Political History of the Eighteenth Century," Providence, 1884. In two parts, constituting Number 19 of " R. I. Historical Tracts." In Part i. 199–208, is a list of the existing writings of Hopkins, consisting of pamphlets, official papers, letters, etc.

[2] From " Liberty : A Poem, in Five Parts," by James Thomson. The motto is from Part iv. See " The Complete Works of James Thomson," ed. by George Gilfillan, New York and Edinburgh, 1854, p. 248.

[3] " The Rights of Colonies Examined," 8. The copy which I have used belongs to the library of Harvard University. Hopkins's pamphlet was reprinted by Almon in London in 1766, under this title : " The Grievances of the American Colonies Candidly Examined." This English alteration in the title was in itself a tribute to the author.

5

renowned for liberty, from a constitution founded on compact, from a people of all the sons of men the most tenacious of freedom ? '' [1]

Without dwelling upon the claim to political rights as
founded on the original charters—a subject which had been
already handled by Otis—Hopkins argues with much force
that the parliament had '' always understood their rights in
the same light.'' [2]   Moreover, these rights, thus resting
upon sanctions so august, have always been enjoyed by the
British colonies even until now.   But now the scene is
changing.   The last parliament '' passed an act, limiting,
restricting, and burdening the trade of these colonies much
more than had ever been done before; . . . enlarging
the power and jurisdiction of the courts of admiralty in the
colonies ''; and resolving upon the establishment of '' stamp
duties and other internal taxes.''   These various measures,
enacted and impending, '' have caused great uneasiness and
consternation among the British subjects on the continent
of America,'' [3] and for very good reasons.

As to the proposed Stamp Act, the mere announcement
of it '' hath much more, and for much more reason, alarmed
the British subjects in America, than anything that had
ever been done before ! . . .   For it must be confessed
by all men that they who are taxed at pleasure by others,
cannot possibly have any property; . . . they who
have no property, can have no freedom, but are indeed
reduced to the most abject slavery,—are in a condition far
worse than countries conquered and made tributary.   For
these have only a fixed sum to pay, which they are left to
raise among themselves, in the way that they may think
most equal and easy; and having paid the stipulated sum,
the debt is discharged, and what is left is their own.   This
is more tolerable than to be taxed at the mere will of others,
without any bounds, without any stipulation and agreement, contrary to their consent, and against their will.'' [4]

---

[1] '' The Rights,'' etc., 8.   [3] Ibid. 10
[2] Ibid.   [4] Ibid. 15–16.

It does not help the case to say that "those who lay these taxes upon the colonies, are men of the highest character for their wisdom, justice, and integrity; . . . for one who is bound to obey the will of another, is as really a slave, though he may have a good master, as if he had a bad one."[1]

Nor will it be any alleviation of the hardship of such taxation, that the money thus drawn from the colonies "will be laid up and set apart for their future defense. This serves only the more strongly to mark the servile state of the people. Free people have ever thought, and always will think, that the money necessary for their own defense, lies safest in their own hands, until it is wanted immediately for that purpose."[2]

Therefore, it is unfair to denounce as unseemly the loud outcry now raised in the colonies against such attacks as these; for, as Dean Swift says, "a man on a wreck was never denied the liberty of roaring as loud as he could."[3] And "is the defense of liberty become so contemptible, and pleading for just rights so dangerous? Can the guardians of liberty be thus ludicrous?"[4]

But it is said that England has gone to great cost on behalf of the colonies, and now deserves some return from them in kind. To what cost has England gone on their behalf? In truth, nearly all the colonies were established without the cost to the government of England of a single penny; from the beginning even until now, they have themselves been at the chief cost of their own defense; while in all England's wars in America against the power of France, the Americans have always contributed in enterprise, treasure, and human life far more than their full proportion.[5]

Nor is it right to say that if the colonies are exempted from taxation by parliament, "they are therefore exempted from bearing their proper share in the necessary burdens of

---

[1] "The Rights," etc., 16.
[2] Ibid. 17.
[3] Ibid. 19.
[4] Ibid.
[5] Ibid. 20–21.

government. This by no means follows. Do they not support a regular internal government in each colony, as expensive to the people here, as the internal government of Britain is to the people there ? Have not the colonies here, at all times when called upon by the crown, raised money for the public service, doing it as cheerfully as the parliament have done on like occasions ? Is not this the most easy, the most natural, and most constitutional way of raising money in the colonies ? What occasion, then, to distrust the colonies ? What necessity to fall on an invidious and unconstitutional method, to compel them to do what they have ever done freely ? Are not the people in the colonies as loyal and dutiful subjects as any age or nation ever produced ? And are they not as useful to the kingdom, in this remote quarter of the world, as their fellow subjects are who dwell in Britain ? The parliament, it is confessed, have power to regulate the trade of the whole empire; and hath it not full power, by this means, to draw all the wealth of the colonies into the mother country at pleasure ? What motive, after all this, can remain to induce the parliament to abridge the privileges and lessen the rights of the most loyal and dutiful subjects,—subjects justly entitled to ample freedom, who have long enjoyed, and not abused or forfeited, their liberties, who have used them to their own advantage in dutiful subserviency to the orders and interests of Great Britain ? Why should the gentle current of tranquillity, that has so long run with peace through all the British states, and flowed with joy and happiness in all her countries, be at last obstructed, be turned out of its true course into unusual and winding channels, by which many of those states must be ruined, but none of them can possibly be made more rich or more happy ? " [1]

" We finally beg leave to assert," pleads this gallant and dexterous champion, " that the first planters of these colonies were pious Christians, were faithful subjects, who, with a fortitude and perseverance little known and less considered,

---

[1] " The Rights," etc., 21–22.

settled these wild countries by God's goodness and their own amazing labors; thereby added a most valuable dependence to the crown of Great Britain; were ever dutifully subservient to her interests; so taught their children, that not one has been disaffected to this day, but all have honestly obeyed every royal command and cheerfully submitted to every constitutional law; have as little inclination as they have ability to throw off their dependency; have carefully avoided every offensive measure, and every interdicted manufacture; have risked their lives as they have been ordered, and furnished their money when it has been called for; have never been troublesome or expensive to the mother country; have kept due order, and supported a regular government ; have maintained peace and practised Christianity, and in all conditions, and in every relation, have demeaned themselves as loyal, as dutiful, and as faithful subjects ought; and that no kingdom or state hath, or ever had, colonies more quiet, more obedient, or more profitable, than these have ever been.

" May the same Divine Goodness that guided the first planters, protected the settlements, inspired kings to be gracious, parliaments to be tender, ever preserve, ever support, our most gracious king; give great wisdom to his ministers, and much understanding to his parliaments; perpetuate the sovereignty of the British constitution, and the filial dependency and happiness of all the colonies." [1]

The impression made by this strong and sober-minded pamphlet was very great throughout the colonies, in nearly every one of which it was reprinted.[2] Moreover, its tone was so temperate and so conciliatory that both in England and in America, it made its way and carried conviction to many minds that would have been repelled by the brusqueness and asperity of Otis.

[1] " The Rights," etc., 24.
[2] W. E. Foster, " Stephen Hopkins," ii. 57–58, 59, gives facts to indicate the wide influence of this pamphlet.

III.

Thus far, the whole current of American opinion seemed to be setting in one direction—that of dissent from the new colonial policy of the government; and had these criticisms been confined to the usual limits of political opposition—to arguments, for example, against mere details of the policy in question—it is doubtful if the current of American opinion, thus vigorously running in the channel of dissent, would have ever encountered any serious resistance either in America or in England. In all these discussions, however, though pervaded by ardent and honest avowals of love for England and of delight in membership of the British empire, was to be discovered the germ of a doctrine which, under every valid form of government, has been deemed inadmissible,—a doctrine which, under our present form of government, has been sternly condemned, in battle and blood, as a pestilent political heresy,—the doctrine of Nullification ! It was in opposition to just this heresy, in its incipient stage,—a heresy which tainted the argument of Stephen Hopkins, as it had already done that of Thacher and of Otis,—that our first Loyalist writer took up his pen. Moreover, it is a token of the unequal conditions under which the debate was thenceforward to be conducted by the two opposite parties, that this first Loyalist writer thought it needful to hide himself under the double concealment of a pseudonym and of an alibi.

Hopkins's pamphlet, as will be remembered, had first appeared in December, 1764, in Providence; and it was in February, 1765, that there was published at Newport a pamphlet in reply, entitled " A Letter from a Gentleman at Halifax, To His Friend in Rhode Island." This enigmatic gentleman at Halifax writes to his apocryphal friend in Rhode Island that he has been reading Hopkins's pamphlet, which he finds " a labored ostentatious piece," and quite inferior to that of Otis, " who, though unhappily misled by popular ideas, and at the head of the tribunitian veto, yet appears to be a man of knowledge and parts."[1] The writer hopes that Hopkins's pamphlet does not accurately represent the prevailing temper of the colonists, whom he advises by all means to meditate on the seriousness of the act of affronting a power like that of England; and then, without more ado, he proceeds to attack the central doctrine, which is also the central fallacy, of Hopkins's pamphlet,—" that the colonies have rights independent of, and not controlled by, the authority of parliament."[2] This doctrine—this fallacy—is itself founded on two propositions, both of them fallacious: first, that the American colonists have under their charters all the political rights of Englishmen at home; and, secondly, that they may not be taxed by parliament unless they themselves send members to parliament.

Against the first of these propositions he argues that, as the colonies are in law mere corporations created by the crown, their privileges are precisely those which are fixed and ascertained by their charters. " I fancy," he goes on to say, " when we speak or think of the rights of freeborn Englishmen, we confound those rights which are personal with those which are political. . . . Our personal rights, comprehending those of life, liberty, and estate, are secured to us by the common law, which is every subject's birthright, whether born in Great Britain, on the ocean, or in the colonies; and it is in this sense we are said to enjoy all the rights and privileges of Englishmen. The political rights of the colonies, or the powers of government communicated to them, are more limited ; and their nature, quality, and extent depend altogether upon the patent or charter which first created and instituted them. As individuals, the colonists participate of every blessing the English constitution can give them; as corporations created by the crown, they are confined within the primitive views of their institution. Whether, therefore, their indulgence is scanty òr liberal, can be no cause of complaint; for when they accepted of

---

[1] "A Letter," etc., 4.   [2] Ibid. 6.

their charters, they tacitly submitted to the terms and conditions of them." [1]

Against the second of these propositions, that because the colonists do not elect members to parliament, therefore they cannot be taxed by parliament, he argues that, by every sound view of the constitution, the jurisdiction of the British parliament must be supreme throughout the whole extent of the British empire; that the American colonies have received from their charters " no exemption from the jurisdiction of parliament "; indeed, that " no grant of the king could exempt them from this jurisdiction, because the common law . . . confessedly reaches the colonies, and brings with it that jurisdiction, and announces its force and operation over them "; finally, that the members of the house of commons, by whomsoever elected, are from that moment the " representatives of every British subject wherever he be, and therefore, to every useful and beneficial purpose, the interests of the colonists are as well secured and managed by such a house, as though they had a share in electing them." [2] " Let me ask," he continues, " is the Isle of Man, Jersey, or Guernsey represented ? What is the value or amount of each man's representation in the kingdom of Scotland, which contains near two millions of people, and yet not more than three thousand have votes in the election of members of parliament ? . . . Let us take into the argument the moneyed interest of Britain, which, though immensely great, has no share in this representation. A worthless freeholder of forty shillings per annum can vote for a member of parliament, whereas a merchant, though worth one hundred thousand pounds sterling, if it consists in personal effects has no vote at all. But yet let no one suppose that the interest of the latter is not equally the object of parliamentary attention with the

---

[1] "A Letter," etc., 8–9.

[2] The clauses quoted in the above sentence are from a summary of his own argument in this pamphlet, but given by the author himself in his later pamphlet, "A Defence," etc., 13.

former. Let me add one example more. Copyholders in England of one thousand pounds sterling per annum . . . cannot by law vote for members of parliament ; yet we never hear that these people ' murmur with submissive fear and mingled rage.' . . . In truth, my friend, the matter lies here: the freedom and happiness of every British subject depends, not upon his share in elections, but upon the sense and virtue of the whole British parliament ; and these depend reciprocally upon the sense and virtue of the whole nation." [1]

As to the ancient constitutional formula—" No taxation without representation "—of course it is true in the sense intended by the men who originated it and who have handed it down to us; but it is not true when " taken in a literal sense," as it is now taken by so many Americans; and being by them thus " ill understood " and falsely applied, it " has made all the mischief in the colonies," where its perpetual incantation has had effects only to be compared to those once produced by " the song of Lillibullero." [2]

As to the dispute now arising between the colonies and the mother country, it has two issues: first, concerning the jurisdiction of parliament, and, secondly, concerning the merits of the particular measures now undertaken by parliament in the exercise of its jurisdiction. If the colonies are wise, they will abandon the former issue, and concentrate themselves upon the latter. Let them object to any act of parliament, if they will,—but never because it is an act of parliament, and only because it is not a wise or good act of parliament. Therefore, the colonists " are at full liberty to remonstrate, petition, write pamphlets and newspapers without number, to prevent any improper or unreasonable legislation. Nay, I would have them do all this, with that spirit of freedom which Englishmen " have always carried into their political discussions.' All serious difficulties may be overcome, all real wrongs may be righted, if only the agita-

---

[1] " A Letter," etc., 12–13.　　[2] Ibid. 11.　　[3] Ibid. 21.

tion be conducted with patience and good humor, or at any rate within the old lines of the constitution. In response to demands presented in this spirit, " the supreme legislature of the nation " may be expected in due time " to frame some code of laws, and therein adjust the rights of the colonies with precision and certainty." [1]

In conclusion, though the writer has no ambition to appear in print, he yet permits the publication of his letter, should its publication seem likely to be of use; and this permission he gives all the more cheerfully for the reason that, " notwithstanding the frequent abuse poured forth in pamphlets and newspapers against the mother country, not one filial pen in America hath as yet been drawn . . . in her vindication." [2]

Upon the whole, it must be admitted that the Loyalists of the American Revolution here make their entrance into American literature in a form not at all discreditable either to their intelligence, or to their character, or to their manners. This " Letter from a Gentleman at Halifax to his Friend in Rhode Island " is an able and an impressive political statement. Temperate in thought and in personal allusion, not lacking in sarcasm, and yet never abusive or unparliamentary, it rests upon a clear and a strong basis both in constitutional law and in sound policy. It indicates, moreover, no little familiarity with literature, and especially with English poetry. Of course, it is in no sense a work of genius; but in thought and in form it is quite above the ordinary level of political controversy. It was evidently the work of an able lawyer, of a man of sense and a man of affairs; and being in its tone at once firm, patriotic, moderate, and gentlemanlike, it would be apt to carry along with it a considerable number of the class of fair-minded men—unless already otherwise committed. Its genuine power was shown in the instant and angry rebound against it.

---

[1] " A Letter," etc., 22.   [2] Ibid.

IV.

So instant and so angry was the rebound against the " Letter from a Gentleman at Halifax," that before it had been many days in the hands of the public, the deputy-governor of Rhode Island went before the lower house of the general assembly, asking them to take the offensive pamphlet into their consideration, and to proceed either against the printer of the pamphlet or against the pamphlet itself. This proposition was supported by " some warm members " of the house, who denounced the pamphlet as a libel, and demanded that the printer should be sent for, and that the pamphlet should be burned by the common hangman.[1]

Then, for some time, over this first literary manifesto of the Loyalist party, raged a war of words,—witty or witless, —here hard-hitting arguments, there only coarse noises as of coarse men falling upon one another in a brutal fray. Stephen Hopkins himself, whose pamphlet had given immediate occasion for the onslaught of the Halifaxian, now deals with his assailant, after his own reasonable and dignified fashion, in sundry articles published in " The Providence Gazette."[2] James Otis, too, takes a hand in the mêlée, partly because it was never easy for him to keep out of any good fight that might be going on in his neighborhood, and partly because he had himself been a target for the fleering compliments of the foe. The peculiar vivacity which he thus contributes to the quarrel, by his " Vindication of the British Colonies against the Aspersions of the Halifax Gentleman," may be inferred from a single sentence of his pamphlet, wherein, after the classic manner of controversy in those days, he describes the tractate of his opponent as containing " the quintessence of a mere martial legislator, the insolence of a haughty and imperious minister, the indolence and half-thought of a petit maître, the flutter of a

---

[1] "A Defence," etc., 28.

[2] For February 23, March 2, March 9, and April 8, 1765. Also W. E. Foster, " Stephen Hopkins," ii. 61.

coxcomb, the pedantry of a quack, and the nonsense of a pettifogger."[1] Of course, a debater so competent as Otis, though lapsing thus into occasional vituperation, could never need to rest his cause on mere spiteful balderdash. Accordingly, taking up one by one the chief arguments of the Halifax Gentleman, he confers upon that still visored combatant many a neat and telling stroke; as when, replying to his claim that since but few people in Great Britain could vote for members of parliament, therefore the Americans need not murmur because none of them could do so, he says:—" Many great and good men have complained of the inequality of the representation in Great Britain. This inequality can never be a reason for making it more so."[2]

This screed of James Otis against the Halifax Gentleman was delivered to the public, probably, in March, 1765; and in April, probably, the Halifax Gentleman made his second and his final appearance in the lists, retorting both upon Otis and upon Hopkins. This he did in a pamphlet published at Newport, and entitled " A Defence of the Letter from a Gentleman at Halifax to His Friend in Rhode Island." Like the former production of this writer, it bears not a few marks of literary cultivation; and compared with most controversial writing in that period, whether in America or abroad, it seems rather notable for its urbanity. As though holding some vantage of superiority to partisan passion and tumult, and constantly chaffing his adversaries with a contemptuous humor all the more insufferable because so cool and so effortless, he proceeds to trace the origin and development of the American idea of nullifying the legislative authority of parliament; he cites passages from American newspapers to illustrate the new spirit of colonial disregard for the mother country,—that " unfilial disposition " against which, in his former pamphlet, he had directed his censures. For this service, he had been covered with " illiberal opposition and multiplied abuse . . .

---

[1] "A Vindication of the British Colonies," etc., 46.
[2] Ibid. 20.

from various quarters,"[1] especially from " two very distinguished personages,"[2] " the exactest models of politeness,
urbanity, and softness of manners, perhaps, in America."[3]

One of these, " the Providence writer," he teases for a
time in his nonchalant fashion, charging him, also, with
being a politician who had lately turned his coat. As to
" the Boston writer," he declines to take that gentleman
seriously, although he admits that the reading of Otis's
latest pamphlet is a very serious business. He had, indeed,
" with great travail and perseverance, waded through this
dreary waste of thirty-two pages. In attempting to explore
it, chaos seemed to be come again. The patience he exercised on that dark and gloomy occasion, has fitted him for
any misfortune or disappointment in life. Pain he will no
more consider as an evil. Nay, should he be forced to pass
the Stygian river, and drink its poisonous vapors, it would
be more than Elysian compared with the misery of reading
through this pamphlet." At the conclusion of his paper,
he announces that whatever treatment he may now receive,
he will not further engage in " a controversy which his
antagonists have already made personal, and therefore can
answer no end but to sour and provoke one against another.
Recrimination throws no light upon the enquiry, and the
subject becomes lost in a torrent of abuse. . . . He
will give no occasion for the further production of human
depravity and baseness, lest he should lose that philanthropy which at present administers to him the greatest
contentment, next to that he derives from the esteem and
friendship of good and virtuous men."[4]

V.

It was not in the nature of James Otis to permit an antagonist thus to fold his robes about him and in haughty
composure to retire from the field, without at least having
his garments ruffled by a farewell shot from himself. This

---

[1] "A Defence of the Letter," etc., 3.   [2] Ibid. 4.   [3] Ibid. 14.   [4] Ibid. 29.

farewell shot, accordingly, Otis sent with his usual promptitude, in the shape of a pamphlet of about forty pages,
entitled " Brief Remarks on the Defence of the Halifax
Libel on the British American Colonies " [1]: a piece of
writing the least worthy of respect, probably, of all that
ever fell from that unsteady hand,—a confused mixture of
controversial ingredients, with which the impetuous patriot,
quite out of temper, ostentatiously carries the dispute down
to the level of a street-fight.   Pointing out his antagonist
as a citizen, not of Halifax, but of Newport,—then the
seat of a great maritime commerce and of the most cosmopolitan community in America,—he bespatters him as one
of a motley crowd of political desperadoes in that town, who,
having not long before been deep in treason as conspirators
for the Pretender, are now posing as the peculiar champions of the House of Hanover: " a set of gentry who are
in combination to vilify the colonies, and depreciate every
service they have rendered the crown. . . . Such is
the little, dirty, drinking, drabbing, contaminated knot of
thieves, beggars, and transports . . . collected from
the four winds of the earth, and made up of Turks, Jews,
and other infidels, with a few renegado Christians and
Catholics, and altogether formed into a club of scarce a
dozen at Newport.[2]   From hence proceed Halifax letters,
petitions to alter the colony forms of government, libels
upon all good colonists and subjects, and every evil work
that can enter into the heart of man.   These are some of
the gentry who, all of a sudden, have become the most

---

[1] Of this pamphlet, but nine copies are known to be in existence.   The copy
used by me, now belonging to the library of Cornell University, formerly belonged to E. B. O'Callaghan.   There need be no doubt that Otis was the author
of it.   By some mistake, possibly a mere slip of the pen, William Tudor, on
the 188th page of his " Life of Otis," published in 1823, spoke of the pamphlet
as the work of Stephen Hopkins; and from this misleading statement, apparently, the pamphlet has been often since then attributed to Hopkins, rather
than to Otis.   A perfectly satisfactory account of the whole matter has been
given by W. E. Foster, in his "Stephen Hopkins," ii. 227-230, Appendix I.,
"A Question of Authorship."

[2] The text reads, N—p—t.

loyal subjects in America, and have had the impudence to attempt to persuade all England that the rest of the colonists are as great rebels as ever appeared in arms for the Pretender." [1]

VI.

At the time when Otis was preparing this parting salute for the clever pamphleteer who had so much irritated him, it had become pretty well known that the " Gentleman at Halifax " was, in reality, none other than a very eminent gentleman of Newport, Martin Howard by name, an accomplished lawyer, and a politician of such note that so early as the year 1754 he had been associated with Stephen Hopkins as a delegate from Rhode Island in the Albany Congress. Roughly as Martin Howard was now handled by Otis for the offense of disagreeing with the new doctrine and the new party of colonial Nullification, he was soon to experience far rougher treatment, and for the same offense, at the hands of his own fellow-townsmen, who, in contending for " the cause of liberty," did not understand by that term the liberty to hold, upon the question then in dispute, any opinions other than those which they themselves held. Accordingly, on Tuesday, the 27th of the following August, at about nine o'clock in the morning, an angry crowd of people in Newport " brought forth the effigies of three persons, in a cart, with halters about their necks, to a gallows twenty feet high, placed near the town-house, where they were hung to public view till near night, when they were cut down, and burnt under the gallows, amidst the acclamations of thousands." Of these three effigies, one was meant to personate Martin Howard. On the next evening, also, the same mob assembled once more, and beset the house of Martin Howard, which they did not leave until they had thoroughly gutted it, had burned or smashed his furniture, and had injured his person; whereupon he him-

---

[1] " Brief Remarks," etc., 5.

self, being at last houseless and well-nigh friendless, and
fearing for his life even there in the place of his kindly
engendrure, " took shelter in the *Signet* man-of-war, and
soon after departed for Great Britain." [1]

[1] My account of the mobbing of Howard is derived chiefly from a contemporary narrative in Almon, " Prior Documents," 14. In the " Records of the
Colony of R. I.," vii. 216, 217, is given Howard's own claim against the government of Rhode Island for damages sustained by him in this riot, followed by
the grimly humorous award thereon as made by the legislative committee in 1773.
For the single item as to the injury then done to his person, I depend on the
modern narrative of Sabine, in his " Loyalists of the Am. Rev.," i. 547. The
plan of Sabine's book is praiseworthy as calling for a treatment of the American
Revolution in a spirit of historic disinterestedness far in advance of his own time ;
but the execution of the work is slovenly and inaccurate. At the page above
cited, the reader may find a brief sketch of Howard's subsequent career as a
magistrate in North Carolina down to 1778, when he finally made his escape to
England, where he died in 1781 or 1782. I have been unable to meet with any
evidence to confirm Sabine's statement as to the bad personal character of
Howard. The loose remark that " careful pens speak of his profligate character and of his corrupt and wicked designs," leaves us still regretting that we have
not the advantage of knowing just who held these " careful pens," or just how
much their testimony might happen to be worth.

CHAPTER IV.

THE AMERICAN DEBATE AS ENLIVENED BY A BRITISH PAMPHLETEER: 1765.

I.—The literary character of Soame Jenyns—His lively pamphlet entitled " The Objections to the Taxation of Our American Colonies, Briefly Considered "—An example of ease and gayety in the solution of difficult problems—His discussion of the maxim, " No taxation without representation " —Admiration of this pamphlet in England—Its great immediate success as a political irritant.

II.—Otis's reply to Soame Jenyns, in " Considerations on Behalf of the Colonies, in a Letter to a Noble Lord," September, 1765—The controversial method of this pamphlet—Otis ridicules the doctrine of virtual representation—Scoffs at the pretense that the colonies need protection—His serious discussion of constitutional questions—Advises the British government to be careful of the affections of the American colonists.

I.

EARLY in the year 1765, not far from the time when the new political heresy of colonial Nullification was receiving at the hands of Martin Howard its first literary attack in America, it received in England a literary attack still more effective at the hands of the noted wit, politician, and man of letters, Soame Jenyns, then for more than twenty years a member of parliament, and for about ten years one of the commissioners of the board of trade: a writer of whom Dr. Johnson said that, even in the discussion of a subject the most difficult and the most solemn, he seemed to have " an affectation of ease and carelessness, as if it were not suitable to his character to be very serious about the matter." [1]

[1] Boswell, " Life of Johnson," ed. by Birkbeck Hill, iii. 288. Gerard Hamilton told Malone that Jenyns could not readily be made " to comprehend an argument. If, however, there was anything weak or defective or ridiculous in what another said, he always laid hold of it and played upon it with success. He looked at everything with a view to pleasantry alone." Prior, " Life of Malone," 375.

Precisely this was his tone in dealing with the American question. All the complexities of that sombre problem which was then lowering over the English-speaking race, he dispatches in a nimble-footed pamphlet of about twenty pages of coarse print, entitled " The Objections to the Taxation of Our American Colonies by the Legislature of Great Britain, Briefly Considered," [1] wherein he touches, as was his wont, the tips and fringes of the subject, doing so in that style of argumentative banter, and of jocular facility in disposing of other people's difficulties, which had already procured for him among his contemporaries extraordinary admiration as being a man of fashion who also knew how to transact the business of Grub Street with the high-bred ease, the sparkle, and the persiflage of the court. To some, indeed, the subject of American taxation might have seemed too technical and too dry to be capable of lending itself to the purposes of a mere purveyor of literary confectionery and of philosophical small-talk; yet even upon this unpromising theme, such was his lightness of touch, his gayety, his shrewdness, his air of social superiority, and his apparent proffer to his readers of the ripe fruits of political wisdom without any cost or toil to them, that his little book leaped at once into considerable vogue, as furnishing out the fashionable world with a complete stock of replies— of short, sharp, conclusive, and not too serious replies—to all possible objections against the taxation of America by parliament.

The right of parliament to tax America, and the expediency of its doing so, are, according to Soame Jenyns, propositions so perfectly plain, that no one would dare to undertake their defense, " had not many arguments been

[1] Two editions of this pamphlet appeared in London in 1765. My references are to the second ed., which differs from the first only in a slightly different paging. See, also, the " Works of Soame Jenyns," ii. 189–204. It is no part of my plan in the present work to include English writings on the American dispute, excepting when, as in the present case, such writings need to be briefly described in order to indicate the occasion and character of the American comments upon them.

lately flung out, both in papers and conversation, which, with insolence equal to their absurdity, deny them both.'' Moreover, these arguments '' are usually mixed up with several patriotic and favorite words, such as liberty, property, Englishmen, and so forth, which are apt to make strong impressions on that more numerous part of mankind, who have ears but no understanding.'' [1]

In looking over this rabble of arguments against the taxation of the colonies by parliament, he finds one which appears to him to be '' the great capital argument,'' and which, '' like an elephant at the head of a nabob's army, being once overthrown, must put the whole to confusion.'' [2] This argument may be stated thus: '' No Englishman is or can be taxed, without the consent of the majority of those who are elected by himself and others of his fellow-subjects, to represent them.'' Now, this statement is simply not true; '' for, every Englishman is taxed, and not one in twenty is represented. Copyholders, leaseholders, and all men possessed of personal property only, choose no representatives. Manchester, Birmingham, and many more of our richest and most flourishing trading towns send no members to parliament; consequently, cannot consent by their representatives, because they choose none to represent them. Yet are they not Englishmen, or are they not taxed ?'' [3] Well, then, '' if the towns of Manchester and Birmingham, sending no representatives to parliament, are notwithstanding there represented, why are not the cities of Albany and Boston equally represented in that assembly ? Are they not alike British subjects ? Are they not Englishmen ? Or, are they only Englishmen when they solicit for protection, but not Englishmen when taxes are required to enable this country to protect them ?'' [4]

But the Americans, not being tyros in debate, nor ever without resource in any logical stress or emergency whatsoever, are here ready with a reply: '' that the colonies are by their charters placed under distinct governments, each of

---

[1] '' The Objections,'' etc., 3–4.   [2] Ibid. 4–5.   [3] Ibid. 7.   [4] Ibid. 9.

which has a legislative power within itself, by which alone it
ought to be taxed; that if this privilege is once given up,
that liberty which every Englishman has a right to, is torn
from them,—they are all slaves, and all is lost!'' [1]   A
most plausible plea, to be sure! And yet how much of
truth does it hold ?   In the first place, '' ' The liberty of an
Englishman ' is a phrase of so various a signification—having within these few years been used as a synonymous term
for blasphemy, bawdry, treason, libels, strong beer, and
cider—that I shall not here presume to define its meaning;
but I shall venture to assert what it cannot mean,—that is,
an exemption from taxes imposed by the authority of the
parliament of Great Britain.''   '' Nor,'' in the second place,
'' is there any charter that ever pretended to grant such a
privilege to any colony in America; and had they granted
it, it could have had no force,—their charters being derived
from the crown, and no charter from the crown can possibly
supersede the right of the whole legislature. Their charters
are undoubtedly no more than those of all corporations,
which impower them to make by-laws and raise duties for
the purposes of their own police, forever subject to the
superior authority of parliament. And, in some of their
charters, the manner of exercising these powers is specified
in these express words—' according to the course of other
corporations in Great Britain.' And, therefore, they can
have no more pretense to plead exemption from this parliamentary authority, than any other corporation in England.'' [2]

Finally, as regards the question of right, it has been suggested that the whole difficulty might be solved by a very
simple process—that of introducing into parliament members elected from the several colonies. '' I shall not here
consider the impracticability of this method, nor the effects
of it, if it could be practised, but only say, that I have
lately seen so many specimens of the great powers of speech
of which these American gentlemen are possessed, that I
should be much afraid that the sudden importation of so

---

[1] '' The Objections,'' etc., 9–10.   [2] Ibid. 10–11.

much eloquence at once, would greatly endanger the safety and government of this country. . . . If we can avail ourselves of these taxes on no other condition, I shall never look upon it as a measure of frugality, being perfectly satisfied that in the end it would be much cheaper for us to pay their army, than their orators.'' [1]

The literary and especially the polemic cleverness of this pamphlet cannot be justly estimated without some comparison of it with the mass of pamphlets, English and American, which were produced at about the same time, and upon the same subject. A recent English historian has spoken of it as containing '' the most powerful reasoning in favor of American taxation '' that he has ever met with.[2] Most writers of that period, however, if upon the opposite side of the question, seem to have been impressed rather by its exasperating qualities—the very qualities, probably, which its author most desired it to have—particularly, its deft unscrupulousness in fastening upon a few available points of the case, and in stating these so adroitly, with such derisive humor, with such an air of easy infallibility, as to seem to settle the whole question off-hand and as a matter of course, for all but dunces and scoundrels. It could hardly be expected that American writers in opposition, being themselves very much in earnest, and profoundly convinced of the strength and the importance of their cause, should be able to read with entire patience a writer who insisted on dealing with them as the perpetrators of a sort of political joke which had the disadvantage of being both stupid and impudent. The irritation which they betrayed in their replies to Soame Jenyns may perhaps have given him the very evidence he most coveted of his own success.

---

[1] '' The Objections,'' etc., 17–18.

[2] Sir Edward Creasy, '' The Imperial and Colonial Constitutions of the Britannic Empire,'' 149 n.

II.

One of the most notable of these replies was by James Otis, and was, in fact, his last service in this form of writing,—" Considerations on Behalf of the Colonies, in a Letter to a Noble Lord " [1]: a capital specimen of the jaunty, slashing, controversial pamphlet of the period ; without urbanity or dignity; catching at all occasions for personal retort upon his opponent, and anon flinging at him some blunt epithet, just as one would fling a brick; at the same time, having abundant dialectic skill, legal sense, political sagacity, flashes of noble sentiment, and the sort of popular effectiveness which comes of a Gothic mixture of keenness, bitterness, and buffoonery.

Upon the very title-page of Soame Jenyns's tract occurs a phrase which seems to have had a peculiarly rasping effect on his American critic—the phrase, " our American colonies." " Whose colonies," exclaims Otis, " can the creature mean ?   The minister's colonies ?   No, surely.   Whose then,—his own ?   I never heard he had any colonies: ' Nec gladio, nec arcu, nec astu vicerunt.'   He must mean his majesty's American colonies.   His majesty's colonies they are, and I hope and trust ever will be. . . . Every garreteer, from the environs of Grub Street, to the purlieus of St. James's, has lately talked of ' his,' and ' my,' and ' our ' colonies, and of the ' rascally colonists.' . . . I cannot see why the American peasants may not with as much propriety speak of their cities of London and Westminster, of their isles of Britain, Ireland, Jersey, Guernsey, Sark, and the Orcades, and of the ' rivulets and runlets thereof,' and consider them all but as appendages to their sheepcotes and goose-pens." [2]

Perhaps the most effective thing in Soame Jenyns's pamphlet was its well-handled attempt to put out of court the

---

[1] Originally printed in " The Boston Gazette," over the signature " F. A.," and dated 4 Sep., 1765.   Reprinted by Almon in London in 1765, where it passed through two editions within that year.

[2] " Considerations," etc., 13–14.

colonial plea against parliamentary taxation, by showing
that there were in England itself vast unrepresented popula-
tions which could as justly go into court with the same plea.
" To what purpose is it," retorts Otis, " to ring everlasting
changes to the colonists on the cases of Manchester, Birmingham, and Sheffield, who return no members ? If these
now so considerable places are not represented, they ought
to be! Besides, the counties in which those respectable
abodes of tinkers, tinmen, and pedlars lie, return members;
so do all the neighboring cities and boroughs. In the
choice of the former, if they have no vote, they must naturally and necessarily have a great influence. I believe every
gentleman of a landed estate, near a flourishing manufac-
tory, will be careful enough of its interests. Though the
great India Company as such returns no members, yet many
of the company are returned, and their interests have been
ever very carefully attended to. Mr. Jenyns¹ says, ' by far
the major part of the inhabitants of Great Britain are non
electors.' The more is the pity! ' Every Englishman,' he
tells us, ' is taxed; and yet not one in twenty is represented.' . . . So, a small minority rules and governs
the majority ! . . . What ' ab initio ' could give an
absolute unlimited right to one twentieth of a community,
to govern the other nineteen by their sovereign will and
pleasure ? . . . His way of reasoning would as well
prove that the British house of commons, in fact, represent
all the people on the globe, as those in America. . . .
Should the British empire one day be extended round the
whole world, would it be reasonable that all mankind should
have their concerns managed by the electors of Old Sarum
and the occupants of the Cornish barns and ale-houses ? "
" It is in my humble opinion as good law, and as good
sense too, to affirm that all the plebeians of Great Britain
are in fact or virtually represented in the assembly of the
Tuscaroras, as that all the colonists are in fact or virtually
represented in the honorable house of commons of Great

---

¹ The text reads, J——s.

Britain, separately considered as one branch of the supreme and universal legislature of the whole empire." [1]

Then, too, James Otis, like many another American, had winced under the taunt which Soame Jenyns flung at them when he asked, if the colonists are " only Englishmen when they solicit for protection, but not Englishmen when taxes are required to enable this country to protect them ? " " I ask in my turn," replies Otis, " when did the colonies solicit for protection ? They have had no occasion to solicit for protection, since the happy accession of our gracious sovereign's illustrious family to the British diadem. His majesty, the father of all his people, protects all his loyal subjects of every complexion and language, without any particular solicitation. But, before the ever memorable Revolution, the northern colonies were so far from receiving protection from Britain, that every thing was done, from the throne to the footstool, to cramp, betray, and ruin them. Yet, against the combined power of France, Indian savages, and the corrupt administration of those times, they carried on their settlements, and under a mild government for these eighty years past, have made them the wonder and envy of the world." [2] And, then, as to protection, now and in the future, against whom are we to be protected ? " Against whom ? Why, a few ragged Indians, thousands and ten thousands of whose fathers, without European aid when we most wanted it, were sent to the infernal shades ! " [3]

But the real strength of Otis's pamphlet lies, not in its repartees, but in its direct presentments of policy—of sound and statesmanlike policy—touching all those questions then inflaming the relations of the American colonies with the mother country. First, as a good constitutional lawyer, Otis admits and proclaims the principle of the supremacy of parliament throughout the entire extent of the British empire: " True it is, that from the nature of the British constitution, and also from the idea and nature of a supreme

---

[1] " Considerations," etc., 6–10, 51.   [2] Ibid. 11–12.   [3] Ibid. 29.

legislature, the parliament represent the whole community or empire, and have an undoubted power, authority, and jurisdiction over the whole; and to their final decisions the whole must and ought peaceably to submit."[1] But, secondly, having conceded this, he demands that parliament, in the exercise of its supremacy over all, should be lenient toward the American colonies, and, as a matter of equitable and politic forbearance, should refrain from imposing heavy taxes on them, especially " while their trade and commerce are every day more than ever restricted."[2] To be thus indulgent is, indeed, to exercise a wise discrimination which parliament has been wont to exercise upon many occasions. For example, " great tenderness has been shown to the customs of particular cities and boroughs; and, surely, as much indulgence might be reasonably expected towards large provinces, the inhabitants of which have been born and [have] grown up under the modes and customs of a subordinate jurisdiction."[3] And, finally, who and what are these American provinces on behalf of which such consideration is demanded ? " I affirm, and that on the best information, the sun rises and sets every day in the sight of five millions of his majesty's American subjects, white, brown, and black. . . . Five millions of as true and loyal subjects as ever existed, with their good affections to the best civil constitution in the world, descending to unborn myriads, is no small object. God grant it may be well attended to!· Had I the honor to be minister to the first, the best, monarch in the universe, and trustee for the bravest people, except perhaps one, that ever existed, I might reason in this manner: ' The Roman Eagle is dead. The British Lion lives. Strange revolutions ! The savage roving Britons, who fled before Julius Cæsar, who were vanquished by his successors, Hengist and Horsa, who cut the throats of the Lurdanes,[4] and fell under the Norman bondage, are,

---

[1] "Considerations," etc., 9.   [2] Ibid. 10.   [3] Ibid. 9–10.

[4] " Spenser's Scholiast says, ' loord' was wont, among the old Britons, to signify a lord ; therefore the Danes that usurped their tyranny here in Britain, were called, for more dread than dignity, ' lurdanes,' i. e., Lord Danes."—Johnson's Dictionary, sub. Loord.

after all, the masters of the sea, the lords of the ocean, the terror of Europe, and the envy of the universe! Can Briton rise higher? Yes. How? . . . Revolutions have been. They may be again. Nay, in the course of time, they must be. Provinces have not been ever kept in subjection. What, then, is to be done? Why, it is of little importance to my master, whether a thousand years hence the colonies remain dependent on Britain or not; my business is to fall on the only means to keep them ours for the longest term possible. How can that be done? Why, in one word, it must be by nourishing and cherishing them, as the apple of your eye. All history will prove that provinces have never been disposed to independency, while well treated. Well treated, then, they shall be!'"[1]

---

[1] "Considerations," etc., 30–32.

CHAPTER V.

THE STAMP ACT AS A STIMULANT TO POLITICAL DISCUSSION: AUGUST, 1765 – JANUARY, 1766.

I.—The Stamp Act finds the Americans already alarmed on account of their political dangers—Johnson's lines in Goldsmith's " Traveller "—His unconsciousness of the gravity of pending legislation.

II.—John Adams—His literary response to the news of the passage of the Stamp Act, August, 1765—His range and boldness as a political thinker—His literary vivacity.

III.—John Adams regards the Anglo-American dispute as but one chapter in a world-wide dispute between individualism and corporate authority—Such authority he finds embodied in the canon and feudal law—The old confederacy of kings and priests—This confederacy partly broken up by the Reformation.

IV.—John Adams deems the Reformation as the true cause of English settlements in North America—Hence American antagonism to all civil and ecclesiastical tyranny—The Stamp Act is but another effort of aggression on behalf of such tyranny—To resist it is to do battle for human nature everywhere—The Americans as heirs of the ancient spirit of English liberty —The publication of John Adams's essays in Boston and in London.

V.—The political essays of a Connecticut pastor, Stephen Johnson, September and October, 1765—Their clear warning of danger to the American connection with Great Britain.

VI.—Daniel Dulany's " Considerations," October, 1765—His personal history —His high standing as a lawyer in the Middle and Southern Colonies.

VII.—Dulany's great argument against the doctrine of virtual representation.

VIII.—Dulany denies that his disproof of virtual representation involves the denial of the legislative authority of parliament—He advises his countrymen to be loyal and orderly, but to make parliamentary taxation unprofitable to Great Britain—Let America produce all she consumes.

IX.—Dulany remains faithful to his doctrine of orderly and legal opposition— In later years is persecuted as a Tory—His argument makes a deep impression both in America and in England—His influence seen in the speeches of Pitt on the repeal of the Stamp Act, January and February, 1766.

X.—The public papers of the Stamp Act Congress, October, 1765—Their great political and personal significance.

XI.—"The Late Regulations respecting the British Colonies," by John Dickinson, December, 1765—The doctrine of Nullification boldly advocated in "Considerations upon the Rights of the Colonists," early in 1766.

XII.—American political anxiety and indignation passionately expressed by an American verse-writer in London—His Satire of "Oppression," 1765—Outline of the poem.

I.

ALL students of the American Revolution, who have been accustomed to view the passage of the Stamp Act, in March, 1765, as the initial event in a famous series that became sufficiently long and tragic, are likely to find some difficulty in accounting for the seeming suddenness with which the American people then sprang up, from what is thereby assumed to have been a previous condition of profound colonial content, into one of universal alarm and anger, as well as of clearly-defined and highly-matured constitutional opposition. In truth, however, there never was in America that previous condition of profound colonial content, although, until the removal, through the Peace of Paris in 1763, of the greater danger from France, the American colonists had submitted with as much reticence as possible to the lesser danger from England. Ever since their earliest settlements here, which began in the reigns of the first James and the first Charles, these Englishmen in America had retained and exercised their hereditary race-qualities: they had always been sensitive to the encroachments of prerogative, and they had always been political grumblers. Moreover, the specimens of American political literature which have thus far received our attention, all show the peculiar alertness of political suspicion which had been awakened among them for at least two years before the passage of the Stamp Act, as well as the clear development of their political philosophy and political purpose touching those extraordinary constitutional dangers which, during the same two years, had been steadily gathering head.

Within the last few weeks of the year 1764—that year of premonition to the American colonies—was first published, in London, Goldsmith's poem of " The Traveller "; and among the ten closing lines of it, written, as is well known, by Dr. Johnson, are these two :—

" How small, of all that human hearts endure,
  That part which laws or kings can cause or cure ! " [1]

The events which occurred both in England and in America, during the subsequent twelve months, furnish a rather derisive comment on the limited range of the poet's vision when he wrote this sonorous couplet, and especially on his entire unconsciousness of the vast and bitter burdens, for millions of human hearts, actually to be created by laws just then under consideration in London,—an unconsciousness in which, probably, Samuel Johnson was surpassed by no other great man in England, excepting always his good friend, the King.

II.

Among the most striking of the literary responses to the news that, in disregard of all appeals from America, the Stamp Act had become a law, was one by a writer of extraordinary vigor in argument, of extraordinary affluence in invective, who chose to view the whole problem as having logical and historical relations far more extensive than had then been commonly supposed,—relations far more serious to mankind in general, than would attach to a mere dispute in Anglo-American politics. This writer was John Adams, then but thirty years old, a rising member of the bar of Massachusetts, already known in that neighborhood for his acuteness, fearlessness, and restless energy as a thinker, and for a certain truculent and sarcastic splendor in his style of speech. To the very end of his long life, even his most off-hand writings, such as diaries and domestic letters, reveal in

---

[1] " The Works of Oliver Goldsmith," i. 21.

him a trait of speculative activity and boldness: they show
that his mind teemed and bubbled and sparkled with ideas;
that he was all the time building theories of society, government, religion, literature, education, conduct; that he was
for ever piercing with his virile and dauntless intelligence
the past, present, and future, the qualities and relationships
of all beings in time and eternity, in heaven, and earth, and
hell. Moreover, his ideas are never cool, never colorless.
His brain was not insulated from his heart; nay his heart,
and even his conscience, poured their warm streams through
his brain, and gave to his words a moral and emotional
thoughtfulness which is at least stimulating, often whole-
some and refreshing. This quality makes John Adams's
writings interesting,—which, of course, is not always a test
of value, or of real impressiveness. With the exception of
Jefferson, he is the most readable of the statesmen of the
Revolutionary period. While his intellect was ever alert,
active, and coruscating, it was not high enough or calm
enough to look all around any subject, and to take in the
whole case as a serious quest for truth. Never could he
have been a great judge, or a great historian, or a supreme
statesman, or a supreme thinker. He was by nature an
orator and an advocate; his frankest discussions of a subject
always have the note of partisanship and sophistication.

III.

What, then, to John Adams was the meaning of this
incipient rupture between England and America in 1765,
over the imposition of the Stamp Act? To him it seemed
but one passage in that ancient, world-wide, inappeasable
feud which ever rages among men between corporate authority on the one hand, and individualism on the other. Particularly since the advent of Christianity, corporate authority
has, according to John Adams, found its most perfect development in the canon and the feudal law,—words which he
uses as synonyms for " ecclesiastical and civil tyranny." [1]

---

[1] " Works," iii. 451.

" By the former of these, the most refined, sublime, extensive, and astonishing constitution of policy that ever was conceived by the mind of man, was framed by the Romish clergy for the aggrandizement of their own order." [1] " In the latter, we find another system, similar in many respects to the former; which, although it was originally formed, perhaps, for the necessary defense of a barbarous people against the inroads and invasions of her neighboring nations, yet for the same purposes of tyranny, cruelty, and lust which had dictated the canon law, it was soon adopted by almost all the princes of Europe, and wrought into the constitutions of their government." [2] The climax of misfortune to mankind was reached when, between the two systems of tyranny above described, a confederacy was established. " It seems to have been even stipulated between them, that the temporal grandees should contribute everything in their power to maintain the ascendency of the priesthood, and that the spiritual grandees in their turn should employ their ascendency over the consciences of the people, in impressing on their minds a blind, implicit obedience to civil magistracy. Thus, as long as this confederacy lasted and the people were held in ignorance, liberty, and with her, knowledge and virtue too, seem to have deserted the earth, and one age of darkness succeeded another, till God in his benign providence raised up the champions who began and conducted the Reformation." [3]

IV.

It was, then, the uprising of individualism against corporate authority which gave us the Reformation, even as it was the Reformation which peopled North America with Englishmen—with Englishmen, that is, who were champions of individualism. " I always consider the settlement of America with reverence and wonder, as the opening of a grand scene and design in Providence for the illumination of

---

[1] " Works," iii. 449.   [2] Ibid. 450.   [3] Ibid. 450–451.

the ignorant, and the emancipation of the slavish part of mankind all over the earth." [1]　These Englishmen in America " formed their plan both of ecclesiastical and civil government, in direct opposition to the canon and the feudal systems." [2]　" Tyranny in every form, shape, and appearance was their disdain and abhorrence." [3]　" They saw clearly that popular powers must be placed as a guard, a control, a balance, to the powers of the monarch and the priest, in every government, or else it would soon become the man of sin, the whore of Babylon, the mystery of iniquity, a great and detestable system of fraud, violence, and usurpation. . . . They saw clearly, that of all the nonsense and delusion which had ever passed through the mind of man, none had ever been more extravagant than the notions of absolutions, indelible characters, uninterrupted successions, and the rest of those fantastical ideas derived from the canon law, which had thrown a glare of mystery, sanctity, reverence, and right reverend eminence and holiness, around the idea of a priest, as no mortal could deserve, and as always must, from the constitution of human nature, be dangerous in society.　For this reason, they demolished the whole system of diocesan episcopacy; and, deriding, as all reasonable and impartial men must do, the ridiculous fancies of sanctified effluvia from episcopal fingers, they established sacerdotal ordination on the foundation of the Bible and common sense."　In like manner, they organized their governments in disdain of the feudal law.　They " had an utter contempt of all that dark ribaldry of hereditary, indefeasible right,—the Lord's anointed,— and the divine, miraculous original of government, with which the priesthood had enveloped the feudal monarch in clouds and mysteries, and from whence they had deduced the most mischievous of all doctrines—that of passive obedience and non-resistance.　They knew that government was a plain, simple, intelligible thing, founded in nature

---

[1] " Works," iii. 452 n.　　　　[3] Ibid. 452.
[2] Ibid. 451.　　　　　　　　[4] Ibid. 452–454.

and reason, and quite comprehensible by common sense.''[1]
They knew that ''nothing could preserve their posterity from
the encroachments of the two systems of tyranny . . .
but knowledge diffused generally through the whole body of
the people.''[2] And the Stamp Act—what is it but a
master stroke on behalf of ecclesiastical and civil tyranny,
another effort of aggression on the part of the confederated
enemies of mankind, a device expressly framed '' to strip
us in a great measure of the means of knowledge, by loading the press, the colleges, and even an almanac and a
newspaper, with restraints and duties; and to introduce the
inequalities and dependencies of the feudal system, by taking from the poorer sort of people all their little subsistence,
and conferring it on a set of stamp officers, distributors, and
their deputies.''[3]

Therefore, in taking our stand against the enforcement of
the Stamp Act, we are but placing ourselves in that mighty
line of heroes and confessors and martyrs who since the
beginning of history have done battle for the dignity and
happiness of human nature against the leagued assailants of
both. Herein, let no one dare to accuse us of being over-
bold. Nay, '' the true source of our sufferings has been our
timidity. We have been afraid to think. We have felt a
reluctance to examining into the grounds of our privileges,
and the extent in which we have an indisputable right to
demand them, against all the power and authority on
earth.''[4] Nor may we be told that this attitude of ours
toward Great Britain is unbecoming the children of a fond
mother: '' Is there not something exceedingly fallacious in
the commonplace images of mother country and children
colonies ? Are we the children of Great Britain, any more
than the cities of London, Exeter, and Bath ? Are we not
brethren and fellow subjects with those in Britain, only
under a somewhat different method of legislation, and a
totally different method of taxation ? But, admitting we

---

[1] '' Works,'' iii. 452–454. [3] Ibid. 464.
[2] Ibid. 455. [4] Ibid. 458–459.

7

are children, have not children a right to complain when their parents are attempting to break their limbs, to administer poison, or to sell them to enemies for slaves ? Let me entreat you to consider, will the mother be pleased when you represent her as deaf to the cries of her children,— when you compare her to the infamous miscreant who lately stood on the gallows for starving her child,—when you resemble her to Lady Macbeth in Shakespeare (I cannot think of it without horror) who

> ' Had given suck, and knew
> How tender 't was to love the babe that milked her,'

but yet who could,

> ' even while 't was smiling in her face,
> Have plucked her nipple from the boneless gums,
> And dashed the brains out.'

" Let us banish for ever from our minds, my countrymen, all such unworthy ideas of the king, his ministry, and parliament. . . . Let us presume, what is in fact true, that the spirit of liberty is as ardent as ever among the body of the nation, though a few individuals may be corrupted. Let us take it for granted, that the same great spirit which once gave Cæsar so warm a reception, which denounced hostilities against John till Magna Charta was signed, which severed the head of Charles the First from his body, and drove James the Second from his kingdom, the same great spirit (may Heaven preserve it till the earth shall be no more) which first seated the great-grandfather of his present most gracious majesty on the throne of Britain, is still alive and active and warm in England; and that the same spirit in America, instead of provoking the inhabitants of that country, will endear us to them for ever, and secure their good-will." [1]

---

[1] " Works," iii. 461–462.

Such was the teaching, and such the temper, of a series of four essays by John Adams, which were first published, though without his name and without any descriptive title, in the " Boston Gazette," in August, 1765. By their wide range of allusion, their novelty, audacity, eloquence, by the jocular savagery of their sarcasms on things sacred, they easily and quickly produced a stir, and won for themselves considerable notoriety. At the instigation of Thomas Hollis, they were almost immediately reproduced in the " London Chronicle "; and in 1768, also by Hollis's act, they were welded together into a single document, and as such were published in London under the somewhat misleading title of " A Dissertation on the Canon and the Feudal Law."[1]

V.

On the sixth of September, 1765, there appeared in a newspaper published in New London the first of a series of five essays addressed " To the Freemen of the Colony of Connecticut," and traversing in grave tone and with masterful intelligence the troublesome matters thrust upon public attention by the Stamp Act. " It is the most critical season," said the writer, "that ever this colony of America saw,—a time when everything dear to us in this world is at stake."[2] Certainly, if parliament may now begin to encroach upon those ancient rights which were secured to us by royal grants and charters,—these being in reality compacts entered into for a valid consideration,—at what point can the encroachments of parliament be expected to end ? If they " have a right to impose a stamp tax, they have a right to lay on us a poll tax, a land tax, a malt tax, a cider tax, a window tax, a smoke tax; and why not tax us for the light

---

[1] It thus formed the last article in a collection of American political writings entitled " The True Sentiments of America"; but is now most easily accessible in " The Works of John Adams," iii. 445-464.

[2] " The New London Gazette," 6 Sept., 1765.

of the sun, the air we breathe, and the ground we are buried in ?[1]   If they have a right to deny us the privilege of trial by juries, they have as good a right to deny us any trials at all, and to vote away our estates and lives at pleasure."[2] Thus, in plain, pungent fashion, level to the common mind, this writer argues against the constitutionality of the Stamp Act as well as of every other form of colonial taxation by the British parliament, exposing at every turn the enormous menace it involves to the most valued rights of Americans —to their very existence, in fact, in any civil rank higher than that of slaves.

Though the authorship of these trenchant essays was at first carefully concealed,[3] they were soon known as the work of a Congregational pastor in Connecticut, Stephen Johnson, sprung from the oldest and best stock in that colony, a graduate of Yale in the class of 1743, a man of pure life, of humane and active sympathy, a sturdy thinker, a strong writer, and of a patriotism so rugged as to show itself on the battlefields of the Revolution as well as in those intellectual combats which led to them.   With a boldness which perhaps no other American writer had then equalled, twice in that year, 1765, this Connecticut pastor gave sharp warning to the mother country that if the policy then in vogue should be persisted in, a bloody revolution would follow, and England would suffer " the loss of two millions of the best affected subjects."[4]   " We cannot think it within any power to make our rights no rights."[5]   " The American

---

[1] A similar thrust at taxation, even at the hands of the colonial legislature, had been made in Massachusetts by Samuel Cooper in 1754.   Both passages in these American writings mildly anticipate, by half a century or more, the point of Sydney Smith's celebrated witticism on the all-pervasiveness of British taxation. " Works of Sydney Smith," ii. 117.

[2] " The New London Gazette," 6 Sept., 1765.

[3] W. Gordon, " History of the . . . Independence . . . of the U. S.," i. 129.

[4] " The New London Gazette," 4 Oct., 1765 ; also " Some Important Observations," etc., 19–20.

[5] " The New London Gazette," 11 Oct., 1765.

colonies can't be enslaved and ruined but by their own folly, consent, or inactivity." [1]

VI.

On the fourteenth of October, 1765, while the members of the Stamp Act Congress were in the midst of their labors upon the great problem of the hour, there came from a printing office in Annapolis a pamphlet, of portly dimensions, dealing with the same problem, and doing so with a degree of legal learning, of acumen, and of literary power, which gave to it, both in America and in England, the highest celebrity among the political writings of this period. It was entitled " Considerations on the Propriety of Imposing Taxes in the British Colonies, for the Purpose of Raising a Revenue by Act of Parliament." The pamphlet was without the author's name; and, still further to obscure its origin, it bore on the title-page, for the place of publication, merely the words " North America." Moreover, the preface was dated " Virginia,"—another device for throwing the reader off the true scent; for, in reality, Maryland was the colony to which its author belonged, and in which, undoubtedly, his pamphlet was written. [2]

All this machinery for self-occultation failed to accomplish its purpose. The marks which the pamphlet bore of its author's individuality, were too definite and too unusual to

---

[1] " The New London Gazette," 1 Nov., 1765. For manuscript copies of these five essays as published in the New London paper, I am indebted to the courtesy of Professor E. E. Salisbury of Yale University. Other writings of Johnson which I have met with are : " Some Important Observations Occasioned by and Adapted to the Public Fast," December 18, 1765, published at Newport in the following year ; the Election Sermon before the General Assembly of Connecticut, 1770 ; and " The Everlasting Punishment of the Ungodly," New London, 1786,—an able theological treatise of nearly four hundred pages, written in a spirit of candor and moderation.

[2] The copy used by me is a London reprint of 1766, calling itself " Second edition." I have seen at the Lenox Library a copy bearing the imprint " Annapolis, 1765," and likewise calling itself " Second edition." In the same library, is a copy of a New York reprint of the year 1765.

permit him to remain long undiscovered. The men then living in the colonies who were capable of handling such a problem in such a manner, were not many and could not be obscure; and, before very long, it was everywhere known as the work of Daniel Dulany, then the foremost lawyer of Maryland, for many years the secretary of the province, and one of its most accomplished and influential citizens. Born in Maryland in 1721, Daniel Dulany had been sent to England for his education, which he received at Eton College, at Clare Hall, Cambridge, and at the Temple. Returning in due time to his native colony, he was admitted to the bar in 1747, his own father being at that time one of its most eminent members. It was not many years before his own extraordinary abilities and his lofty personal character raised him to the very head of his profession not only in Maryland but in the middle colonies. His authority was so great that the courts of his own province were accustomed to submit to him the most difficult questions which came before them; his opinion was also sought from England upon abstruse matters of law; while in some parts of Virginia it was no unusual thing for cases to be withdrawn from their own courts, and even from the hands of the Lord Chancellor in England, in order to leave them to him for settlement.[1] Finally, his great gifts for the understanding of the law, were accompanied by those which contribute to its persuasive exposition,—powerful oratory, felicity of literary allusion, and a fine and gracious personality. William Pinkney, who could have known Dulany only in his later years and who had a familiar acquaintance also with the great orators of England near the close of the eighteenth century, is said to have been of the opinion " that even amongst such men as Fox, Pitt, and Sheridan," was no one superior to this barrister in an American province.[2]

---

[1] McMahon, "An Hist. View of the Government of Maryland," i. 356 n.

[2] Ibid. 356–357 n. Some additional facts relating to Dulany may be found in Scharf, " History of Maryland," i. 544–546 ; and especially in a monograph by John H. B. Latrobe, entitled " Biographical Sketch of Daniel Dulany," published in " The Pa. Mag. of History and Biography," iii. 1–10.

VII.

The logical expertness of Dulany as a debater is apparent in the skill with which, at the beginning of his pamphlet, he fixes the true issue. For, in the very preamble of the Stamp Act, he finds an assumption which seems to him to lie at the bottom of every question in dispute between the colonies and the mother country: it is the assumption whereon parliament undertakes to " give and grant " certain portions of the property of the people of America. " What right had the commons of Great Britain to be thus munificent at the expense of the commons of America ? " [1] Upon one point, at least, all parties are agreed, namely, that nowhere can British subjects be taxed except " with their own consent given by their representatives." [2] Are, then, the commons of Great Britain the representatives of the people of America ? It is not pretended that we have ever elected any members of the house of commons. How, then, can the members of that house be our representatives ? The answer is, that this is a case of virtual representation,—precisely such representation as subsists between the house of commons and the vast majority of the people of Great Britain itself, who likewise have no votes for members of that body. Now, this non-voting majority of the people of Great Britain, though not actually represented in the house of commons, are understood to be virtually represented by that house; and they accept the relation as a valid, even if imperfect, compliance with the old constitutional maxim, and submit themselves, accordingly, to such taxes as are imposed upon them by parliament. But, as regards the privilege of voting for members of parliament, the situation of those British subjects in Great Britain is the same as that of all British subjects in America; and, consequently, though the latter are not actually, they are virtually, represented by the house of commons; hence, they also should accept this virtual

---

[1] " Considerations on the Propriety," etc., 1-2.   [2] Ibid. 2.

representation as a valid compliance with the old constitutional maxim, and should submit themselves to the taxes that may be laid upon them by the imperial legislature, which represents them and their interests as truly as it does the vast non-voting population of the mother country.

This imposing analogy between the situation, and therefore between the obligations, of the non-voting people of Great Britain and the non-voting people of America, it is the chief purpose of Dulany's pamphlet to break down and destroy,—as resting on an argument which, in his opinion, " is totally defective," since " it consists of facts not true, and of conclusions inadmissible."[1] " I shall," he says, " undertake to disprove the supposed similarity of situation, whence the same kind of representation is deduced of the inhabitants of the colonies, and of the British non-electors; and if I succeed, the notion of a virtual representation of the colonies must fail,—which, in truth, is a mere cobweb spread to catch the unwary, and to entangle the weak." Accordingly, he goes on to point out a number of particulars in which the situation of the America non-electors is radically different from that of the British non-electors. Thus, in Great Britain, the interests " of the non-electors, the electors, and the representatives, are individually the same, to say nothing of the connection among neighbors, friends, and relations. The security of the non-electors against oppression is that their oppression will fall also upon the electors and the representatives. The one can't be injured, and the other indemnified. Further, if the non-electors should not be taxed by the British parliament, they would not be taxed at all; and it would be iniquitous, as well as a solecism in the political system, that they should partake of all the benefits resulting from the imposition and application of taxes, and derive an immunity from the circumstance of not being qualified to vote. Under this constitution, then, a double or virtual representation may be reasonably supposed. The electors, who are inseparably connected in their

---

[1] "Considerations on the Propriety," etc., 3.

interests with the non-electors, may be justly deemed to be
the representatives of the non-electors, at the same time
they exercise their personal privilege in their right of election, and the members chosen, therefore, the representatives
of both." [1] On the other hand, " the inhabitants of the
colonies are, as such, incapable of being electors, the privilege of election being exercisable only in person ; and,
therefore, if every inhabitant of America had the requisite
freehold, not one could vote, but upon the supposition of
his ceasing to be an inhabitant of America and becoming a
resident in Great Britain,—a supposition which would be
impertinent, because it shifts the question." [2] Furthermore, " should the colonies not be taxed by parliamentary
impositions, their respective legislatures have a regular,
adequate, and constitutional authority to tax them; and,
therefore, there would not necessarily be an iniquitous and
absurd exemption, from their not being represented by the
house of commons." [3] Finally, " there is not that intimate
and inseparable relation between the electors of Great
Britain and the inhabitants of the colonies, which must
inevitably involve both in the same taxation. On the contrary, not a single actual elector in England might be immediately affected by a taxation in America, imposed by a
statute which would have a general operation and effect
upon the properties of the inhabitants of the colonies. The
latter might be oppressed in a thousand shapes, without any
sympathy, or exciting any alarm in the former. Moreover,
even acts oppressive and injurious to the colonies in an
extreme degree, might become popular in England, from
the promise or expectation that the very measures which
depressed the colonies, would give ease to the inhabitants
of Great Britain. It is, indeed, true that the interests of
England and the colonies are allied, and an injury to the
colonies, produced into all its consequences, will eventually
affect the mother country. Yet, these consequences, being
generally remote, are not at once foreseen; they do not

[1] " Considerations on the Propriety," etc., 4–5.   [2] Ibid. 9.   [3] Ibid.

immediately alarm the fears and engage the passions of the English electors,—the connection between a freeholder of Great Britain and a British American being deducible only through a train of reasoning which few will take the trouble, or can have an opportunity, if they have capacity, to investigate. Wherefore, the relation between the British Americans and the English electors is a knot too infirm to be relied on as a competent security, especially against the force of a present, counteracting expectation of relief.'' In conclusion, then, '' if the commons of Great Britain have no right by the constitution to ' give and grant ' property not belonging to themselves but to others, without their consent actually or virtually given; . . . if it appears that the colonies are not actually represented by the commons of Great Britain, and that the notion of a double or virtual representation doth not with any propriety apply to the people of America; then the principle of the Stamp Act must be given up as indefensible on the point of representation, and the validity of it rested upon the power which they who framed it, have to carry it into execution.'' [1]

VIII.

Having, by this brilliant stroke of debating ability, broken the very centre of the enemy's line—their famous doctrine of virtual representation—Dulany finds himself for a moment embarrassed by the very extent of his own success. Has he not proved too much ? For, if the colonies may not be taxed without being either actually or virtually represented, and if, indeed, they are represented neither actually nor virtually, then the alarming inference seems to follow, that '' the subordination or dependence of the colonies, and the superintendence of the British parliament, cannot be consistently established.'' [2] If, indeed, he has proved all that, he has proved far more than either he or his fellow colonists had then desired to prove, and far more, of

---

[1] '' Considerations on the Propriety,'' etc., 9–11.   [2] Ibid. 15.

course, than their fellow subjects in Great Britain can hear
of without abhorrence and dismay. To meet this embar-
rassment, is his next important step. Does, then, the
denial of the right of parliament to tax unrepresented colonies, involve the denial of the general authority of parliament over them ? By no means. The real question at issue
is not one of all power or none, but merely of power sufficient for the unity and welfare of the whole empire. Surely,
the general authority of parliament may be exerted to every
useful purpose required for the due subordination of the
unrepresented colonies, without proceeding to the extent of
laying taxes upon them. Who does not see that parliament
may leave to the colonies their ancient privilege of taxing
themselves for the general support of the empire, without
by that act dissolving the connection of those colonies with
the empire, or their due allegiance to the empire? " May
not, then, the line be distinctly and justly drawn between
such acts as are necessary or proper for preserving or securing the dependence of the colonies, and such as are not
necessary or proper for that very important purpose ? " [1]
" Because the parliament may, when the relation between
Great Britain and her colonies calls for an exertion of her
superintendence, bind the colonies by statute, therefore a
parliamentary interposition in every other instance is justifiable,—is an inference that may be denied." [2] " If,
moreover, Great Britain hath an equitable claim to the
contribution of the colonies, it ought to be proportioned to
their circumstances; and they might, surely, be indulged
with discharging it in the most easy and satisfactory manner
to themselves. If ways and means convenient and conciliating would produce their contribution, as well as oppressive and disgusting exactions, it is neither consistent with
humanity nor policy to pursue the latter. A power may
even exist without an actual exercise of it; and it indicates
as little good sense as good nature to exercise it, only that
the subjects of it may feel the rod that rules them." [3]

---

[1] " Considerations on the Propriety," etc., 17.   [2] Ibid. 18.   [3] Ibid. 24.

But what, finally, is the practical use which this powerful debater would make of his apparent victory over the advocates of parliamentary taxation ? He seems to have shown that the theory of a virtual representation of the colonies is untenable. What then ? In case parliament should still persist in taxing those colonies, what course of action does Daniel Dulany recommend to them ? A nullification of such acts of parliament ? A total rejection of the authority of parliament ? Armed resistance ? Revolution ? Independence ? Heaven forbid ! " I would be understood. I am upon a question of propriety, not of power; and though some may be inclined to think it is to little purpose to discuss the one, when the other is irresistible, yet are they different considerations; and, at the same time that I invalidate the claim upon which it is founded, I may very consistently recommend a submission to the law—whilst it endures." [1]

And is this all ? Nay, but while we make no unlawful resistance to the authority of parliament, we should so shape our affairs as to render such an exertion of its authority quite unprofitable to those who have advised it. " If in consequence of . . . the imposition of taxes upon their properties, the colonies should only be driven to observe the strictest maxims of frugality, . . . to use new methods of industry, and to have recourse to arts for a supply of necessaries, the difficulty in succeeding would prove less than the apprehension of miscarrying, and the benefit greater than the hope of it." [2] " For food, thank God, they do not, and for raiment they need not, depend upon Great Britain." [3] " Let the manufacture of America be the symbol of dignity, the badge of virtue, and it will soon break the fetters of distress. A garment of linsey-woolsey, when made the distinction of real patriotism, is more honorable and attractive of respect and veneration, than all the pageantry, and the robes, and the plumes, and the diadem

---

[1] " Considerations on the Propriety," etc., 4.
[2] Ibid. 63–64.   [3] Ibid. 64–65.

of an emperor without it. Let the emulation be not in the richness and variety of foreign productions, but in the improvement and perfection of our own. Let it be demonstrated that the subjects of the British empire in Europe and America are the same—that the hardships of the latter will ever recoil upon the former.

" In theory it is supposed that each is equally important to the other,—that all partake of the adversity and depression of any. The theory is just, and time will certainly establish it. But if another principle should be ever hereafter adopted in practice, and a violation, deliberate, cruel, ungrateful, and attended with every circumstance of provocation, be offered to our fundamental rights, why should we leave it to the slow advances of time . . . to prove what might be demonstrated immediately ? Instead of moping, and puling, and whining, to excite compassion, in such a situation we ought with spirit, and vigor, and alacrity, to bid defiance to tyranny, by exposing its impotence, by making it as contemptible as it would be detestable. By a vigorous application to manufactures, the consequence of oppression in the colonies, to the inhabitants of Great Britain, would strike home, and immediately, and none would mistake it. Craft and subtlety would not be able to impose on the most ignorant and credulous ; for, if any should be so weak of sight as not to see, they would not be so callous as not to feel it. Such conduct would be the most dutiful and beneficial to the mother country. It would point out the distemper when the remedy might be easy, and a cure at once effected by a simple alteration of regimen." [1] " In common life, a tameness in bearing a deprivation of part of a man's property, encourages rapacity to seize the rest." [2] " Any oppression of the colonies would intimate an opinion of them I am persuaded they do not deserve, and their security, as well as honor, ought to engage them to confute." [3] " If the case supposed should

---

[1] " Considerations on the Propriety," etc., 66–67.
[2] Ibid, 68.   [3] Ibid.

really happen, the resentment I should recommend would
be a legal, orderly, and prudent resentment, to be expressed
in a zealous and vigorous industry, in an immediate use and
unabating application of the advantages we derive from our
situation.'' [1]

IX.

To the plan of American opposition thus outlined by
Daniel Dulany—that of denying the propriety of parliamentary taxation, while resorting to all manly and lawful
measures for convincing parliament of the impolicy of such
taxation—to this plan, he himself remained faithful through
the remainder of the conflict. When, however, his fellow
colonists passed the bounds of constitutional opposition and
resorted to measures which were seditious and revolutionary, he declined, with perfect consistency, to take any further part in the movement; and for this he was bitterly
denounced as a Tory, his property was confiscated, and the
safety of his person imperilled. Though he could not join
with those of his fellow colonists who had resolved upon
measures which seemed to him to be unwise and unjustifiable, neither could he bring himself to take up arms against
them. He therefore went into complete seclusion, from
which he never afterward emerged.

There can be no doubt that the line of colonial policy
thus advocated by Daniel Dulany, with so much legal ability and with so much literary skill, made a deep impression
upon a vast number of his fellow colonists, whom it convinced of the duty and the wisdom of making a fearless
stand against the measures of the ministry, but without
any rupture of allegiance. It is apparent, also, that the
learning, the logical force, the boldness, and the fair-
mindedness of Dulany's pamphlet had no small effect upon
the leaders of liberal politics in England, and especially
upon William Pitt, all of whom it seems to have aided in

---

[1] " Considerations on the Propriety," etc., 68–69.

defining and justifying the policy which they themselves should advocate in parliament with respect to the American colonies. For example, on the fourteenth of January, 1766, just three months after the publication of Dulany's pamphlet, Pitt appeared in the house of commons for the first time after a long absence, and spoke with tremendous power in favor both of an immediate repeal of the Stamp Act, and of the final abandonment of all measures looking towards the taxation of the colonies by parliament. In one of the speeches which he made in the course of that debate, he held up Dulany's pamphlet to the approval and the admiration of the imperial legislature; and though but a meagre outline of his speech is now in existence, even from such outline it is made clear that in all but one of the great features of his argument as to the constitutional relations of Great Britain to her colonies, he followed the very line of reasoning set forth by Daniel Dulany,—an old Eton boy like himself.[1]

---

[1] This may be sufficiently shown by the following passages from Dulany's pamphlet on the one hand, and from the outline of Pitt's speeches on the other :—

DULANY.

"In the constitution of England, the three principal forms of government, monarchy, aristocracy, and democracy, are blended together in certain proportions ; but each of these orders, in the exercise of the legislative authority, hath its peculiar department, from which the others are excluded. In this division, the granting of supplies, or laying taxes, is deemed to be the province of the house of commons, as the representative of the people. All supplies are supposed to flow from their gift ; and the other orders are permitted only to assent or reject generally, not to propose any modification, amendment, or partial alteration of it." i.

PITT.

"In legislation, the three estates of the realm are alike concerned, but the concurrence of the peers and the crown to a tax is only necessary to close with the form of a law. The gift and grant is of the commons alone." Hansard, "Parl. Hist.," xvi. 99.

DULANY.

"For the preamble sets forth, that the commons of Great Britain had resolved to 'give and grant' the several rates and duties imposed by the act. But

X.

No other American writings, in immediate response to the passage of the Stamp Act, are stronger in thought, or nobler in form, or more precious to us now as authentic utterances of the very mind and conscience and heart of the American people in that awful crisis of their affairs, than are the several papers put forth by the Stamp Act Congress,— a renowned assemblage, which was convened in the city of New York, and which transacted its entire work within the space of seventeen days of the month of October, 1765. Its public papers consist, in the first place, of fourteen formal declarations of rights and grievances; and, in the second

---

what right had the commons of Great Britain to be thus munificent at the expense of the commons of America?" 1-2.

PITT.

"When, therefore, in this house we 'give and grant,' we 'give and grant' what is our own. But in an American tax, what do we do? We, your majesty's commons of Great Britain, 'give and grant' to your majesty—what? Our own property? No. We 'give and grant' to your majesty the property of your majesty's commons of America. It is an absurdity in terms." Hansard, xvi. 99-100.

DULANY.

"The notion of a virtual representation of the colonies . . . is a mere cobweb, spread to catch the unwary, and entangle the weak." 4.

PITT.

"The idea of a virtual representation of America in this house, is the most contemptible idea that ever entered into the head of a man : it does not deserve a serious refutation." Hansard, xvi. 100.

DULANY.

"By their constitutions of government, the colonies are empowered to impose internal taxes." 17. "The right of exemption from all taxes without their consent, the colonies claim as British subjects. They derive this right from the common law, which their charters have declared and confirmed ; and they conceive that when stripped of this right, . . . they are at the same time deprived of every privilege distinguishing free men from slaves. On the other hand, they acknowledge themselves to be subordinate to the mother country,

place, of three elaborate addresses, one to the king, one to the house of lords, and one to the house of commons.[1]

He who would truly estimate the moral as well as the intellectual quality of American resistance to the claims of the British parliament, at the moment when the issue was first squarely made and met, will find it needful to read these official announcements of political faith touching imperial problems, the first ever issued by an inter-colonial body of American-Englishmen, then for the first time united against a common danger, and standing up, as their ancestors in the old home had often done before them, against dangerous encroachments upon their rights. Expressed in legal and constitutional language, and employing many of those aphorisms of justice and of civic courage which had been freely used by Englishmen ever since Magna Charta— exactly five hundred and fifty years before—they constitute the first group in that wonderful series of state-papers which the American colonists, speaking through their official representatives, sent forth to the world during the period of their Revolution. In whatever light we may view them,

---

and that the authority vested in the supreme council of the nation may be justly exercised to support and preserve that subordination." 37. " But though the right of the superior to use the proper means for preserving the subordination of his inferior is admitted, yet it does not necessarily follow, that he has a right to seize the property of his inferior when he pleases." 16. " May not, then, the line be distinctly and justly drawn between such acts as are necessary or proper for preserving or securing the dependence of the colonies, and such as are not necessary or proper for that very important purpose ?" 17.

PITT.

" The commons of America, represented in their several assemblies, have ever been in possession of the exercise of this, their constitutional right, of ' giving and granting' their own money. They would have been slaves if they had not enjoyed it. At the same time, this kingdom, as the supreme governing and legislative power, has always bound the colonies by her laws, by her regulations and restrictions in trade, in navigation, in manufactures, in everything —except that of taking their money out of their pockets without their consent. Here I would draw the line. ' Quam ultra citraque nequit consitere rectum.'" Hansard, xvi. 100.

[1] All reprinted in Niles, " Principles and Acts of the Revolution." 457–460.
8

these papers of the Stamp Act Congress are masterly and impressive pieces of political statement,—learned, wise, firm, temperate, conservative, even reverent, — as far removed from truculence as from fear. As mere indices of personal character, as materials on which to frame a wise and safe imperial policy, they should have been invaluable to the leaders of English statesmanship at that time. Obviously, a people capable of such political statements were of stuff unfit to make slaves of. Had the king of England been equal to his great opportunity, he would have recognized these men as politicians too clear-headed to be caught by any sophisms of prerogative, as subjects too self-respecting to lie down in quiet under the violation of their ancient rights; and, instead of trying to trample them into any sort of political subordination, he would have made haste to welcome them, for the loftiness and efficiency of their characters, to the fullest privileges of the empire.

XI.

In December, 1765, in the midst of the ferment occasioned by the fact that the Stamp Act, which was then nominally in force in all the American colonies, was practically nullified in thirteen of them, there appeared in Philadelphia, in opposition to the policy out of which that Act had sprung, a notable pamphlet, the peculiar strength of which lay in its good sense united with good humor and expressed in good English. It was entitled " The Late Regulations respecting the British Colonies on the Continent of America, Considered in a Letter from a Gentleman in Philadelphia to his Friend in London." It was immediately republished in London; and " though," as a contemporary observer wrote, " the town has been in a manner glutted with pamphlets on America, yet its sale has been rapid. It . . . has gained the author much reputation." [1] The author, whose reputation as a political writer

---

[1] Quoted in Dickinson's " Political Writings," Ford ed., i. 210.

was thus breaking upon the world, was John Dickinson, who, as a member of the Stamp Act Congress, had drafted at least two of its public papers, and whose later literary services on behalf of the Revolution were so brilliant as to win for him the title of its " Penman."

Early in the year 1766, and before the hope of a speedy repeal of the offensive Stamp Act had reached these shores, there was published in New York another striking pamphlet on the same side of the question, bearing some of the ear-marks of John Dickinson, though perhaps bolder in thought and more trenchant in phrase: " Considerations upon the Rights of the Colonists to the Privileges of British Subjects, introduced by a Brief Review of the Rise and Progress of English Liberty, and concluded with some Remarks upon our Present Alarming Situation." The real aim of this writer comes out in his open avowal of that doctrine of Nullification which was already going into practice there amid multitudinous curses and groans: " Let us at once boldly plead to the jurisdiction of parliament. Let us totally disallow the force of that Act so evidently calculated to enslave us." [1]

XII.

While the Americans in America were thus pondering the anxious problems thrust upon them by the new taxing-policy of the mother country, it happened that an American man of letters, just then in London, was moved by the same cause to give utterance to his own indignant emotion, in the form of a somewhat pugnacious satire in verse, entitled " Oppression." [2] This poem, which bears on every

---

[1] " Considerations," etc., 25–26.

[2] A copy of the original London edition is in the Harvard library, where I first read it ; but it happens that my quotations are from the Boston reprint of the same year, now in the library of the Mass. Hist. Society, where I read it the second time. Sabine speaks of a New York reprint, also of the year 1765 ; but of this edition I have seen no copy. Hildeburn gives the title, and suggests a Philadelphia reprint.

page the note of Charles Churchill, was probably written in the latter part of 1764. It made its first appearance in London in 1765. The author, not revealing his name, but describing himself as

" An uncouth genius from a western wood,
    Who 've neither wealth, election votes to bribe,
    Nor will to hackney falsehood for a tribe," [1]

has been watching with alarm and indignation the arbitrary measures and the corrupt methods of the court and parliament, all under the malefic leadership of Lord Bute. As a British subject, he feels the disaster which all this threatens to public and private life in the mother land,—to the very integrity and benignity of the imperial constitution itself; but as a British subject of American birth and connections, he is simply enraged to see with what frivolity, in what a riot of wantonness and scorn, the most sacred rights, the dearest interests, of his far-off and unvoiced fellow colonists are here bartered away. This, then, is the broad ground and justification of his satiric wrath :—

" When gathering murmurs spread throughout the realm,
    And favorite pilots bungle at the helm ;
    When tyrants skulk behind a gracious throne,
    And practice—what their courage dare not own ;
    When ministers like screening Grenville rule,—
    A pendant talker and a Butean tool ;
    When law is chained, when Mansfield holds the rod,
    And justice trembles at his partial nod ;
    When naught but fawning, flattery and lies
    Are the just emblems of our brave and wise ;

    .   .   .   .

    When countries groan beneath Oppression's hand,
    And pensioned blockheads riot through the land ;
    When colonies a savage excise pay,
    To feed the creatures of a motley day ;

    .   .   .   .

---

[1] " Oppresion," 4–5.

When dunce on dunce successive rules our state,
Who can't love Pitt, and who a Grenville hate ?
When all these ills, and thousands yet untold,
Destroy our liberty, and rob our gold,
Should not then Satire bite with all its rage,
And just resentment glow through every page ?
Who can indignant bear to hear such crimes,
And not commence an author of the times ? " [1]

But, in the very sordidness and hypocrisy of politics about the court, and in the facility with which the claims of America have been betrayed there even by her own sons, there seems to him to be the added and most impressive reason why he, an American in England, should not succumb to influences that would either keep him silent, or make him false :

" And shall I mingle with the courtly throng,
When truth and reason tell me they are wrong?
Or, if poetic madness seize my brain,
Shall I not rhyme, when conscience guides my strain ?
Shall I subscribe to every dunce's nod,
Call Pitt a villain, or Lord Bute a god ?

  .   .   .   .

Shall I extol the late severe excise,
Call it mere naught, and damn myself by lies ?
Shall I my country, at thy distant call,
Not mark vile H . . . [2] that first proposed thy fall?

---

[1] " Oppression," 1-2.

[2] The person thus bitterly referred to as a renegade American, would be easily identified at the time as John Huske, a native of New Hampshire, then a merchant in London, a member of parliament from Malden, and for his supposed activity in bringing about the Stamp Act greatly detested in America. His effigy, with that of Grenville, was hung upon the Tree of Liberty in Boston in 1765. Hutchinson, " History of Massachusetts, iii. 135. These suspicions against him may have been unfounded. At any rate, he was active in bringing about the repeal of the Stamp Act. During Franklin's examination before the house of commons, Huske was one of the members who by their questions tried to aid in developing the testimony so as to tell in favor of the American cause. Franklin described him as a " friend." " Works of Franklin," Bigelow ed., iii. 451.

Or shall I turn a traitor to my clime,
And be, like him, accursed to latest time?

. . . .

I want no places at a servile court,
To be the dupe of ministerial sport ;
Where honesty sincere but seldom dwells ;
Where every tongue with adulation swells ;
Where great fools smile, though greater fools may laugh ;
Where fawns our H . . . at best a mere state calf ;
Where miscreants in every scene of strife,
Get bread, for bastards and themselves, for life ;
Where favorite falsehood only seems to charm,
And statesmen promise never to perform ;

. . . .

Where public virtue meets with abject hate,
Gives way to pleasure and intrigues of state ;
Where men devoid of decency as grace,
Get titles, pensions, perquisites, and place ;
Where every ill that now annoys our state,
Have their fell source—from thence their baleful date." [1]

Following the precedent then abundantly established among English writers in opposition, this American satirist proceeds to single out and to imprecate Lord Bute as the author and the arch manipulator of all these political woes, particularly of the vexations and calamities now brought upon America :

" Do not our shores now swarm by your command,
With licensed officers by sea and land ?—
A crew more dreadful than our savage foes,
A locust tribe that feed on others' woes ? " [2]

And this execrable colonial policy that

" half the Western World annoys,
That mars their trade, their liberty destroys,
That makes them slaves, or mere mechanic tools
To work for nought, as fools do work for fools," [3]

---

[1] " Oppression," 3–5.   [2] Ibid. 13–14.   [3] Ibid. 10.

is in no way redeemed by the method of its administration
in America at the hands of Lord Bute's hirelings, who,
indeed, contrive by their insolence to crown the whole
system with the last refinements of vexation:—

> " Must it not fill all men of sense with scorn,
> To see a muckworm of the earth low born,—
> A creature but at best a custom clerk,
> The chance production of some amorous spark,
> In ignorance supreme, profoundly dark,—
> To see him seat his mighty self in state,
> With arms akimbo deal to each his fate ;
> To see the hornèd scribbler force along
> And elbow here and there the busy throng ?
> What awful consequence transforms his face,
> To show the importance of his mighty place,
> As if in him all excise solely hung,
> And fates of kingdoms balanced on his tongue ! " [1]

But, now, these wrongs, great or petty, inflicted upon
the colonies by the hard policy of Lord Bute,—all these
stings and stabs of oppression,—how long can America be
expected to endure them ?　The poet's answer to that
question takes the form of a prophecy which to us may
seem almost droll in its moderation, but which may also
have an interest for us as being a very early example of
those numerous hypothetical Declarations of Independence
which were pronounced during the ten or twelve years preceding the real one, and which unconsciously heralded its
advent:—

> " Ere five score years have run their tedious rounds,—
> If yet Oppression breaks o'er human bounds,
> As it has done the last sad passing year,
> Made the New World in anger shed the tear,—
> Unmindful of their native, once-loved isle,
> They 'll bid Allegiance cease her peaceful smile,
> While from their arms they tear Oppression's chain,
> And make lost Liberty once more to reign." [2]

---

[1] " Oppression," 15–16.　　　[2] Ibid. 21.

Yet not with such a menace could even this fierce lover of
liberty permit his satire to close; and in a relenting strain
which has in it the very pathos of filial supplication, he
affirms the affectionate fidelity of the colonies to the empire
of which they would gladly remain a part:—

> " But let them live, as they would choose to be,
>   Loyal to king, and as true Britons free,
>   They 'll ne'er by fell revolt oppose that crown
>   Which first has raised them, though now pulls them down ;
>   If but the rights of subjects they receive,
>   'T is all they ask—or all a crown can give." [1]

[1] Ibid. 22.   Excepting the citation of the title of this notable poem, as given
by Sabin and by Hildeburn, I do not remember to have seen any allusion to it
by any writer.   I first stumbled upon it at the Harvard library, and could not
fail to observe its political and literary significance in relation to the subject of
this book.   Neither Hildeburn nor Sabin has anything to suggest as to its
author.   I am inclined, from internal evidence, to attribute it to the once celebrated Arthur Lee, who was born in Virginia in 1740, was educated at Eton
College and at the University of Edinburgh, and having settled as a physician
in his native colony, went back to England at the outbreak of the great dispute
intending to become a lawyer and a politician.   His biographer writes very
loosely as to dates, and mentions this event as occurring "about the year 1766."
" Life of Arthur Lee," by Richard Henry Lee, i. 15.   He had a knack both
for rhyme and for vituperation ; and may have tried, in 1765, to imitate the
satire of Churchill, as, a few years later, he tried to imitate the invective of
Junius.

CHAPTER VI.

AN EARLY PULPIT-CHAMPION OF COLONIAL RIGHTS: 1766.

I.—Death of Jonathan Mayhew shortly after the repeal of the Stamp Act—His gifts for intellectual and moral leadership—His special influence on the young radicals of the Revolutionary period.

II.—Outline of his career—His early break with New England ecclesiasticism —His activity as a writer—His published writings.

III.—A champion of individualism—His traits as a sermon-writer—His rationalism—His defiance of authority—His demand that religious thinking be practical—His rancorous denunciation of theological rancor.

IV.—His use of the pulpit for the discussion of all topics of the time—The avowed sources of his political opinions—His statesmanlike view of public questions—His political foresight.

V.—His particular antagonism, on behalf of civil liberty, to the Roman and Anglican Churches—A leader in the American crusade against Anglican bishops—Important connection of that excitement with the popular suspicions as to the political purposes of the English government—Mayhew's invective against the Church of England, and especially against bishops.

VI.—His " Discourse concerning Unlimited Submission "—Reflects the influence of Milton's political tracts—Mayhew's ridicule of the saintship and martyrdom of Charles the First—The right of the people to disown and resist bad rulers.

VII.—Immediate effects of Mayhew's preaching on the Stamp Act riots in Boston—His last political discourse, " The Snare Broken," celebrates the repeal of the Stamp Act—His last message to James Otis pleads for a permanent union of the colonies as a defense against evils to come.

I.

ON the ninth day of July, 1766,—in the first lull of a political storm which he had done almost as much as any man to raise,—there died in Boston, in his forty-sixth year, Jonathan Mayhew, minister of the West Church in that town; a great master of the art of rational and passionate speech, and for the previous twenty years, from his coigne

of vantage in the pulpit, a robust and fiery antagonist of
almost every form of arbitrary authority in church or state;
a man of such boldness of character, splendor of diction,
wit, sarcasm, invective, of such enthusiasm for all spacious
and breezy views of freedom and duty, that he had become
a sort of tribune of the people,—particularly, the companion
and inspirer of many of those young radicals in politics
who, long before the final onset of the American Revolution, were unconsciously beating out a path for it.   More
than half a century afterward, one of those young radicals
—still young at eighty-three—in a review of the beginnings
of the Revolutionary movement, fixed upon the years 1760
and 1761 as the time when was produced '' an awakening
and a revival of American principles and feelings, with an
enthusiasm which went on increasing till, in 1775, it burst
out in open violence, hostility, and fury.   The characters
the most conspicuous, the most ardent and influential, in
this revival, from 1760 to 1766, were, first and foremost,
before all and above all, James Otis ; next to him was
Oxenbridge Thacher, next to him, Samuel Adams; next to
him John Hancock; then, Dr. Mayhew.'' [1]   Another of
these young radicals, Robert Treat Paine, carried with him
through life such an impression of the greatness of Mayhew
as a dauntless pioneer of mental and political emancipation,
that, even from a distant retrospect, he named him as '' the
father of civil and religious liberty in Massachusetts and
America.'' [2]   Ninety years after the death of Mayhew, his
last successor in the pulpit of the West Church—himself a
man of fine genius—described a certain sermon of Mayhew's
preached in 1750, as '' the first peal on the trumpet of freedom in this western land, blown clear and loud enough to
be heard over land and water far and wide.'' [3]   '' He had a
truly public soul, an ability in action, a genius for affairs,
which made him the worthy compeer of all the civil authors

[1] John Adams, '' Works," x. 284.

[2] Alden Bradford, '' Memoir of the Life and Writings of Rev. Jonathan
Mayhew, D.D.," 118 n.

[3] Cyrus Augustus Bartol, '' The West Church and its Ministers," 104.

of our national freedom and fundamental institutions; nor does the figure of the elder Samuel Adams or Otis . . . stand out in more distinct relief on the canvas that shows the sublime forms of our political sires, than does that of this religious preacher of the gospel." [1] " I must, for grandeur of aim, and mighty will to bring to pass his purposes, put him in the first rank of human spirits." [2]

And while these tributes bespeak for Mayhew the recognition of posterity for his strong and lofty character—for his purity, nobility, sagacity, and force in practical leadership—they who in his lifetime yielded to his spell, could not refrain from testifying, likewise, to the brilliance of those literary gifts which gave instant splendor and renown to all he did. The writer of a sketch of Mayhew, published just after his death, mentions that he was then generally esteemed " to be as brilliant a genius as ever this country produced." [3] The biographer, John Eliot, a contemporary of Mayhew, speaks of his unsurpassed literary eminence: " No American author ever obtained higher reputation." [4] John Adams, who was not wont either to bless or to curse by halves, does not stick at speaking of Mayhew as a " transcendent genius " [5]; of his writings as sure to be esteemed as long as " wit, spirit, humor, reason, and knowledge " are admired in this part of the world [6]; and of the " wit and satire " that seasoned Mayhew's famous sermon on the saintship and martyrdom of King Charles the First, as " superior to any in Swift or Franklin." [7]

As if conscious that his life was to be a short one, he began to shed its literary fruitage early; and the tone and manner in which he did this, help us to mark some traits of him which his eulogists have not deemed it needful to mention. Never, in his lifetime or since, could he have been

---

[1] Cyrus Augustus Bartol, " The West Church and its Ministers," 86.

[2] Ibid. 84.

[3] In appendix to Ebenezer Gay's two sermons on the death of Mayhew, Boston, 1766.

[4] " Biographical Dictionary," 323.

[5] " Works," x. 288.   [6] Ibid. iv. 29.   [7] Ibid. x. 287-288.

spoken of as a representative of any known species of humility, either intellectual or spiritual,—humility being, apparently, one of those Christian graces which he had to content himself with eloquently commending to the practice of others. The special work he had to do in the world, could have been done, perhaps, only by a man unembarrassed by self-distrust or by too much deference for others. From first to last, as we read what he wrote and spoke and printed, we are made aware of a man born with so sumptuous a supply of self-reliance, as to have little room left in him for such qualities as caution, diffidence, hesitation, reverence; a man quite incapable of suspecting that his own illumination on any subject was not a match for that of all other men and of all past ages; his humor, wit, sharpness, severity, affluence, arrogance, and love of applause, finding their opportunity in the large, uncontrolled freedom of a rationalistic pulpit, before which, in that age of universal rupture with the past, there ascended the ceaseless incense of admiration from disciples most grateful to him for his aid in enabling them to form so good an opinion of their own times, and of themselves. In the case of common men, this uncommon self-esteem is apt to be described by words that do not veil its offensiveness. Even in the case of so privileged a person as Mayhew, there were some onlookers who made bold to apply such words to him,—as John Adams's friend, Veasy, who in 1760 ventured the opinion that Dr. Mayhew had " haughty spirits and vanity "[1]; or, as the author of some verses published in 1763, who thus frankly apostrophized that much belauded man :

" By nature vain, by art made worse,
    And greedy of false fame ;
    Through truth disguised, and mobs deceived,
        Thou fain would'st get a name." [2]

---

[1] J. Adams, " Works," ii. 86.

[2] " Verses on Doctor Mayhew's Book of Observations," etc., 16. The author of these verses is called " a gentleman of Rhode Island," and is said by E. F. Slafter to have been John Alpin.

II.

He was born on the eighth of October, 1720, on the island of Martha's Vineyard, of a line of saintly men who, for three generations before him, had tilled the soil and preached the gospel in that lovely place. He was graduated at Harvard College in 1744, highly distinguished for the ease and elegance with which he wrote Latin, and for his skill in dialectics. Three years after his graduation, he was settled as pastor of the prominent church in Boston, in the service of which he spent his brief life. At his ordination there, the leading clergymen of the neighborhood were conspicuous by their absence,—this being on account of an odor of heterodoxy already perceptible about his person, and in no way lessened as the years went on. He is said to have been the first minister among the New England churches openly to attack and spurn the five great buttresses of the system of John Calvin, and openly to deny the doctrines of the Trinity, and the divinity of Jesus Christ; while the church of which he was pastor, was the first one in that region to avow itself as Unitarian.[1] Standing up thus alone as an incipient heretic in a town then prodigiously devoted both to orthodoxy and to church-going, young Mayhew made from the first a gallant and a winning fight for recognition and influence. He had an eye for the strategic uses of the printing-press as an ally of the pulpit ; and while the thoughtfulness, force, and vivacity of his spoken sermons soon made his meeting-house a resort for men and women of advanced ideas—a mart for the exhibition and interchange of many sorts of theological and political novelties —those same sermons, being frequently flung into print and scattered hither and yon in this country and in England, soon lifted his name into a distinction unrivalled, probably, by any of his contemporaries in the American pulpit. Of the industry and fearlessness with which he thus prosecuted his trade of authorship, the reader may judge

---

[1] Bradford, " Life of Mayhew," 24, 464.

by a mere glance at the long list of his published writings:
In 1749,—"Seven Sermons . . . Preached as a Lecture in the West Meeting House"[1]; in 1750,—"A Discourse concerning Unlimited Submission and Non-Resistance
to the Higher Powers; With some Reflections on the Resistance made to King Charles the First, and on the Anni-
versary of his Death,—in which the Mysterious Doctrine of
that Prince's Saintship and Martyrdom is unriddled"[2]; in
1751,—"Sermon . . . on the Death of Frederick,
Prince of Wales"; in 1754,—the Massachusetts election
sermon; in 1755,—"Two Sermons, . . . November
23, . . . Occasioned by the Earthquakes . . . on
the Tuesday Morning and Saturday Evening preceding";
"A Discourse . . . Occasioned by the Earthquakes in
November, . . . delivered December 18 following";
and a volume of fourteen sermons on subjects of speculative
and practical importance[3]; in 1758,—"Two Discourses
delivered November 23, . . . being a Day of Public
Thanksgiving, relating more especially to the Success of his
Majesty's Arms and those of the King of Prussia the last
year"; in 1759,—"Two Discourses delivered October
25, . . . being . . . a Day of Public Thanksgiving for the Success of his Majesty's Arms, more particularly
in the Reduction of Quebec"; in 1760,—"A Sermon
occasioned by the Great Fire in Boston," "Two Discourses
delivered October 9, . . . being a Day of Public
Thanksgiving for the Success of his Majesty's Arms, more
especially in the entire Reduction of Canada," "A Discourse occasioned by the Death of the Honorable Stephen
Sewell," and a volume of thirteen "Practical Discourses
delivered on Occasion of the Earthquakes in November,
1755"[4]; in 1761,—"A Discourse occasioned by the Death

---

[1] Reprinted in London, 1750.

[2] Reprinted in Boston, 1818.

[3] Reprinted in London, 1756.

[4] In an advertisement for April 1, 1760, at the end of his sermon on the
"Great Fire," this volume is announced as then first published.

of King George the Second, and the Happy Accession of
his Majesty King George the Third," and two sermons on
" Striving to Enter in at the Strait Gate"; in 1763,—" Two
Sermons on the Nature, Extent, and Perfection of the
Divine Goodness"; a volume of eight sermons, to young
men, on " Christian Sobriety," and a pamphlet entitled
" Observations on the Charter and Conduct of the Society
for the Propagation of the Gospel in Foreign Parts "; in
1764,—two pamphlets in defense of the one just mentioned
and in reply to the criticisms of Archbishop Secker and
others, and " A Letter of Reproof to Mr. John Cleaveland
of Ipswich, occasioned by a Defamatory Libel published
under his Name "; in 1765,—the Dudleian lecture, on
" Popish Idolatry "; in 1766,—" The Snare Broken: A
Thanksgiving Discourse preached . . . Friday, May
23, 1766, occasioned by the Repeal of the Stamp Act,"—
this sermon having been delivered less than seven weeks
before its author's death.[1]

III.

Whoever glances through this long series of publications,
will be likely to note the early and persistent action of
Mayhew's mind in the direction of individualism, on behalf
of which he proves himself from first to last a staunch and
dashing fighter—a scornful and a merciless one:

> " A latter Luther, and a soldier-priest ;
>
> . . . . . .
>
> —— no Sabbath-drawler of old saws
> Distill'd from some worm-canker'd homily ;
> But spurred at heart with fiercest energy."

[1] The foregoing list was made by me from the documents themselves, either
in my own possession, or in the libraries of Harvard University, the Massachusetts Historical Society, and the Congregational House, Boston. A list
is given in Sprague, "Annals," etc., viii. 26 ; and in Bradford, " Life of
Mayhew," 29 n.

As to method and form, his sermons have never the quality of mere essays—placid and disinterested statements of thought: they are essentially orations, not to say, fulminations,—their sentences being framed, or rather born, for strong and passionate utterance, and swelling into climaxes of argument and emotion.   He has a towering and soaring sort of eloquence.   He nobly wields majestic Biblical language.   He compacts his pages with edged and pointed diction, concentrated sayings, epigrams.   Even in the most serious moods, his discourse is in danger of crackling into caustic humor and satire; so that a sentence begun in solemnity and even pathos may end in a jocular detonation, —the height and triumph of his argument being celebrated at times by flashes and coruscations of intellectual fire, even as the rocket bursts into a shower of sparkling jets at the summit of its flight.   As is apt to be the case with such men, he was at times the victim of his own cleverness,—his gift for satire tempting him to indulge it at the expense both of charity and of reverence.[1]

The distinctive trait of Mayhew's work is intellectuality, with fervor and force.   For fervor and force without intellectuality, he expresses uncontrollable contempt,—as when in his early ministry, he went one day to hear Whitefield, and then, writing to his father, said of the sermon: " It was as low, confused, puerile, conceited, ill-natured, enthusiastic a performance as I ever heard."[2]   Everywhere he insists on the dignity and worth of the intellect in all matters of faith and sentiment.   He declares himself to be a rationalist in religion, and Christianity a consummate sys-

---

[1] Instances of the former may be found in nearly all of his allusions to the Roman and Anglican Churches; and in many of his comments upon his own Protestant antagonists in New England—especially in his " Letter of Reproof " to the Rev. John Cleaveland.   Notable examples of the latter are to be met with in his note professing to explain why the " Song of Solomon " was admitted into the sacred canon ("Sermons upon the Following Subjects," etc., 349); and in his parody on the Athanasian creed, for the purpose of ridiculing the alleged deification of the Virgin Mary (Ibid. 323 n.).

[2] Bradford, " Life of Mayhew," 102.

tem of rationalism: "Our anointed Lord, the author and finisher of our faith, constantly appealed to the senses and the reason of mankind, as the proper judges of his miracles, divine commission, and doctrine. He did not demand of men an implicit, blind belief in himself, without offering matter of conviction to their understandings; but put them on examining, in a rational way, whether he were authorized by heaven, or were an impostor, and whether his doctrines were of God, or whether he spake of himself." [1] Mayhew seems always to think with emotion, often with passion, but he thinks; and he requires that they who hear him or read him shall think. Not even the love of God is to be deemed a thing of sentiment only: it is not to be confounded, says Mayhew, with "those flashy and rapturous sallies of the heart towards God, which may proceed from a fond conceit that we are singled out to be the particular favorites of heaven. . . . The love of God is a steady, solemn, calm, and rational thing, the result of thought and consideration. It is, indeed, a passion, but a passion excited by reason presenting the proper object of it to the mind." [2] Constantly, even in times of general excitement, as after an earthquake, or a great fire, or a great tempest,—the entire community then thrilling and throbbing with terror,—this preacher demands that men and women shall keep their heads, and not lose them. On the very morning after the town of Boston had been thrown into consternation by an earthquake—the second one within the space of three days—he went into his pulpit, and said: "It is not my intention to address myself merely to the passions of my hearers, much less to take this opportunity, when the minds of many people may be ruffled and discomposed, to promote the cause of superstition. . . . I shall, therefore, address myself to you as to men and reasonable creatures. . . . And this will so much the rather be the manner of my address, because I am persuaded from

---

[1] From sermon reprinted in part in Bradford, "Life of Mayhew," 54–55.
[2] "Seven Sermons," etc., 95.

9

my own observation, that no religious impressions can be of the right kind, durable, and of lasting benefit to the subjects of them, besides those which are made, or at least fixed, by rational, sober, and honest methods, with the concurrence and blessing of Him who worketh all in all.''[1]

Of course, the preacher who thus reveres the sovereignty of the intellect, is one who will claim, for himself and for every man, the right to use it freely, even in opposition to all external authority, whether of kings, or bishops, of ancient creeds, ancient churches, or modern ones. In short, here stands before us an uncommonly fierce champion of the right of private judgment,—a right which, he declares, he will never yield up to the authority of '' all the good Fathers of the Church, even with that of the good Mothers added to it.''[2] '' Did I say, we have a right to judge and act for ourselves ? It is our solemn duty to do it. We cannot relinquish the right, nor neglect to use it, without being highly culpable. We may dispose of our temporal substance, if we please, but God, and reason, and the gospel of Christ enjoin it upon us, as a duty, to maintain the right of private judgment, and to worship God according to our consciences, as much as they enjoin it on us to give alms to the poor, to love God and our neighbor, and to practise all righteousness. They are all duties, and not simply rights ; duties founded in the reason of things ; duties equally commanded by the same God; duties equally enjoined by the same Lord; duties equally required by the same gospel. And the neglect of the duty of private judgment, may be attended by worse consequences to ourselves and fellow-men, than the neglect of any other. For he who does not examine for himself what is right and true, acts entirely in the dark, and may run into the most irregular and destructive practices which can be conceived of, just as his weak or wicked guides are pleased to prompt him. He is fit only for a tool to the devil and his emissaries; and

[1] '' Two Sermons . . . on Earthquakes," etc., 9–10.
[2] From dedication to volume of '' Sermons," published in 1755.

may flatter himself that he is doing God service, when he is imbruing his hands in the blood of the innocent, and persecuting the true church of Christ.'' [1]

Moreover, while Mayhew insists on the necessity of thought in every sphere of religion, he demands that the chief aim of religious thinking should be not speculative but practical: '' Those things which have kept the Christian world in an eternal ferment, which have sharpened the spirits of men, and set little angry bigots a snarling and growling at one another, are nice metaphysical fooleries, scholastic distinctions without any difference, and mere words without a meaning. These are the things—or rather the nothings—which have been disputed about to the neglect of the weightier matters of the gospel, and even to the destruction of all piety and brotherly love—of everything becoming a man and a Christian. So hot and furious have many professed Christians been in all ages, and so wrathful their contentions about nothings or mere trifles, that one unacquainted with the genius of their religion would be apt to think it a very different thing from what it is. He might be apt to think that the Master of these furious, railing, and burning disputants had left it in express charge, as the distinguishing character of his disciples, not that they should ' be wise as serpents and harmless as doves,' not that they should ' love one another,' and practise mutual forbearance and condescension, and do unto all men as they would be done by, but that they should be venomous and malicious as serpents—hate one another with all their hearts—do to every one as they would be willing to be done to by none—go together by the ears about words and sounds—drag each other to gaols and gibbets, to dungeons and flames, and consign all over to hell fire at last who could not immediately pronounce their uncouth shibboleths. But, O blessed Jesus ! thou Saviour of the world! is this, for thy disciples to love one another as thou hast loved them ? Or didst thou mercifully make peace

---

[1] From sermon reprinted in part in Bradford, '' Life of Mayhew,'' 71–72.

between God and man by the blood of thy cross, that men, being at peace with God, might thus make war upon one another, and inhumanly shed each other's blood ? '' [1]

IV.

Like nearly all the New England preachers of that day, this preacher by no means confined himself to topics concerning individual thought and conduct, but launched out habitually on Sundays into those great matters of state— civil, ecclesiastical, even military—which his people were thinking about during the week,—the deaths and the coronations of English kings; the rise and fall of English ministries; the conflicts of England with her rivals in all lands and seas; the glorious deeds of Frederick of Prussia as champion of Protestant power throughout the world; the appalling menace to the American colonies presented by the mere existence of French colonies in North America; the alarming aggressions of the English government upon the political rights of Americans; the rightful limits of submission, the rightful spirit and method of resistance, on the part of subjects to their sovereign.

In the very last of his sermons on public questions, Mayhew avows the chief sources of his ideas as to civil liberty, saying that in his youth he had imbibed them from '' Plato, Demosthenes, Cicero, and other renowned persons among the ancients,'' and from Sidney, Milton, Locke, and Hoadly among the moderns; above all, that earlier still he had '' learnt from the holy scriptures, that wise, brave, and virtuous men were always friends to liberty; that God gave the Israelites a king, or absolute monarch, in his anger, because they had not sense and virtue enough to like a free commonwealth, and to have Himself for their King; that the Son of God came down from heaven to make us ' free indeed '; and that ' where the spirit of the Lord is, there is liberty.' '' [2]

---

[1] '' Seven Sermons,'' etc., 155–156.   [2] '' The Snare Broken,'' 35.

It must be admitted that in his discussion of national and international topics, there is often a statesman-like largeness of view, a dignity and strength of thought, a magnificence of expression, which make his discourse very noble and inspiring. He had such a grasp, also, on the import of passing events, that, at times, his interpretation of them was prophecy; as when, in the Massachusetts election sermon for 1754, he virtually announced the approach of the Seven Years' War, and the final conflict between Englishmen and Frenchmen for the possession of North America: " We are morally sure . . . that there must sooner or later be some great turn of affairs upon this continent, which will put it out of our power, or out of theirs, to dispute about boundaries. . . . We are peaceably extending our settlements upon our own territories ; they are extending theirs beyond their own, by force of arms. We must meet at length—which cannot be without violent concussion—and the time seems not to be far off. . . . The continent is not wide enough for both; and they are resolved to have the whole.'' [1]

V.

In Mayhew's day, almost every question of church was also a question of state; and he believed himself to be battling for the cause of civil liberty in assaulting and execrating, at every opportunity, the Church of Rome and, more especially, the Church of England. The fire, the fury, the venom of his attacks upon these two great bodies of Christians, and, in particular, his expressions of anger and of horror at the possible introduction of Anglican bishops into America, would, in the light of our present knowledge, seem like the ravings of an eloquent maniac, were we not also aware that his words on that subject expressed the sincere thought of multitudes of his most rational contemporaries, and that they set before us, in

---

[1] Massachusetts election sermon for 1754, 36–37.

most authentic form, one of the chief sources of American alarm, between 1763 and 1775, over the taxing-policy of the English government, and, therefore, one of the profoundest of the remoter causes of the American Revolution. " When we consider," said Mayhew, in 1763, " the real constitution of the Church of England, and how alien her mode of worship is from the simplicity of the gospel, and the apostolic times; when we consider her enormous hierarchy, ascending by various gradations from the dirt to the skies; when we consider the visible effects of that church's prevailing among us, to the degree that it has; when we reflect on what our forefathers suffered from the mitred, lordly successors of the fishermen of Galilee, for nonconformity to a non-instituted mode of worship, which occasioned their flight into this western world; when we consider that, to be delivered from their unholy zeal and oppressions, countenanced by sceptred tyrants, they threw themselves, as it were, into the arms of savages and barbarians; when we reflect that one principal motive to their exchanging the fair cities, villages, and delightful fields of Britain for the then inhospitable shores and deserts of America, was that they might here enjoy unmolested God's holy word and ordinances, without such heterogeneous and spurious mixtures as were offensive to their well-informed consciences; when we consider the narrow, censorious, and bitter spirit that prevails in too many of the Episcopalians among us, and what might probably be the sad consequence, if this growing party should once get the upper hand here and a major vote in our houses of assembly,—in which case the Church of England might become the established religion here, tests be ordained, as in England, to exclude all but conformists from posts of honor and emolument, and all of us be taxed for the support of bishops and their underlings;—when we consider these things, and too many others to be now mentioned, we cannot well think of that church's gaining ground here to any great degree, and especially of seeing bishops fixed among us, without

much reluctance. Will they never let us rest in peace,—
except where all the weary are at rest ? Is it not enough
that they persecuted us out of the Old World ? Will they
pursue us into the New ?—to convert us here, compassing
sea and land to make us proselytes, while they neglect the
heathen and heathenish plantations ? What other New
World remains as a sanctuary for us from their oppressions,
in case of need ? Where is the Columbus to explore one
for us, and pilot us to it, before we are consumed by the
flames, or deluged in a flood, of Episcopacy ? " [1]

VI.

Probably no production of Mayhew's pen is now so interesting as his famous " Discourse concerning Unlimited
Submission," [2] preached on the Sunday immediately after
the 30th of January, 1750; none reveals to us more clearly
the great features of his mind as a writer, preacher, political
thinker; none indicates, in a more comprehensive way, his
special contribution to those moral forces which, accumu-
lating in the very heart of American society in the middle
of the eighteenth century, bore the American people forward into the audacity of concerted resistance to the prerogative and power of Great Britain. In this discourse, also,
perhaps more than in any other of his, one is reminded of
Mayhew's own avowal of his interest in the political writ-

---

[1] " Observations on the Charter," etc., 155–156. It may afford the reader
some amusement—indeed, it should afford him, also, some instruction—to recall
the fact, that Jonathan Mayhew's only surviving child, a daughter, became the
mother of a man, who, bearing the name and inheriting many of the brilliant
gifts of his grandfather, became a distinguished Anglican bishop in America—
Jonathan Mayhew Wainwright, of the diocese of New York. It was, in fact,
this grandson of Jonathan Mayhew, the bishop-hater, who, replying to the epigram of Rufus Choate, that the Pilgrim Fathers had founded " a state without
a king " and " a church without a bishop," made the famous retort : " There is
no church without a bishop."

[2] A reprint of this discourse may be seen in John Wingate Thornton, " The
Pulpit of the American Revolution," 39–104.

ings of John Milton;—for here, as is apparent, the disciple has caught, not only all of his master's ideas as to bishops and kings, but much of his master's vehement and brilliant scurrility in uttering them.[1] He describes the Anglican commemoration of the death-day of Charles the First, as "the mystery of nonsense as well as iniquity,"[2] and as the result of "an impious bargain struck up betwixt the sceptre and the surplice, for enslaving both the bodies and the souls of men."[3] After a denunciation, not at all self-restrained, of the public and private crimes of the monarch thus annually exalted as a saint and a martyr, the preacher comes, in characteristic fashion, to the climax of his blazing indictment: "King Charles was really a man black with guilt. . . . He lived a tyrant; and it was the oppression and violence of his reign that brought him to his untimely and violent end at last. Now, what of saintship or martyrdom is there in all this? What of saintship is there in encouraging people to profane the Lord's day! What of saintship in falsehood and perjury? What of saintship in repeated robberies and depredations? What of saintship in throwing real saints and glorious patriots into gaols? What of saintship in overturning an excellent civil constitution, and proudly grasping at an illegal and monstrous power? What of saintship in the murder of thousands of innocent people, and involving a nation in all the calamities of a civil war? And what of martyrdom is there in a man's bringing an immature and violent death upon himself, by being wicked overmuch? Is there any such thing as grace, without goodness?—as being a follower of Christ, without following him? —as being his disciple, without learning of him to be just,

---

[1] Of course, I here refer to "A Defense of the People of England, in Answer to Salmasius's Defense of the King"; to "The Second Defense of the People of England, against an anonymous Libel, entitled 'The Royal Blood crying to Heaven for Vengeance on the English Parricides'"; and to "Eikonoklastes, in Answer to a Book entitled 'Eikon Basilike, the Portraiture of His Sacred Majesty in his Solitudes and Sufferings.'" "The Prose Works of John Milton." London, Henry G. Bohn, volume 1.

[2] "Discourse," etc., 51.   [3] Ibid. 52.

and beneficent ?—or as saintship, without sanctity ? If not, I fear it will be hard to prove this man a saint. And, verily, one would be apt to suspect that that church must be but poorly stocked with saints and martyrs, which is forced to adopt such enormous sinners into her calendar, in order to swell the number ! '' [1] Nevertheless, in Mayhew's opinion, even the colossal absurdity of this commemoration of the death of king Charles the First was to have at least one good result, if it should '' prove a standing memento that Britons will not be slaves, and a warning to all corrupt councillors and ministers, not to go too far in advising to arbitrary despotic measures! '' [2] Such, in 1750, was Mayhew's unconscious premonitory advice to the future ministers of the future king George the Third.

But to Mayhew's countrymen, far more urgent than the question as to the character of king Charles the First, became the question as to the right of the people to resist, and to put to death, any king, if he be at all as bad a king as that particular one was represented to be. In Mayhew's treatment of that question we find, in most explicit and trenchant form, the idea that made inevitable the armed opposition which, some twenty-five years later, the American subjects of a British king were to institute, and to carry on, against him. In the case before us, the preacher has to meet the argument for unlimited submission to rulers, based on the Scriptural statement that '' their power is from God.'' But, says Mayhew, '' rulers have no authority from God to do mischief. . . . It is blasphemy to call tyrants and oppressors God's ministers. They are more properly the messengers of Satan to buffet us. No rulers are properly God's ministers, but such as are ' just, ruling in the fear of God.' When once magistrates are contrary to their office and the end of their institution, when they rob and ruin the public, instead of being guardians of its peace and welfare, they immediately cease to be the ' ordinance ' and ' ministers ' of God, and no more deserve that

---

[1] '' Discourse,'' etc., 49–51.   [2] Ibid. 54.

glorious character than common pirates and highwaymen." [1]
" It will not follow that, because civil government in gen-
ral is a good institution, and necessary to the peace and
happiness of human society, therefore there are no suppos-
able cases in which resistance to it can be innocent." [2]   " If
it be our duty, for example, to obey our king merely for
this reason, that he rules for the public welfare—which is
the only argument the apostle makes use of—it follows, by
a parity of reasoning, that when he turns tyrant, and makes
his subjects his prey to devour and to destroy, instead of
his charge to defend and cherish, we are bound to throw off
our allegiance to him, and to resist." [3]

VII.

Surely, the preacher who, in the placid times of 1750,
could light up in his soul such a flame of consuming wrath
merely against hypothetic and imagined tyranny, would be
likely to have something warm and enkindling to say when,
fifteen years later, there should appear before him in
America a form of tyranny which he believed to be actual.
Writing to a friend in England, on the eighth of August,
1765, just before the outbreak in Boston of the popular fury
against the supposed friends of the Stamp Act, Mayhew
put much of his political philosophy into small compass
when he pithily remarked, " No people are under a religious
obligation to be slaves, if they are able to set themselves at
liberty." [4]   At such times, speculative statements as to the
right of resistance are apt to receive an application rougher
and more headstrong than the teacher has in mind; and on
the morning after the sack and destruction of Hutchinson's
house, one of the rioters confessed that he had been incited
to take part in that barbarous proceeding by the sermon
which he had heard from Dr. Mayhew on the previous
Sunday, from the text,—" I would they were even cut off

---

[1] " Discourse," etc., 23-24.   [2] Ibid. 19.   [3] Ibid. 29-30.
[4] Given in Bradford, " Life of Mayhew," 418.

which trouble you. For, brethren, ye have been called unto liberty; only use not liberty for an occasion to the flesh, but by love serve one another.''[1]

The last political discourse ever uttered by Mayhew was one of great joy,—therein interpreting the general ecstasy of his countrymen over the news of the repeal of the Stamp Act. But to a far-seeing mind like Mayhew's, no joy under such circumstances could be without its deep tinge of solicitude; and on the morning of the second Sunday after this sermon of his on '' The Snare Broken,''[2] being about to start upon a fatiguing journey which, in fact, brought on the illness that proved fatal to him, he wrote to his friend, James Otis, a hurried note conveying to that kindred soul what proved to be a legacy of incomparable value for all his countrymen,—his statesmanlike project for a permanent union of the American colonies, so recently united by the bond of a common peril:—'' To a good man all time is holy enough, and none is too holy, to do good, or to think upon it. Cultivating a good understanding and hearty friendship between these colonies, appears to me so necessary a part of prudence and good policy, that no favorable opportunity for that purpose should be omitted. I think such an one now presents. Would it not be proper and decorous for our assembly to send circulars to all the rest, on the late repeal of the Stamp Act, and the present favorable aspect of affairs . . . expressing a desire to cement and perpetuate union among ourselves, by all laudable methods? . . . It is not safe for the colonies to sleep; for it is

---

[1] Galatians, v. 12–13. Compare Hutchinson, '' History of Massachusetts Bay,'' iii. 123, with the correspondence between Hutchinson and Mayhew as given in Bradford, '' Life of Mayhew,'' 420–422. Mayhew was horrified at the charge that his preaching had incited to these lawless and savage acts ; and he wrote to Hutchinson, '' I had rather lose my right hand, than be an encourager of such outrages as were committed last night.'' He complained, as many a preacher has had to do, before and since, that his congregation, instead of taking the whole text, took that part of it which they liked best.

[2] A reprint of this sermon may be found in '' The Patriot Preachers of the American Revolution,'' 9–48.

probable they will always have some wakeful enemies in Great Britain. But if they should be such children as to do so, I hope there are some, too much of men, and too great friends to them as well as to liberty, to rock the cradle, or to sing lullaby to them. You have heard of the communion of churches; and I am to set out to-morrow morning for Rutland, to assist at an ecclesiastical council. Not expecting to return this week, while I was thinking of this in my bed, the great use and importance of a communion of colonies appeared to me in a strong light,— which led me immediately to set down these hints to transmit to you." [1]

---

[1] The whole letter is in Bradford, " Life of Mayhew," 428–430.

CHAPTER VII.

DESCRIPTIONS OF NATURE AND MAN IN THE AMERICAN WILDERNESS: 1763-1775.

I.

IN the year 1763, at the close of that famous war which resulted in the acquisition of Canada by the English, there was in New England an enterprising young American soldier, named Jonathan Carver, stranded as it were amid the

141

threatened inanities of peace and civilization, and confronting a prospect that was for him altogether insipid through its lack of adventure, and especially of barbaric restlessness and discomfort. " I began to consider," so he wrote a few years afterward, " having rendered my country some services during the war, how I might continue still serviceable, and contribute, as much as lay in my power, to make that vast acquisition of territory, gained by Great Britain in North America, advantageous to it. It appeared to me indispensably needful that government should be acquainted, in the first place, with the true state of the dominions they were now become possessed of. To this purpose, I determined, as the next proof of my zeal, to explore the most unknown parts of them, and to spare no trouble or expense in acquiring a knowledge that promised to be so useful to my countrymen. . . . What I chiefly had in view, after gaining a knowledge of the manners, customs, languages, soil, and natural productions of the different nations that inhabit the back of the Mississippi, was to ascertain the breadth of that vast continent, which extends from the Atlantic to the Pacific Ocean, in its broadest part between forty-three and forty-six degrees northern latitude. Had I been able to accomplish this, I intended to have proposed to government to establish a post in some of those parts about the Straits of Annian, which, having been first discovered by Sir Francis Drake, of course belong to the English. This, I am convinced, would greatly facilitate the discovery of a northwest passage, or a communication between Hudson's Bay and the Pacific Ocean,—an event so desirable, and which has been so often sought for but without success. Besides this important end, a settlement on that extremity of America would answer many good purposes, and repay every expense the establishment of it might occasion. For it would not only disclose new sources of trade, and promote many useful discoveries, but would open a passage for conveying intelligence to China and the English settlements in the East Indies, with greater expedition than a tedious voyage by the Cape of Good Hope or the Straits of Magellan will allow of." [1]

Here, then, in the latter half of the eighteenth century was an American Englishman in whom shone some of the best traits of Elizabethan Englishmen two centuries before, —strong-limbed and strong-brained men, with a love of letters and a love of deeds, not always content with home-keeping employments, scornful of ease whenever any tough matter was to be attended to, able to fight and to write, to sail a boat into strange seas or to lead a band of hardy men through a wilderness, proud of their country and their race, having the power and the passion to spread afar through the world the sway of both. Certainly, the project thus clearly wrought out in 1763 by this obscure provincial captain in New England, anticipated by forty years the American statesmanship which, under President Jefferson, sent Merriwether Lewis and William Clark to penetrate the passes of the Rocky Mountains and to pitch their tents by the mouth of the Columbia River; even as it anticipated by a hundred years the Canadian statesmanship which, under Sir John Macdonald, has in our time beaten out an iron way across the continent at its greatest breadth, and has made the waters that splash against Vancouver Island neighborly and friendly to those which ripple under the ramparts of Quebec.

II.

It seems to have taken Carver about three years to complete his preparations for the tremendous enterprise which then inspired him. Not until June, 1766,—in the political lull occasioned by the repeal of the Stamp Act,—was he able to start. After passing Albany, he plunged at once into the wilderness which then stretched its rough dominion over the uncomputed spaces to the western sea,—a realm populous with a set of gentlemen rather too fond, as was

---

[1] Carver, " Travels through the Interior Parts of North America," Introd. i.–ii. ; v.–vi.

supposed, of tampering with the scalps of harmless travelers that might be journeying their way. Having stopped awhile at the English fort at Niagara, he again pushed on until he reached Michillimackinac, "a fort distant from Boston 1300 miles. This being the uttermost of our factories towards the northwest, I considered it as the most convenient place from whence I could begin my intended progress, and enter at once into regions I designed to explore. . . . Having here made the necessary dispositions for pursuing my travels, and obtained a credit from Mr. Rogers, the governor, on some English and Canadian traders who were going to trade on the Mississippi, and received also from him a promise of a fresh supply of goods when I reached the Falls of St. Anthony, I left the fort on the third of September, in company with these traders. It was agreed that they should furnish me with such goods as I might want for the presents to the Indian chiefs, during my continuance with them, agreeable to the governor's order. But when I arrived at the extent of their route, I was to find other guides, and to depend on the goods the governor had promised to supply me with." [1]

Setting out from Michillimackinac in canoes, he and his companions arrived in fifteen days at those beautiful islands which are strung along the entrance of Green Bay. "On the largest and best of these islands stands a town of the Ottawas, at which I found one of the most considerable chiefs of that nation, who received me with every honor he could possibly show to a stranger. But what appeared extremely singular to me at the time . . . was the reception I met with on landing. As our canoes approached the shore, and had reached within about three-score rods of it, the Indians began a feu-de-joie in which they fired their pieces loaded with balls; but at the same time they took care to discharge them in such a manner as to fly a few yards above our heads. During this they ran from one tree or stump to another, shouting and behaving as if they

---

[1] "Travels," etc., 17, 20-21.

were in the heat of battle. At first, I was greatly surprised, and was on the point of ordering my attendants to return their fire, concluding that their intentions were hostile; but being undeceived by some of the traders, who informed me that this was their usual method of receiving the chiefs of other nations, I considered it in its true light, and was pleased with the respect thus paid me.

"I remained here one night. Among the presents I made the chiefs, were some spirituous liquors, with which they made themselves merry; and all joined in a dance that lasted the greater part of the night. In the morning when I departed, the chief attended me to the shore, and, as soon as I had embarked, offered up, in an audible voice and with great solemnity, a fervent prayer in my behalf. He prayed that the Great Spirit would favor me with a prosperous voyage; that he would give me an unclouded sky, and smooth waters by day, and that I might lie down by night on a beaver blanket, enjoying uninterrupted sleep and pleasant dreams; and also that I might find continual protection under the great pipe of peace. In this manner he continued his petitions till I could no longer hear them."[1]

Thus Carver passed on and on into the wilderness lying westward of Lake Michigan; up the Fox River to "the great town of the Winnebagoes"; thence to the Wisconsin River; and finally to the Mississippi. Having reached this mighty stream, he parted from the traders who had thus far been his companions; and with only two servants,—one a French Canadian, the other a Mohawk of Canada,—he began his voyage up the Mississippi in a single canoe. In due time, he reached the Falls of St. Anthony, whence after some delay he continued his ascent of the great river until he arrived at the mouth of the River St. Pierre. Up this river, likewise, he forced his way, having the pipe of peace fixed at the bow of his canoe and the English colors flying at the stern, until, after about two hundred miles, he came to the country of "the Naudowessies of the Plains."

---

[1] "Travels," etc., 23-25.

Receiving from these people the most friendly hospitality, he dwelt among them during that winter—seven months long.

And now a great disappointment was to befall him. Though he had already proceeded so far into the wilderness, there still remained more than two thousand miles of wilderness yet to be traversed before he could reach the goal for which he had started—the Straits of Annian, on the Pacific. For such a journey through strange lands and fierce peoples, no success could be expected without an ample supply of those goods for presents which, by the promise of the governor of Michillimackinac, were to await him at the Falls of St. Anthony. Thither, accordingly, he sent for them, but only to find, with great bitterness of heart, that the governor's promise had not been fulfilled; that the necessary goods could not then be procured from others; and that the completion of his vast project must, for that time at least, be abandoned.[1]

Spending the summer and autumn of 1767 in energetic and very important explorations among the lands and waters and peoples between the Mississippi and Lake Superior, he finally coasted along the northern shore of that immense lake, and early in November, 1767, he arrived once more at Michillimackinac. During the fourteen months which had passed since his departure from this fort, he had traveled on foot and by canoe nearly four thousand miles, and had formed acquaintance with twelve nations of Indians, besides making geographical discoveries of no little importance. At Michillimackinac he was obliged to remain until the opening of navigation in June, 1768, when he began his journey homeward. In the October following, he reached Boston, '' having,'' as he says, '' been absent from it on this expedition two years and five months, and during that time traveled near seven thousand miles. From thence, as soon as I had properly digested my journal and charts, I set out for England, to communicate the discov-

---

[1] '' Travels,'' etc., 92–93, 131.

eries I had made, and to render them beneficial to the kingdom.'' [1]

III.

Arriving in England in 1769, he petitioned the government for some recognition of his labors and of his losses in the public service,—in the hope, also, of being thus enabled to resume and to complete his great tour of discovery across the continent. To the lords of trade and plantations, he submitted his journals and his charts; by these great officers he was examined in person respecting his travels ; he received from them a gracious permission to publish his discoveries—and that was all that he received from them,—even that, also, being soon withdrawn.

Of course, for the business to which he desired to draw their attention, the time was most inopportune. The dispute with the colonies, which had been allayed by the repeal of the Stamp Act, and had been revived by the legislation of the following year, was now fast ripening into its later fierceness and violence. No doubt the project then pressed by Carver upon the attention of the government was an important one. Unfortunately, however, it was not the project then first in order. Before the British government could properly incur the cost of ascertaining the extent of its American possessions, it needed to incur the cost of ascertaining whether it was destined to have any American possessions at all. When, at last, the dispute with the colonies passed from words to blows, Carver became still more embarrassed. Soldier as he was, he shrank from taking service on either side; he would not draw his sword against his king, nor had he the heart to draw it against his own countrymen. Unable, therefore, to return to America— where his neutrality would have been an offense; with no funds at his command in England; with no claims upon the government which the government could then recognize, he

---

[1] '' Travels,'' etc., 177.

was forced for his livelihood to become a hack-writer, and to bow himself down to such ill-paid tasks as the booksellers of London might choose to employ him in. In 1778, nine years after his arrival there, he succeeded in bringing out his noble and fascinating book of " Travels through the Interior Parts of North America." On account of the reputation which this book brought to him, he was enabled in the following year to gain something by the sale of his name for a compilation entitled " The New Universal Traveler." [1] In the same year, also, in the hope of stimulating an industry then made important by the cutting off of the usual supply of tobacco from America, he published in Dublin " A Treatise on the Culture of the Tobacco Plant, with the Manner in which it is usually cured: adapted to Northern Climates, and designed for the Use of the Landholders of Great Britain and Ireland." [2]

IV.

All these, however, were employments which, if they brought him some immediate distinction, brought him little else. Baffled at every turn, submitting himself at last to the abject labors of a clerk in a lottery office, working and worrying beyond his strength in the effort to save his English [3] wife and children from starvation, even his robust

---

[1] It is a further token of the reputation which his " Travels " brought to him, that in " A New and Complete Collection of Voyages and Travels," compiled by John Hamilton Moore, and published in London (n.d., but probably) about 1780, Carver is chosen as the last of the famous travelers to represent American exploration. What is given of his book extends in double columns from page 874 to page 895 of the second volume of this " Collection."

[2] Of this very rare book, the only copy I have ever met with is in the library of Mr. John Nicholas Brown, of Providence, R. I.

[3] Nothing is here said of any efforts made by him for the support of his American wife and children. Jonathan Carver was in many ways so gallant a fellow that one is quite sorry to be compelled to mention, even in the privacy of a footnote, the one serious stain which rests upon his character. Was it, perhaps, due to his prolonged residence among the Indians, that, after he had gone to the other side of the Atlantic, it became somewhat easy for him to yield himself to the polygamic custom? At any rate, it must not be concealed that, " at

constitution finally gave way; and in the year 1780, " after rendering, at the expense of fortune and health and the risk of life, many important services to his country," Jonathan Carver " perished through want in the first city of the world." [1] With this man's sorrowful history, is bound up another touching fact—a fact most worthy of remembrance, as a token of the solidarity and of the interchanging benignity of literature in England and America. It was in consequence of the publication, soon after his death, of the tale of Carver's career as an explorer in America, and especially of the struggles and the miseries he encountered as an American man of letters in London, that, for the relief in future of deserving men of letters there, the foundation was laid for that munificent endowment, now so celebrated under the name of " The Royal Literary Fund." [2]

Every one who has come to some acquaintance with Jonathan Carver, will be glad to think that his name is not likely to be forgotten among those vast, intelligent, and powerful communities now filling that portion of the Northwest which he explored so lovingly, and at a cost to himself so great. [3] It is, however, to something more than to a local remembrance in this country that he seems destined. His best monument is his book. As a contribution to the history of inland discovery upon this continent, and especially to our materials for true and precise information

---

the time of his marriage in England, he had a wife and five children living in America." J. Westby-Gibson, in " Dictionary of National Biography," ix., 238.

[1] These words are from the " Account of the Author," prefixed to the third edition of Carver's " Travels " published in London in 1781. See pages 18–19.

[2] F. S. Drake, " Dic. of Am. Biog.," 167.

[3] In 1867,—just one hundred and one years from the date of his arrival in that region,—a commemoration of him was held not far from St. Paul, at the cave which bears his name ; and a report of the ceremony has been published under the title of " The Carver Centenary." His name has been again brought to public attention by Mr. Paul Leicester Ford, who in 1890 reprinted from " The Royal Magazine," for September, 1759, " A Short History and Description of Fort Niagara, with an Account of its importance to Great Britain. Written by an English Prisoner, 1758," and signed " J. C——r."

concerning the "manners, customs, religion, and language of the Indians," Carver's book of "Travels" is of unsurpassed value. Besides its worth for instruction, is its worth for delight; we have no other "Indian book" more captivating than this. Here is the charm of a sincere, powerful, and gentle personality—the charm of novel and significant facts, of noble ideas, of humane sentiments, all uttered in English well-ordered and pure. In evidence, also, of the European celebrity acquired by his book, may be cited the fact that it seems to have had a strong fascination for Schiller, as, indeed, might have been expected; and Carver's report[1] of a harangue by a Naudowessian chief over the dead body of one of their great warriors—being itself a piece of true poetry in prose—was turned into verse by the German poet, and became famous as his "Nadowessiers Totenlied,"[2]—a dirge which pleased Goethe so much that he declared it to be among the best of Schiller's poems in that vein, and wished that his friend had written a dozen such.[3]

V.

Robert Rogers, who was born in New Hampshire in 1727 and who died in London near the close of the century, was a noted American officer in the service of the crown during the two great wars which occurred in America in his time. He is also to be remembered for his intelligent contributions to the history of the first of these wars, and for his descriptions, as an eye-witness, of the lands and peoples immedi-

---

[1] " Travels," 399–400.

[2] " Schillers sämtliche Werke in fünfzehn Bänden. Mit Einleitungen von Karl Goedeke." i. 162–163.

[3] Schiller's versification of the Indian harangue as given by Carver, was translated into English by Sir Edward Bulwer-Lytton, and was published, first, as " The Indian's Death-Song," in " Blackwood's Magazine" for December, 1842, p. 765 ; again, as " The Indian Death-Dirge," in " The Poems and Ballads of Schiller," Tauchnitz ed., Leipzig, 1844, pp. 26–27 ; and still again, and much improved, as " The Nadowessian Death-Dirge," in the London edition of the volume last named. Of this London edition an American reprint appeared in New York in 1866, wherein this song is given on pages 55–56.

ately concerned therein. Being present at the siege of
Detroit in the war with Pontiac, in 1763, he kept "A Journal" of it, beginning with the sixth of May, and breaking
off suddenly on the eighth of August.[1] Two years afterward, he published in London "Journals of Major Robert
Rogers: containing an Account of the several Excursions
he made under the Generals who commanded upon the
Continent of North America, during the late War."[2] In
the same year, and in the same city, he also published "A
Concise Account of North America," devoted to descriptions of the several British colonies there, and of especial
value for its sketches of the Indians and of the outlying
countries then occupied by them. Both of these books
have the worth which attaches to direct testimony from a
competent witness. In both of them, also, the author
writes with a manly and soldierlike straightforwardness,
saying simply the thing he has to say, and being therewith
content.[3]

VI.

In proof of the almost insatiable interest of the public in
direct facts touching the American Indians and the way to
deal with them, may be mentioned the temporary celebrity,
both in America and in Europe, acquired by "An Historical Account of the Expedition against the Ohio Indians,
in the Year 1764, under the Command of Henry Bouquet,
Esquire, Colonel of Foot and now Brigadier General in

[1] This "Journal" seems to have been sent off by him, during the siege, to
Sir William Johnson, among whose manuscripts in the New York State Library
it was found about forty years ago. It was edited by Franklin B. Hough, and
published in 1860, forming pages 121–135 in the fourth number of "Munsell's
Historical Series."

[2] The pretended reprint of this work at Concord, New Hampshire, in 1831,
under the title of "Reminiscences of the French War," etc., is a slovenly and
fraudulent piece of work: it tampers with the text in an abominable way.

[3] The literary versatility of this bold soldier is further seen in a tragedy written by him, and founded on his knowledge of the great Indian chieftain, Pontiac.
For this, the reader of the present work is referred to the chapter dealing with
our early dramatic writings.

America," published first in Philadelphia in 1765, next in London in 1766, and next in Amsterdam in 1769, the last being a French translation by C. G. F. Dumas. The conspicuous matter in the book is the military journal, which was written by the gallant Bouquet during his campaign beyond the Alleghanies, and which was retouched, diluted, and somewhat conventionalized by an editor who is here content to describe himself as " a Lover of his Country "— under which designation long lay concealed the versatile William Smith, Provost of the College in Philadelphia.[1] The real value and the fascination of the book were also much enhanced by the insertion of a series of " military papers" treating of the traits and resources of the Indians in their favorite capacity as fighters; likewise, of the prudent method of forming English settlements along that frontier—so horrid with its menace of the terror by night and of the arrow that flieth by day.[2]

VII.

" A Description of East Florida,"[3] by William Stork, first published in London in 1766, is a skillful and a delightful account of a country then but little known to the rest of the world, and especially to England to which it belonged. In a style pure, flexible, and graceful, with a charming forbearance from over-emphasis and with frequent touches of humor, the author contrives to pack his thirty or forty pages full of the most readable information about Florida, under the several divisions of " climate and situation," " soil," " natural productions," and " cultivation." As might be expected of so deft an advocate, his optimism is

[1] Horace Wemyss Smith, " Life and Correspondence of the Rev. William Smith," i. 392.   Until recently it has been supposed that the compiler of the book was Thomas Hutchins ; and to him it is ascribed by Rich, William Allen, Allibone, and others.

[2] " Historical Account of Bouquet's Expedition," etc., 93–156, reprinted in " Ohio Valley Historical Series," Cincinnati, 1868.

[3] Third ed., London, 1769.

equal to almost any draught that may be made upon it by the circumstances of his lovely client,—as, for instance, in connection with so troublesome a topic as that of the insects and reptiles of Florida: " If one considers the extent of East Florida, and the small number of inhabitants it has had these sixty years since the native Indians were exterminated by the Creeks, one would be apt to think it must of course be overrun with venomous insects and reptiles. Several writers who mention Florida have taken it for granted to be so: amongst others, the gentleman who lately wrote Major Rogers's 'History of North America,' tells us East Florida would be a fine country, were it not for the innumerable venomous insects with which it is infested. The fact is quite otherwise. If we except the alligator, East Florida has fewer insects than any other province in America. During my stay there, I saw but two black snakes. Mr. Rolle, who for eighteen months lived constantly in the woods, has seen but one rattlesnake. If East Florida is so happy as to have but few venomous creatures, it is not owing to a supernatural or miraculous cause, like the blessings of St. Patrick upon Ireland, but to a very plain and natural one, which is, that the hunting parties of the Creek Indians, who are dispersed through the whole province, continually set the grass on fire, for the conveniency of hunting; by which means, not only the insects but the eggs are destroyed.

" Alligators are here very numerous. They do not excite any fear, as there has not yet occurred any instance of their attacking men, either in the water or upon the land.

" There is an insect in East Florida, not known in other parts of America; which is a large yellow spider. The hind part of his body is bigger than a pigeon's egg, and the rest in proportion; its web is a true yellow silk, so strong as to catch small birds, upon which it feeds. The bite of this spider is attended with a swelling of the part and great pain, but no danger of life.

" A great variety of lizards are found here, some of them

very beautiful—changing their color like the cameleon : they are quite harmless." [1]

VIII.

In 1775, just as the physical conflict of the Revolution was beginning to redden our fields, there was published in London a somewhat stately quarto volume of nearly five hundred pages, entitled " The History of the American Indians,"—the author, James Adair, being described on the title-page as " a trader with the Indians, and resident in their country for forty years." This book, then, is a true product of the American wilderness. " Most of the pages," says he, " were written among our old friendly Chickasaw, with whom I first traded in the year 1744. . . . Never was a literary work begun and carried on with more disadvantages. The author was separated by his situation from the conversation of the learned, and from any libraries; frequently interrupted, also, by business, and obliged to conceal his papers, through the natural jealousy of the natives. The trader's letters of correspondence aways excited their suspicions, and often gave offense. Another difficulty I had to encounter, was the secrecy and closeness of the Indians as to their own affairs, and their prying disposition into those of others,—so that there is no possibility of retirement among them. . . . One great advantage my readers will here have : I sat down to draw the Indians on the spot—had them many years standing before me—and lived with them as a friend and brother. . . . The public may depend on the fidelity of the author, and that his descriptions are genuine, though perhaps not so polished and romantic as other Indian histories and accounts they may have seen." [2]

The style of the book throughout comports with these tokens,—the style of an honest man and a manly Englishman,—plain, frank, sinewy. Nor is the book lacking in pas-

---

[1] " A Description," etc., 21–22.   [2] Preface.

sages of vivid force and picturesqueness, having that sincerity and fulness of statement which comes of a direct handling of the facts in the case, all apparently quickened and guided by motives humane and patriotic. As mere testimony it has this weakness: its author had adopted the theory of the Jewish origin of the American Indians, and was led thereby to marshall a part of his statements in the form of twenty-three " arguments " in support of that hypothesis. Nearly one half of the book is thus taken up with what one of his contemporaries described as " ingenious extravagance." [1] After he makes his escape, however, from this perilous bog of preconceived theory, he proceeds to tell the remainder of his story for its own sake, and not for the sake of a bit of speculation which he is anxious to bolster up. By far the most important part of the book, therefore, is the latter part. Through all those solid pages —about two hundred and fifty of them—he gives his testimony like an honest and clear-headed witness, unfolding the things that he himself knows, and knows entirely: namely, the results of forty years of observation and experience among those powerful and fierce tribes of Indians who then dwelt in the lands south of the Ohio and east of the Mississippi. As a piece of sustained narration and description pertaining to that subject, the book has an unrivaled value and charm. No lapse of time can diminish the interest attaching to the modest and graphic tales he here tells of his own thrilling adventures[2]; or to his clear-cut delineations of those ferocious but still fascinating bipeds with whom he had to deal—strange survivals of the stone age of human culture[3]; or, even, to the brusque and fearless words with which, in the very capital of the empire and within ear-shot of the king's palace, he speaks out his sympathy with his fellow-colonists in that crisis of their

---

[1] B. S. Barton, " New Views," etc., Prelim. Descrip., iii.

[2] For example, see pages 276–278 ; also, pages 298–302.

[3] See pages 388–399.

danger, and his disdain for the petty English statesmanship which was then presuming to govern an empire with an amount of wit which would hardly have sufficed for the government of a village.[1]

---

[1] See pages 266–267 ; also, pages 462–464.

CHAPTER VIII.

BEGINNINGS OF NEW LIFE IN VERSE AND PROSE: PHILA-
DELPHIA, PRINCETON, AND NEW YORK. 1763–1775.

I.

IN the year 1772, amid all the heat and uproar of politics
then raging up and down these sea-board communities in
America, there was published in Philadelphia a volume so
unique as to contain absolutely no reference to politics,—
to wit, " Poems on Several Occasions, with Some Other

Compositions," by Nathaniel Evans.   The writer, a native
of Philadelphia, a master of arts in its college, and a clergyman of the Anglican Church, had died five years before, at
the age of twenty-five, leaving behind him, throughout a
wide circle of acquaintance, the impression of something
very rare in literary capacity, as well as very sweet and
noble in personal character.   Nearly all of the writings here
huddled together into print—after he was gone and could
neither explain nor protest—were but the playthings of a
sensitive but still undeveloped mind, the finger-practice of
a youth of poetic instincts, who was training himself for
maturer work but still under pernicious leadership, and in
opposition to a host of disadvantages in his outward life.
That he had in him the likelihood of an ultimate escape
from the wooden tyranny of his poetic models, may partly
appear from these lines, " To Melancholy " :

> " Come, thou queen of pensive air,—
>   In thy sable, sooted car,
>   By two mournful turtles drawn,—
>   Let me meet thee on yon lawn,
>   With decent vestments wrapt around,
>   And thy brows with cypress bound !
>   Quickly come, thou sober dame,
>   And thy musing poet claim.
>   Bear me where thou lov'st to rove
>   In the deep, dark, solemn grove,
>   Where, on banks of velvet green,
>   Peace, with Silence, still is seen ;
>   And Leisure, at the sultry noon,
>   On flowery carpet flings him down.
>   There, sweet queen, I 'll sing thy pleasures
>   In enthusiastic measures,
>   And sound thy praise through the lone vale,
>   Responsive to the hollow gale ;
>   The murmuring rills shall spread it round,
>   And grottoes the wild notes rebound." [1]

---

[1] " Poems on Several Occasions," 135.

A still more valid token of poetic promise in Nathaniel Evans is furnished us by some lines of his, struck off with playful strokes,—"An Ode, Attempted in the Manner of Horace," and addressed to his boon companion in poetry and in poverty, Thomas Godfrey.[1] At the time when these verses were written, Godfrey was earning his daily bread in some commercial employment in North Carolina, while Evans was doing the same thing in the same way in Philadelphia,—both lads being full of literary aspiration, both hampered by the hard limitations of their lives, and both conscious of some deadly chill in the surrounding atmosphere, charged as it was with the maxims and ambitions of commerce:

> "While you, dear Tom, are forced to roam,
>   In search of fortune, far from home,
>   O'er bogs, o'er seas, and mountains,
>   I, too, debarred the soft retreat
>   Of shady groves, and murmur sweet
>   Of silver-prattling fountains,
>
> "Must mingle with the bustling throng,
>   And bear my load of cares along,
>   Like any other sinner :
>   For, where 's the ecstasy in this—
>   To loiter in poetic bliss,
>   And go without a dinner ?
>
> "Flaccus, we know, immortal bard,
>   With mighty kings and statesmen fared,
>   And lived in cheerful plenty ;
>   But now, in these[2] degenerate days,
>   The slight reward of empty praise
>   Scarce one receives in twenty.

---

[1] I have given an account of Godfrey, in my "History of Am. Lit. during the Colonial Time," ii. 244–251.

[2] The text reads, "those"—evidently a misprint.

" Well might the Roman swan along
The pleasing Tiber pour his song,
   When blest with ease and quiet ;
Oft did he grace Mæcenas' board,
Who would for him throw by the lord,
   And in Falernian riot.

" But, dearest Tom ! those[1] days are past,
And we are in a climate cast
   Where few the Muse can relish ;
Where all the doctrine now that 's told,
Is that a shining heap of gold
   Alone can man embellish.

" Then since 't is thus, my honest friend,
If you be wise, my strain attend,
   And counsel sage adhere to :
With me, henceforward, join the crowd,
And like the rest, proclaim aloud,
   That money is all virtue !

" Then may we both, in time, retreat,
To some fair villa, sweetly neat,
   To entertain the Muses ;
And then life's noise and trouble leave—
Supremely blest, we 'll never grieve
   At what the world refuses." [2]

II.

It is rather for her possible, than for her actual, poetic achievement, that Elizabeth Fergusson, a woman of brilliant social gifts, survives among the literary traditions of the Revolution. Belonging to a family of considerable note in the middle colonies, much of her life was passed at Graeme Park, a somewhat stately country-seat eighteen

---

[1] The text reads " these,"—evidently a misprint.
[2] " Poems on Several Occasions," 50–52.

miles northwest of Philadelphia.[1] But little of her work as a writer was ever permitted to go into print; and what she did make public seems commonly to have been hidden under some form of literary disguise. It is probable that her hand may be traced in the rather striking, even if sombre, verses which, with true feminine appropriateness, were added as " A Postscript " to an anonymous poem entitled " Resignation,"[2] published at Philadelphia in 1764:

> " Why mourn the dead ?   You wrong the grave—
>   From storm that safe retreat ;
> We are still tossing out at sea—
>   Our Admiral in port !
>
> " Was death denied, this world—a scene
>   How dismal and forlorn !
> To Death we owe that 't is to man
>   A blessing to be born.
>
> .   .   .   .
>
> " How happy that no storm or time
>   Of Death can rob the just,—
> None pluck from their unaching heads
>   Soft pillows in the dust ! "[3]

Examples of her sprightlier and more carnal moods are to be seen in a series of little poems[4] produced by her, under the name of " Laura," in the course of a literary duel of badinage and flirtation with the poet, Nathaniel Evans. To this charming young bachelor, then settled as an Anglican clergyman in Gloucester County, New Jersey, she

---

[1] An account of her is given in " Memoirs of the Hist. Soc. of Pa.," i. 459–463.

[2] I found this volume in the library of the Pa. Hist. Society ; and in attributing these lines to Elizabeth Fergusson, I follow the lead of local information inscribed upon the title-page.

[3] " Resignation," etc., 71.

[4] These are in Evans, " Poems on Several Occasions," etc., 149–150, 152–154, 159–160.

11

addressed what she called " A Parody," playfully descanting on the supposed felicities of his unwedded life in that parochial solitude:

" How happy is the country parson's lot !—
Forgetting bishops, as by them forgot ;
Tranquil of spirit, with an easy mind,
To all his vestry's votes he sits resigned.
Of manners gentle, and of temper even,
He jogs his flocks with easy pace to heaven.
In Greek and Latin pious books he keeps ;
And while his clerk sings psalms, he soundly sleeps.
His garden fronts the sun's sweet orient beams,
And fat churchwardens prompt his golden dreams.
The earliest fruit in his fair orchard blooms ;
And cleanly pipes pour out tobacco's fumes.
From rustic bridegroom oft he takes the ring ;
And hears the milkmaid plaintive ballads sing.
Backgammon cheats whole winter nights away,
And Pilgrim's Progress helps a rainy day." [1]

III.

On the morning of a certain day in August, 1776, John Adams, member of the Continental Congress then in session at Philadelphia, unbent his mind from the cares of state by taking a walk into Arch Street, and visiting there the studio of the portrait-painter, Charles Wilson Peale; and in a letter to his wife on the following day, the sturdy Puritan politician gave a näive sketch of the persons and things he had seen there,—a sketch first of the painter himself, then of his paintings, and finally of a fellow-congressman who

---

[1] " Poems on Several Occasions," etc., by N. Evans, 149–150. These lines will be recognized as a parody on that part of Pope's " Eloiza to Abelard," which begins :

" How happy is the blameless vestal's lot !
The world forgetting, by the world forgot" ;

and extending from line 207 to line 222. " Works of Alexander Pope," Warburton's edition, London, 1753, ii. 24–39.

happened to be at the studio as a visitor like himself. " At this shop," he says, " I met Mr. Francis Hopkinson, late a mandamus councillor of New Jersey, now a member of the Continental Congress, who, it seems, is a native of Phila-delphia, . . . was liberally educated, and is a painter and a poet. I have a curiosity to penetrate a little deeper into the bosom of this curious gentleman, and may possi-bly give you some more particulars concerning him. He is one of your pretty, little, curious, ingenious men. His head is not bigger than a large apple, less than our friend Pemberton, or Doctor Simon Tufts. I have not met with anything in natural history more amusing and entertaining than his personal appearance,—yet he is genteel and well bred, and is very social." The unconscious humor of this final concession lingers on into the words of the next sen-tence, revealing, as the entire letter does, the mind of a practical, aspiring, New England lawyer and politician of that period, just waking up to the perception of a form of culture with which up to that time he had had no contact; of which, indeed, he could not help speaking with a sort of condescension; and yet to the acquisition of which even he could almost be willing betimes to let himself down. " I wish," he adds, " I had leisure and tranquillity of mind to amuse myself with those elegant and ingenious arts of painting, sculpture, statuary, architecture, and music. But I have not." [1]

But, now, this queer little congressman whom John Adams thus met in Peale's studio, and who seemed to the New Englander to be as amusing a specimen of natural history as he had ever met with,—who and what was he ? The range of this little man's versatility was by no means fully indicated in the remark that he had been a mandamus councillor, and was at that time a member of congress, a painter, and a poet. Even in these days, Francis Hopkin-son would have been regarded as a man of quite unusual cultivation, having in reality many solid as well as shining

---

[1] " Letters of John Adams, Addressed to His Wife," i. 156–157.

accomplishments.   He was a distinguished practitioner of
the law; he became an eminent judge; he was a statesman
trained by much study and experience; he was a mathema-
tician, a chemist, a physicist, a mechanician, an inventor, a
musician and a composer of music, a man of literary knowledge and practice, a writer of airy and dainty songs, a
clever artist with pencil and brush, and a humorist of
unmistakable power.   For us Americans, the name of
Francis Hopkinson lives—if indeed it does live—chiefly on
account of its presence in the august roll-call of the signers
of the Declaration of Independence; and through all the
strenuous years which preceded and followed that great
avowal, this man served the cause therein set forth, not
only as a patriot of austere principle, as a statesman of
genuine sagacity, as a citizen of high civic courage, but as
a wit and a satirist,—the edge of his sarcasm cutting into
the enemy as keenly as any sword, and the ruddy glow of
his mirth kindling good cheer over all the land on many a
grim day when good cheer was a hard thing to be had on
his side of the fight.[1]

IV.

He was born in Philadelphia on the second of October,
1737.   His father, Thomas Hopkinson, a barrister of English birth and education, had settled in Philadelphia in early
life, arriving there, probably, in 1731; and thenceforward,
until his premature death in 1751, he had risen steadily in
the public esteem, not only as a lawyer and a judge, but as
a man of literary and scientific training, and as a friend of

[1] Of Francis Hopkinson no adequate biography has yet been written.   An
early sketch of him in "Delaplaine's Repository," vol. ii. part i. pp. 125–
138, seems to be founded on an earlier sketch by some writer not named by
Delaplaine, but contemporary with Hopkinson.   Other sketches of him are in
Sanderson, "Biography of the Signers," ii. 187–204; in "The National Portrait Gallery" for 1836, 5th article; and in "The Pa. Mag. of Hist. and
Biog.," ii. 314–324.   The last is by Charles R. Hildeburn; and though it contains one quite serious lapse from accuracy, it is upon the whole the best account
of Hopkinson now to be had.

every good cause.[1]   The son, thus left an orphan at the age of fourteen, received the best education then to be had in that neighborhood.   He happened to be the first pupil to enter the new College of Philadelphia, and was in the class of its first graduates,—receiving his bachelor's degree in 1757, and his master's degree in 1760.   He studied law in the office of Benjamin Chew, the attorney-general of Pennsylvania; he was admitted to the bar in 1761; he devoted himself zealously and with success to the work of his profession; and to the very end of his life, he showed, as his father had done before him, a fine versatility of talent, and an active interest in all things tending to the public good.[2]

On the 26th of May, 1766, almost at the very moment of the news that the Stamp Act had been repealed, Hopkinson set sail for England,—where he was to pay a long visit among his kinsfolk on that side of the sea.   It is a touching fact that almost the last glimpse which the young American barrister then had of his own country, as his ship moved down the Delaware, was of the popular illuminations at Newcastle over the news which was then making all Americans so glad.[3]   As his ship sailed away from those happy

---

[1] Thomas Hopkinson became judge of the Vice-Admiralty for Pennsylvania, member of the Council of Pennsylvania, and first president of the American Philosophical Society.   He is named by Provost William Smith as the first of four men most active in the founding of the College of Philadelphia, now the University of Pennsylvania.   He was also a member of Franklin's Junto, and one of Franklin's very intimate friends ; and it was to him that Franklin acknowledged himself as indebted for the discovery of the power of metallic points "to throw off the electrical fire."   "Works of Franklin," Sparks' ed., v. 182.

[2] It helps one to ascertain the quality and range of this man's gifts to note, that besides devoting himself to his profession as a lawyer, and to experimental researches in chemistry and physics, and to much study of literature, and at one time even to the business of a conveyancer and of a shop-keeper, he was able, on behalf of the public, to serve as secretary of the Library Company of Philadelphia for several years, as its librarian for more than one year, and as its director for more than two years ; also, for various periods, as secretary to the vestry of the united parishes of Christ Church and St. Peter's, and as warden of St. Peter's.   For awhile, also, he tried to improve the services of the two parishes by teaching their children to sing.

[3] Hopkinson to his mother, 2 July, 1766, in "The Pa. Mag. of Hist. and Biog.," ii. 316–317.

signals, and carried him out into the double mystery of the ocean and of the future, no doubt those lights blazing upon the shore seemed to him to be a token of the end of all the dangerous disputes that could arise for many a year between the colonies and the mother country.   So little, in fact, did he dream of the fiercer and the less extinguishable flames that were soon to be kindled all along the continent, that when, during the period of this very visit in England, parliament passed its acts for laying new customs duties on the colonies and even for setting up in America a board of commissioners for collecting such duties, Hopkinson himself became an eager applicant for a place on that board, and suffered deep disappointment in consequence of his failure to get it.[1]

In England, he spent about fourteen months,—having access to the best society there.   A near kinsman of his was the Bishop of Worcester; and Hopkinson made long visits at that prelate's palace at Hartlebury.   In London, his acquaintance was among interesting and distinguished people.   One day he speaks of having a whitebait dinner at Greenwich with Benjamin West and his family; and, on another day, of dining with John Penn, the proprietor of Pennsylvania, and with Lord North.[2]   Finally, having seen something of the world beyond his own horizon, and having gained, doubtless, something of the catholicity of mind and the polish of manners which a year or two of the best English life could give to an observant and tractable young fellow like him, Hopkinson returned home in the latter part of 1767.   One year afterward, he was married to Ann Borden, of Bordentown, New Jersey, granddaughter of the man who founded the town; and through his alliance with that wealthy and influential family, he was gradually drawn to be a citizen of New Jersey.   The young politician who had dined with Lord North in 1767, had evidently made a good impression on that powerful statesman; for, in 1772,

---

[1] Letter of Hopkinson's, "The Pa. Mag. of Hist. and Biog.," ii. 318.
[2] Ibid. 317.

through Lord North's favor, Hopkinson was given the office of collector of customs at Newwcastle, with the privilege of discharging its duties by deputy; and, in 1774, he became by royal appointment a member of the council of New Jersey.

Meantime, the square issue was forming between the colonies on the one side, and the British government on the other. How would Francis Hopkinson stand, with respect to that issue ? This flattering kindness of Lord North, this profitable sinecure office at Newcastle, this seat in the aristocratic branch of the legislature of New Jersey,—all these were dangerous lures to an ambitious American politician of that period. The firmness of many a member of the opposition went down, in those times, under such temptations. Concerning Francis Hopkinson, however, there seems not to have been any serious doubt. In June, 1776, when the question of national Independence had suddenly become the master-question of the hour, he was sent by New Jersey as one of her delegates in Congress. On the 28th of June, he presented his credentials, and took his seat; on the second of July, he voted for the resolution favoring Independence; two days later, he voted for the Declaration itself; on the second of August, when the engrossed copy of the Declaration came into the house for signatures, he put his signature there where it belonged; and from the midst of all those perilous proceedings, he wrote to a friend in Baltimore these modest and manly words: " If my poor abilities can be of the least service to my country in her day of trial, I shall not complain of the hardship of the task." [1]

Thus, as it appears, this same " pretty, little, curious, ingenious man "—this member of congress who was to John Adams an amusing specimen of natural history—this lawyer and statesman who could also write songs and set them to music of his own, who could play daintily on the harpsichord, and could draw in crayon exquisite portraits of

[1] Hopkinson to Dr. Coale, of Baltimore, in " The Pa. Mag. of Hist. and Biog.," ii. 319.

the beauties of Bordentown and of Philadelphia, and who
had a head " not bigger than a large apple "—had a heart
also quite as big perhaps as John Adams's, and a soul kindred to his, likewise, in central gravity, and in valor, and in
the power of self-sacrifice.   Beneath the elegant exterior of
that traveled and polished little gentleman, not spoiled by
any dilettanteism of his, nor made frivolous by his irrepressible gift of mirth, nor seduced by the smiles of the great
man in England who stood nearest to the king, was a nature
as clear-eyed, as pure-handed, as firm-footed, and as solidly
good, we may suppose, as belonged to the most ponderous
and unadorned patriot-father in all the august Congress at
Philadelphia.

V.

But before we drift quite away into those angry times in
which Francis Hopkinson acted his rare and effective part,
let us stay a moment for one glimpse at a far different aspect
of his mind and life.   As one thinks of that extremely serious collection of personages—the signers of the Declaration
of Independence—whose faces, looking down upon us from
their squares of canvas in Independence Hall, seem to have
solidified themselves into a preternatural and somewhat
ligneous gravity, as if to confront the perpetual stare of an
admiring posterity; as one remembers the wise, operose,
valiant, sedate, and altogether considerable things those
solemn gentlemen did in their times,—it is not quite easy
to conceive of any one of them as ever having had in this
grim life such a thing as a lyric mood, a solitary hour uncon-
cerned enough to have permitted him to write, and to set
to music, and even to sing, say, a dainty, defiant, little love-
song like this—a song not unworthy of the touch of Herrick
or of Lovelace:

I.

" My generous heart disdains
     The slave of love to be ;
I scorn his servile chains,
     And boast my liberty.

This whining
And pining
And wasting with care,
Are not to my taste, be she ever so fair.

2.

"Shall a girl's capricious frown
Sink my noble spirits down?
Shall a face of white and red
Make me droop my silly head?
Shall I set me down and sigh
For an eye-brow, or an eye?
For a braided lock of hair,
Curse my fortune and despair?
My generous heart disdains, etc.

3.

"Still uncertain is to-morrow,
Not quite certain is to-day—
Shall I waste my time in sorrow?
Shall I languish life away?
All because a cruel maid
Hath not love with love repaid?
My generous heart disdains, etc." [1]

And who would have imagined that, among all those
plodding and pragmatical members of the Continental Congress, engaged in their portentous task of hunting out of
the land sundry herds of Hessians and their British employ-
ers, was one who could, at any time, have written a merry
little sporting-song like this,—a song for the fox-hunters,—
a song having lightness of touch, swiftness, airy melody,
and genuine lyric feeling?

---

[1] " Poems on Several Subjects," 190–191; separate paging in vol. iii. of
Hopkinson's " Miscellaneous Essays and Occasional Writings." These volumes,
printed as they were after Hopkinson's death, contain an unusual number of
typographical errors.

" O'er the hills far away, at the birth of the morn,
I hear the full tone of the sweet-sounding horn ;
The sportsmen with shoutings all hail the new day,
And swift run the hounds o'er the hills far away.
Across the deep valley their course they pursue,
And rush thro' the thickets yet silver'd with dew :
Nor hedges nor ditches their speed can delay—
Still sounds the sweet horn o'er the hills far away." [1]

And, surely, no reader seeking for other verses of Hopkinson's which may still be worth recalling, is likely to overlook this little thing,—the song of the young wife of Jemmy the Sailor, after Jemmy the Sailor has gone to sea:

I.

" My love is gone to sea,
    Whilst I his absence mourn,
No joy shall smile on me
    Until my love return.
He ask'd me for his bride,
    And many vows he swore ;
I blush'd—and soon complied,
    My heart was his before.

2.

" One little month was past,
    And who so blest as we ?
The summons came at last,
    And Jemmy must to sea.
I saw his ship so gay
    Swift fly the wave-worn shore ;
I wip'd my tears away—
    And saw his ship·no more.

3.

" When clouds shut in the sky,
    And storms around me howl ;

---

[1] " Poems on Several Subjects," 190.

When livid lightnings fly,
     And threat'ning thunders roll ;
All hopes of rest are lost,
     No slumbers visit me ;
My anxious thoughts are tost
     With Jemmy on the sea." [1]

VI.

On the eighteenth of December, 1832, an old man,
sprightly and vigorous under the weight of nearly eighty-
one years, started, just as the evening was coming on, to
walk from the village of Monmouth, in New Jersey, to his
home in the open country, a distance of about two miles.
At that home, a paternal estate of a thousand acres, this
man had passed, at intervals, many years of his long life—
filled as it had been with manifold employments on land
and sea.   He was still a fine specimen of active and manly
old age; in person somewhat below the ordinary height,
but muscular and compact; his face pensive in expression
and with a care-worn look; his dark gray eyes sunken deep
in their sockets, but sending out gleams and flashes of fire
when aroused in talk; his hair once abundant and beautiful, now thinned and bleached by time; stooping a little as
he walked; to those who knew him, accustomed to give
delight by a conversation abounding in anecdotes of the
great age of the American Revolution.   On the evening
just referred to, he had started alone on his walk towards
his home, but the night passed away without his arrival
there; and the next morning his lifeless body was found in
a swampy meadow, into which, as it seemed, he must have
wandered,—missing his way in the darkness, and in his
exhaustion and bewilderment surrendering at last to death.

That dead old man was Philip Freneau, incomparably the
bitterest and the most unrelenting, and, in some respects
the most powerful, of the satirical poets belonging to the
insurgent side of the Revolution.   His long life, beginning

---

[1] "Poems on Several Subjects, 186–187.

on the second of January, 1752, twenty-four years before
the Declaration of Independence, had spanned a period
which included such events as the British conquest of
Canada, the American Revolution, the futile experiment of
the confederation, the establishment of the national constitution, the rise and fall and extinction of the Federalist
party, the whole tragedy of the French Revolution, the
earliest dawn and the final setting of the career of Napoleon,
our second war with England, the expansion of our national
domain to the breadth of the continent, the development
of the American slave-power into an aggressive territorial
and political propaganda, the inception of the triumphant
anti-slavery movement in America, the second election of
Andrew Jackson, and the assertion by South Carolina of
the doctrine of nullification. The poor old man, thus
found dead on the lonely New Jersey moor, had undoubtedly some sweetness in his heart; but he permitted very
little of it to work its way down to the tip of his pen.
With that pitiless pen of his he had fought many a fierce
fight. in his day; but the one fierce fight most worthy of
him and most likely to keep his name alive in the memory
of his countrymen, was that which he fought on behalf of
the American Revolution. For such a fight he was born.
He was the poet of hatred, rather than of love. He had a
passion for controversy. His strength lay in attack; his
characteristic measure was the iambic. Among all his
verses, the reader finds scarcely one lyric of patriotic enthusiasm, nor many lines to thrill the hearts of the Revolutionists
by any touch of loving devotion to their cause, but everywhere lines hot and rank with sarcasm and invective against
the enemy. He did, indeed, give ample proof that he had
the genius for other and higher forms of poetry; yet it was
as a satirist that he won his chief distinction,—as a satirist,
likewise, doing always the cruelest work of that savage
vocation with the greatest relish. In this respect, Philip
Freneau correlates, upon the Whig side, to Jonathan Odell
on the side of the Tories. Like Odell, Freneau was a good

hater; his was the wrathful muse; his chosen warfare was grim, unsparing, deadly. He was the satirical gladiator on behalf of the Revolution, even as Odell was the satirical gladiator in opposition to it.

VII.

He came of heroic stock—that of the Huguenots; and if, from the moment of the first American alienation, he quickly learned to hate the British with a hate uncommon even for an American Revolutionist, he perhaps inherited the aptitude for doing so, along with his French name and his French blood. At Princeton, where he received his education, he had for classmates two or three men of note in after years,—Samuel Spring, Hugh Henry Brackenridge, and James Madison. Already the odor of insurrection was in the air; and these young collegians—as is apt to be the case with young collegians—sniffed it eagerly, though perhaps they did not quite realize what the wild fragrance meant that pleased them so. The part which Freneau took on commencement day, in 1771, was that of an interlocutor in a metrical dialogue, written by himself and by Brackenridge, on " The Rising Glory of America "[1]—one of a thousand tokens that already among these colonists was born a spirit of national self-consciousness which must soon snap the cords of provincial subordination, and even fling off at some time the tremendous and indeed the unwholesome fascination with which Europe predominated over the American spirit.

Already, too, before his departure from Princeton, Fre-

---

[1] The entire poem was published in Philadelphia in 1772. The portion written by Freneau was afterward printed by itself in the first edition of his collected verses, entitled "The Poems of Philip Freneau," 37–51, Philadelphia, 1786. This edition is extremely rare. After much enquiry, I have met with but one copy,—that belonging to the Massachusetts Historical Society, and formerly the property of George Ticknor. Fortunately, this edition has been reprinted in a form that places it within easy reach, by John Russell Smith, London, 1861. To this reprint I always refer in citing the above title.

neau had caught another infection—a more fatal one, even, than that of incipient rebellion—the infection of verse-making. When but sixteen years old, he wrote a consider-able poem, vigorously conceived, and in well-wrought rhymed pentameters, on the rather discouraging topic of " The Prophet Jonah "; and, a year later, a dramatic frag-ment in blank verse, on " The Pyramids of Egypt." Both are examples of really strong and promising poetic work.

It is not easy to learn just how he was employed during the years immediately following his graduation. Very likely, with an inward preference for a literary life, he found in the commercial and maritime connections of his family an occupation not altogether unfriendly to his favorite studies. As the war came on, though he had a passionate interest in its problems, and took in it a fierce and a great part with his terrible pen, he seems never to have fought in it with musket or sword. It is known that both before and during the war he often went to sea, at times in command of a ship, being thus engaged in commercial transactions in the West Indies.

Indeed, he appears to have been greatly attracted by life upon the ocean; and among his poems, both political and non-political, not a few refer to the sea, and to traits of his own experience upon it, and to those fascinating tropical realms into which his voyages had so often brought him as a pilgrim. It is obvious, too, that in the watch he kept of the unfolding fortunes of the Revolution, he was especially drawn to those incidents which appealed to him as a sailor-poet. Moreover, for the purposes of humorous verse, he was not slow to perceive and to use the comic phases of nautical life—even of nautical coarseness and irreverence; as is to be seen, for example, in some playful lines written by him on finding that the crew of a ship on which he hap-pened to be, was made up of men bearing, absurdly enough, the names of several famous English divines:

> " In life's unsettled, odd career
> What changes every day appear,

To please or plague the eye !—
A goodly brotherhood of priests
Are here transformed to swearing beasts
That heaven and hell defy.

" Here Bonner, bruised with many a knock,
Has changed his surplice for a frock ;
Old Erskine swabs the deck ;
And Watts, that once such pleasure took
In writing hymns, here turned a cook,
Sinners no longer vex.

" Here Burnet, Tillotson, and Blair,
With Jemmy Hervey, curse and swear ;
Here Cudworth mixes grog ;
Pearson the crew to dinner hails,
A graceless Sherlock trims the sails,
And Bunyan heaves the log." [1]

VIII.

The note of playfulness in these lines is, however, a rare
one in Freneau's work, whether for land or sea; but still
other examples of it may be seen in " The Village Merchant," [2] in " The Desolate Academy," [3] in " Epitaph
intended for the Tomb-stone of Patrick Bay, an Irish Soldier and Inn-holder, killed by an ignorant Physician," [4] and
especially in " Crispin O'Connor's Answer," [5] wherein the
said Crispin thus explains why he had left Ireland and come
to America:

" I could not bow to noble knaves
Who equal rights to men deny ;
Scornful I left a land of slaves,
And hither came—my axe to ply.

---

[1] " Poems on Several Occasions," Monmouth, 1795, 161.
[2] Ibid. 9–15.
[3] " The Poems of Philip Freneau," 72–73.
[4] Ibid. 31–32.
[5] " Poems on Several Occasions," 160–161.

"The axe has well repaid my toil :
  No king, no priest, I yet espy—
To tythe my hogs, to tax my soil,
  And suck my whiskey-bottle dry.

" In British land what snares are laid !—
  There, royal rights all right defeat :
They taxed my sun, they taxed my shade,
  They taxed the wretched crumbs I eat ;

" They taxed my hat, they taxed my shoes,
  Fresh taxes still on taxes grew ;
They would have taxed my very nose,
  Had I not fled, dear friends, to you ! "

Too seldom, however, was the playful note allowed to give its relief to Freneau's work. His prevailing tone is not only serious, but severe. Rarely does he permit a smile to ripple upon his own face, or upon ours; and though he did attempt, with a successs that is unmistakable, some of the nobler forms of poetry, it was to satire that he felt himself called, if not by the limitations of his own genius, at least by the cricumstances of his own time. Indeed, upon this subject we are not left to conjecture; for in a little poem of his, called " The Author," he expressly tells us that, in his opinion, an American poet was then debarred by the very conditions of American life, from every form of poetry but satire :

" On these bleak climes by Fortune thrown,
  Where rigid Reason reigns alone,
  Where flowery Fancy holds no sway,
  Nor golden forms around her play,
  Nor Nature takes her magic hue—
  Alas ! what has the Muse to do ?
  An age employed in pointing steel,
  Can no poetic raptures feel ;
  No fabled Love's enchanting power,
  Nor tale of Flora's shady bower,

Nor woodland haunt, or murmuring grove,
Can its prosaic bosom move.
The Muse of Love in no request,
I 'll try my fortune with the rest.
Which of the Nine shall I engage,
To suit the humor of the age ?
On one, alas ! my choice must fall,
The least engaging of them all !
Her visage stern, severe her style,
A clouded brow, a cruel smile,
A mind on murdered victims placed—
She, only she, can please the taste." [1]

Perhaps for immediate recognition, especially under the political and commercial tests of the American literary market, Freneau's conclusion may have been the wise one. At any rate, it is impossible not to regret that the circumstances of his life, and especially the intellectual cravings of the public to which his appeal was confined, did not encourage him to give more of his strength to other muses than to her of the " visage stern." Surely, an American poet from whom Thomas Campbell, " in his best day, thought it worth while to borrow an entire line," and that, too, without taking the trouble to mention the fact, need not have confined himself to the field of satire for lack at least of " fine tact and delicate handling " [2] in the higher work of poetry. In Campbell's mystic and most musical love-tale, —" O'Connor's Child; or, The Flower of Love Lies Bleeding,"—that fastidious poet thus sings of the dead warrior, Connocht Moran, and of the living lady who still loved him :

" Bright as the bow that spans the storm,
  In Erin's yellow vesture clad,
A son of light, a lovely form,
  He comes and makes her glad.

---

[1] " Poems on Several Occasions," 327.

[2] Duyckinck, " Cyclopædia of American Literature," ed. by M. L. Simons, i. 349.

12

> Now on the grass-green turf he sits,
>   His tasseled horn beside him laid ;
> Now o'er the hills in chase he flits—
>   The hunter and the deer—a shade ! " [1]

The truth of history compels us to mention that the last line
in that exquisite passage, which is also its best line, had
already appeared in print several years before, in a little
poem of Freneau's entitled " The Indian Burying Ground,"
and in this fine stanza :

> " By midnight moons, o'er moistening dews,
>   In vestments for the chase arrayed,
> The hunter still the deer pursues,
>   The hunter and the deer—a shade." [2]

Moreover, a similar depredation was committed upon Freneau by a writer of far greater genius than Campbell, and
under far less need than he to help himself in that way to
other people's property. Every reader of " Marmion " will
have noticed a certain fine stroke in the " Introduction to
Canto Third," where the poet, in his apostrophe to the
heroic Duke of Brunswick, exclaims,—

> " Lamented chief !—not thine the power
> To save in that illustrious hour,
> When Prussia hurried to the field,
> And snatched the spear—but left the shield." [3]

Here, again, the last and the best line of the passage is borrowed—with the change of a single word, and also without
acknowledgment—from a poem of Freneau's entitled " To
the Memory of the Brave Americans, under General Greene,
who fell in the Action of September 8, 1781," [4] a poem of
which Sir Walter Scott long afterward said, that it was

---

[1] " The Complete Poetical Works of Thomas Campbell," 58.

[2] " Poems on Several Occasions," 89.

[3] " The Poetical Works of Sir Walter Scott," ii. 130.

[4] " The Poems of Philip Freneau," 203–204.

" as fine a thing as there is of the kind in the language." [1] Perhaps, however, in all the record that might be made of these oblique transmarine tributes to the poetic worth of Philip Freneau, nothing is more notable for its generous largeness of furtive appreciation, than the homage which was paid to him by a high-born British lady—a sister of Sir Everard Home—one Mistress Anne Hunter, who, in 1802, published a volume of poems wherein she gave prominence to a plaintive ballad which she entitled " The Death Song," and which, putting it forward as her own, she described as having been " written for, and adapted to, an original Indian air." In an ingenuous note, the good lady sweetly tells us just how the idea of writing the poem had first occurred to her, and just what was her artistic purpose in writing it, namely, " to give something of the characteristic spirit and sentiment of those brave savages." [2] Twenty-five years afterward, among the verses chosen by Alexander Dyce to represent her work in his " Specimens of British Poetesses," a place was given to " The Death Song"; whereupon, the editor of " Blackwell's Magazine " singled out this particular poem of hers as the one most worthy of praise. " Her ' Death Song,' " said he, " is a noble strain, almost worthy of Campbell himself." [3] Would any British critic, in that acrimonious time, have bestowed such applause on Mrs. Hunter's " Death-Song," had he known that, except for a few mutilations, it was not Mrs. Hunter's at all, but Philip Freneau's, by whom it had been published in an American magazine [4] many years before, over his own name, and under the full title of " The Death-Song of a Cherokee Indian " ? At any rate, the poet who was capable of producing lines fit to be thus blended with their own

---

[1] This was said to Mr. Henry Brevoort, who reported the conversation to the brothers Duyckinck. " Cyclopædia of American Literature," i. 349.

[2] Mrs. Hunter's volume I have not seen. These sentences are cited by Duyckinck, ibid. 355 n, from Maria Edgeworth's " Rosamond," where once more poor Freneau's work is quoted—and the honor given to some one else.

[3] " Blackwood's Magazine," xli. 409.

[4] " The American Museum," i. 77, in 1787.

by Thomas Campbell and Walter Scott, and of such true lustre as to catch the eye of any critical reader, as they sparkled among those gems of poetic strass with which they were intermingled by the honorable lady who had condescended to claim them as her own, was not forced into the field of satire for lack of genius to succeed in some higher sphere of poetry.

IX.

It is a striking proof of the genuine poetic life then beginning to spring up in America—though soon to be crushed down again by the turbulence of the times—that the year 1770—the year in which Wordsworth was born—proved to be for Philip Freneau, then a college lad of eighteen, a year of uncommon prolificacy in the production of verse, and of verse which, like Wordworth's, and of course long before Wordsworth's, was emancipated from the poetic mannerisms of that age. For example, " The Power of Fancy," in rhymed tetrameters—alert, elastic, full of music and motion —wholly discards the sing-song, the artificial phraseology, and the stilted movement then so common in English poetry, and breathes out a lively and sweet note, at once reminiscent of the minor verse of Milton in the century before, and prophetic, also, of some strains of the Lake Poets in the century after :

> " Wakeful, vagrant, restless thing,
>   Ever wandering on the wing,
>   Who thy wondrous source can find,
>   FANCY, regent of the mind !
>   .   .   .   .   .
>   On the surface of the brain
>   Night after night she walks unseen ;
>   Noble fabrics doth she raise
>   In the woods or on the seas,
>   On some high, steep, pointed rock,
>   Where the billows loudly knock,

And the dreary tempests sweep
Clouds along the uncivil deep.

" Lo ! she walks upon the moon,
  Listens to the chimy tune
  Of the bright harmonious spheres,
  And the song of angels hears ;
  Sees this earth a distant star,
  Pendent, floating in the air ;
  Leads me to some lonely dome,
  Where Religion loves to come,
  Where the bride of Jesus dwells,
  And the deep-toned organ swells
  In notes with lofty anthems joined—
  Notes that half distract the mind.

" Now like lightning she descends
  To the prison of the Fiends,
  Hears the rattling of the chains,
  Feels their never-ceasing pains—
  But, O never may she tell
  Half the frightfulness of hell.

  .   .   .   .   .   .

" Lo ! she leads me wide and far,
  Sense can never follow her—
  Shape thy course o'er land and sea,
  Help me to keep pace with thee,
  Lead me to yon chalky cliff,
  Over rock and over reef,
  Into Britain's fertile land
  Stretching far her proud command :
  Look back and view, through many a year,
  Cæsar, Julius Cæsar, there.

  .   .   .   .   .   .

" FANCY, thou the Muses' pride,
  In thy painted realms reside,
  Endless images of things,
  Fluttering each on golden wings,

Ideal objects, such a store,
The universe could hold no more :
FANCY, to thy power I owe
Half my happiness below ;
By thee Elysian groves were made,
Thine were the notes that Orpheus played ;
By thee was Pluto charmed so well
While rapture seized the sons of hell ;
Come, O come, perceived by none,
You and I will walk alone." [1]

So, too, in Freneau's little poem called " Retirement,"
written probably a year or two after Wordsworth was born,
one catches tones that anticipate the poetic and spiritual
traits of that mighty maker and master of the new era of
English song,—his love of nature and of solitude, his moral
independence, his serenity, his joyous unworldliness, even
his simplicity of form :

" A hermit's house beside a stream,
With forests planted round,
Whatever it to you may seem,
More real happiness I deem
Than if I were a monarch crowned.

" A cottage I could call my own,
Remote from domes of care ;
A little garden, walled with stone,
The wall with ivy overgrown,
A limpid fountain near,

"Would more substantial joys afford,
More real bliss impart,
Than all the wealth that misers hoard,
Than vanquished worlds, or worlds restored,—
Mere cankers of the heart !

---

[1] " The Poems of Philip Freneau," 21–25.

" Vain foolish man ! how vast thy pride,
How little can thy wants supply !—
'T is surely wrong to grasp so wide—
To act as if we only had
To triumph—not to die !" [1]

---

[1] " The Poems of Philip Freneau," 52.

CHAPTER IX.

BEGINNINGS OF NEW LIFE IN VERSE AND PROSE: NEW ENGLAND. 1763–1775.

I.

FROM the earliest colonial days, the town of Boston had been the chief seat of intellectual activity in New England; but such activity had there found its favorite employment in religious discourse, in historical narrative, and in controversy—theological or political. This was particularly the case during the period of the Revolution. Able sermon-writers there were then in eastern Massachusetts, clever

184

political essayists, and two or three historians of no contemptible ability; but the most persevering search into
what has survived of the writings produced in that neighborhood, between the years 1763 and 1783, has thus far
failed to reveal to our eyes any token of promise for genuine work in poetry in that part of the world. Even those
highly-wrought fabrications in the nature of classical tragedy, which were elaborated by Mercy Otis Warren during
the anguish of that time, furnish no materials for an exception to the statement just made. Indeed, the depth of the
poetic poverty into which that very cultivated community
had then fallen, can perhaps be indicated in no more conclusive way than by a frank mention of the two most conspicuous verse-writers whom Boston has to offer to our
notice for the entire period now under consideration.

One of these was Benjamin Church, physician, politician,
essayist, and poet,—a man of glib and fervid expression,
with numerous showy gifts, but shallow, volatile, false. He
was born in 1734; he was graduated at Harvard in 1754; he
was thereafter for some time a student of medicine in London; and from the date of his return to Massachusetts,
about the year 1756, to that of his enforced and ignominious
departure from it, about twenty years later, he was lavish
in his literary tributes to the public,—the chief of them
being, in 1757, a didactic poem, entitled " The Choice ";
in 1761, a poem in " Pietas and Gratulatio "; in 1765,
" The Times, a Poem by an American," being a rather
toothless satire on the Stamp Act and other political atroci-
ties [1]; in 1766, an " Elegy on the Death of the Reverend
Jonathan Mayhew "; in 1769, a poem in vituperation of Sir
Francis Bernard, entitled " An Address to a Provincial
Bashaw "; in 1770, " An Elegy to the Memory of . . .
the Reverend Mr. George Whitefield "; and, in 1773, the
municipal oration on the Boston massacre.[2] No complete

---

[1] A full reprint of this satire may be found in Kettell, "Specimens of American Poetry," i. 149–156.

[2] Reprinted in Niles, " Principles and Acts," etc., 8–12.

report can now be made, or would be worth making, of this
man's other scribblements,—beyond number or recognition,
in prose and verse, argumentative, sentimental, comic, eulo-
gistic, abusive,—the writer himself masquerading under
various pseudonyms, and advocating with equal zeal the
opposite sides of the same political question.   Finally, of
all the productions of this loquacious charlatan, nothing
seems deserving of further recall, unless it be two stanzas in
his tribute to Jonathan Mayhew, wherein, apparently
unconscious of the possible application to himself of the
latter part of them, he gives it as the function of the Muse:

> " Deep into times rolled by, to dart her ken ;
>   At the tribunal of the lordly mind,
> T' arraign the conduct of the mightiest men,
>   Acquit, or doom, the Nimrods of mankind ;

> " To sift the motive stript of wily glare,
>   And through each cell the lurking guilt pursue,—
> The heart dissecting, till the bottom bare
>   Betrays the villain to the naked view." [1]

The other prominent representative of the town of Boston in the poetry of this period is Phillis Wheatly, a gentle-
natured and intelligent slave-girl, whose name still survives
among us in the shape of a tradition vaguely testifying to
the existence of poetic talent in this particular member of
the African race.   Unfortunately, a glance at what she
wrote will show that there is no adequate basis for such
tradition, and that the significance of her career belongs
rather to the domain of anthropology, or of hagiology, than
to that of poetry—whether American or African.   Her
verses, which were first published in a collected form in
London in 1773, under the title of " Poems on Various
Subjects, Religious and Moral," attracted for a time consid-

---

[1] " Elegy on —— Mayhew," 4.   By the courtesy of the Boston Athenæum
I had the use of its copy of this poem,—a copy which once belonged to A. Eliot,
and in which the poem is attributed to Church.

erable curiosity, both in England and in America,—not at all, however, because the verses were good, but because they were written by one from whom even bad verses were too good to be expected. In 1784, under her new name of Phillis Peters, she published in Boston a poem entitled "Liberty and Peace," suggested by the happy ending of the Revolutionary war. ⸱This production, however, makes no change in the evidence touching her poetic gifts.[1]

II.

To any one who may care to bring together and to scrutinize the multitudinous productions of American writers for the period now under review, it will become plain that, at about the year 1770, the chief hope for a new and stronger life among us, either in poetry or in prose, lay in the destinies of two very young men, one of them, Philip Freneau, an undergraduate at Princeton, the other, John Trumbull, a graduate-student still in residence at Yale; both of them at about that time doing things that denoted the presence here of finer poetic genius than had yet spoken out on this side of the Atlantic; both of them, also, afterward driven by the storms of the Revolution, at first reluctantly and under protest, into the service of the country as political satirists. In a previous chapter, some account has been given of the early training and equipment, and of the early poetic work, of Freneau. A similar account has now to be given of Trumbull, especially for the period of his literary life prior to his engulfment in the ferocious controversies of the Revolution.[2]

---

[1] A little book, entitled "Letters of Phillis Wheatly, the Negro-Slave Poet of Boston," and edited by Charles Deane, was privately printed in Boston in 1864,—at a time when testimony as to the intellectual capacity of the negro race was much desired. But poor Phillis's efforts in prose have no more value in that direction than have her efforts in verse,—these letters being little else than pious and almost infantile platitudes expressed in extremely stilted English.

[2] For his livelihood, Trumbull early adopted the profession of the law,—a profession which, in America, has thus far been the receptacle and the tomb for much talent that under other conditions would have found a more congenial

John Trumbull was born in Waterbury, Connecticut, on the 24th of April, 1750. Both on his father's side and on his mother's he was of the pure Brahmin stock of New England,—a stock prolific of scholars, teachers, magistrates, and divines. Moreover, the very name of Trumbull, if we may yield our faith to a picturesque tradition, was originally the coinage and the grateful gift of an English king, who owed his life to the valor of the earliest perceptible ancestor of this family. As King Henry—the tradition very properly shuns the vulgarity of being too specific—was one day walking in the park, a mad bull, which had escaped from Smithfield and was filled with a diabolical spirit of murder, made at his majesty, and was about to gore his sacred person, when a yeoman of his guard rushed upon the scene, and, at the peril of his own life, saved that of the king. For this good deed, the king gave his yeoman a pension of one hundred marks a year; also the expressive name of Turnbull; likewise a coat-of-arms copiously enriched with the appropriate taurine imagery, to wit, " three bulls' heads, with their fronts displayed, and a bull's head for the crest." [1]

and a more illustrious employment in literature. In spite of frequent interruptions from frail bodily health, Trumbull became an eminent lawyer. In due time, he was made State Attorney for the County of Hartford, member of the legislature, a Judge of the Superior Court of the State, and finally a Judge of its Supreme Court of Errors. In the year 1825, being then seventy-five years of age, he went to live with his daughter, Mrs. William Woodbridge, at Detroit —at that time a petty though ancient post in the depths of the American wilderness. Soon after setting forth upon that long and arduous journey, the old lawyer and poet tarried awhile in New York, where he was entertained at a great banquet given in his honor by the lawyers and men of letters of that city. In Detroit he remained until his death in 1831 ; and his grave, marked by a fitting monument, is in the beautiful cemetery of Elmwood, near that city. Through the friendship of his grandson, Mr. Dudley Bradstreet Woodbridge, —a friendship which began between us in my own boyhood,—I have had access to the private papers of John Trumbull ; and from these I have been enabled, in the present volume, to make considerable additions to what has hitherto been known in our time concerning the very striking early work, both in prose and in verse, of the author of " M'Fingal." To these papers I shall refer in my footnotes as Trumbull MSS.

[1] Trumbull MSS.

Sometime afterward, one of this yeoman's posterity, having married an heiress in the west of England, and being anxious to disguise the plebeian suggestiveness of his name, —which in sooth might bespeak an ancestral butcher or herdsman quite as well as hero,—procured the same to be changed to Trumbull. Although the most noted American branch of the family wear their patronymic in this transposed form, something of the fearlessness which gained for the original Turn-bull his valor-breathing name, seems to have survived in that particular member of the family, whose acquaintance we are now about to make, and who, as a social and political satirist, went forth betimes and defied the horns of many a monster, madder perhaps, and more dangerous, than the mad bull of Smithfield.

Should John Trumbull cease to be remembered among us for his achievements as a grown-up man, it may be safe to say that he will still deserve some sort of renown for the prodigies he wrought while yet in his babyhood, and immediately after that brilliant epoch in his career. In the records of intellectual precocity, scarcely anything can be cited more remarkable than some of the things that are recorded of this amazing little creature at a period of life when ordinary mortals are sufficiently employed in absorbing and digesting a lacteal diet and in getting forward with their primary set of teeth. Before he was two years old, he could say by heart all the verses in the "Primer," and all of Watts's "Divine Songs for Children." As soon as he had reached the considerable age of two, he began to learn to read; which mystery he acquired within the next half-year. Even prior to the age of four, he had read the entire Bible through; and by that year he had also read all of Watts's "Lyrics,"[1] and was able to repeat them all without book. Emulous, no doubt, of the laurels of the heavenly and much desired Watts, he began at about the age of four to

---

[1] Stiles, "Itinerary," iv. 204, MS. Probably an American selection from the "Horæ Lyricæ" is meant.

make verses for himself, as much as possible in the true
Wattsian manner; but not having as yet advanced so far in
learning as to be able to write, he could only preserve these
valuable productions by storing them away in his memory.
At five, being still unable to write, he hit upon the device
of transcribing his verses by imitating printed letters.   His
first attempt of this kind consisted of four stanzas of an
original hymn, and his " scrawl of it filled a complete sheet
of paper." [1]   Having perceived a want of connection
between the third and the fourth lines of one of his stanzas,
this weird urchin was greatly perplexed thereby; but " after
lying awake some nights," meditating upon the problem,
he finally solved it by the proper verbal corrections.   Near
the end of his fifth year, his father, who was the village-
pastor at Waterbury, received into his house as a pupil, to
be instructed for admission to Yale College, a lad of seventeen years, one William Southmayd.   At the outset, this
lad was required to learn both the Latin Accidence and
Lilly's Latin Grammar; also, with the help of a translation,
to construe the Select Colloquies of Corderius.   While the
anguish of this task was in progress, the pastor's little boy,
loitering unobserved in the study, was accustomed to listen
to the Latin words which were spoken by teacher and
pupil; and in this way, before his father knew of it, he had
learned one half of Lilly's Grammar.   For example, he
" learned ' Quæ genus ' by heart in a day."   When at last
the pastor became aware of these secret depredations upon
classical knowledge on the part of his son, he allowed the
little fellow to join regularly in the work, in which indeed
the youngster soon outstripped the elder student; and in
September of the following year, 1757, the two lads, one
being nineteen years of age, and the other seven, " were
presented at college, examined by the tutors, and admitted as members." [2]   On this occasion, a boy of twelve
years, Nathaniel Emmons, afterward famous as a theologian, held the little candidate on his lap, while the exam-

---

[1] Trumbull MSS.   [2] Trumbull, " Poetical Works," ed. 1820, Mem. 10.

ination proceeded.[1] What were the requirements at that time exacted for admission to Yale College may be seen in the following statute printed in the year 1759: " Admissionem in hoc Collegium Nemo expectet, nisi qui é Præsidis et Tutorum Examine, Tullium, Virgilium et Testamentum Græcum extemporè legere, ad Unguem redere, ac grammaticè resolvere, et Prosâ veram Latinitatem scribere potuerit; et Prosodiæ ac Arithmetices vulgaris Regulas perdidicerit: atque Testimonium idoneum de Vitâ ac Moribus inculpatis exhibuerit." [2] Long afterward, Trumbull himself stated to President Stiles that within the year and a half now referred to he had " learned Cordery, Tully's XII Select Orations, Virgil's Eclogues, and all the Æneid (not Georg.), and 4 Gospels in Greek." [3]

It need not surprise us that the success of so young a boy in passing these requirements, seemed at that time a marvel fit to be chronicled in the newspapers. " The Connecticut Gazette," for September 24, 1757, mentions it in these words: " At the Commencement in this Town the 14th Instant, . . . among those that appear'd to be examined for Admission, was the Son of the Rev'd Mr. Trumble, of Waterbury, who passed a good Examination, altho' but little more than seven Years of Age; but on account of his Youth his Father does not intend he shall at present continue at College." [4]

In consequence of this sensible decision on the part of the " Rev'd Mr. Trumble," our juvenile phenomenon was kept at home six years longer; during which period, of course, his brain could not remain idle. For one thing, he then made a still more extended reading of the Greek and Roman authors, especially of Homer, Horace, and Cicero.

[1] E. A. Park, in " Works of Emmons," i. page clxviii.

[2] For a copy of this statute, I am indebted to Professor F. B. Dexter, M.A., Registrar of the Faculty, and author of " Sketch of the History of Yale University," and of two volumes of " Biographical Sketches of the Graduates of Yale College."

[3] Stiles, " Itinerary 1785-8," iv. 204-5, MS.

[4] J. Hammond Trumbull, " The Origin of M'Fingal," 6 n.

Not many books in English literature were to be found in his father's library, which consisted chiefly of theological writings and of the ancient classics. At the age of eight, however, the boy read for the first time " Paradise Lost," Thomson's " Seasons," an English version of " Telemachus," and, above all, " The Spectator "; and upon this not ill-assorted stock of modern literature, he continued to nourish his spirit until he went to college.[1] Before he reached the age of nine, he had put into English verse one half of " The Psalms of David "; but in the midst of this labor, he happened to fall in with Watts's version, whereupon, in despair, he " laid aside and burnt his own."[2] Moreover, he had a memory so quick and tenacious that, even as a child, he was sometimes induced to test its powers by feats performed for a wager. Thus, when nine years old, he attempted under such stimulus to commit to memory in a quarter of an hour the Hungarian version of the Lord's Prayer, as given in Salmon's " Geographical and Historical Grammar." He more than won the bet; for, after learning the Lord's prayer in the Hungarian language, he had time enough left over to learn it in Malabar also; and both versions he retained in memory as late as twenty-nine years afterward, when he repeated one of them to President Stiles.[3]

III.

In September, 1763, being then thirteen years of age, he was deemed old enough to take up his residence at the college; but as he had by that time read nearly all the Greek and Latin authors studied there, he was advised by his tutor to give his chief attention to algebra, geometry, and astronomy, which he did during the first three years of his course as an undergraduate.[4] In his senior year, however, he went back to his earlier studies in English literature, having, of course, access to a much wider range of authors

---

[1] Stiles, " Itinerary," M.S.   [2] Ibid.   [3] Ibid.
[4] Trumbull, " Poetical Works," ed. 1820, Mem. 11.

than he had enjoyed at his father's house. Taking his first degree in 1767, he continued to reside at the college as Dean's Scholar until 1770, in which year he received the degree of Master.

Those years, from 1767 to 1770, were for him a period of the most delightful and the most fruitful activity in literary culture. His time was his own; he had the stimulus of congenial literary companionship; and he seems to have given himself up, with unbounded enjoyment, to a prolonged and critical study of what was then called " polite literature." During those years he read, in some cases for the second or third time, " all the Greek and Latin classics, especially the poets and orators "; while to the writers then dominant in English literature, he surrendered himself with great zest, delighting in their gayety of tone and in their lightness of touch, and trying to reproduce their manner in literary experiments of his own. It should be mentioned, too, that there were among his contemporaries at Yale several young fellows of unusual ability, and with literary tastes not unlike his own,—such as Joseph Howe, Buckingham St. John, Timothy Dwight, Joseph Buckminster, and David Humphreys,—young fellows of Puritan ancestry and of Puritan nurture, and with an ineradicable strain of Puritan earnestness, yet elate like himself with brilliant gifts, full of the fire, mirth, and ambition of youth, and all aglow with enthusiasm for the later English poets, essayists, and satirists, whose writings brought to them the spell of a higher and a finer literary method than had hitherto been known in America; and sent the unwonted charm of urbane criticism and of high-bred playfulness down into the ponderous and uncouth erudition, the grimness, the provincialism, the controversial truculence, then to some degree characteristic of the intellectual life of New England.

IV.

Trumbull's earliest literary undertaking was a series of essays, the form and tone of which he caught from the

13

Queen Anne writers, particularly Addison and Steele. These essays, which bore the happy title of " The Meddler," and were " chiefly of the moral, critical, and poetical kind, upon miscellaneous and mostly disconnected subjects," [1] made their appearance in " The Boston Chronicle," beginning with the 4th of September, 1769, and ending with the 22d of January, 1770. [2] Each number is decorated with a Latin quotation, usually from Persius, or Horace, or Vergil. Under the masque of his pseudonym, the author makes playful allusion to his own pretended foibles, and to those of a few literary friends whom he meets at his club,— such as Mr. Thomas Freeman, John Manly, Esq., and " the youthful gay Jack Dapperwit, who is lineally descended from the famous Tom Dapperwit." Moreover, in this literary undertaking, he frankly avows an æsthetic purpose, as something quite aside from that practical, strenuous, and hortatory function to which literature had been commonly subjected in that quarter of the world. " My essays," says he, " are chiefly designed for the entertainment of those who have some acquaintance with polite literature ; but among the various subjects I shall discuss, I hope every person may find something of humor, instruction, or amusement, that will repay the trouble of a perusal. In the

---

[1] Trumbull, MSS. My citations from the early prose essays of Trumbull are made from copies which he left in his own handwriting, and which are now in my possession.

[2] The following are the dates of the publication of the entire series :—

No. 1, Sep. 4–7, 1769 ;
No. 2, Sep. 14–18 ;
No. 3, Oct. 23–26 ;
No. 4, Oct. 30–Nov. 2 ;
No. 5, Nov. 9–13 ;
No. 6, Nov. 30–Dec. 4 ;
No. 7, Dec. 18–21 ;
No. 8, Dec. 28, 1769–Jan. 1, 1770 ;
No. 9, Jan. 11–15 ;
No. 10, Jan. 18–22.

Numbers 4, 6, and 9 are probably not by Trumbull, but by one or more of his literary associates. In ascertaining the foregoing dates, I used the file of " The Boston Chronicle " belonging to the library of Yale University.

meantime, I think myself well employed in contributing my assistance (how trifling soever it may be) towards instructing the ignorant, diverting and improving the learned, rectifying the taste and manners of the times, and cultivating the fine arts in this land." [1]

His aptitude for the work of censor of conversation and manners, is well shown in the second essay, which is an exposition of true and false wit. " True wit is always accompanied with good nature, politeness, and a fine taste; the false, with the grossest offenses against modesty, good manners, and good sense. I shall not say much at present concerning wit in writing. We are happily passed the age or era of Pun, Crambo, Anagram, and Acrostic. Yet I cannot but observe that the magazines and such miscellaneous repositories have lately been stuffed with a new kind of vermin, begotten between the Anagram and Riddle, called the Rebus, which is the most pure, refined, and sublimated kind of nonsense that hath appeared in any age." Among the several kinds of false wit then often displayed in conversation, is that special form of raillery " which consists in putting modest people to the blush, by insulting and exposing them for every folly or defect that is reported of them, of their relations, or the town or country to which they belong. Whosoever would succeed in this way, must be possessed of the most matchless and unparalleled impudence; must be a perfect master of scandal and defamation; and must apply himself with the greatest assiduity to studying the noble art of lying. . . . When by these means he has attained to perfection, I will engage that his practice shall be crowned with the laughter of fools, the blushes of the modest, and the contempt of the wise." [2]

In the fifth number is introduced a contributor who describes himself " as a member of the fraternity of authors." " I have for a long time," he adds, " been a retailer, or rather a peddler, in wit; but my stock is so small and my credit so low, that I am in danger of bankruptcy.

---

[1] Trumbull MSS. [2] Ibid.

I have published essays, songs, jests, satires, almanacs, controversy, politics, prophecies, and letters to a friend; all which the ungrateful world have neglected and despised; so that I must abandon the trade, unless I obtain your speedy assistance." " In my productions," he goes on to say, " I shall assume the title of a Schemer,—for which I think myself pretty well qualified ; having always been obliged to live by my wits, and employ myself in contriving schemes for the payment of an old debt, or the contraction of a new one. . . . I have in writing innumerable schemes on all subjects, having in happier days been schemer to one general, two prime ministers, several misers, and many neglected marriage-seekers of both sexes, for whom I have invented infallible schemes to win a place, an estate, a battle, a husband, or a wife, according to the respective wants of each petitioner. I have farther, as became my circumstances, deeply studied the rules of praise and commendation, and read critically the productions of flattery in all ages. . . . From these, especially from the poetical addresses of Dryden, the odes of Boileau in praise of the French king, the ministerial writers of the present day, and the whole herd of moneyless poets, I have extracted and compounded an essay which I esteem the quintessence of panegyric and the very marrow of dedication. This, if a few blanks were filled with the name and titles of some person of quality, would make a splendid appearance at the beginning of your ' Meddler,' if ever those papers should be published in a volume by themselves." [1]

In the essays which follow, this lively and versatile contributor makes his appearance more than once, and each time with something which adds to their piquant flavor. Here, for example, is an advertisement which he has prepared for the use of a young lady at the successful close of a series of four annual campaigns which she had conducted for the capture of a husband:

---

[1] Trumbull MSS.

" Advertisement.

To Be Sold At Public Vendue,

The Whole Estate Of

Isabella Sprightly, Toast and Coquette,

(Now retiring from Business).

" Imprimis, all the Tools and Utensils necessary for carrying on the Trade, viz. Several bundles of Darts and Arrows, well-pointed, and capable of doing great execution; A considerable quantity of Patches, Paint, Brushes, and Cosmetics, for plastering, painting and whitewashing the face; a complete set of caps, ' a la mode a Paris,' of all sizes from five to fifteen inches in height; With several dozens of Cupids, very proper to be stationed on a ruby lip, a diamond eye, or a roseate cheek.

" Item, as she proposes by certain ceremonies to transform one of her humble servants into an husband, and keep him for her own use, she offers for sale, Florio, Daphnis, Cynthio, and Cleanthes, with several others, whom she won by a constant attendance on business during the space of four years. She can prove her indisputable right thus to dispose of them, by certain deeds of gifts, bills of sale, and attestations, vulgarly called love-letters, under their own hands and seals. They will be offered very cheap, for they are all of them either broken-hearted, consumptive, or in a dying condition. Nay, some of them have been dead this half year, as they declare and testify in the above-mentioned writings.

" N.B. Their hearts will be sold separately." [1]

In another essay, the same vivacious contributor enters into that great controversy between the moderns and the ancients, which was one of the burning questions of the

---

[1] Trumbull MSS.

eighteenth century: " The moralists of our time . . . complain that men are dwindling down in arithmetical progression from the gigantic size of our forefather Goliath, towards a pygmean stature, to which they expect posterity will in a few centuries arrive. But they more especially maintain that we fall short of the ancients in the height, length, and breadth of our understandings; and seem to think that nature at first dealt out the stock of brains, designed for man, with too lavish a hand, and that we are now forced to take up with the scrapings of the dish. I have always wondered that this opinion hath been so long maintained; and that for two very substantial reasons: first, because I have observed that no one will, as to his particular self, allow that he is in the least degree less wise than his ancestors; and, secondly, because I do not think the opinion itself is founded either in truth or reason. For I cannot discover from Scripture or tradition that Adam was one inch above six feet high, or had more wit to avoid being cheated than thousands of the present generation.'' He then proceeds to demonstrate that the moderns, instead of being inferior to the ancients, are actually superior to them '' in all the polite arts and sciences.'' '' By these,'' he continues, '' I mean dress, dancing, compliments, curses, drinking, swearing, gaming, poetry, fighting, and dying, and in a word every qualification of a gentleman and a man of honor in the modern acceptation of those titles.'' Then follows some excellent drollery on these several claims, in the course of which he has a capital parody on the pompous style then so much admired in Hervey's '' Meditations.'' After dealing with several matters of dress and society, in which he asserts superiority for the moderns, he comes to '' the art of cursing and swearing,'' which, as he argues, '' is almost wholly of modern invention. Aristophanes, Plautus, Terence, Horace, and a few others who might perhaps have been gentlemen, had they lived in these days, do indeed make a few slight attempts at the practice; but they have not an oath or a curse fit for the mouth of a modern gentleman. I cannot but congratulate my contemporaries on their improvements in this art, which they have carried to such wonderful length, that the lowest dregs of the people have attained to a facility and perfection that cannot be excelled by the politest of the nobility." As to the single item of poetry, however, he is obliged to confess that the superiority of the moderns is not quite so easy to prove: " Poetry being looked upon as the lowest qualification of a gentleman, is indeed somewhat neglected in this age. As advocate for the moderns, I will use the best argument I can in their favor. It is a well known maxim, that every poet is a fool. If this be true, I believe no one who has read thus far, will doubt of our ample qualifications for that office. As to the duration of modern poetry, we indeed make no great pretensions. The ancient art of embalming, which extended to their writings, as well as to their bodies, hath been for many ages lost and unknown; and our works, like the good man's, follow us into the grave."[1]

The tenth and last of these essays has for its motto a few words from Juvenal,[2]

" Nostri farrago libelli est."

As might be expected from such a text, the discourse which follows is itself a medley of disconnected topics, some of which, indeed, have a very sparkling treatment. " My entertainments," says the author, " have usually consisted of one or two plain dishes; but finding some people desire a greater variety, I shall at present furnish out my table with a mixture of olios, fricassees, ragouts, tarts, and sweetmeats, and beg of the reader, without making any wry faces, to sit down and fall on without any ceremony." One of the tarts which the host thus sets before his guests is this: " Many of my country readers have wondered at my description of the gentry in town, in my last essay, where I represented them as rising at noon, and making the after-

---

[1] Trumbull MSS.   [2] " Saturæ," i. 86

noon the only busy part of the day. I will therefore tell them, for their further information, that by the encouragement and assistance of people in great towns, the Afternoon hath of late made great encroachments upon its neighbors, and strangely justled and discomposed the other parts of the day. It hath driven forward the Morning from its proper station, and forced it to take refuge in the habitation of Noon; it hath made Breakfast and Dinner shake hands, and been the total destruction of Supper; it hath devoured a large portion of Night, and unless a speedy stop be put to its motion, may probably swallow up the whole four and twenty Hours.'' And here is one of the sweetmeats: '' There is no figure more employed by the present race of wits and satirists than the Periphrasis, or, in modern language, the Circumbendibus. To call a man a hog, is by no means allowable; but if we exalt the expression, and say he is that animal before which we are commanded not to throw pearls, it becomes extremely witty, polite and delicate, and may be used by a Doctor of Divinity with the greatest facility and pleasure.'' [1]

Stirred by the new forms of literary expression which Trumbull and his friends had found in later English literature, these young men began to take a somewhat contemptuous and even a revolutionary attitude toward the narrow scope and the hard jejune methods then prevailing in the curriculum at Yale, as well as toward the tone and spirit of nearly the entire body of writers who, in that neighborhood, then had the ear of the public. Indeed, the whole field of American letters seemed at that time to be abandoned to controversy, political, theological, and otherwise. Such controversy, moreover, was carried on with the absurd pedantry, the unrelenting partisanship, the extravagance of misrepresentation, the anger, the coarseness, the barbarous incivility with which, in those days, even cultivated persons thought it proper to convey to one another their ideas on subjects concerning which they happened to

---

[1] Trumbull MSS.

disagree. As Trumbull himself long afterward described the situation, " Every pamphlet, every newspaper, was filled with metaphysics; the press groaned with controversy; and the world was stunned with Sermons, Letters of Debate, Replies and Rejoinders, Dialogues between Ministers and Parishioners, and such like weapons of this spiritual warfare, whose names it would tire one to reckon up." [1]

V.

Here, then, as it seemed to the young satirist, looking down upon it from his cheery watch-tower in the college, was a situation which could best be dealt with by ridicule; and in his next series of essays, to which he was prompted by his recognition of this fact, we may once more observe something of the new tone that was coming into American letters,—urbanity, perspective, moderation of emphasis, satire, especially satire on its more playful side,—that of irony. It was in February, 1770, that he began publishing in " The Connecticut Journal and New Haven Post-Boy," a series of essays which he entitled " The Correspondent," and which are also avowedly framed after the model of " The Spectator." Though the writer was then but a youth of twenty, these essays show in him no inconsiderable maturity of thought and keenness of observation, and no slight success in catching the method of his literary masters. Already he was too much of an artist to flaunt in the face of his readers the serious motive of his work; and they who should find it out, were to come upon it unawares in the midst of the light-hearted mirth which pervades his sentences.

As his first essay is devoted chiefly to the task of self-introduction, it opens with a neatly turned explanation of the title which had been chosen by the author for the entire series. " There is," he says, " in the present age a most

[1] Trumbull MSS.

wonderful tendency to letter-writing. Every book that outgrows the size of a pamphlet, is ushered into the world by an epistolary dedication. Party and politics take on them the form of Letters to Lords and Members of Parliament; Religion and Morality, of Letters to a Friend. Nay, so far hath this humor been carried that the writers of weekly essays, not content with an universal correspondence, have sometimes on particular emergencies condescended to compose Letters to Themselves.

" But on account of the difficulties which some have met with in finding out proper persons to patronize their letters, I conceived it necessary that somebody should assume the character of an universal Correspondent, to receive letters from all the world, to return suitable answers, and to patronize such writings as nobody else would take notice of. Whether I am qualified for this post or not, the reader will best determine by giving me an opportunity to display my abilities. I therefore do hereby send greeting to all Scribblers whatsoever, to whom these presents shall come, whether Poets, Politicians, Almanack-Makers, Metaphysicians, or Writers of Advertisements, whose nightly toils for their country's edification have been rewarded only by the contempt of the world, promising that in every distress or perplexity, they shall find in me a most friendly patron, and be favored with my best advice and assistance. As the strongest instance of my universal charity and disinterested benevolence, even to the lowest objects of literary compassion, I desire the ' Plain Dealer,' [1] if ever he writes again, to dedicate his next essay to me; and on that condition, I engage my word and honor to read over every sentence of it, without one smile of derision at the unmeaning flourish of his style, or the barefaced sophistry of his reasoning: desiring him, however, for the sake of my credit with the rest of

---

[1] The name assumed by a " disciple of the metaphysical party," who had written much in the same paper, but of whom, after this, no more was heard.

the world, to avoid the usual custom of dedicators, and not be very lavish to me of his praise and panegyrics.

" But since it may be thought proper that I should follow my own rule, and throw my essays into the form of Letters, I do by these presents constitute the World for my Patron, and shall address myself to it in the following epistle. Though the method be a little singular, I hope it will give the reader as much satisfaction, as if it had been inscribed to a Member of Parliament, to my Lord What-d'-ye-call-him, to Messieurs Printers, to J. W., Esq., or from A Gentleman in the East to his Friend in the West: premising, in the first place, that if the reader find in it anything obscure and unintelligible, I desire him to suppose it very deep and mysterious, and to believe me a great genius and profound reasoner, and the matter far above his comprehension; by which means he may have an opportunity of extending his charity to me, in the same manner as it hath been often extended to other candidates for the metaphysical laurel." [1]

The essays which he thus began were continued from the 23d of February, until the 6th of July, 1770, at which date they had reached eight numbers; but few as they were, they attracted great attention, and were read with vast relish by a public unaccustomed to so sprightly a mode of discussion; and to the end of his life Trumbull himself felt pride in the fact that he had been the first in that neighborhood " who dared by satire to oppose the party of controversial scribblers," and to " set this part of America an example of the use of ridicule and humor " in controlling " the whims of dogmatical enthusiasts." [2] The very titles of the books of these dogmatical writers he parodies in sundry droll announcements of pretended works which he was about to give to the world, such as:

" Creeds and Catechisms Made and Mended by D.D.[3] &

---

[1] Trumbull MSS.   [2] Ibid.
[3] Rev. Joseph Bellamy, D.D.

Company: Being the Substance of many Treatises that have lately made a Noise in the World."

"The Art of Quarreling; Being a Curious and Entertaining History of Some late Transactions."

"An Essay on Dancing [1]; Proving from the Examples of King David and others that it is a most grievous Iniquity, and directly contrary to the Eternal Fitness of Things.   By the Pious ——."

"An Easy and Compendious Method of becoming a Great Man; With a few Hints on the Art of Climbing."

"The Art of Second-Sight, Shewing an Easy and Infallible Method of Discovering any Person's Character, Principles, Practices, State of Body and Soul, future Happiness or Misery, &c.; far Superior to Palmistry, Astrology, or any other Method of Fortune-telling: First introduced by a renowned Stage Player, [2] and since brought to Perfection by the united Labors of a certain Set of Philosophers." [3]

Some of the devices for self-display and for defamation, which were often resorted to by authors in the construction of the title-pages and advertisements of their books, he satirizes in the following kind and helpful suggestions addressed by him to his brethren of the literary guild:

"As to the decorations of your book, be sure to frame a very pompous title; for I can assure you there is much virtue in a title-page, and I have often known it, when duly managed, to contain all the wit and the greatest part of the arguments in the book. If you choose to answer some former writer, it may not be amiss to advertize him in the newspapers, after this manner:

---

[1] A great outcry had just then been raised against this sinful practice.
[2] The Rev. George Whitefield.
[3] Trumbull MSS.

' Now in the Press

and will speedily be published,

A VINDICATION OF TRUE RELIGION,

FROM THE CAVILS OF IGNORANCE AND HERESY;

Being an Answer to the remarks of

The Rev'd Dunscotus:

" ' Wherein is clearly proved that the Remarker is clearly unacquainted with the true Spirit of the Gospel, that he hath wholly mistaken the subject of controversy, and hath been guilty of the most palpable blunders and absurdities: Concluding with a Catalogue of his Contradictions, and an Appendix shewing the coincidence of his opinions with those of Hobbes, Spinoza, and the Atheists and Deists in all ages.' " [1]

Then, too, as a satire on the self-complacence and the self-stultification often exhibited by those charming writers whose traits he has subjected to such careful study, he offers to the public " A New System of Logic," of which the two grand principles are: " First, That the common sense and reason of mankind is so weak and fallacious a guide, that its dictates ought never to be regarded; Secondly, That nevertheless nothing is so great that it can surpass, or so perplexing that it can entangle, the understanding of a true metaphysician." " I take these points to be so nearly self-evident," he continues, " that although I can say very little in proof of them, the reader ought for this very reason the more firmly to believe them. For such is the nature of every self-evident proposition that no arguments can be brought to prove it. . . . Hence, it is plain (if I have any skill in metaphysics) that when a point is very difficult

---

[1] MSS. This burlesque has allusion to Dr. Samuel Hopkins, whose answer to Mills gives a catalogue of about forty contradictions he professes to find in the work of the latter; also, to Dr. James Dana, whose answer to Jonathan Edwards's treatise on the Will contains several pages of extracts from Hobbes, Gordon, and other deistical writers, collated with extracts from Edwards.

to be proved, and all the arguments you can urge in its favor very weak and little to the point, it is not far from being a self-evident proposition." [1]

Furthermore, still personating the character of a disputatious metaphysician, and speaking in the name of his entire class, he goes on to explain the feud existing between themselves and that vulgar standard of opinion for which a superstitious esteem was still cherished among the non-metaphysical rabble: " A great enmity hath in all ages subsisted between metaphysics and common sense. They were, indeed, partly reconciled some years ago by a certain great author [2] among us, and continued pretty good friends for a considerable time. By these means, metaphysics was introduced into the best company, and was greatly esteemed by the most sensible part of the world ; but having naturally a disposition to ramble and change sides, it hath been again seduced to revolt from common sense, and they are now at greater variance than ever. Therefore, by all the rules of justice, we who fight under the banner of metaphysics have a right to treat common sense as a common enemy, to speak all the ill we can of it, and to regard it as little as possible, both in conversation and writing." [3]

Finally, he reaches the culmination of his satirical eulogy upon his literary brethren, by showing the great and peculiar service they are constantly rendering to the bewildered race of mortals : " Though the world of itself be in a state of darkness and chaos, yet it is not destitute of every spark and glimmering. The metaphysicians, those burning and shining lights, to our great advantage, are kindled up in various parts of our land ; and to their praise be it spoken, they do not seem disposed to hide their candle under a bushel, but very generally set it up in the most conspicuous places, to lead the lonely and benighted traveler on his journey. I am not

---

[1] Trumbull MSS.

[2] Probably refers to Berkeley, whose " Alciphron " was written in New England.

[3] Trumbull MSS.

ignorant that some evil-minded persons will pretend that
they deserve rather to be compared to an ' ignis fatuus,'
or one of those vapory fires that appear by night in the
meadows,—affirming that the cold marshes where the latter
is generated, are a type of a metaphysician's brain; that
each of them hath the faculty of shining only in the dark;
and that they serve their followers alike, leading them into
ponds and quagmires, from which they may thank their
stars if they ever get out again. Much might be said in
answer to these malicious insinuations; but as my time is
too precious to be employed in such trifles, I desire the
reader to get rid of the objection as well as he is able, and
attend to certain points of far greater importance, which I
am now preparing to discuss." [1]

In the course of the first seven numbers of " The Correspondent," the author had perhaps sufficiently diverted
the public at the expense of his too pugnacious literary
brethren; but it was not at all needful that he should now
stay his hand, merely for lack of other objects worthy of his
satirical attention. Accordingly, in the eighth number he
turns toward an entirely different class of his fellow-citizens,
—those noble-minded American philanthropists and Christians who were deriving large wealth from an active participation in the African slave-trade. This essay, which closed
the series, is a fusillade of witty and stinging satire, and
deserves attention in any study of anti-slavery opinion in
America prior to the Declaration of Independence. [2]

---

[1] Trumbull MSS.

[2] This first series of " The Correspondent " appeared in " The Conn. Journal
and New Haven Post-Boy," at the following dates :

    No. 1, Feb. 23, 1770 ;
    No. 2, March 2 ;
    No. 3, March 9 ;
    No. 4, March 23 ;
    No. 5, April 6 ;
    No. 6, April 27 ;
    No. 7, June 1 ;
    No. 8, July 6.

In ascertaining the dates of these essays, I have had the privilege of using the

VI.

From the task of writing this satire against the American traffic in African slaves, Trumbull must have turned to that of writing " An Essay on the Use and Advantages of the Fine Arts," [1] a composition partly in prose and partly in verse, which he delivered at the commencement in New Haven on the 12th of September, 1770, on taking his master's degree.   Giving to literature the highest place among the fine arts, he points to the unhappy neglect of them in America : " They are considered as matters of trifling amusement, and despised in comparison with the more solid branches of learning."   Nevertheless, " they ennoble the soul, purify the passions, and give the thoughts a better turn.   They add dignity to our sentiments, delicacy and refinement to our manners.   They set us above our meaner pursuits, and make us scorn those low enjoyments, which perhaps we once esteemed as the perfection of human felicity.   .   .   .   These are the delights which humanize the soul, and polish away that rugged ferocity of manners, which is natural to the uncultivated nations of the world." [2]

But why bring forward a theme so untimely ?   In this crisis of desperate controversy, when Americans are contending for those primary rights without which the fine arts are but the diversions and gew-gaws of slaves, why interrupt serious business by so inopportune a plea ?   Nay, retorts our juvenile champion of æsthetic culture, in every land, in every age, these arts have most bloomed and flourished in conjunction with " the unconquered spirit of freedom " and with the ambition for " heroic deeds."   " Learning and glory walk hand in hand through the world."   " The same ardor of ambition, the same greatness of

---

exceedingly rare file of " The Conn. Journal," in the possession of Miss Elizabeth Lyon Linsley, Elmwood, Stratford, Conn.

[1] New Haven, printed by T. & S. Green.   The copy in my possession was Trumbull's, and has corrections in his handwriting.

[2] "An Essay," etc., 3-4.

thought, which inspires the warrior to brave danger in the conquering field, when diffused among a people will call forth genius in every station of life, fire the imagination of the artist, and raise to sublimity the aspiring muse." [1]

This, then, was the burden of the young poet's message to his fellow-countrymen, on that September day in 1770, while the air all about them was vibrant with the clangor of political debate, and trembling with whispered premonitions of some earth-shaking strife. And to justify his message, he then sketches the history of the fine arts, particularly of literature, in ancient and in modern times, closing it with a masterly outline of the great periods of English literature.

From this survey of literature in other times and among other peoples, he next turns to his own: "America hath a fair prospect in a few centuries of ruling both in arts and arms. It is universally allowed that we excel in the force of natural genius; and although but few among us are able to devote their whole lives to study, perhaps there is no nation in which a larger portion of learning is diffused through all ranks of the people." "The heroic love of liberty, the manly fortitude, the generosity of sentiment, for which we have been so justly celebrated, seem to promise the future advancement and established duration of our glory. Many incidents, unfortunate in themselves, have tended to call forth and sustain these virtues. Happy, in this respect, have been our late struggles for liberty! They have awakened the spirit of freedom; they have rectified the manners of the times; they have made us acquainted with the rights of mankind, recalled to our minds the glorious independence of former ages, fired us with the views of fame, and by filling our thoughts with contempt of the imported articles of luxury, have raised an opposition, not only to the illegal power, but to the effeminate manners of Britain." "This land hath already begun to distinguish itself in literature. . . . Our late writers in the cause

---

[1] "An Essay," etc., 5–6.

14

of liberty have gained the applause of Europe. Many elegant essays have been produced in the style of wit and humor; nor hath poetry been entirely uncultivated among us.'' Then, rising prophet-like into metrical utterance, he foretells the day when American poets shall

> " with lofty Milton vie ;
> Or wake from nature's themes the moral song,
> And shine with Pope, with Thomson, and with Young.
> This land her Steele and Addison shall view,
> The former glories equal'd by the new ;
> Some future Shakespeare charm the rising age,
> And hold in magic chains the list'ning stage ;
> Another Watts shall string the heav'nly lyre,
> And other muses other bards inspire." [1]

VII.

Soon after the occasion on which young Trumbull had thus pleaded the cause of the fine arts in America, and especially of good letters, he removed to Wethersfield, probably for the purpose of beginning the study of the law ; but the impression which his own work as a man of letters had already made upon his readers is indicated by some lines of verse which, at about that time, greeted the publication of his commencement address :

> " All that for future times he bids us hope,
> We see in him, as England saw in Pope." [2]

After twelve months passed in Wethersfield, he was recalled to Yale College as a tutor, and entered upon his duties there in the autumn of 1771.   There were but two other tutors in the college at that time, Joseph Howe and Timothy Dwight ; and all three were agreed in enthusiasm for English literature, and in the purpose of giving a more modern and a more literary tone to the studies of the place.

---

[1] " An Essay," etc., 11–15.
[2] " Connecticut Journal," for Nov. 30, 1770.

In this employment, Trumbull continued for the next two years,—a period standing out in his life not only as the last one passed by him in academic retirement, but as in itself very fruitful in literary products which denote his diligent self-training as a scholar, as well as his struggle to keep alive some function for letters apart from, and above, that rage for political controversy that was then drawing all thoughts into its bitter service. His interest in philosophical studies during this period is seen in seven " Speculative Essays " on such subjects as " The Limits of Human Reason," " Our Idea of Infinity," and so forth.[1] As a writer of verse, the work he then did shows how carefully he was studying the models at that time most admired in English literature. Thus, in December, 1771, he wrote some twenty pentameter quatrains, " On the Vanity of Youthful Expectations: an Elegy,"[2] which is little else than a succession of echoes of Goldsmith and of Gray. In " The Owl and the Sparrow: a Fable,"[3] written in 1772, one traces the influence of John Gay and of Samuel Butler, —this being perhaps the earliest example of his use of that Hudibrastic verse which afterward became his favorite weapon as a satirist. To this period, also, belongs his " Ode to Sleep,"[4] written in 1773, a composition resonant of noble and sweet music, and making, if one may say so, a nearer approach to genuine poetry than had then been achieved by any American, excepting Freneau:

I.

" Come, gentle Sleep !
    Balm of my wounds and softner of my woes,
    And lull my weary heart in sweet repose,
  And bid my sadden'd soul forget to weep,
    And close the tearful eye ;
  While dewy eve with solemn sweep,
    Hath drawn her fleecy mantle o'er the sky,

---

[1] Trumbull MSS.   [2] " Poetical Works," ed. 1820, ii. 165–168.
[3] Ibid. 149–154.   [4] Ibid. 113–120.

And chased afar, adown th' ethereal way,
The din of bustling care and gaudy eye of day.

II.

" Come, but thy leaden sceptre leave,
    Thy opiate rod, thy poppies pale,
        Dipp'd in the torpid fount of Lethe's stream,
        That shroud with night each intellectual beam,
And quench th' immortal fire, in deep Oblivion's wave.
    Yet draw the thick impervious veil
O'er all the scenes of tasted woe ;
    Command each cypress shade to flee ;
    Between this toil-worn world and me,
Display thy curtain broad, and hide the realms below.

III.

" Descend, and graceful in thy hand,
With thee bring thy magic wand,
And thy pencil, taught to glow
In all the hues of Iris' bow.
And call thy bright, aërial train,
    Each fairy form and visionary shade,
        That in the Elysian land of dreams,
            The flower-enwoven banks along,
        Or bowery maze that shades the purple streams,
            Where gales of fragrance breathe th' enamor'd song,
    In more than mortal charms array'd,
People the airy vales and revel in thy reign.

IV.

" But drive afar the haggard crew,
    That haunt the guilt-encrimson'd bed,
    Or dim before the frenzied view
    Stalk with slow and sullen tread ;
While furies with infernal glare,
Wave their pale torches through the troubled air ;
And deep from Darkness' inmost womb,

Sad groans dispart the icy tomb,
And bid the sheeted spectre rise,
'Mid shrieks and fiery shapes and deadly fantasies.

V.

" Come and loose the mortal chain,
That binds to clogs of clay th' ethereal wing ;
And give th' astonished soul to rove,
Where never sunbeam stretch'd its wide domain ·
And hail her kindred forms above,
In fields of uncreated spring,
Aloft where realms of endless glory rise,
And rapture paints in gold the landscape of the skies.

VI.

" Then through the liquid fields we 'll climb,
Where Plato treads empyreal air,
Where daring Homer sits sublime,
And Pindar rolls his fiery car ;
Above the cloud-encircled hills,
Where high Parnassus lifts his airy head,
And Helicon's melodious rills
Flow gently through the warbling glade ;
And all the Nine, in deathless choir combined,
Dissolve in harmony th' enraptured mind,
And every bard, that tuned th' immortal lay,
Basks in th' ethereal blaze, and drinks celestial day."

Surely, the poetic apprentice who was capable of such
work as this, was not far from Apollo's kingdom.

VIII.

Trumbull's continued fondness for Steele and Addison is
shown by his activity, during the second year of his tutorship at Yale, in the writing of many prose essays after their
sprightly manner, on current topics in society, letters, and

politics. For these new essays, he revived the old title of
" The Correspondent," which he had already made so
popular; and counting the later series as a mere continua-
tion of the earlier one, he kept up the publication in " The
Connecticut Journal and New Haven Post-Boy," from the
12th of February, 1773, to the 3d of the following September. About three-fourths of the entire number were written
by himself, the remainder by his literary friends.[1] As may
be imagined, much inequality of merit is noticeable in these
essays; but the hand of Trumbull is easily traced in the
11th number, which contains a ludicrous burlesque on the
prevailing New England fashion as to obituary notices; in
the 18th and 19th numbers, which satirize medical quackery
as then and there practised; in the 21st number, which deals
caustically with common beggary and its proper treatment;
in the 33d number, which gives to the public a sad warning
of the approaching demise of their benefactor and friend,
" The Correspondent"; in the 37th number, which duly
chronicles that melancholy event; and, finally, in the 38th
number, which closes the series with the last will and
testament of the deceased, and a full recantation of every
opinion hitherto expressed by him which had given the
slightest disturbance to anybody's mental repose.[2]

IX.

The most remarkable fact respecting this period of Trumbull's residence at Yale College is that he seems then to have

---

[1] His own statement. MSS.

[2] This second series of " The Correspondent" appeared in " The Conn.
Journal and New Haven Post-Boy " at the following dates, for the opportunity
of tracing which I was also indebted to the courtesy of Miss Linsley, of Stratford :
No. 9, Feb. 12, 1773 ; No. 10, Feb. 19 ; No. 11, Feb. 26 ; No. 12, March 5 ;
No. 13, March 12 ; No. 14, March 19 ; No. 15, March 26 ; No. 16, April 2 ;
No. 17, April 9 ; No. 18, April 16 ; No. 19, April 23 ; No. 20, April 30 ; No.
21, May 7 ; No. 22, May 14 ; No. 23, May 21 ; No. 24, May 28 ; No. 25,
June 4 ; No. 26, June 11 ; No. 27, June 18 ; No. 28, June 25 ; No. 29, July
2 ; No. 30, July 9 ; No. 31, July 16 ; No. 32, July 23 ; No. 33, July 30 ; No.
34, Aug. 6 ; No. 35, Aug. 13 ; No. 36, Aug. 20 ; No. 37, Aug. 27 ; No. 38,
Sep. 3.

found out his final place and function in letters,—that of satirist. Long afterward, he expressed the opinion that his vocation to satire was but the accident of circumstances. " Formed," said he, " with the keenest sensibility and the most extravagantly romantic feelings, . . . I was born the dupe of imagination. My satirical turn was not native. It was produced by the keen spirit of critical observation, operating on disappointed expectation, and avenging itself on real or fancied wrongs." [1] Whether or not this account of the matter be anything more than an old man's conjecture operating on a supposed reminiscence, it is plain that Trumbull's satirical turn did manifest itself very early in his life, in the midst of the gayety of his undergraduate days, and before he could have known much of disappointed expectation, or of the sombre passion for avenging himself either on real or on fancied wrongs. In actual result, too, his satire ranged over almost every form,—playful, delicate, broad, coarse, ludicrous, severe, scathing, savage, pitiless.[2] Finally, his satirical turn was cultivated not only by abundant exercise, in prose and in verse, on every sort of subject, but by an intense and critical study of the great masters of satire, particularly in English, French, and Latin.

His first deliberate and elaborate publication as a satirist in verse, was " The Progress of Dullness," [3] consisting of three separate poems under that single title. Of this satirical trilogy, the first part, " On the Adventures of Tom Brainless," was written during the first year of his tutorship, and was evidently begotten of sundry observations made by him under the advantages of that position. It is simply a satire on collegiate education as then practised in New England—its shams, incongruities, stupidities—especially as to the qualifications required for the sacred ministry.

In a New England farm-house, Farmer Brainless is talking with his wife concerning the future of their son Tom, who is really a drone and a dunce. The conclusion of the

---

[1] Trumbull MSS. [2] Many examples of these are among his MSS.
[3] " Poetical Works," ii. 7–90.

whole matter is this: Tom shall not follow his father in that
hard vocation—a long anguish in plucking subsistence from
a rocky and barren soil. No, he shall go to college; he
shall seize hold of life by a pleasanter handle; he shall have
a profession. First of all, then, Tom must be fitted for
college:

> " So to the priest in form he goes,
> Prepared to study or to doze."

After two years thus spent in sham preparation, dieting
" on husks of Lily," murdering Vergil, turning Tully into
farce, and gaining just skill enough to blunder through a
chapter of the Greek Testament, Tom goes to college,
where he passes triumphantly a sham examination, and
settles down within its learned walls to four years of sham
study. Very soon he is seized by " the college-evil," to
wit, indisposition—an indisposition to do any manner of
work—a mysterious delicacy of health which is offended by
all labor in the preparation of lessons, or in attendance upon
lectures:

> " Then every book which ought to please,
> Stirs up the seeds of dire disease ;
> Greek spoils his eyes, the print 's so fine,
> Grown dim with study, or with wine ;
> Of Tully's Latin much afraid,
> Each page he calls the doctor's aid ;
> While geometry, with lines so crooked,
> Sprains all his wits to overlook it.
> His sickness puts on every name,
> Its cause and uses still the same,—
> 'T is tooth-ache, colic, gout, or stone,
> With phases various as the moon ;
> But though through all the body spread,
> Still makes its cap'tal seat, the head.
> In all diseases, 't is expected,
> The weakest parts be most infected.
> Kind Head-Ache, hail ! thou blest disease,

The friend of idleness and ease ;
Who, mid the still and dreary bound
Where college walls her sons surround,
In spite of fears, in justice' spite,
Assum'st o'er laws dispensing right,
Set'st from his task the blunderer free,
Excused by dullness and by thee.
Thy vot'ries bid a bold defiance
To all the calls and threats of science,
Slight learning, human and divine,
And hear no prayers, and fear no fine." [1]

Such are the achievements of drones and of dunces at
Yale !   But as to those who are neither dunces nor drones ?
Ah, surely, true scholars do exist there, and they perform
most famous work, with their dead and deadening erudition !   These be the mighty book-worms who

" Despising such low things the while,
As English grammar, phrase, and style,
Despising every nicer art
That aids the tongue or mends the heart,
Read ancient authors o'er in vain,
Nor taste one beauty they contain,

.   .   .   .   .   .

And plodding on in one dull tone,
Gain ancient tongues and lose their own." [2]

With a like audacity does this irrepressible young reformer
then proceed to hold up to derision other outworn notions
and methods of education then prevailing in the college of
which he is tutor,—the preposterous ways, for example, in
which they there teach logic, rhetoric, mathematics, and
metaphysics.   Returning from his irreverent raid into the
field of collegiate reform, the satirist resumes the history of
his typical dunce, Tom Brainless:

---

[1] " Poetical Works," ii. 15–16.   [2] Ibid. 17.

"Four years at college dozed away
In sleep and slothfulness and play,
Too dull for vice, with clearest conscience,
Charged with no fault but that of nonsense,
(And nonsense long, with serious air,
Has wandered unmolested there,)
He passes trial, fair and free,
And takes in form his first degree." [1]

Armed with his diploma, Tom now goes forth to prey upon a much-enduring world. First, that he may put immediate money into his purse, he begins his career by taking a school, where,

. . . "throned aloft in elbow chair,
With solemn face and awful air,
He tries with ease and unconcern,
To teach what ne'er himself could learn ;
.   .   .   .   .   .
Holds all good learning must depend
Upon his rod's extremest end,
Whose great electric virtue 's such,
Each genius brightens at the touch ;
.   .   .   .   .   .
Thinks flogging cures all mortal ills,
And breaks their heads to break their wills." [2]

At the end of a year, Tom gives up the school, and enters upon his professional studies. In the house of a famous minister, he undertakes to learn the art of preaching; he

. . . "settles down with earnest zeal
Sermons to study, and to steal ;
.   .   .   .   .   .
Learns with nice art, to make with ease
The Scriptures speak whate'er he please ;
With judgment, unperceived to quote
What Poole explained, or Henry wrote ;

---

[1] "Poetical Works," 23-24.   [2] Ibid. 26.

To give the gospel new editions,
Split doctrines into propositions,
Draw motives, uses, inferences,
And torture words in thousand senses ;
Learn the grave style and goodly phrase,
Safe handed down from Cromwell's days,
And shun, with anxious care, the while,
The infection of a modern style."

At length, Tom stalks abroad a grave divine, having received a license to preach ;—for

  . . . "though his skull be cudgel-proof,
He 's orthodox, and that 's enough."

Next follows a period during which this would-be heaven-expounder roves and raves as a candidate :

"Now in the desk, with solemn air,
Our hero makes his audience stare ;
Asserts with all dogmatic boldness,
Where impudence is yoked to dullness ;
.   .   .   .   .   .
Two hours his drawling speech holds on,
And names it preaching when he 's done."

At last established for life in a town which is sufficiently described by saying that its mental condition was happily suited to his own, he

  . . . "deals in preaching and in prayer,
And starves on sixty pounds a year ;
And culls his texts, and tills his farm,
Does little good, and little harm ;
On Sunday, in his best array,
Deals forth the dullness of the day ;
And while above he spends his breath,
The yawning audience nod beneath."

The first part of " The Progress of Dullness " [1] was published at New Haven, probably in August, 1772. This was followed, in January, 1773, by the second part,—" On the Life and Character of Dick Hairbrain," [2]—an effective delineation of the career of a rich and vulgar New England fop of the period, from his pampered boyhood, his unstudious and ruffianly years in college, and the sensual frivolities of his foreign tour, onward to that terribly accelerated stage of existence, when, for him,

> " Lone age with hasty step comes on,"

and when, elbowed aside by younger fops, the palsied dandy

> " sinks forlorn—
> Of all, and even himself, the scorn."

This powerful satire was followed in July, 1773, by the third part of the trilogy,—" On the Adventures of Miss Harriet Simper," [3]—a satire on the wrong and the folly of excluding women from the higher education,—portraying the world of shallow thought, of frivolous occupation, of blighting disappointment, to which women in fashionable life are doomed, if without the dignity and the consolations conferred by intellectual pursuits.

No wonder that a notable stir was made by these three satires, so fresh and ruddy with the tints of real life, so fearless in their local tone and color, so pungent with contemporary and local criticism, and coming as they did in so rapid succession from the academic solitude of that portentous young tutor. They seemed to announce the arrival of a rather uncomfortable inhabitant,—a satirist from whose glance no folly or obliquity would be likely to hide itself. And even yet, and for us, the whole work has a masterful aspect. Though far less subtle than his later and greater satire, " M'Fingal," it deals with subjects more universal and more permanent. Moreover, like all of Trumbull's work, it shows the training of the scholar, the technical

---

[1] " Poetical Works," ii. 27–33.   [2] Ibid. 35–57.   [3] Ibid. 59–90.

precision of the literary artist. Each poem has a unity
of its own, and holds up to laughter the despicable or
the detestable traits of a single type of character. To
all three poems an artistic unity is given, by a correla-
tion, not only of topics, but of incidents, the latter of
which just sufficiently entangle their chief personages at
the end. Here, also, one finds ample facility and variety
of literary allusion, unblinking observation of the follies and
vices of society, an eye for every sort of personal foible, a
quick sense of the ludicrous, a sure command of the vocab-
ulary of ridicule and invective. Then, too, the genuine
power of these satires was shown by evidence that could
not be contradicted,—the outcry of punctured vanity with
which they were greeted,—an outcry so vociferous, so sibi-
lant, from so many quarters, as to prove how well each
arrow had found its mark. Finally, the author then began
to let the public know something of his remarkable gift
for epigram in verse—for those neat forth-puttings of shrewd
humor which have carried so many of Trumbull's lines far
out into the current of popular proverbs. Then it was that
people began to pass from one to another some sayings of
his, which, though they soon forgot the fact, they had
gathered from the pages of " The Progress of Dullness,"
such as this—

> " For metaphysics, rightly shown,
> But teach how little can be known " [1] ;

or this—

> " Whoe'er at college points his sneer,
> Proves that himself learn'd nothing there " [2] ;

or this—

> " First from the dust our sex began,
> But woman was refined from man " [3] ;

or this—

> " For weighty works men show most sloth in,
> But labor hard at doing nothing " [4] ;

or this—

> " Good sense, like fruits, is rais'd by toil.
> But follies sprout in every soil." [5]

---

[1] " Poetical Works," ii. 22. [2] Ibid. 52. [3] Ibid. 65. [4] Ibid. 69. [5] Ibid. 70.

CHAPTER X.

THE REKINDLING OF THE GREAT DISPUTE: 1766–1769.

I.—The study of American political writings resumed—Happiness of the colonies over the repeal of the Stamp Act in the Spring of 1766.

II.—Commencement exercises at the College of Philadelphia, 20 May, 1766—The prize by John Sargent for the best essay on " A Perpetual Union between Great Britain and her American Colonies "—Provost Smith's congratulations on the news of repeal received the day before—Publication of the four essays written for the Sargent prize—Their political note—Francis Hopkinson's avowal of American identity with England.

III.—American political confidence disturbed by the Declaratory Act—Political anxiety as uttered in " Virginia Hearts of Oak," May, 1766.

IV.—A great stride in American theories as to the legislative authority of parliament—The new doctrine as set forth by Richard Bland, in his " Enquiry into the Rights of the British Colonies," 1766—Jefferson's praise of this pamphlet.

V.—American distrust greatly increased by the proceedings of parliament in 1767 under the lead of Charles Townshend—His three measures reviving the American controversy—Their effects in America as described by Lecky—Great stimulus thus given to American political literature—Traits of this literature.

VI.—The supreme significance of John Dickinson's " Letters from a Farmer in Pennsylvania," December, 1767, to February, 1768—Purpose and method of these essays—Their unrivaled success in America and Europe—The renown thus won by Dickinson—His enormous popularity.

VII.—The arrival of the customs commissioners at Boston—They are driven by the populace to take refuge on an island in the harbor, June, 1768—British troops summoned from Halifax to quell American resistance—Dickinson's " Liberty Song," in response to these proceedings, July, 1768.

VIII.—The gravity of the situation as revealed in other writings of this year—Speech at the dedication of a Tree of Liberty at Providence—A New York pamphlet entitled " The Power and Grandeur of Great Britain founded on the Liberty of the Colonies "—The political tension prolonged into the year 1769—" Liberty, a Poem lately Found in a Bundle of Papers said to be Written by a Hermit in New Jersey."

IX.—American writers then resident abroad—Their sympathy with their countrymen at home—Arthur I ee—His chief political writings.

I.

THE interval of rest from the strife of political tongues, which the repeal of the Stamp Act brought to the Americans in the spring of 1776, has thus been used by us for the purpose of forming some acquaintance with the several groups of non-political writings which belong to the first decade of the Revolutionary period, and which may give us a clew as to the course which American literature would have taken during the latter half of the eighteenth century, had not its method and tone, as well as its topics, been roughly turned aside by the inrushing flood of Revolutionary passion. It is now time for us to come back to those political writings which, if not the most delightful, were at least the most characteristic, expression of the thought and life of the period we are dealing with, and which, after this brief lull in the storm of controversy, once more spoke out with accents of wounded affection, of alarm, of remonstrance, finally of wrath, and scorn, and defiance.

We should find it hard to overstate the happiness which, for a few weeks, filled the hearts of the American people at the news that the detested Stamp Act had been repealed. As, in 1765, through the bond of a common fear, the thirteen colonies had been brought for the first time into some sort of union, so in 1766, that union was for a while prolonged through the bond of a common joy. Certainly, never before had all these American communities been so swept by one mighty wave of grateful enthusiasm and delight. As the news passed up and down the land, business was suspended, bells were set a ringing, bonfires were lighted, the imperial colors were unfurled; and thus, with processions, and banquets, and barbecues, and even with more sedate assemblages crowding their places of worship, they gave themselves up for a time to their own spontaneous manifestations of pleasure at having been delivered from a humiliating political stigma, from an appalling political peril. Statues were voted to the king and to the great commoner; and to them, as well as to the ministry, and to Barré, and Conway, and Lord Camden, were sent addresses all aglow with loyalty and love.

"The repeal of the Stamp Act," wrote an American politician,[1] in his diary for the third of November, 1766, "has hushed into silence almost every popular clamor, and composed every wave of popular disorder into a smooth and peaceful calm." "I am bold to say," declared Edmund Burke,[2] "that so sudden a calm, recovered after so violent a storm, is without a parallel in history."

II.

The true note of this universal joy may still be heard by us as then uttered in its most refined and most discriminating form, at an academic festival, the commencement exercises of the College of Philadelphia, on the 20th of May, 1766,—which happened to be only one day after the confirmation there of the news of the repeal of the Stamp Act. Some months before, a noble-minded Englishman, a member of parliament, John Sargent of London, being desirous of helping to check the growth of discord between the two great branches of the English race, had offered a gold medal to be given to any graduate or undergraduate of the college, for the best essay on "The Reciprocal Advantages of a Perpetual Union between Great Britain and her American Colonies." Near the close of his address bestowing this medal and saying the usual farewell words to the young graduates, the provost of the college, William Smith, paused for an instant, and then added: "And here I ought to conclude—but the joyous occasion calls me to return particular thanks to this splendid audience for the countenance they have given us this day, and to congratulate them on the glorious and happy turn in the affairs of America, whereof yesterday gave us the certain and confirmed accounts. When I look back on the dreadful state of suspense, in which these colonies have been so long

[1] John Adams, "Works," ii. 203.   [2] Burke, "Works," ii. 61.

agitated; when, in the room of foreboding doubt and painful solicitude, I behold joy in every look, the clouds dispersed, the sun breaking in upon us again, and an assembly around me, in which every man rejoices to salute his neighbor as free, I feel,—I feel, a sympathy unutterable, and an exultation of soul never felt before. O glorious day! O happy America! if now we but know how to prize our happiness! The unguarded sallies of intemperate zeal will soon be forgotten; but the steadfast, the noble, the patriotic efforts of cool and good men, in the vindication of native and constitutional rights, will more and more claim the regard of all the free, in every clime and age, and perhaps be consecrated by time into one of the brightest transactions of our story; asserting our pedigree and showing that we were worthy of having descended from the illustrious stock of Britons.'' [1]

So perfectly did the theme of the prize-essay suit the feeling of the time, that, along with the three other essays which had been written on the same subject, it was immediately published both in Philadelphia and in London. These four papers on behalf of the perpetual unity of the English-speaking race, furnish to us now a striking exhibition of the most cultivated American thought and sentiment at that moment,—a firm resolve for civil rights, this resolve being blended with passionate love for the mother country and with pride and happiness in the fact of American membership of the British empire. '' Were it possible,'' wrote one of these essayists, '' for Great Britain, with an high and arbitrary hand, to think of snatching from her colonies the essential privileges of Englishmen, . . . it would be to dress her slaves in livery, and deck America in robes of paper, to make her the contempt and derision of every other nation.'' '' But why should the mutual connection between the parent country and her colonies ever come into

---

[1] '' Four Dissertations.'' etc., 9–10.

[2] '' Four Dissertations on the Reciprocal Advantages of a Perpetual Union between Great Britain and her American Colonies.''

15

question ? Are we not one nation and one people ? And do we not own obedience to one common king ? . . . We of America are in all respects Englishmen, notwithstanding that the Atlantic rolls her waves between us and the throne to which we all own allegiance. Nor can we, though in ever so flourishing a state, throw off our dependence, or dissolve this union, without breaking the very bonds of nature." " How detestable, then, must the politician be, who shall ever attempt to kindle the destructive flames of jealousy between two friends, whom nature seems to have united in the closest bonds, and whose hearts and interests are and ever ought to be one ! Should any one ever succeed in this (which God forbid) I doubt not but that, after much cruel contention and unnatural bloodshed, each would rush into the other's arms, and emphatically cry out—' We are both in the wrong !' " [1]

III.

Nevertheless, through all the exclamations of joy with which, in the spring and early summer of 1766, the Americans everywhere welcomed the news of the repeal of the Stamp Act, one may still detect a note of disquietude. As so often before and since, the British government had then chosen to do a gracious act in an ungracious way. The repeal of the law had been accompanied by what seemed to the Americans to be a lurking menace,—namely, the declaration that parliament had the right " to bind the colonies in all cases whatsoever." This declaration—which, indeed, merely expressed a sound constitutional principle in a form needlessly harsh—had the effect which was afterward well described by Lord Shelburne when, in a letter to Pitt, he said that it had kept alive " an unfortunate jealousy and distrust of the English government throughout the colonies." [2] Accordingly, before many months the joy of the gratified colonists began to die away into a gloomy suspicion that the government had then drawn back its arm

---

[1] " Four Dissertations," etc., 108, 109, 111–112. These sentences are from the dissertation by Francis Hopkinson.

[2] Quoted in Bryant and Gay, " A Popular History of the U. S.," iii. 351.

from smiting them, only to gain the opportunity for giving them a more stunning blow. It was a most distressing doubt. To one who now reads the writings of that period, nothing is plainer than that the colonists then loved England, not only sincerely but passionately,—giving to her, in fact, an inordinate and a thoroughly provincial reverence. It was, therefore, a terrible pang which they experienced in this unrevoked need of distrusting her; and the deep solicitude of all that time during which even exultation had to keep room for suspicion, is vividly interpreted for us in an anonymous political song that then rose from the loyal but troubled heart of Virginia. This crude lyric was entitled " Virginia Hearts of Oak "; and it is of special interest to us now, not only for its own sake, but as being, perhaps, the first of a considerable series of political and military songs written during the Revolution after the same model,—that model being David Garrick's famous sailor-song called " Hearts of Oak,"—a song of British freedom, of British pluck, and especially of the pride of Britain in her sailors and in her sovereignty of the sea. At least two stanzas of Garrick's song we must here recall, as being quite necessary to the appreciation of this and every subsequent American echo of it:

> " Come, cheer up, my lads ! 't is to glory we steer,
> To add something more to this wonderful year :
> To honor we call you, not press you like slaves,
> For who are so free as the sons of the waves ?
>> Hearts of oak are our ships,
>> Gallant tars are our men,
>>> We always are ready ;
>>> Steady, boys, steady ! "

> " Britannia triumphant, her ships sweep the sea ;
> Her standard is Justice,—her watchword, ' Be Free ! '
> Then cheer up, my lads ! with one heart let us sing,
> ' Our soldiers, our sailors, our statesmen, our king.'
>> Hearts of oak," etc. [1]

---

[1] The whole song is given by James T. Fields and Edwin P. Whipple, in their " Family Library of British Poetry," 388.

Remembering the troubled mood which still lingered in the hearts of the Americans through all their joy over the several steps in the progress of the repeal of the Stamp Act, and how, even then, beneath all other purposes, was their purpose to obey their English instincts which disdained cowardice even toward England, and which disdained to be enslaved even by England, we shall not fail to notice how perfectly, with what neat implications, all this complexity and tumult of emotion finds itself uttered in the " Virginia Hearts of Oak," wherein, indeed, the sturdy sentiment of Garrick's song is simply transplanted and Americanized, and its very nobility of enthusiasm for courage, for freedom, for patriotism, is turned, like a captured battery, against any and all aggressions on the part of the British ministry :

> " Sure never was picture drawn more to the life,
> Or affectionate husband more fond of his wife,
> Than America copies and loves Britain's sons,
> Who, conscious of freedom, are bold as great guns.
>   Hearts of oak are we still ;
>   For we 're sons of those men
>   Who always are ready—
>   Steady, boys, steady—
>   To fight for their freedom again and again.

> " Though we feast and grow fat on America's soil,
> Yet we own ourselves subjects of Britain's fair isle ;
> And who 's so absurd to deny us the name ?—
> Since true British blood flows in every vein.
>   Hearts of oak, etc.

> " Then cheer up, my lads, to your country be firm !
> Like kings of the ocean, we 'll weather each storm :
> Integrity calls out, fair Liberty, see,
> Waves her flag o'er our heads, and her words are—' Be Free ! '
>   Hearts of oak, etc.

" To King George, as true subjects, we loyal bow down,
But hope we may call Magna Charta our own :
Let the rest of the world slavish worship decree,
Great Britain has ordered her sons to be ' Free ' !
    Hearts of oak, etc.
    .   .   .   .   .   .

" On our brow while we laurel-crowned liberty wear,
What Englishmen ought, we Americans dare :
Though tempests and terrors around us we see,
Bribes nor fears can prevail o'er the hearts that are ' Free.'
    Hearts of oak, etc.

" With Loyalty, Liberty let us entwine,
Our blood shall for both flow as free as our wine ;
Let us set an example what all men should be,
And a toast give the world,—' Here 's to those who 'd be ' Free.'
    Hearts of oak, etc." [1]

IV.

Moreover, how immense was the stride which political suspicion then prompted some of the colonial leaders to take in the development of opinion touching the authority of the general government, may be seen in the fact that in this very year of pacification was first promulgated the startling doctrine that the British colonies in America were united to the empire only through the British crown, and not at all through the British parliament, and that to the acts of the latter they owed no more obedience than did the king's dominion of Hanover. Although not many Americans were then ready for this prodigious innovation in constitutional doctrine, yet as a working theory, first, for the preservation of the union with Great Britain, and, afterward, as it proved, for the dissolution of that union, it seems to have occurred almost at the same time to three different chiefs of American opposition, and in three widely

---

[1] This ballad was first printed in the " Virginia Gazette " for May 2, 1766. It contains seven stanzas, and is given in full in Duyckinck, " Cyclopædia of American Literature," i. 451. In that copy, the toast given in the last line reads : " Here 's to those dare be free."

separated places,—to Joseph Hawley in Massachusetts,[1] to Benjamin Franklin in London,[2] and to Richard Bland in Virginia.

From the aspect of immediate publicity as well as of elaborateness of presentation, special notice may be claimed for the plea then put forward by the last of these three politicians,—a man of substance and renown in his own colony, who for his supposed learning in Anglo-American history was then styled "the Antiquary." It was in his pamphlet bearing the title of "An Enquiry into the Rights of the British Colonies," first published in 1766, that Richard Bland boldly announced the proposition that, though a part of the British empire, "America was no part of the kingdom of England," and that, having been "settled by Englishmen at their own expense, under particular stipulations with the crown,"[3] it was under no obligation to receive laws from the parliament. It was to the crown alone that the colonies owed their existence; it was to the crown alone that they owed allegiance.

The surname of this writer by no means describes his style, which, besides being somewhat jerky and harsh, is tinged by the acerbity of a high-spirited man keeping angry vigil over those enemies of his country who, as he thought, were trying "to fix shackles upon the American colonies— shackles which, however nicely polished, can by no means sit easy upon men who have just sentiments of their own rights and liberties."[4] Forty-nine years after the publication of this brochure, it received from Jefferson the extravagant praise of being "the first pamphlet on the nature of the connection with Great Britain which had any pretension to accuracy of view on that subject."[5] It is evident that by "accuracy of view" Jefferson meant, as usual, conformity to his own view. Without doubt, Bland's pamphlet is

[1] W. M. Sloane, "The French War and the Revolution," 147.
[2] "Works of Franklin," Bigelow ed., iii. 483, 485, 490–491.
[3] "An Enquiry," etc., 16.   [4] Ibid. 5.
[5] "Writings of Jefferson," H. A. Washington ed., vi. 485.

both acute and ingenious; but accurate it is not, even as to
the facts of history, and probably not as to the principles of
constitutional law. Finally, the argument is lacking both
in unity and in consistency; and, in the case of well-read
persons, it could hardly have been convincing except to
those who were convinced already or were already determined to be.[1]

V.

The returning political distrust which in America soon
mastered and silenced the "jocund strains" of the year
1766, was constantly nourished and inflamed by the tidings
which kept coming from England during the year 1767; as
that, so early as in January, Charles Townshend, chancellor
of the exchequer, had openly avowed in the house of
commons his purpose, through some form of taxation, to
procure from America a revenue sufficient to support a military establishment there[2]; and that, a few months later,
and at a time " when Chatham was completely incapacitated,
and when all other statesmen had sunk before the ascendency of Townshend,"[3] this brilliant but reckless leader had
carried through parliament three drastic measures admirably
contrived, as Pownall then said of one of them, to be " the
beginning of a series of mischiefs."[4] These three measures
were, first, the famous act for laying a port-duty in America
on several prominent articles of Anglo-American commerce,
to-wit, glass, red lead, white lead, paper, paint, and tea[5];
secondly, " an act to enable his majesty to put the customs
and other duties in the British dominions in America, and
the execution of the laws relating to trade there, under the
management of commissioners to be appointed for that pur-

---

[1] Other writings by Bland are "A Fragment of the Pistole Fee Claimed by
the Governor of Virginia," 1753, edited from the original manuscript by W. C.
Ford, and published in 1891 ; also, " A Letter to the Clergy of Virginia," 1760.

[2] Lecky, " A History of England," iv. 107. [3] Ibid. 109.

[4] Hansard, " The Parliamentary History of England," xvi. 341.

[5] " The Statutes at Large," 7 Geo. iii. c. 46, 56.

pose, and to be resident in the said dominions '' [1]; and, thirdly, the act suspending the functions of the legislature of New York until it should be ready to provide British troops stationed there, not only with suitable quarters, but with '' fire, candles, vinegar, and salt, bedding, utensils for dressing victuals, and small beer, cider, or rum.'' [2]

If, as Lord Chatham then facetiously said of the Americans, '' the Stamp Act of most unhappy memory '' had '' frightened those irritable and umbrageous people quite out of their senses,'' [3] it should not have required supernatural gifts for the king and his ministers to foresee that these new acts of parliamentary aggression were likely to produce in America even more serious effects—for a description of which we may safely depend upon the great English historian who in our time has so fairly reviewed the several stages of the American Revolution. '' A period of wild and feverish confusion followed. Counsels of the most violent kind were freely circulated, and for a time it seemed as if the appointment of the new board of commissioners would be resisted by force; but Otis and some of the other popular leaders held back from the conflict, and in several colonies a clear sense of the serious nature of the struggle that was impending exercised a sobering influence. Georgia, which had been inclined to follow the example of New York, was brought to reason by the prospect of being left without the protection of English troops in the midst of the negroes and the Indians. The central and southern colonies hesitated for some time to follow the lead of New England. Hutchinson wrote to the government at home that Boston would probably find no other town to follow her in her career of violence; and DeKalb, the secret agent of Choiseul, who was busily employed in fomenting rebellion in the colonies, appears for a time to have thought it would all end in words, and that England, by keeping her taxes with-

---

[1] '' The Statutes at Large,'' 7 Geo. iii. c. 46, 56.

[2] Ibid. c. 59; also 5 Geo. iii. c. 33.

[3] '' The Correspondence of William Pitt,'' etc., iii. 193.

in very moderate limits, would maintain her authority. Massachusetts, however, had thrown herself with fierce energy into the conflict, and she soon carried the other provinces in her wake. Non-importation agreements, binding all the inhabitants to abstain from English manufactures, and especially from every article on which duties were levied in England, spread from colony to colony, and the assembly of Massachusetts issued a circular addressed to all the other colonial assemblies denouncing the new laws as unconstitutional, and inviting the different assemblies to take united measures for their repeal. The assembly at the same time drew up a petition to the king and addresses to the leading English supporters of the American cause. These addresses, which were intended to act upon English opinion, were composed with great ability and moderation; and while expressing the firm resolution of the Americans to resist every attempt at parliamentary taxation, they acknowledged fully the general legislative authority of parliament, and disclaimed in the strongest language any wish for Independence.'' [1]

The quick and ever-deepening excitement thus created in America through the abrupt abandonment by the British government in 1767 of the statesmanlike colonial policy it had proclaimed only twelve months before, found a most vivid expression in the prodigious crop of political writings, in prose and verse, which then came into life under such stimulus. Thenceforward, for at least eight years, the colonial printing-presses had to toil hard in order to deliver to the public the pamphlets, broadsides, handbills, and other fugitive productions which dealt with the terrible problem once more thrust upon the country, some of them doing so, no doubt, in language almost profligate in its violence. Even now the reader who has access to so rare and precious a souvenir of those times as a file of American newspapers for any portion of the period between the years 1767 and 1775, may almost feel for himself the thrill of that

---

[1] Lecky, `` A History of England,'' iv. 113–114.

fiery passion—noble and ignoble—which seems yet to throb and burn along the dingy pages of these old journals,—astonishment, wounded affection, grief, anger, resentment, disdain, defiance, with here and there, also, the demagogue's mean joy in popular disquiet, and the demagogue's lust for notoriety and profit to be got by him out of the general breaking up of the ancient bonds of popular faith and order. "It is mournful to notice," says the English critic from whom we have just quoted, "how the field of controversy had widened and deepened, and how a quarrel which might at one time have been appeased by slight mutual concessions, was leading inevitably to the disruption of the empire." [1]

VI.

Among all the political writings which were the immediate offspring of this baleful revival of a dispute that had been so recently and so well set at rest, there stand out, as of the highest significance, certain essays which began to make their appearance in a Philadelphia newspaper in the latter part of the year 1767. These essays very soon became celebrated, on both sides of the Atlantic, under the short title of the "Farmer's Letters." Their full title was "Letters from a Farmer in Pennsylvania to the Inhabitants of the British Colonies." Though published without the author's name, they were instantly recognized as the work of John Dickinson; and their appearance may perhaps fairly be described as constituting, upon the whole, the most brilliant event in the literary history of the Revolution.

One distinction attaching to them is that they were written by a man who shared in the general excitement over the new attack upon colonial rights, but who desired to compose it rather than to increase it, and especially to persuade his countrymen so to bear their part in the new dispute as to save their rights as men, without losing their happiness as British subjects. However it may have been

[1] Lecky, "A History of England," iv. 111.

with some other American writers of that period, here was
no reckless declaimer, no frantic political adventurer, precipitating public confusion because he had nothing to lose
by public confusion, and eager to run American society
upon the breakers in the hope of gathering spoils from the
common wreck. On the contrary, here was a man of powerful and cultivated intellect, with all his interests and all
his tastes on the side of order, conservatism, and peace, if
only with these could be had political safety and honor.

The dreadful import of the three chief measures of the
British government in 1767 touching the American colonies,
no man saw more clearly, or felt more acutely, than did
John Dickinson; and under the guise of a plain Anglo-
American farmer of patriotic instincts, and with solid possessions at stake, he proceeded to deal with this new problem
in such a manner as to help both Americans and Englishmen to solve it before they should rush any nearer to the
abyss which he saw yawning between them. By a graceful
bit of self-description, he cleverly puts himself, at the
outset, into sympathy with his readers, and then proceeds
to take up for consideration the recent acts of parliament,
trying to show both their incompatibility with the principles
of the British constitution, and their fatal bearing upon the
liberties of America and the well-being of the whole empire.
His chief object, he declares, is " to convince the people of
these colonies, that they are, at this moment, exposed to
the most imminent dangers; and to persuade them, immediately, vigorously, and unanimously, to exert themselves,
in the most firm but most peaceable manner, for obtaining
relief." [1] The cause of liberty, he tells them, " is a cause of
too much dignity, to be sullied by turbulence and tumult.
It ought to be maintained in a manner suitable to her
nature. Those who engage in it should breathe a sedate
yet fervent spirit, animating them to actions of prudence,
justice, modesty, bravery, humanity, and magnanimity." [2]

---

[1] " The Political Writings of John Dickinson," ed. of 1801, i. 167.
[2] Ibid. 168.

He expresses a hope that they and their " posterity, to the latest ages," may be guided by such a spirit " that it will be impossible to determine whether an American's character is most distinguishable for his loyalty to his sovereign, his duty to his mother country, his love of freedom, or his affection for his native soil." [1]   " Let us behave like dutiful children, who have received unmerited blows from a beloved parent.   Let us complain to our parent; but let our complaints speak at the same time the language of affection and veneration." [2]   He protests against any thought· of Independence as of a fatal calamity.[3]   Nevertheless, " let these truths be indelibly impressed on our minds: that we cannot be happy, without being free; that we cannot be free, without being secure in our property; that we cannot be secure in our property, if, without our consent, others may, as by right, take it away; that taxes imposed on us by parliament, do thus take it away." [4]   " Let us take care of our rights, and we therein take care of our prosperity.   ' Slavery is ever preceded by sleep.'   Individuals may be dependent on ministers, if they please : states should scorn it." [5]   " Americans have that true magnanimity of soul, that can resent injuries, without falling into rage." [6]   " Though your devotion to Great Britain is the most affectionate, yet you can make proper distinctions; and know what you owe to yourselves, as well as to her." [7]

No other serious political essays of the Revolutionary era quite equaled the " Farmer's Letters " in literary merit, including in that term the merit of substance as well as of form; and, excepting the political essays of Thomas Paine, which did not begin to appear until nine years later, none equaled the " Farmer's Letters " in immediate celebrity, and in direct power upon events.   As they first came forth, from week to week, in the Philadelphia newspaper that originally published them, they were welcomed by the

---

[1] " The Political Writings of John Dickinson," ed. of 1801, i. 169.

[2] Ibid. 173.   [3] Ibid. 171.   [4] Ibid. 275.

[5] Ibid. 277.   [6] Ibid. 282.   [7] Ibid. 282–283.

delighted interest and sympathy of multitudes of readers in that neighborhood, and were instantly reproduced in all the twenty-five newspapers then published in America, with but four known exceptions.[1] Within less than four weeks after the last letter had made its appearance, they were all collected and issued as a pamphlet, of which at least eight editions were published in different parts of America.[2] In the very year in which the pamphlet was first published in America, two editions of it were published in London, and one edition in Dublin,—each one bearing the clever preface written by Franklin. In the year following, a French version, made by Jean Barbeu Dubourg, was published at Amsterdam, and was largely circulated upon the continent.

On both sides of the Atlantic, therefore, the "Farmer's Letters" gained universal attention among people interested in the rising American dispute. The name of John Dickinson became a name of literary renown surpassing that of any other American, excepting Benjamin Franklin. On the continent of Europe, these essays of the Pennsylvania Farmer became, for a time, the fashion: they were talked of in the salons of Paris; the Farmer himself was likened to Cicero[3]; and almost the highest distinction then possible for any man, was bestowed upon him through the notice and applause of Voltaire.[4] Even in England, the success of these writings was remarkable, and was shown quite as much in the censures, as in the praises, which were lavished upon them. They received the compliment of being regarded by Lord Hillsborough as "extremely wild."[5] The "Critical Review,"[6] which honored them

---

[1] P. L. Ford, "The Political Writings of John Dickinson," i. 283; C. R. Hildeburn, "The Issues of the Press of Pennsylvania," ii. 75 n.

[2] In the French edition, published at Amsterdam, it is stated that thirty editions had appeared in America within the first six months. It is probable that newspaper reprints were included in this estimate.

[3] George Bancroft, "History of the United States," 16th ed., vi. 149.

[4] Stillé, "Life of Dickinson," 92.

[5] "The Complete Works of Benjamin Franklin," Bigelow ed., iv. 130.

[6] Volume xxvi. 62. A considerable portion of the notice is given by P. L. Ford, "The Political Writings of John Dickinson," i. 282.

with its scornful disapprobation, expressed the opinion that Dickinson " would have proved himself a much better member of society had he never learned either to read or write," and that his book was " seditious in its principles, superficial in its execution, and tending to the perdition of the country for which " he was " so furious an advocate." On the other hand, among the English admirers of the " Farmer's Letters " was Edmund Burke, who gave his sanction to their principle [1]; while the " Monthly Review " closed a long notice of them by declaring that, if reason was to decide between England and her colonies, the author of these essays would " not perhaps easily meet with a satisfactory refutation." [2]

In America, the admiration and the gratitude of the people was expressed in almost every conceivable form. To this fact we have valid testimony, in the complaint of the royalist governor of Georgia, who, in May, 1768, wrote to Lord Hillsborough that by the Americans the Farmer was " adored," and that " no mark of honor and respect " was " thought equal to his merit." [3] Thanks were voted to him by political associations, by town-meetings, by grand juries. The College of New Jersey conferred on him the degree of Doctor of Laws. He became the favorite toast at public banquets. He was offered the membership of the choicest social clubs. On his entrance, one day, into a court room, whither business called him, the proceedings were stopped in order to recognize his presence, and to make acknowledgment of the greatness and splendor of his services to the country. Songs were written in his praise. Even in the pedestrian homeliness of prose, the resources of language were strained in the effort to celebrate the genius and the virtue of a man, who, as was said in one brochure, had " gloriously distinguished himself by asserting the rights

---

[1] George Bancroft, " History of the United States," 16th ed., vi. 148.

[2] Volume xxxix., 26.

[3] George Bancroft, " History of the United States," 16th ed., vi. 149. The governor of Georgia at that time was Sir James Wright.

and liberties of America, in a manner that renders him an honor to his education, a public blessing to his country, and will immortalize his name with renown to the latest ages of time." [1]

VII.

At the very time when these reverent, cautious, and persuasive essays by John Dickinson were passing into print for the first time, events were in progress which soon gave an almost ghastly tone to Dickinson's avowals of faith in the justice or the wisdom of the British government,—events which, indeed, pushed Dickinson himself a step or two nearer to the doctrine of forcible revolution. The last of the " Farmer's Letters " was published in February, 1768. In the following May, the new commissioners of customs arrived at Boston; in June, these commissioners, attempting to execute their odious office on John Hancock's sloop, " Liberty," were fiercely assaulted by the populace of Boston, and were driven for refuge to Castle William in Boston harbor; whereupon Governor Bernard summoned thither General Gage with his troops from Halifax,—thus replying to all the reason, and the moderation, and the filial tenderness of Dickinson's arguments, by the royal syllogism of gunpowder and cold steel.

Of these most ominous events in Boston, John Dickinson was an observer from his distant home on the Delaware; and even he, with all his deep loyalty and conscientious hesitation, was so stirred by them as then to utter what seems almost a ringing war-cry,—a clarion call to all Americans to stand forth together with united and undaunted front, and to the men over-sea who were pushing forward such mad measures, a stern clear undernote of warning. Taking for his model Garrick's "Hearts of Oak "—the air of which was then so familiar to every one—he wrote the

---

[1] " An Elegy to the Infamous Memory of Sir F. B." The words quoted are from the dedication to the author of the " Farmer's Letters." Boston, 1769.

stanzas which he christened " A Song for American Freedom,"—a bit of versification obviously the work of a man
neither born nor bred to that business. With some natural
tremors of maidenly coyness, Dickinson at once sent the
manuscript of his poem to his friend James Otis, in Boston ;
and by Otis, who knew real poetry when he saw it, the
demerits of this song in that regard were freely pardoned
for its practical value in giving sonorous voice to the emotion which was then beating in all hearts. At the instance
of Otis, it was printed for the first time in the " Boston
Gazette " for July 18, 1768, whence it was reprinted in
nearly all the newspapers of the country ; and being quickly
caught up into universal favor under the endearing name of
the " Liberty Song," its manly lines soon resounded over
all the land ; and thenceforward, for several years, it remained the most popular political song among us. Interpreted by the events of that anxious summer of 1768, with
the customs commissioners driven off by the populace to a
fortified island in Boston harbor, and with Gage's troops
hurrying thither to introduce on behalf of the government a
very different method of conducting the discussion, the
singing of that rough song all about New England and far
back along the wooded slopes of the western frontier, and
all the way down the coast toward the Carolinas and Georgia, denoted in the American people the existence of a spirit
not safe for kings and prime ministers to tamper with,—a
spirit before which even a royalist governor and an armed
British official might well have paused:

> " Come join hand in hand, brave Americans all,
>   And rouse your bold hearts at fair Liberty's call ;
>   No tyrannous acts shall suppress your just claim,
>   Or stain with dishonor America's name.
>   In freedom we 're born, and in freedom we 'll live ;
>   Our purses are ready,—
>   Steady, friends, steady,—
>   Not as slaves, but as freemen, our money we 'll give !

" How sweet are the labors that freemen endure,
That they shall enjoy all the profit secure ;
No more such sweet labors Americans know,
If Britons shall reap what Americans sow.
    In freedom, etc.

" Swarms of placemen and pensioners soon will appear,
Like locusts deforming the charms of the year ;
Suns vainly will rise, showers vainly descend,
If we are to drudge for what others shall spend.
    In freedom, etc.

.   .   .   .   .   .

" All ages shall speak with amaze and applause
Of the courage we 'll show in support of our laws :
To die we can bear—but to serve we disdain,
For shame is to freemen more dreadful than pain.
    In freedom, etc.

" This bumper I crown for our sovereign's health,
And this for Britannia's glory and wealth ;
That wealth and that glory immortal may be,
If she is but just, and we are but free.
    In freedom, etc." [1]

VIII.

Just seven days after John Dickinson's " Liberty Song "
was, through the columns of a Boston newspaper, first given
to the public, there was performed at Providence a symbol-
ical and somewhat weird ceremony very expressive of the
spirit which had begun to rule the time,—the dedication of
a Tree of Liberty. The discourse which was spoken at this
singular function reached its climax in a few words which
betokened the general consciousness of the gravity of the
struggle into which the American people were being forced,
and their sense of kinship therein with all free-minded and
resolute people in other parts of the world: " We do therefore, in the name and behalf of all true Sons of Liberty in

---

[1] Given in full by F. Moore, in " The Ballad History of the American Revolution," 20–21.

America, Great Britain, Ireland, Corsica, or wheresoever they are dispersed throughout the world, dedicate and solemnly devote this tree, to be a Tree of Liberty. May all our counsels and deliberations under its venerable branches, be guided by wisdom, and directed to the support and maintenance of that liberty which our renowned forefathers sought out and found under trees and in the wilderness. May it long flourish, and may the Sons of Liberty often repair hither to confirm and strengthen each other. When they look toward this sacred Elm, may they be penetrated with a sense of their duty to themselves, their country, and their posterity." [1]

The look of bitter joy, the shudder of proud pain, with which many noble-minded Americans then began to dwell upon the possibilities involved in all these hurrying events, may still be perceived by us in a pamphlet, published in New York in 1768, and bearing this striking title, "The Power and Grandeur of Great Britain Founded on the Liberty of the Colonies"; wherein the unknown writer describes himself, as "one who wishes to see an inviolable union formed between his majesty's American and British subjects; to see the British empire advanced to the highest pinnacle of earthly glory; to see it the sovereign of the world, and, at the same time, the protector of the liberties of mankind; to see her an example and encourager of every civil and religious virtue; to see America enjoying peace and plenty and the best of civil governments under her protection. . . . But if, for our sins, Providence should suffer pride, party-spirit, envy, and avarice to defeat the measures of the real well-wishers of their country, I see Britain reduced in her trade, depopulated by the transmigration of her people to America, her populous trading and manufacturing cities deserted, her nobles for want of ten-

---

[1] "A Discourse delivered in Providence . . . upon the 25th Day of July, 1768, at the Dedication of the Tree of Liberty," by a Son of Liberty. Providence, 1768, p. 16. I met with this pamphlet at the library of the American Antiquarian Society.

ants tilling their own grounds, and calling on oppressed disaffected America to relieve and defend her against the power of her enemies; in short, I see Britain in America, and America in Britain.'' [1]

The political tension of the year 1768, prolonged into the year 1769, was then still further increased, on the one hand, by several resolutions of parliament in support of the ministerial policy, one of them directing that persons accused of treason in America should be brought to England for trial; and, on the other hand, by several resolutions against the ministerial policy passed by the colonial assemblies, and especially by a general agreement throughout the colonies to boycott all British commerce until the ministry and parliament should come to a better mind.

In the vast throng of American writings dealing with these harassing topics, we may find it to our purpose to delay a moment before one piece of vigorous and high-spirited verse, entitled '' Liberty, a Poem: Lately Found in a Bundle of Papers Said to be Written by a Hermit in New Jersey.'' For its motto, it bore the noble sentence which during all that period was quoted in America more frequently, perhaps, than any other,—'' Whoever would give up essential liberty to purchase a little temporary safety, deserves neither liberty nor safety.'' Nowhere has this poem a line which in austerity of principle falls below that legend. The thought which throughout asserts itself most forcibly, is that if the Americans are indeed insubmissive to the base lessons which would teach them to be slaves, it is because they have in their veins the blood of Britons, and before their eyes the example of Britons in standing up for liberty against whatsoever odds:

> '' And shall we want the spirit to be free?
> That spirit, Britain, we derived from thee.
> We are thy offspring—and we 'll sooner part
> With every drop that flows around the heart,

---

[1] '' The Power and Grandeur of Great Britain,'' etc., 23–24.

Than tamely yield our birthright.   If it must,
Let ruin crush our cities into dust ;
Let madness arm thy self-destroying hand
To drench with civil blood this peaceful land,
Or make us fly from tyranny's control,
Beyond the limits of the frozen pole.
We are thy offspring.   Heavens ! how have we loved
Our mother's name, and with what ardor proved
Our duty and our love ; and were she still
But kind and just, how gladly would we spill
That blood for her which, now, at freedom's call,
Perhaps must turn to bitterness and gall." [1]

IX.

At about this time, also, several American writers [2] then resident abroad began to manifest in a public way their sympathy with the political solicitude that had once more taken possession of their countrymen at home.   Notable among such transmarine Americans was Arthur Lee, a writer whose high literary reputation among his contemporaries rests upon no materials which can justify its revival at the hands of posterity.   He was born in Virginia in 1740, the youngest of six brothers, all of whom rose to distinction in their day.   He was a scholar of Eton College, a graduate in medicine of the University of Edinburgh, then a member of one of the Inns of Court in London, afterward for many

---

[1] " Liberty, a Poem," etc., 9.

[2] Among these writers, for whom I do not think it necessary to make room in the text, may here be named Edward Bancroft, a singularly versatile and successful American scoundrel then living in England, who in later years made his fortune partly by the process of compound interest from well-paid rascality, —now selling the secrets of his own country to England, and then selling the secrets of England to his own country.   The best sketch of him known to me, is by Paul Leicester Ford, in his edition of Bancroft's treacherous " Narrative of the Objects and Proceedings of Silas Deane as Commissioner of the United Colonies to France : Made to the British Government in 1776."   This is the gentleman, who, in 1769, published in London a rather clumsy piece of political statement on the colonial side of the question, entitled " Remarks on the Review of the Controversy between Great Britain and Her Colonies."

years active in the foreign service of the American Congress. A man of ability, integrity, and patriotism, the value of all that he did or said was constantly hurt by an inordinate and a fussy sense of his own importance, by a morbid jealousy of others, and by an invincible habit of suspicion, opposition, and disparagement.[1] His chief contributions to the political literature of the Revolution are, first, " The Monitor," a series of seven essays, published in London in 1768, after having been previously published in Virginia[2]; secondly, " The Political Detection; or, the Treachery and Tyranny of Administration, both at Home and Abroad, displayed in a Series of Letters signed Junius Americanus," published in London in 1770; and, thirdly, " An Appeal to the Justice and Interests of the People of Great Britain, in the present Disputes with America," published in London in 1774, under the feigned authorship of " an old Member of Parliament."[3]

---

[1] It was difficult for him to agree exactly with any statement on any subject as made by anybody but himself. Thus, being caught in a shower, Lee met under a shed a gentleman who, by way of affability, ventured upon a remark which he probably thought a safe one: " It rains very hard, sir." To this, however, Lee replied: " It rains hard, sir ; but I don't think you can say it rains very hard." George Tucker, " Life of Jefferson," i. 180.

[2] The London reprint was in " The American Gazette," number ii. 189–218, and is of the date as given above. I used the copy in the Harvard library. For the year of the publication of " The Monitor," Jefferson, in his " Notes on Virginia," happened to mention 1769 ; and most writers who have had occasion to refer to the subject,—as Allen, Drake, Allibone, and the writer of the article on Arthur Lee in " Appleton's Cyclopædia of Am. Biog.,"—appear to have followed one another back to this wrong date as started by Jefferson.

[3] Considerable portions of Arthur Lee's personal and official correspondence are given in his " Life," by Richard Henry Lee, Boston, 1829. A " Calendar of the Arthur Lee Manuscripts in the library of Harvard University " was published in 1882, and forms the eighth number of " Bibliographical Contributions," edited by Justin Winsor. These papers were given to the Harvard library by Richard Henry Lee in 1827, and are bound in eight volumes.

CHAPTER XI.

BRITISH TEA AS A POLITICAL INTOXICANT IN AMERICA: 1770–1774.

I.—The grotesque prominence given to Tea in the Anglo-American controversy—Outline of the history of ministerial measures which forced on this result—These measures derided by Junius, and by Edmund Burke.

II.—Jests by English opponents of the ministry on its policy of forcing the Americans to drink Tea.

III.—The American verse-writers imprecating Tea as the bearer of political woes—" Virginia Banishing Tea "—" The Blasted Herb "—The malediction of Tea in " The American Liberty Song "—" The Cup infused with Bane "—" A Lady's Adieu to Her Tea-Table "—A jocose anathema of Tea in " A New Song to an Old Tune."

IV.—A humorous version of the Tea-troubles given in " The First Book of the American Chronicles of the Times."

V.—How the controversy over Tea brought on American political Union, through the First Continental Congress in 1774.

I.

IN our effort to trace the development of thought and emotion behind the historic events which form the outward framework of the American Revolution, we now reach a point where the tragedy of this most bitter race-quarrel enters upon a phase which may seem not only comic but even frivolous,—as though the gods themselves, coming down from Olympus and mixing in the tumults of men, were trying to show us the absurdity of our grandiose attempts at important business, and were all the time laughing at us for taking ourselves so seriously.

It is doubtful if anything could be invented more effective as burlesque upon the supposed rationality and dignity of what then called itself statesmanship, than is furnished by the bald facts embodying the successive measures of minis-

246

terial policy toward the American colonies during the dozen
years prior to that of the Declaration of Independence.
For, in 1763, having then greatly enlarged both her dominions and her debts, England gives fair notice that, in her
opinion, the time has come for us Americans, having always
shared in the benefits of the empire, at last to share also in
its general costs. To this reasonable demand we make no
grave objection, only insisting that the amount of our contribution for imperial expenses, being indicated from year to
year by royal requisitions, shall be raised by us in the usual
way—that is, in the constitutional and English way—
through our local legislatures, these being composed of persons chosen by ourselves and empowered to act for us in
the public expenditure of our money. Unhappily, however, upon this question of mere method in the doing of a
thing which both parties deem proper and right, comes the
first, and also the fatal, breach,—a breach which through
preposterous mismanagement grows wider and wider till it
divides two kindred peoples by a space more enormous
than that of the sea which rolls between them. Under the
American revenue act of 1764, and in order to enable us
to do what we are already quite willing to do—to pay our
fair share of imperial expenses—the very method is chosen
which we are obliged to regard as both unconstitutional and
dangerous: our money is to be taken, not through the free
action of our own legislatures, but under the imposition of a
legislature three thousand miles away. Having thus chosen
an improper method of doing a proper thing, the government naturally proceeds to intensify our consciousness of
the fact by a second and a more accentuated use of that
method, namely, by the requirement of revenue stamps in
America for nearly all professional and commercial transactions between civilized men. These revenue stamps,
accordingly, we refuse to buy, or even to tolerate in the
land ; and in giving rather animated expression to this
refusal, we cause such an uproar, that, in the following year,
1766, the government abandons its plan for taking our

money in that particular way, at the same time declaring to us its perfect right to take our money either in that way or in any other. This theoretical assertion of right we could have borne, if only it had remained theoretical[1]; but, in 1767, it is made practical, and consequently offensive and even alarming, by a new measure, which places duties on six great articles of import,—glass, red lead, white lead, paper, painters' colors, and especially tea. Whereupon we proceed to bind ourselves to an agreement that, so long as this law remains in force, we will endeavor to get on without purchasing from our English brethren their glass, their red lead, their white lead, their paper, their painters' colors, and especially their tea. Then for three angry years, follows much debate, recrimination, hubbub,—all the while the item of tea becoming more and more prominent in the column of items on which the obnoxious tax is levied; and, at the end of that time, that is, in the spring of 1770, the ministry inform us that, in view of our objections, they have concluded to withdraw the offensive tax on the first five articles, leaving, however, the same offensive tax on the sixth article—the article of tea—merely to mark a principle. Instead of relieving the strain, this announcement only increases it; since it never was either the subject of the tax or the size of the tax, but always the principle of the tax, which had disturbed us. In other words, these Wise Men in the East undertake to pacify a loyal and a generous but a proud people to whom the revenue act of 1767 has given serious annoyance, by so amending that Act as to retain in it everything that was ever seriously annoying. In 1770, therefore, the other articles of taxation being withdrawn, the dispute respecting the mere principle of taxation is left to be waged around this single article of tea. Then, against the lovely little tea plant alone, we proceed to frame our solemn leagues and covenants; and we make and take mighty oaths to the effect that we will not import it, nor buy it, nor sell it, nor drink it, nor have anything whatso-

---

[1] " Works of Franklin," Bigelow ed., iii. 423.

ever to do with it excepting to curse it. Then pass by
three years more of ever-deepening discord and exasperation, after which time, in April, 1773, upon motion of Lord
North, the government falls back upon its favorite and
sovereign remedy of a bribe,—allowing such a drawback on
all tea exported from England to America as will enable the
Americans to buy their tea, even though loaded with the
three-penny tax, at a much lower price than the same tea is
sold for in England.[1] The inventors of this noble piece of
political chicanery " have no idea," says Franklin,[2] " that
any people can act from any other principle but that of
interest ; and they believe that three pence in a pound of
tea, of which one does perhaps drink ten pounds in a year,
is sufficient to overcome all the patriotism of an American." " No man ever doubted," exclaims Burke, in the
house of commons, " that the commodity of tea could
bear an imposition of three pence. But no commodity will
bear three pence, or will bear a penny, when the general
feelings of men are irritated, and two millions of people are
resolved not to pay." [3] And when, in accordance with this
palpable trick for accomplishing by an appeal to our avarice
what could not be accomplished by an appeal to any other
motive, several shiploads of the tea are brought hither in
the latter part of 1773, we angrily reject the bribe—all the
more angrily, perhaps, because we half suspect the stability
of our own virtue in rejecting it ; and then in our anger
giving way to lawlessness, we proceed to destroy much valuable property belonging to subjects of the king. We
smash the tea-chests, and we pitch their contents overboard,
in one place ; from two other places, we send the ships with
their cargoes back to England ; we burn the tea to ashes,
in another place ; we deposit it in a damp cellar and so spoil
it, in another place. Naturally, the boldest and the most
flagrant of these acts of insubmission—that which occurred

---

[1] Lord North's resolutions were introduced April 27, 1773. Hansard, " Parliamentary History," xvii. 840–841.

[2] " Works," Bigelow ed., v. 147.   [3] " Works," ii. 17.

in the harbor of Boston—is selected by the government for its most conspicuous measure of punishment: that port is by law hermetically sealed up, and the poorer inhabitants of a city dependent on maritime commerce are given over to starvation. Immediately, the doom which thus falls upon the single colony of Massachusetts, is accepted by her sisters as the doom of all. Then, as never before, the Thirteen Colonies rally to one common standard, and face together the common peril; then, as never before, are very busy their committees of correspondence; then comes the Continental Congress, then the gathering of military stores, the mustering of armed men, and, finally, as was to be expected, the accident of a little bloodshed; and then, of course, over land and sea is heard the song of the weird sisters, followed by eight years of hurly-burly, these to be followed perhaps by endless years of international hate.

Such was the process of the American Revolution. Was ever statesmanship so blind ? Was ever the birth of an implacable race-feud so needless ? And, indeed, even while these measures of the government were in progress, and before they had reached the stage of fatal culmination, their fatuity was exposed by many great writers and orators in England, as by Junius, who, so early as in 1769, with his most bitter wit derided them as pitifully inconsistent, as having already " alienated the colonies," [1] as having made the reign of George the Third " a reign of experiments." [2]
" Nothing in all the world," said Edmund Burke, in 1774, " can read so awful and so instructive a lesson . . . upon the mischief of not having large and liberal ideas in the management of great affairs. Never have the servants of the state looked at the whole of your complicated interests in one connected view. They have taken things by bits and scraps, some at one time and one pretense, and some at another, just as they pressed, without any sort of regard

---

[1] This was a leading topic for invective in the first letter of Junius, dated January 21, 1769. "Junius," i. 107–109.

[2] Ibid. 171.

to their relations or dependencies. They never had any kind of system, right or wrong; but only invented occasionally some miserable tale for the day, in order meanly to sneak out of difficulties into which they had proudly strutted." [1] " What woful variety of schemes have been adopted; what enforcing, and what repealing; what bullying and what submitting; what doing and undoing; what straining and what relaxing; what assemblies dissolved for not obeying, and called again without obedience; what troops sent out to quell resistance, and, on meeting that resistance, recalled; what shiftings, and changes, and jumblings of all kinds of men at home, which left no possibility of order, consistency, vigor, or even so much as a decent unity of color, in any one public measure." [2] " By such management, by the irresistible operation of feeble councils, so paltry a sum as three pence in the eyes of a financier, so insignificant an article as tea in the eyes of a philosopher, have shaken the pillars of a commercial empire that circled the whole globe." [3]

II.

The latent comedy of the situation flashes upon us now from the grotesque prominence then given, in the politics of the British empire, to this coy and quiet-loving tea plant—thus selected to stand alone and bear the whole brunt of colonial enmity to parliamentary taxation. By a sort of sarcasm of fate, it happened that between the years 1770 and 1775, this ministress of gentleness and peace—this homelike, dainty, and consolatory shrub of Cathay—came to be regarded, both in America and in England, as the one active and malignant cause of nearly all the ugly and disastrous business that filled up those years. Perhaps it was not altogether in jest, that an explanation of the American revolt then commonly offered, connected it with England's seeming determination to compel her colonial children to drink tea—a species of liquid nourishment for which they

---

[1] " Works," ii. 14. [2] Ibid. 69. [3] Ibid. 14–15.

were ironically said to have an extreme dislike. This was the view frequently presented by the oppositionist newspapers in England, which delighted to chaff the ministry over their preposterous policy in treating the Americans with so much harshness merely for their alleged disinclination to that particular beverage. Not long after the arrival in London of the tidings of the Bunker Hill fight, the " St. James's Chronicle " burlesqued the statesmanship which had brought so hideous an event to pass, by representing the ministerial troops as addressing the women of Boston in these bland words:

> " O Boston wives and maids, draw near and see
> Our delicate Souchong and Hyson tea ;
> Buy it, my charming girls, fair, black, or brown,—
> If not, we 'll cut your throats, and burn your town ! " [1]

That a war with England had actually broken out in Massachusetts, seemed to be the effect of the news from Lexington, Concord, and Bunker Hill; but just what the war was about, and especially just which party was to blame for it, was tersely set forth by a London newspaper in some half a dozen verses which seemed to put the American Iliad of that time into a nutshell:

> " Rudely forced to drink tea, Massachusetts in anger
> Spills the tea on John Bull—John falls on to bang her :
> Massachusetts, enraged, calls her neighbors to aid,
> And gives master John a severe bastinade !
> Now, good men of the law, pray who is in fault,—
> The one who begins, or resists the assault ? " [2]

A few months later, a newspaper writer in London sent over to New York the important information that the ministry, having found among the Americans so great a repug-

---

[1] F. Moore, " Diary of the Am. Rev.," i. 140.

[2] Republished, from " a London newspaper," in " The Constitutional Gazette" for Nov. 25, 1775 ; and reprinted in F. Moore, " Diary of the Am. Rev.," i. 168.

nance to tea, were about to make matters right by supplying them with an altogether different drink : " Several contractors have set off for Rome for a fresh supply of Jesuits' bark; as tea does not agree with an American stomach, being apt to produce the heartburn. There is a rumor the new parliament intends to force the bark upon the Yankees, especially as Doctor Bute recommends it as a great specific for the Fever of Rebellion."[1] Even the English punsters in the pay of the ministry may have supposed themselves to be dealing in philosophy as well as wit, when they characterized the political storm then rising in America, as only a tempest in a teapot!

III.

In this way, too, it happened that in the writings produced among us from 1767 to 1770, and especially from 1770 to 1775, the most precious interests of the American people seem to be imperiled and the peace of the whole world to be disturbed by this hitherto amiable and pacific tea plant. Through a ludicrous metonomy in our political rhetoric, the harmless thing comes to be regarded by us with detestation as the very embodiment of political outrage and shame; so that at last upon it alone are concentrated and wreaked all the suspicions and all the animosities of a quarrel that finally broke asunder a great empire and smote two continents with the thunders and sorrows of war. The innocent shrub, which the gentlest of English poets was soon afterward to glorify as giving to its devotees those

> . . . " cups
> That cheer but not inebriate,"[2]

seldom receives in our literature for these years any less lurid description than that of " the detestable plant," or " the pestilential herb." Just south of the Potomac, a

---

[1] " The New York Packet," Jan. 4, 1776 ; reprinted in F. Moore, "Diary of the Am. Rev.," i. 190.

[2] " The Task," Book iv. lines 39–40. This poem was first published in 1785.

much-excited young woman, addicted, as she supposed, to poetry as well as to politics, sends forth to the world a number of stanzas entitled " Virginia Banishing Tea," wherein that valorous colony exclaims,—

> " Begone ! pernicious, baleful Tea,
> With all Pandora's ills possessed ;
> Hyson, no more beguiled by thee
> My noble sons shall be oppressed." [1]

A rhymester in New Hampshire fires at it a tremendous broadside of poetical hot shot :

> " Rouse, every generous thoughtful mind,
> The rising danger flee ;
> If you would lasting freedom find,
> Now, then, abandon Tea !" [2]

Another rhyming patriot, whose scorn of English tyranny seems to extend even to the tyranny of English grammar, vituperates it in words that make no effort to seem mild— words that bespeak a pent-up rage which is doubtless noble, even if slightly profane :

> " The State-bunglers shall see
> We despise their curs'd Tea,
> Since a way for Oppression it paves.
>
> .   .   .   .   .   .
>
> Vain foolish curmudgeons,
> To think we, like gudgeons,
> Swallow baits that of Freedom bereaves ;
> Tea, nabobs, and minions,
> With their dire opinions,
> May be damned—but we 'll not be slaves." [3]

---

[1] The entire ballad is given in F. Moore, " Ballad History of the Am. Rev.," 170.

[2] " The Blasted Herb," originally published in " The New Hampshire Gazette," afterward printed in broadside and sung to a sacred tune. The ten stanzas composing it are given in F. Moore, " Ballad History," etc., 171–172.

[3] From " The American Liberty Song," in thirteen stanzas, published in broadside without date, but probably about 1773. The only copy I remember to have seen is in the library of the Pa. Hist. Soc.

On the very day on which a certain agreement for total abstinence from tea was to go into effect, another poet, more pensive than the others, salutes it in these words of political austerity, written with a diamond on a pane of glass :

> " Ah, fated plant of India's shore !
> Thy wonted steams must rise no more
>   In Freedom's sacred land.
> This day her genuine sons ordain,
> To dash the cup infused with bane
>   By North's insidious hand.
> The period fixed—thy banished time—
> A diamond celebrates in rhyme,
>   And marks the patriot day ;
> While Phœbus, from his heavenly arch,
> Sheds lustre on the first of March,
>   And points it with a ray." [1]

As the drinking of tea was supposed to be a peculiarly feminine luxury, the Whig ladies in most of the colonies abjured its use from the date fixed upon by public resolution; and it is among the picturesque traditions of the period how these patriotic housewives, as the fatal day drew on, sealed up their stocks of tea and laid them away— not to be touched till the troubles should be over. Even then, there were some who did not fail to see a certain ludicrous quality in this vast continental uprising against the delicate and blameless beverage, as in these lines, entitled " A Lady's Adieu to her Tea-Table,'' in which the melancholy event of parting with it is set forth with mock pathos and half-comic gravity :

> " Farewell the tea-board, with its gaudy equipage
> Of cups and saucers, cream-bucket, sugar-tongs ;
> The pretty tea-chest, also, lately stored
> With Hyson, Congo, and best Double-Fine.

---

[1] First printed in " The New York Journal," March 23, 1775 ; reproduced in F. Moore, " Ballad History," etc., 340.

Full many a joyous moment I 've sat by ye,
Hearing the girls tattle, the old maids talk scandal,
And the spruce coxcombs laugh—maybe—at nothing !
No more shall I dish out the once-loved liquor—
    Though now detestable ;
Because I 'm taught, and believe it true,
Its use will fasten slavish chains upon my country ;
For Liberty 's the goddess I would choose
To reign triumphant in America." [1]

As showing how, even in America, and even after the fighting began, the same dramatic prominence continued, in the popular imagination, to be given to tea as the chief baleful factor in the fiercer politics of the year 1775, may here be cited a sprightly street ballad, " A New Song to an Old Tune," written between the Lexington and Concord day and the day of Bunker Hill, and after the arrival at Boston of the three famous British generals, Clinton, Howe, and Burgoyne :

" What a court hath Old England of folly and sin—
    Spite of Chatham, and Camden, Barrè, Burke, Wilkes, and
        Glynne !
    Not content with the Game Act, they tax fish and sea,
    And America drench with hot water and tea.
        Derry down, down, hey derry down.

" Lord Sandwich, he swears they are terrible cowards,
    Who can't be made brave by the blood of the Howards ;
    And to prove there is truth in America's fears,
    He conjures Sir Peter's ghost 'fore the Peers.

" Now, indeed, if these poor people's nerves are so weak,
    How cruel it is their destruction to seek !
    Dr. Johnson 's a proof, in the highest degree—
    His soul and his system were changèd by tea.

---

[1] F. Moore, " Ballad History of the Am. Rev.," 46.

" But if the wise council of England doth think,
They may be enslaved by the power of drink,
They 're right to enforce it,—but then, do you see ?
The colonies, too, may refuse, and be free.

" There 's no knowing where this oppression will stop ;
Some say—' There 's no cure but a capital chop ' [1] :
And that I believe 's each American's wish,
Since you 've drenched them with tea, and deprived 'em of fish.

" The birds of the air, and the fish of the sea,
By the gods, for poor Dan Adam's use were made free,
Till a man with more power than old Moses would wish,
Said—' Ye wretches, ye sha'n't touch a fowl or a fish ! '

" Three Generals these mandates have borne cross the sea,
To deprive 'em of fish and to make 'em drink tea ;
In turn, sure, these freemen will boldly agree,
To give 'em a dance upon Liberty Tree.

" Then freedom 's the word, both at home and abroad,
And—every scabbard that hides a good sword !
Our forefathers gave us this freedom in hand,
And we 'll die in defense of the rights of the land.
    Derry down, down, hey derry down." [2]

IV.

For this entire phase of the Revolutionary conflict, there
exists a somewhat remarkable piece of humorous literature,
entitled " The First Book of the American Chronicles of

---

[1] If this jocose expression suggests anything more than the decapitation of a
wicked prime-minister, it must be the cutting of the cord that then bound
America to the British empire,—another proof of the fact that the doctrine of
Independence was not taken up and advocated by responsible statesmen in
America until many months after it had found more or less open championship
among the song-writers and newspaper humorists who, protected by their obscurity, thus flung up into the air a dangerous thought which was already slowly
fermenting in the minds of the people.

[2] F. Moore, " Ballad History," etc., 176–177.

the Times."[1] This little book, itself but the beginning of an unfinished work, consists of some six chapters which seem to have been first printed serially in the latter part of 1774 and in the early part of 1775. It is probable, also, that in consequence of the change in motive and method brought about by the Lexington and Concord fights, the further development of this amusing satire came to an unintended close. Not a little of the humor of the book is due to its literary form—that of scriptural parody; for it undertakes to narrate contemporary events after the manner of the historical books of the Old Testament, particularly of the Kings and the Chronicles,—a species of literary mirth very effective among a people addicted from childhood to the reading of the Hebrew Scriptures. Employing very cleverly this quaint phraseology, and getting at times extremely droll effects through the clash of modern inci-

---

[1] This vivacious specimen of American humor, which made a considerable mark at the time of its publication, seems to have fallen almost entirely out of men's notice since then. Excepting in a library catalogue, and in Hildeburn, "Issues of the Pa. Press," ii. 179, I do not remember to have seen any mention of it. I first came across it in 1880 in the library of my lamented friend, Mr. C. Fiske Harris, of Providence, who, however, was unable to give me any information about it; and when, in the following year, I read some parts of it to another valued friend, now also gone from us, Mr. Charles Deane, of Cambridge, I was told by him that he had never before heard of it. Since that time, I have met with two other copies; one belonging to the Massachusetts Historical Society, another to the Library Company of Philadelphia. The Fiske Harris copy is without title-page or page numbers; and each of its five chapters ends with the words, "[To be continued] Boston, Printed and Sold by John Boyle, 1775." The copy belonging to the Massachusetts Historical Society has the same five chapters; at the end of each chapter the imprint of D. Kneeland, in Queen Street; but at the end of the third chapter, the date 1775, also the announcement that, at the printer's may be had "complete setts of these Chronicles." The copy belonging to the Library Company of Philadelphia was printed and sold by B. Towne in Philadelphia; it contains six chapters; and by the imprint at the end of each, it appears that the first was issued there in October, 1774, the second in November, and the third and fourth in December, of the same year, while the fifth and sixth were issued in February, 1775. A third edition of the first chapter was also announced. I am inclined to think that the work was not written in New England, but in the neighborhood of Philadelphia: its humor is as the humor of Francis Hopkinson.

dents with ancient and venerable associations, it gives a ludicrous version of Anglo-American history during the later stages of the tea-troubles, especially from the autumn of 1773 to the autumn and winter of 1774, wherein all our calamities are seen to flow from the fact that the king has set up for our worship the god of the heathen—the Tea-Chest, whose length is three cubits, and the breadth thereof one cubit and a half.

The story begins in the true epic manner: it plunges into the midst of things, by telling of the wrath of King George the Third at the horrid tidings, early in 1774, of the destruction of the tea in Boston harbor in December of the previous year:

" 1. And behold! when the tidings came to the great city that is afar off, the city that is in the land of Britain, how the men of Boston, even the Bostonites, had arose, a great multitude, and destroyed the Tea, the abominable merchandise of the east, and cast it into the midst of the sea:

" 2. That the Lord the King waxed exceeding wroth, insomuch that the form of his visage was changed, and his knees smote one against the other.

" 3. Then he assembled together the Princes, the Nobles, the Counselors, the Judges, and all the Rulers of the people, even the great Sanhedrim, and when he had told them what things were come to pass,

" 4. They smote their breasts and said, these men fear thee not, O King, neither have they obeyed the voice of our Lord the King, nor worshipped the Tea-Chest, which thou hast set up, whose length was three cubits, and the breadth thereof one cubit and a half.

" 5. Now, therefore, make a decree that their harbours be blocked up, and ports shut, that their merchants may be broke, and their multitudes perish, that there may be no more the voice of merchandise heard in the land, that their ships that goeth upon the waters, may be sunk in the depths thereof, and their mariners dwindle away to nought, that their cods and their oil may stink, and the whale, the great Leviathan, may be no more troubled, for that they have rebelled against thee.

" 6. And it came to pass that the King hearkened unto the voice of these sons of Belial."

This, of course, is meant to give us the origin of the Boston port bill, which became a law in the spring of 1774. While, however, that drastic measure is under consideration, an effort to prevent its adoption is made by an aged and astute counselor, named Mordecai the Benjamite, to-wit, Benjamin Franklin, then colonial agent in London, and likewise deputy postmaster-general for North America:

" 7. Then arose Mordecai, the Benjamite, who was four-score and five years old, an aged man whom the Lord loved, a wise man, a soothsayer, an astrologer, in whom was wisdom from above, and he said unto the King, I pray thee, O King, let thy servant speak.

" 8. And the King commanded that he should speak.

" 9. Then Mordecai spake aloud, in the presence of all the Princes, the Nobles, the Counselors, the Judges, and the Rulers of the people, and said, O King, live for ever.

" 10. Thy throne, O King, is encompassed about with lies, and thy servants, the Bernardites, and the Hutchinsonians, are full of deceit; for be it known unto thee, O King, they hide the truth from thee, and wrongfully accuse the men of Boston; for behold, these letters in mine hand witnesseth sore against them; O King, if thou art wise, thou wilt understand these things.

" 11. And there was present one of the King's Counselors, a Jacobite, a vagabond, a Wedderburnite, and he used foul language, and said unto Mordecai, Thou liest ; and Mordecai answered and said unto him, God will smite thee, thou whited wall ; and Mordecai departed from amongst them.

" 12. And behold the Princes, the Nobles, the Counselors, the Judges, and all the Rulers of the people, cried out vehemently against Mordecai, for they were in fear because of Mordecai's wisdom.

" 13. And they besought the King that he would take from Mordecai his post, for he was in high honour before that time.

" 14. So they prevailed on the King and he took from Mordecai his post and all that he had, and Mordecai was persecuted yet more and more; but he bore it patiently, for Job was his grandfather's great-grandfather; moreover, he knew the times must alter, and the King's eyes would be opened anon."

The chronicler next proceeds to shift the scene from England to America, telling how the King orders one of his generals to take fierce warriors, and sail away in ships, and invade the land of the Bostonites:

" 15. Now in the seventh month, in the fourteenth day of the month, the Lord the King commanded Thomas, the captain of the Gageites, saying,

" 16. Choose thou the valiant men of Britain, by hundreds and by thousands, and get ye together the ships, even the ships of war, the terror of the nations round about, and make your way towards the coasts of the Americanites, the land of the Bostonians, that lieth on the other side of the sea westwards, and cut off all [their men], and utterly destroy all their cities with fire and with sword, for they have rebelled against me.

" 17. Howbeit, the men of Boston had intelligence thereof, for they kept their spies abroad from the east to the west, and from the north to the south; and when the tidings came of these things, they rent their clothes, and fasted, and put on sackcloth, and went softly.

.   .   .   .

" 23. And behold when Thomas, the Gageite, was come into the land of the Bostonites, he threatened them sore, and swore by the life of Pharaoh, insomuch that some of the old women and children lifted up their voices, and wept exceedingly, with bitter lamentations."

Nevertheless, while some of the old women and children among the Bostonites thus exhibit fear at the sight and

sound of these men of war, the people in general, and especially their leaders, do not give way to unseemly fright,
but keep their heads so well as to be able to practice much
mischief upon Thomas the Gageite, especially to tease him
with the subtleties of their politics; whereat he becomes
sore in heart, and much discouraged, and writes a letter of
dolorous complaint to the king:

" 5. O King, thy servant is in a great strait; the men of
New England are stiff-necked, and as stubborn hogs, neither
knoweth thy servant what to make of them; they are worse
unto me than all the plagues of Egypt.

" 6. For they resolve upon resolves, they address, they
complain, they protest, they compliment, they flatter, they
sooth, and they threaten to root me up.

" 7. Now, therefore, O King, I pray thee send able Counselors over, that they may advise and counsel thy servant,
lest they circumvent him, and he appear foolish in the eyes
of all the people; for thou knowest, O King, thy servant is
no conjurer.

" 8. Moreover, all my Counselors have forsaken me, and
resigned, and are become like unto Job's comforters; thy
servant knoweth not what to do.

" 9. For the men of New England are as venomous as
the poison of a serpent, even like the deaf adder that stop-
peth her ears; they give good words with their mouths, but
curse with their hearts; they go to and fro in the evening
and grin like a dog, and run about through the city; they
slander thy servant, they make a byword of him, and
grudge him everything; yet complain if they be not satisfied.

" 10. Surely, O King, the spirit of Oliver or the devil is
got in them."

The effect of this complaint is to convince the king that
his general hath need, not of more men to advise, but of
more men to fight. Wherefore he gathers together another
great host of fierce men of war, and putting them on board
his mighty ships, despatches them over the sea westward.

commanding them to make short work with these disobedient and cunning Bostonites. Already, however, among the Bostonites themselves is some expectation of so dreadful an enlargement of the number of the enemies within their gates; and at last the coming of the mighty host is seen afar off by one of the leaders of the people, named Jeremiah, to-wit, Samuel Adams:

" 27. Now Jeremiah, the son of the prophet, got himself up on high, and climbed on the top of Liberty Tree, and sat there from the morning until the evening, and said,

" 28. Behold yonder I see a dark cloud, like unto a large sheet, rise from the North, big with oppression and desolation, and the four corners thereof are held up by the four great beasts, Bute, Mansfield, Bernard and Hutchinson;

" 29. Carrying a large swarm, like unto locusts, of sycophants, commissioners, duty-gatherers, custom-house officers, searchers, tide-waiters, placemen and pensioners innumerable;

" 30. The bastards and spurious breed of Noble-men, and the children of harlots."

Certainly not even Jeremiah, the son of the prophet, from his high watch on the top of Liberty Tree, could stay the progress of this formidable host bringing succor to Thomas the Gageite; and, accordingly, their arrival in the harbor of Boston, and all the evil they did there, and how they hemmed in the city and cut off its communications with the inhabitants of the back country,—all this is set forth in faithful words, of which the following are a part:

. . . .

" 45. Now, it came to pass when the Gageites had received succor, they prepared to go against the city, in which were men of valor, and old women and children, and the mothers of children, and grandmothers and the mothers of mothers.

" 46. And they brought their battering rams, and their cannon, whose mouths were of the diameter of a cubit, and whose throats were like unto open sepulchres, and which bellowed out fire, and smoke, and saltpetre, and brimstone.

" 47. And they planted them on the neck of the Bostonites, and they laid siege against it, and builded a fort and bulwarks, and cast a mount, and set the camp against it, and laid engines of war against it round about.

" 48. And their ships, even their mighty ships of war, with their iron tiers, their pride and their boast, whose masts are of the stately cedars of Lebanon, and the huge pine from the Norwegian hills, surrounded the posts round about, so that the ships of the merchants that came to traffic from the isles afar off could not enter.

" 49. And they jested one with another, and made mouths, and squinted with their eyes, and said, Let us cut off the communication between the city and country, and pinch them by famine, and they will surely give up, and fall a prey into our hands."

.   .   .   .

" 36. Now it came to pass, while the Gageites abode in the land of the Bostonites, they day by day committed iniquity; they made great clattering with their sackbuts, their psalteries, their dulcimers, bands of music, and vain parade.

" 37. And they drummed with their drums, and piped with their pipes, making mock fights, and running to and fro like shitepokes on the muddy shore.

" 38. Moreover, by night, they abused the watchmen on duty, and the young children of Boston by the wayside, making mouths at them, calling them Yankees. . . .

" 39. And it provoked the young men, and they said unto Aminidab, We cannot bear this; these seven times have they vexed us; for they gape upon us with their mouths, as it were a ramping and roaring lion.

" 40. Now therefore, speak unto Jedediah the priest, that he would blow the ram's horn and conch shells, that we may go and smite the heathen. . . .

" 41. But Jedediah, the priest, answered and said, Nay,

my sons, let us bear with them yet seventy and seven times. . . .

" 42. Only be of good courage and strong, pluck up your hearts, dread not nor be afraid, hold up your heads, and look like young unicorns: for they are a nation void of counsel, neither is there any understanding in them."

V.

Thus, the chronicler brings his story onward to a very great event in the history of those times—the immediate origin of the American Union through the call of the distressed Bostonites for a great council to be held by them and their brethren of the other tribes in the coasts of America. For, when the oppression practiced upon the men of Boston became too great for them to resist or to bear alone, and especially when " Thomas the Gageite, the Captain of the Heathen, came by night to steal away their powder, and their implements of war, and to seize their brethren and send them away captives to Babel, to be tried by the Heathen laws, and peradventure hanged for supposed transgressions,

" 35. Then arose Jedediah the priest, and Aminidab, and Obadiah, and Jeremiah, and lifted up their voices, and spake aloud and said,

" 36. Fathers, brethren, and the children of our fathers, ye have heard of all the evil that has been brought upon our city, the city of our forefathers, the New Canaan, the land of Promise, and behold this day it is desolate, and no man dwelleth therein.

" 37. How doth the city remain solitary that was full of people; she is as a widow: she that was great amongst the nations, and princess among the provinces, is about to be made tributary, and bow down to the Tea Chest, the God of the Heathen. . . .

" 28. Be of good comfort, let us send messengers into all the coasts of our brethren the Americanites, peradventure they will commune with us, for we be one people, and serve one God: If so be they hear us, the Lord is on our side; but if they refuse to hearken unto us, they and we be then slaves to the Gageites, and our substance and all that we have, taken from us, and we be their hewers of wood and drawers of water.

" 29. And all the people shouted, and said with one voice, send and commune with our brethren.

" 30. Now it came to pass that their brethren listened unto them, and they sent messengers backwards and forwards throughout the land, from the east unto the west, and from the north unto the south, even unto the sea coast of the Georgeites.

" 31. And they assembled themselves together, in a Congress in the great city of Philadelphia, in the house of the Carpenters, the builders' house, in the land of Pennsylvania, on the seventh day of the ninth month, with their coaches, their chariots, their camels, their horsemen and their servants, a great multitude, and they communed together."

Thus, even from the clouds of steam rising out of the political teapot in America, there emerges the august figure of the first Continental Congress, which assembled in Carpenters' Hall, Philadelphia, in September, 1774, and which then and there began on behalf of the American people a general government that, under varying forms and with gradually increasing strength, has lasted among us, without one break in its continuity, till the present hour. Indeed, the chief moral of this humorous chronicle of the American tea-troubles, is that of the necessity and the beneficence of American political Union. In the midst of all their dangers and sufferings, as we are here told, " the men of Boston waited patiently the event, for they put their trust in the Lord of Hosts, in the Congress, in themselves, and in Occuncocogeecocacheecacheecadungo; for they said—Two is better than one, and a fourfold cord is not easily broken."

CHAPTER XII.

THE SUMMONS FOR A GREAT AMERICAN COUNCIL: MAY—SEPTEMBER, 1774.

I.—The critical character of the year 1774 in the development of the Revolution—Marks a change in the process of governmental discipline of the colonies—Expectation that the colonies would succumb to the pressure thus laid upon them.

II.—Action of Boston at the news of the port-bill—The response of the twelve colonies to Massachusetts—The summons for the first Continental Congress.

III.—A fresh outburst of political literature immediately prior to the meeting of the Congress—Josiah Quincy's "Observations on the Boston Port-Bill"—James Wilson's "Considerations on the Nature and Extent of the Legislative Authority of the British Parliament."

IV.—"A Few Political Reflections Submitted to the Consideration of the British Colonies, by a Citizen of Philadelphia"—Demands that American opposition should be legal and rational—Anticipates two prominent arguments of Thomas Paine.

V.—The fundamental theory of American opposition challenged in "A Letter from a Virginian to the Members of the Congress"—Taxation and government are inseparable—This writer blames his fellow colonists for their political fickleness and inconsistency—He denounces the proposal for non-importation and non-consumption.

VI.—The assembling of the first Continental Congress—Their meeting is simultaneous with the publication of "A Pretty Story" by Peter Grievous, Esq.—The invitation of the preface.

VII.—Outline of "A Pretty Story" as an allegorical history of the business that brought the Congress together—The story teller stops at the point where the Congress takes it up.

VIII.—The literary charm of "A Pretty Story"—Comparison of it with Arbuthnot's "History of John Bull"—Francis Hopkinson, the author of "A Pretty Story," thus takes his place as one of the three leading satirists on the Whig side of the Revolution—The character of his satire as compared with that of Trumbull and Freneau.

I.

No student of our Revolutionary period can afford to hasten past the year 1774,—the year which divides the entire period into two nearly equal sections. In the deeper meaning of things, this was the most critical year of all the twenty: in it were done the deeds that defined what went before, that predicted what came after. At the beginning of that year, it could not certainly be known from any outward fact, that the one party or the other in the great dispute would not finally give way in time to avert the clash which might produce civil war, the disruption of one English empire, the appearance in its place of two. By the end of that year, events had occurred which made it certain that no essential claim of either party was to be withdrawn; consequently, that the claims of both, being irreconcilable, were also to be pressed to their ultimate issue. In that ultimate issue was included every action and passion of American experience down to the Peace of 1783.

Of course, scarcely any other chapter of history is more familiar to us than the record of this critical year. For the purpose now before us, all that is needed is that, having in mind the salient items of that record, we fail not to note their fresh and tremendous significance as we adjust them to our present point of view.

In all the windings of the controversy during the previous ten years, a certain threefold process had been uniform: first, parliamentary encroachment, then colonial resistance, then parliamentary concession. Will this third term in the process be once more repeated, when, in March, 1774, parliament shall learn of the obstreperous transactions in Boston harbor three months before? If, indeed, under such circumstances, that third term shall be repeated, then any onlooker may foresee that the subsequent decade is not to be essentially different from the previous one. If, however, instead of parliamentary concession, at last shall be substituted parliamentary firmness—an unflinching refusal to concede anything—and if with this shall go its logical adjunct —coercion—then, also, any onlooker may foresee that the subsequent decade is to develop lines of public experience startlingly unlike those which had gone before: either the colonies themselves will yield,—which, indeed, would be something very new,—or the dispute will become a Revolution.

Here, then, in 1774, we mark the point of change in the fatal third term of the process of governmental discipline. Instead of yielding any portion of the policy which had provoked colonial resistance, parliament stood by that policy without flinching, and at once provided for its vindication by four measures of appalling force: the act for closing the port of Boston, the act for exterminating every trace of self-government in Massachusetts, the act for removing to Great Britain for trial any person indicted in Massachusetts for a capital offense, and the act for preventing the colonists south of the St. Lawrence from finding, in their future measures of resistance, allies in the colonists north of that boundary. Still further to indicate the thoroughness of this scheme for stamping out sedition in Massachusetts, its governor, a civilian, was withdrawn, and in his stead was sent there as governor, the commander-in-chief of all the royal forces in America. Thenceforward, the rough murmurings of American discontent were to be met by the frank and simple policy of blood and iron.

What will be the response of the Americans to all this simplicity and frankness? In the presence of so tremendous a display of imperial firmness and force, will not the several colonies be terrorized? And, in their terror, will they not remain politically separated as hitherto? And in their political separation, will they not think each of its own safety only, and thus, one by one, succumb to a power so vastly beyond their ability to cope with? That such would be the effects of the new colonial policy as pushed through the two houses in the spring of 1774, was the confident prediction of the king, of the ministry, of the entire court party, in and out of parliament. What actually happened in America merely proved them to be bad prophets, and worse politicians.

II.

The Boston port-bill—the first of the four great measures then in contemplation—received the royal assent on the 31st of March.   The news of that fact reached the doomed city on the 10th of May.   On the 13th of May, arrived the new governor, General Gage.   Even while he was sailing up the harbor, the people of Boston, in town-meeting assembled, voted that the act of parliament to which their good king had just given his assent, was one of " impolicy, injustice, inhumanity, and cruelty " ; against it they made solemn appeal " to God and the world " ; and they called upon the other colonies not to suffer the colony of Massachusetts to contend alone against a power which, if it should first crush that colony, would be able the more easily to crush all the rest.[1]

By the other colonies, this invocation from Massachusetts was scarcely needed: they were not so obtuse as to be unable of themselves to perceive their own concern in the Boston port-bill.   Indeed, the mere arrival within their borders of printed copies of that act, had produced everywhere an effect even profounder and more impassioned than that produced by the Stamp Act nine years before.   Of the greatness of the danger which then menaced them, they were fully aware; but, instead of terror, was fearless resolve, instead of the blind selfishness of localism and the imbecility of divided councils, was an almost universal demand for political union.   Even those Americans—and there were many—who thought that American opposition had already gone too far, could easily see that the time had come for them all to try, at any rate, to think and act together. Almost at one breath, therefore, from the twelve other colonies went back the word to Massachusetts, that the cause of one was the cause of all, and that on behalf of all must be immediately summoned a great American council, to consider and to announce a common course of action in

---

[1] W. Gordon, " History," etc., i. 361 ; W. V. Wells, " Life of Samuel Adams," ii. 161–164.

the presence of a common danger. This was the call—almost a simultaneous one—which brought to Philadelphia, in September, 1774, the first Continental Congress.

III.

These events, of course, were the signal for a fresh outburst of political literature among us. Within the two or three months prior to the meeting of the Congress, the colonial newspapers teemed and glowed with essays touching the business upon which that body was to deliberate; and these, with the host of political pamphlets then separately issued, discussed with a new intensity the arduous and tragic character of the responsibilities thus thrown upon the American people. Even the men who thought alike as to the injustice and the dangerousness of the new measures of the government, were by no means able to think alike as to the most proper and most politic method of dealing with them. The need, at any rate, of a general American Congress; the right to have such a Congress, even though no express permission to that effect was to be found in any constitutional document; above all, the claims which the Congress should promulgate on behalf of the colonies, and the line of action it should recommend in support of those claims,—such were then the great matters under consideration. Even American jocularity—that inextinguishable resource of this people in times of storm and gloom—seems then to have been almost chastened by the pathos of the situation.

Of the various writings which sprang into life from the midst of these excitements, one of the earliest and one of the most significant was a pamphlet published in Boston in May, 1774, and bearing this title: " Observations on the Act of Parliament commonly called the Boston Port-Bill; with Thoughts on Civil Society and Standing Armies." [1]

---

[1] Reprinted in " Memoir of the Life of Josiah Quincy, of Massachusetts Bay : 1744-1775. By his Son Josiah Quincy, Jr.," 293-376. The dedication is

Its author, who did not here conform to the common usage of anonymous publication, was Josiah Quincy, a well-educated, brilliant, and high-mettled lawyer of Boston, then but thirty years old, already frail from pulmonary disease, and destined to death from that cause in less than a twelve-month thereafter. As if conscious of his fate, he often permits to himself in this pamphlet a hectic intensity of style, which, also, reflects a local habit of that period in its occasional spasms of grandiloquence and in its tiresome repetitions of Greek and Roman commonplaces. There is, however, nothing hectic, nothing rhetorical, in the courage which prompts him to put his name openly upon the title-page of a tract that was not unlikely to bring him to the scaffold:[1] " Legislators who could condemn a whole town unheard, nay, uncited to answer; who could involve thousands in ruin and misery, without suggestion of any crime by them committed; and who could so construct their law as that enormous pains and penalties would inevitably ensue, notwithstanding the most perfect obedience to its injunctions, . . . would undoubtedly imagine the attainder and death of a private individual, for his public animadversions, a less extraordinary act of power. But all exertions of duty have their hazard. . . . He who shall go about to treat of important and perilous concerns, and conceals himself behind the curtain of a feigned signature, gives an advantage to his adversaries, who will not fail to stigmatize his thoughts as the notions of an unknown writer, afraid or ashamed to avow his sentiments; and hence they are deemed unworthy of notice and refutation. Therefore I give the world both my sentiments and my name on the

---

dated Boston, May 14, 1774, only four days after the reception there of the news of the passage of the bill discussed by him. The pamphlet is of great length, and in some parts gives evidence of considerable reading, as well as of some care in writing. Much of it, doubtless, had been written before the immediate occasion which brought it to light,—the author using the excitement produced by the port-bill as a tide on which to float his " Thoughts on Civil Society and Standing Armies."

[1] " Memoir of Josiah Quincy," 130–136.

present occasion." [1] As to the political virtues which in
that trying hour were most needed by his countrymen, he
writes with a solemnity not at all artificial, even if it be
somewhat grandiose: " To divide and conquer was the
maxim of the devil in the garden of Eden, and to disunite
and enslave hath been the principle of all his votaries from
that period to the present. . . . The combinations of
public robbers ought, therefore, to cement patriots and
heroes; and, as the former plot and conspire to undermine
and destroy the commonwealth, the latter ought to form a
compact for opposition,—a band of vengeance." [2]

In broad contrast to the somewhat febrile intensity of
Quincy's pamphlet, is the quiet tone of a pamphlet published anonymously at Philadelphia a few weeks later, and
entitled " Considerations on the Nature and Extent of the
Legislative Authority of the British Parliament," [3] wherein,
with great learning and with great acumen, as well as with
perfect sobriety, the author seeks to influence the policy of
the approaching Congress by an argument in support of the
constitutional paradox that the American colonies were
bound to the empire only through their allegiance to the
British crown, and consequently were beyond the legislative
authority of parliament. Its author was James Wilson, a
lawyer of Philadelphia, at that time but thirty-two years
old, a Scotsman bred at St. Andrew's, Glasgow, and Edinburgh, an accomplished and a courageous politician, then
on the threshold of a great career in the higher walks of
American statesmanship. [4]

---

[1] "Observations," etc., 299–301 of reprint in " Memoir."   [2] Ibid. 372.

[3] Reprinted in the Works of James Wilson, iii. 199–246.

[4] The case of this man would serve to point a moral or adorn a tale as to the
caprice which seems to direct the distribution of fame in this world. Among
the men who founded the Republic, and especially among those who created
and shaped our national constitution, James Wilson stood in his lifetime in the
front rank with John Dickinson and John Jay, with Hamilton and Madison ;
yet during the present century his name has fallen into something like oblivion.
There are some tokens that such oblivion is not always to last ; one being the
recent call for a new edition of his works, which, edited by James deWitt
Andrews, was published in two volumes in Chicago in 1896.

18

IV.

Between the eleventh of June and the fourth of August, 1774, the dominant topic was discussed in the " Pennsylvania Packet " in a series of six essays, which drew upon themselves so much attention that a collected edition of them had then to be struck off. The pamphlet as thus formed was called " A Few Political Reflections Submitted to the Consideration of the British Colonies, by a Citizen of Philadelphia." [1] The uncommon quality of this writer is shown in the fearless manner in which, while approving of the universal rejection of the tax-claim of parliament, he dares to demand that all measures of opposition shall be both lawful and rational.

To begin with, he plants himself squarely upon the proposition that that claim is " so unjust, so unnatural and absurd," that all Americans must unite to oppose it, and that in such opposition, if wisely conducted, they will have the sympathy and support of multitudes of good people in England.[2] The propriety, the necessity, of opposing this tax-claim, then, is admitted; only as to the manner of opposing it, can there be a doubt.

One form of opposition—that through civil war—should be at once and forever discarded: " The ' ultima ratio,' to oppose force to force, is what the heart of every American must revolt at. For with whom should we engage ? Our friends—our countrymen—our kindred ! No ! Let not the profligacy of a ministry abandoned to every principle of virtue and raging for despotism, tempt such near and dear connections to sheathe the sword in each other's bowels. There are surer, safer, means to end the controversy." [3]

And as he would reject the remedy through war, so

---

[1] The copy used by me—the only one that I have ever met with—belongs to the Library Company of Philadelphia. On the fly-leaf is a manuscript note apparently by the late Mr. Lloyd Smith, attributing the authorship of the pamphlet to Richard Wells.

[2] "A Few Political Reflections," 3.   [3] Ibid. 3–4.

would he reject the remedy through mere riot and the wanton destruction of property; and in order to atone for some recent lapses of that kind, he would promptly compensate the East India Company for its pecuniary losses at our hands.

The true remedy, in his opinion, is to be found among the resources of legitimate and honorable commerce. Here, also, there is one resource which, though in itself just, is not wise—that of an agreement for non-exportation; for, just in proportion as we are faithful to it, we merely hurt ourselves. Nevertheless, the true remedy is a commercial one: it is a general agreement for non-importation, which, if honestly adhered to, would break neither the law nor the peace, and would, in due time, compel the ministers either to give up their policy or to go out of office.

This pamphlet has additional interest for us, as developing, on behalf of a larger and freer political life in America, two striking arguments which, eighteen months afterward, were repeated with brilliant amplification by Thomas Paine. One is the argument from our political maturity: the other is the argument from our greatness in territory and in population. Americans, it is here argued, are no longer political infants; they have reached their political majority; the time has come for them to be clothed with all its appropriate rights and duties: "We look to manhood; our muscles swell with youthful vigor; our sinews spring with elastic force, and we feel the marrow of Englishmen in our bones. The day of independent manhood is at hand. . . . In domestic life, we all allow, there is a time when youth shall no longer be subject to the control of age."[1] Finally, in demanding that American greatness in territory and in population should be accepted as having its due weight against any further minute or severe control over us by England, he predicts the ultimate and peaceful transfer to America of the seat of the British empire,—his words to this effect being a sort of prose version of Dean Berkeley's earlier pre-

---

[1] "A Few Political Reflections," 33–34.

diction in verse: " George the First, when called to the throne of England, never harbored so absurd a thought as to wield the English sceptre in the Electorate of Hanover. The centre of his dominion was the place of his choice; nor would the nation have been satisfied without it. How long it may be before a similar translation shall happen in favor of America, I will not undertake to determine. But, should the Georges in regular succession wear the British diadem to a number ranking with the Louises of France, many a goodly prince of that royal line will have mingled his ashes with American dust; and not many generations may pass away, before one of the first monarchs of the world, ascending his throne, shall declare with exulting joy,—' Born and educated amongst you, I glory in the name of American!' " [1]

V.

We should be only misleading ourselves into a morass of historical error, if we were to overlook the fact that in this season of alarm and of earnest consultation, there were many patriotic Americans who gravely challenged the wisdom, even the rectitude, of the chief measures of opposition which, by so many writers, were already pressed upon the attention of the Congress in advance of its meeting. Perhaps the most characteristic example of this political attitude is furnished by a pamphlet, admirable in temper and expression, entitled " A Letter from a Virginian to the Members of the Congress to be held at Philadelphia on the First of September, 1774." [2]

The solicitude of this writer has its deepest root in his own distrust of the soundness of the constitutional theory on which most of the colonial opposition proceeds. That

---

[1] "A Few Political Reflections," 49.

[2] The great impression made by this pamphlet is proved by the numerous reprints of it which were made in spite of the fact that its argument was dead against what appeared to be the popular current. Some copies of it are without place of publication. It was probably first printed at Philadelphia. I am using a Boston reprint of 1774.

the measures of the ministry are impolitic and ought to be withdrawn, he nowhere denies,—but are they unconstitutional ? " We may ring eternal changes upon taxation and representation ; . . . but there is one proposition, a self-evident proposition, to which all the world give their assent, and from which we cannot withhold ours,—that, whatever taxation and representation may be, taxation and government are inseparable." [1]

Granted that the ministerial measures to which we object, do entail hardship and are justly offensive, what course ought we to pursue to obtain their repeal ? For one thing, we ought to pursue a consistent course—a thing we have not been doing the past ten years. And is this long record of our political inconsistency to be extended ? " Shall we, Proteus-like, perpetually change our ground, assume every moment some new and strange shape, to defend, to evade ? Shall we establish distinctions between internal and external taxation one year, and laugh at them the next ? Shall we confound duties with taxes, and regulations of trade with revenue laws ? Shall we rave against the preamble of the law, while we are ready to admit the enacting part of it ? Shall we refuse to obey the tea act, not as an oppressive act, but as a dangerous, a sole precedent of taxation, when every post day shows a precedent which our forefathers submitted to, and which we still submit to, without murmuring ? Shall we move heaven and earth against a trifling duty, on a luxury unknown to nine-tenths of the globe, unknown to our ancestors, despised by half the nations of Europe, which no authority, no necessity, compels us to use ? " [2]

Furthermore, we shall miss the right way for securing the repeal of measures to which we object, if we adopt any plan for merely vexing and distressing the mother country, as that of non-importation and non-consumption : " Beware how you adopt that measure, how you engage in that strange conflict of sullenness and obstinacy, till you have

[1] " A Letter from a Virginian," etc., 26.   [2] Ibid. 22–23.

given it the most calm and serious deliberation." [1] " We may tease the mother country ; we cannot ruin her." [2] " No man of spirit in private life, even on the slightest quarrel, will submit to be bullied, and exposed to the scorn and derision of the little circle he lives in. Can we seriously hope that a great nation, a proud nation, will be insulted and degraded with impunity by her colonies, in the face of every rival kingdom in Europe ? " [3]   Even though our agreement for non-importation and non-consumption should succeed, " it certainly behooves us as men, and as Christians, to be sure that it is a just measure. A combination to ruin or to obstruct the trade of a fellow citizen who happens to differ from us in his religious or political opinions, adopted in passion, prosecuted by the intrigues of a cabal, by innuendoes, insinuations, threatenings, and publicly signed by large numbers of leading men, would, I presume, be a manifest violation of the laws of God and man, and would, on conviction, be severely punished in every court of justice in Christendom. In what colors, then, will appear combinations of a large and respectable body of subjects against the supreme power of the community, adopted from the same motives, prosecuted by the same arts, and publicly signed in the face of the whole world ? " [4] " For the sake of common humanity, gentlemen, disdain to co-operate with handbills, with newspapers, with the high menacing resolves of common town-meetings. Do not conspire with them, to reduce, under the pains and penalties of disgrace and infamy, thousands of your fellow citizens to the cruel alternative of involving themselves, their wives and children, in indigence and wretchedness, or of being publicly branded and pointed out by the frantic multitude as apostates and traitors to their country." [5]

---

[1] " A Letter from a Virginian," etc., 18–19.   [2] Ibid. 20.
[3] Ibid. 25.   [4] Ibid. 20–21.
[5] Ibid. 22. I do not remember to have met with any suggestion as to the authorship of this able pamphlet ; but from its tone both of thought and of expression, I am inclined to attribute it to Jonathan Boucher.

VI.

On Monday morning, the fifth of September, 1774, four-and-forty respectable gentlemen, mostly strangers to one another, but representing twelve " colonies and provinces in North America," quietly made their way into Carpenters' Hall, in Philadelphia, and there sitting down together began " to consult upon the present state of the colonies, and the miseries to which they are and must be reduced, by the operation of certain acts of parliament respecting America, and to deliberate and determine upon wise and proper measures to be by them recommended to all the colonies, for the recovery and establishment of their just rights and liberties, civil and religious, and the restoration of union and harmony between Great Britain and the colonies, most ardently desired by all good men." [1]   Thus came into life the first Continental Congress, and with it the permanent political union of the American people.   As to the task set before those four-and-forty gentlemen, no graver one was ever undertaken since the world began.

As they came out from that hall of anxious deliberation, some of them may have found, on stepping into Mr. John Dunlap's shop not far away, a lively-looking little book, just come from the printer's hands, in which book, under the veil of playful allegory, they could read in a few minutes a graphic and indeed a quite tremendous history of the very events that had brought them together in that place:

A
PRETTY STORY
written in the
YEAR OF OUR LORD 1774,
By
PETER GRIEVOUS, ESQ.,
A.B.C.D.E.
Veluti in Speculo.
PHILADELPHIA.
Printed and sold by John Dunlap.
M. DCC. LXXIV.

---

[1] "Journals of Congress," i. 1–2.

As this title-page,[1] however, gave no clew to the real import of the book, the reader who should then seek for such clew in the preface, would find himself there decoyed and led on by explanations which still failed to give him warning that he was about to peruse a tractate upon Anglo-American politics. " A book," gaily remarks Peter Grievous, with the nonchalant air of a mere story-teller unvexed by things political, " is like a house. The grand portico is the Dedication; the flagged pavement is an Humble Address to the Reader, in order to pave the way for a kind reception of the work; the front door with its fluted pillars, pediment, trigliffs, and modillons, are the Title-page, with its motto, author's name and titles, date of the year, etc.; the entry is the Preface—oftentimes of a tedious length; and the several apartments and closets are the Chapters and Sections of the work itself. As I am but a clumsy carpenter at best, I shall not attempt to decorate my little cottage with any out-of-door ornaments; but as it would be inconvenient and uncomfortable to have my front door open immediately into the apartments of the house, I have made this Preface by way of entry.

" And now, gentle reader, if you should think my entry too plain and simple, you may set your imagination to work, and furnish it with a grand staircase, with cornices, stucco, and paintings. That is, you may suppose that I entered very unwillingly upon this work, being compelled to it by a chain of unforeseen circumstances; that it was written in the midst of a great hurry of other business, and under particular disadvantages of time and place, and that it was only intended for the inspection of a few friends, without any expectations of ever seeing it in the press.

---

[1] In my citations from " A Pretty Story," I have used the edition by B. J. Lossing, published in N. Y., in 1864, under the outside title of " The Old Farm and the New Farm: A Political Allegory." Lossing professes to give an exact reprint of the original edition ; while the copy to be found in Hopkinson's " Miscellaneous Essays," i. 65–91, was more or less tampered with and weakened by himself, in his preparation of it for what proved to be the posthumous publication of his writings.

You may, kind reader, go on to suppose that when my
friends perused my work, they were struck with the energy
of my genius, and insisted that the public ought not to be
deprived of such a fund of amusement and improvement
through my obstinate modesty; and that, after many solicitations and powerful persuasions, I had been prevailed upon
to bless mankind with the fruits of my labor. Or, if you
like not this, you may suppose that the following sheets
were found in the cabinet of some deceased gentleman; or
that they were dug out of an ancient ruin, or discovered in
a hermit's cave, or dropped from the clouds in a hail storm.
In short, you may suppose just what you please. And
when, by the help of imagination, you have seasoned the
Preface to your palate, you may turn over this leaf, and feast
upon the body of the work itself."

VII.

Turning over the leaf, then, in obedience to such persuasion, the reader would soon be in full sail upon a current of
rapid and fascinating narrative in which, under the names
of the Old Farm for England, and the New Farm for
America, the troubled relations between the two, especially
for the ten or twelve years prior to 1774, are depicted in a
very amusing way, and through which, especially, there
runs a vein of delicate raillery and satire upon the entire
spirit and method of the masters of the Old Farm in their
dealing with the settlers of the New. It was the whole
case, then to be considered with so much solemnity by the
first Continental Congress, set forth logically and laughably
in a good-humored little story,—which no one could fail to
read to the end who should once begin it.

" Once upon a time, a great while ago, there lived a certain Nobleman, who had long possessed a very valuable
Farm, and had a great number of children and grand-
children. Besides the annual profits of his land, which were
very considerable, he kept a large shop of goods; and being

very successful in trade, he became, in process of time, exceeding rich and powerful, insomuch that all his neighbors feared and respected him. With respect to the management of his family, it was thought he had adopted the most perfect mode that could be devised; for he had been at the pains to examine the economy of all his neighbors, and had selected from their plans all such parts as appeared to be equitable and beneficial, and omitted those which from experience were found to be inconvenient. Or, rather, by blending their several constitutions together, he had so ingeniously counterbalanced the evils of one mode of government with the benefits of another, that the advantages were richly enjoyed, and inconveniences scarcely felt. In short, his family was thought to be the best ordered of any in his neighborhood." [1] " Now it came to pass that this Nobleman had, by some means or other, obtained a right to an immense tract of wild uncultivated country at a vast distance from his mansion house. But he set little store by this acquisition, as it yielded him no profit; nor was it likely to do so, being not only difficult of access on account of the distance, but was also overrun with innumerable wild beasts [2] very fierce and savage,—so that it would be extremely dangerous to attempt taking possession of it.

" In process of time, however, some of his children, more stout and enterprising than the rest, requested leave of their Father to go and settle on this distant tract of land. Leave was readily obtained; but before they set out, certain agreements were stipulated between them. The principal were —the old Gentleman, on his part, engaged to protect and defend the adventurers in their new settlements; to assist them in chasing away the wild beasts; and to extend to them all the benefits of the government under which they were born,—assuring them that although they should be removed so far from his presence, they should nevertheless be considered as the children of his family, and treated accordingly. At the same time, he gave each of them a

[1] " A Pretty Story," 13–14.   [2] Particularly, the American Indians.

bond for the faithful performance of these promises, in which, among other things, it was covenanted that they should each of them, in their several families, have a liberty of making such rules and regulations for their own good government as they should find convenient, provided the rules and regulations should not contradict or be inconsistent with the general standing orders established in his Farm. In return for these favors, he insisted that they, on their parts, should at all times acknowledge him to be their Father; that they should not deal with their neighbors without his leave, but send to his shop only for such merchandise as they should want.[1] But, in order to enable them to pay for such goods as they should purchase, they were permitted to sell the product of their lands to certain of his neighbors."[2]

Having duly adjusted all these preliminaries, the hardy sons of the old Nobleman set off on their journey. After dangers and hardships almost without number, they at last got comfortably settled on the New Farm; in due time their harvests became abundant; and, keeping up a constant correspondence with the family on the Old Farm, they went to great expense for wagons, horses, and drivers, with which to bring from their Father's shop such goods as they wanted, which they paid for out of the produce of their lands. Thus matters went on very happily until, in an evil day, the old Nobleman's Wife[3] "began to cast an avaricious eye upon the new settlers." In the first place, she issued "an edict setting forth that, whereas the tailors of her family were greatly injured by the people of the New Farm, inasmuch as they presumed to make their own clothes, whereby the said tailors were deprived of the benefit of their custom, it was therefore ordained that for the future, the new settlers should not be permitted to have

---

[1] The Navigation Acts.

[2] "A Pretty Story," 19–21.

[3] The Nobleman's Wife is, of course, the British Parliament. In Arbuthnot's "History of John Bull," also, John Bull's Wife is Parliament.

amongst them any shears or scissors larger than a certain fixed size.[1] In consequence of this, our adventurers were compelled to have their clothes made by their Father's tailors ; but out of regard to the old Gentleman, they patiently submitted to this grievance."[2] Next, she proceeded to lay heavy taxes upon them on various pretences, all the time " receiving the fruits of their industry with both hands. Moreover, she persuaded her Husband to send amongst them, from time to time, a number of the most lazy and useless of his servants, under the specious pretext of defending them in their settlements, and of assisting to destroy the wild beasts, but in fact, to rid his own house of their company, not having employment for them, and at the same time to be a watch and a check upon the people of the New Farm."[3]

As the old Nobleman advanced in years, he came to leave his affairs more and more in the hands of his Steward, who was a very bad man, and had debauched the old Nobleman's Wife,[4] " and by that means gained an entire ascendency over her. She no longer deliberated what would most benefit either the Old Farm or the New, but said and did whatever the Steward pleased. Nay, so much was she influ-

---

[1] For example, no hat maker in America was allowed to have more than two apprentices, or to teach his trade to a negro, or to export his products by loading them on any horse, ass, cart, or sailing vessel whatsoever. All iron manufacture in the colonies was particularly obnoxious. An act was passed by the house of commons, but did not go into effect, whereby no American blacksmith might make so much as a bolt, or spike, or nail ; but later, parliament actually " forbade under penalties the maintaining of iron mills, slitting or rolling mills, plating forges, and steel furnaces in the colonies," " Encyc. Brit.," xxiii. 733. " England made it a fixed maxim of her commercial policy to crush every rising industry in her colonies, that could possibly compete with the home market." Lecky, " A History of England in the 18th Century," ii. 240. " It is to the antagonism of interests " created by such laws, " much more than to the Stamp Act or to any isolated instances of misgovernment, that the subsequent disruption must be ascribed." Ibid. 241.

[2] " A Pretty Story," 26–27.

[3] Ibid. 27–28.

[4] The corruption of parliament by ministerial bribes in the form of money, office, titles, etc.

enced by him, that she could neither utter Aye or No but as he directed. For he had cunningly persuaded her that it was very fashionable for women to wear padlocks on their lips, and that he was sure they would become her exceedingly. He therefore fastened a padlock to each corner of her mouth. When the one was open, she could only say Aye; and when the other was loosed, could only cry No. He took care to keep the keys of these locks himself; so that her will became entirely subject to his power." [1]

Thus, the wicked Steward with the help of the debauched Old Lady was able to work his will against the people of the New Farm, devising all sorts of " ways and means to impoverish and distress them." For one thing, he got the old Nobleman to sign an edict against the new settlers, in which it was declared that it was their duty as children to pay something towards supplying their Father's table with provisions, and to the supporting the dignity of his family.[2] For that purpose, it was ordained [3] that all their spoons, knives and forks, plates and porringers, should be marked with a certain mark, by officers appointed for that end; for which marking, they were to pay a certain stipend; and that they should not, under severe penalties, presume to make use of any spoon, knife or fork, plate or porringer, before it had been so marked, and the said stipend paid to the officer." [4] The attempt to put this edict in force led to a vast amount of trouble both in the Old Farm and in the New, so that at last the Nobleman thought it best to revoke it,[5] though he did this with a very bad grace.[6] Of course, " the Steward continued to hate the new settlers with exceeding great hatred, and determined to renew his attack

---

[1] " A Pretty Story," 30–31.

[2] In 1764, duties were laid on the colonies for the first time for the avowed purpose of increasing the imperial revenue.

[3] The Stamp Act, 1765.

[4] " A Pretty Story," 31–32.

[5] Repeal of the Stamp Act, 1766.

[6] The Declaratory Resolution asserting the power of parliament to bind the colonies in all cases whatsoever.

upon their peace and happiness."¹   Accordingly, he caused
to be proclaimed another decree,² to the effect "that the
new settlers should pay a certain stipend upon particular
goods, which they were not allowed to purchase anywhere
but at their Father's shop."³   Of these goods, the most
important was Water-Gruel, of which the new settlers were
very fond.   Thereupon, they made such a commotion that
the Old Nobleman thought it necessary to repeal this
decree,⁴ only retaining that portion of it which laid a stipend
on Water-Gruel, and this merely for the purpose of showing
that he had the power to do so.   Then followed worse
troubles than before.   For, the new settlers agreed with
one another that so long as the tax on Water-Gruel should
remain, they would drink no Water-Gruel, and would thus
cause the Water-Gruel business to be unprofitable to the
Great Merchants⁵ in the Old Farm, who had it for sale.
Accordingly, these Great Merchants lifted up their voices
and wept, because innumerable casks of the commodity
were lying unsold in their warehouses.   Whereupon the
wicked Steward directed them to load many and great
wagons with these casks of Water-Gruel,⁶ and send them
to the New Farm for sale at a price so low that the settlers
would be tempted to violate their agreement,—he "promising that the accustomed duty which they paid for their
exclusive right, should be taken off from all the Gruel they
should send amongst the new settlers; and that in case their
cargoes should come to any damage, he would take care
that the loss should be repaired out of the old Gentleman's
coffers."⁷   When, however, the people saw the wagons

---

¹ "A Pretty Story," 38.

² The act introduced by Charles Townshend in 1767, laying duties on paper,
painters' colors, glass, and tea.

³ "A Pretty Story," 39.

⁴ The bill introduced by Lord North, 5 March, 1770, repealing that part of
the act of 1767 which laid a duty on paper, painters' colors, and glass, but retaining the duty on tea in order to maintain the parliamentary right of taxation.

⁵ The East India Company.

⁶ Lord North's bill, in 1773, authorizing the East India Co. to send their
commodity to America free of export duty.

⁷ "A Pretty Story," 42.

of Water-Gruel approaching, they " were again thrown into great alarms and confusions. Some of them would not suffer the waggons to be unloaded at all, but sent them immediately back to the Gruel Merchants.[1] Others permitted the waggons to unload, but would not touch the hateful commodity ; so that it lay neglected about their roads and highways until it grew sour and spoiled.[2] But one of the new settlers, whose name was Jack,[3] either from a keener sense of the injuries attempted against him, or from the necessity of his situation, which was such that he could not send back the Gruel because of a number of mercenaries[4] whom his Father had stationed before his house to watch, and be a check upon his conduct,—he, I say, being almost driven to despair, fell to work, and with great zeal stove to pieces the casks of Gruel, which had been sent him, and utterly demolished the whole cargo."[5]

Of course, as soon as these high doings were known at the Old Farm, " great and terrible was the uproar there. The old Gentleman fell into great wrath, declaring that his absent children meant to throw off all dependence upon him, and to become altogether disobedient. His Wife, also, tore the padlocks from her lips, and raved and stormed like a billingsgate. The Steward lost all patience and moderation, swearing most profanely that he would leave no stone unturned until he had humbled the settlers of the New Farm at his feet,[6] and caused their Father to trample on their necks. Moreover, the Gruel Merchants roared and bellowed for the loss of their Gruel; and the clerks and

---

[1] The tea ships were sent back from New York and Philadelphia.

[2] At Charleston the tea was landed, but placed in damp cellars where it spoiled.

[3] Boston.

[4] British soldiers and vessels of war in Boston harbor.

[5] Pages 44–45.

[6] A reverberation of Lord North's too-well-remembered speech in the house of commons in 1768 : " I am against repealing the last act of parliament, securing to us a revenue out of America ; I will never think of repealing it until we see America prostrate at our feet."

apprentices were in the utmost consternation lest the people of the New Farm should again agree to have no dealings with their Father's shop. Vengeance was immediately set on foot, particularly against Jack." For that purpose, a large padlock was prepared, which was " to be fastened upon Jack's great gate," [1] and this was not to be opened again until Jack had paid for the Gruel he had spilt, and had shown other signs of repentance. Moreover, " a large gallows was erected before the mansion house in the Old Farm, and an order made that if any of Jack's children or servants should be suspected of misbehavior, they should not be convicted or acquitted by the consent of their brethren, . . . but be tied neck and heels and dragged to the gallows at the mansion house, and there be hanged without mercy." [2]

Certainly, all this was dreadful for poor Jack. " The great inlet to his farm was entirely blocked up, so that he could neither carry out the produce of his land for sale, nor receive from abroad the necessaries for his family. But this was not all. His Father, along with the padlock aforesaid, had sent an Overseer [3] to hector and domineer over him and his family, and to endeavor to break his spirit by exercising every possible severity; for which purpose, he was attended by a great number of mercenaries, and armed with more than common authorities." [4] On the arrival of the Overseer, Jack and his family received him with all due respect; [5] " for, notwithstanding all that had passed, the people of the new Settlements loved and revered the old Gentleman with a truly filial attachment,—attributing his unkindness

[1] The Boston port bill, 1774.

[2] Pages 45, 46, 47.

[3] General Gage, to whom was given extraordinary powers. He arrived at Boston, May, 1774, bringing four additional regiments.

[4] Page 48.

[5] General Gage " landed at Long Wharf, amid salutes from ships and batteries. Received by the council and civil officers, he was escorted by the Boston cadets, whom Hancock commanded, to the state house, where the council presented a loyal address. . . . He then partook of a public dinner in Faneuil Hall." Bancroft, " Hist. of U. S.," last rev., iv. 7–8.

entirely to the intrigues of their enemy, the Steward. But this fair weather did not last long. The new Overseer took the first opportunity of showing that he had no intentions of living in harmony and friendship with the family. Some of Jack's domestics had put on their Sunday clothes, and attended the Overseer in the great parlor, in order to pay him their compliments on his arrival, and to request his assistance in reconciling them to their Father; but he rudely stopped them short in the midst of their speech, called them a parcel of disobedient scoundrels, and bid them go about their business. So saying, he turned upon his heel, and with great contempt left the room." [1]

In the midst of these troubles, poor Jack turned for help to the other Families on the New Farm. The latter promptly and kindly assured Jack and his family that in their opinion the cause of one was the cause of all,—adding that " they would stand by and support them to the last." But, above all, they " earnestly recommended it to them to be firm and steady in the cause of liberty and justice, and never acknowledge the omnipotence of their Mother-in-Law, nor yield to the machinations of their enemy, the Steward. In the meantime, lest Jack's family should suffer for want of necessaries, their great gate being fast locked, liberal and very generous contributions were raised among the several Families of the new Settlements for their present relief. This seasonable bounty was handed to Jack over the garden wall, all access to the front of his house being shut up." [2]

All these proceedings only the more provoked the hard-fisted Overseer, who, observing " that the children and domestics of Jack's Family had frequent meetings and consultations together, sometimes in the garret, and sometimes in the stable, . . . he wrote a thundering prohibition, much like a Pope's Bull, which he caused to be pasted up in every room in the house; in which he declared and protested that these meetings were treasonable, traitorous, and rebel-

---

[1] Pages 48–49.   [2] Page 51.

19

lious, contrary to the dignity of their Father, and inconsistent with the omnipotence of their Mother-in-Law ;
denouncing, also, terrible punishments against any two of
the Family who should from thenceforth be seen whispering
together, and strictly forbidding the domestics to hold any
more meetings in the garret or stable.

" These harsh and unconstitutional proceedings irritated
Jack and the other inhabitants of the New Farm to such a
degree that . . .

Cætera desunt."[1]

In other words, Peter Grievous is an historian and not a
prophet; and having brought the record down to the point
at which the older members of the several Families on the
New Farm have met together in the hall of the Carpenters,
at Philadelphia, there to make common cause with poor
Jack, and for him and with him to think out wisely what is
further to be done by them all in their common troubles,
the author very properly leaves it to these wise gentlemen
to finish the " Pretty Story " in their own way, and in
doing so to decide whether it shall really turn out to be,
upon the whole, a pretty story or not.

VIII.

To any one in the least degree familiar with the problems
which convulsed the American colonies in the year 1774,
when the troubles growing out of the tea tax had culmi-
nated in the closing of the harbor at Boston and in the
opening of the Congress at Philadelphia, even a glance over
this little book will show that here at last was a writer,
enlisted in the colonial cause, who was able to defend that
cause, and to assail its enemies, with a fine and a very rare
weapon—that of humor. The personages included in " A
Pretty Story " are few; its topics are simple and palpable,

---

[1] Pages 51–52.

and even now in but little need of elucidation; the plot and
incidents of the fiction travel in the actual footsteps of well-
known history; while the aptness, the delicacy, and the
humor of the allegory give to the reader the most delightful
surprises, and are well sustained to the very end. Indeed,
the wit of the author flashes light upon every legal question
then at issue; and the stern and even technical debate
between the colonies and the motherland is here translated
into a piquant and a bewitching novelette. It soon became
known that its author was Francis Hopkinson.

Some critic was good enough, at an early day, to launch
upon the world the opinion that Hopkinson's " Pretty
Story " was closely modelled after Arbuthnot's " History
of John Bull "; and this opinion seems to have held its
own unchallenged since then, and to have thriven on mere
repetition. The truth is, however, that Hopkinson's little
book resembles Arbuthnot's in just one particular—it is an
example of the use of allegory in the facetious treatment of
national or international politics—a use of allegory almost
as old as allegory itself; and, besides this, so far as thought,
or form, or incident is concerned, there is almost no feature
of resemblance between them. It is not to be doubted that
Hopkinson had read " The History of John Bull," for he
was a loving disciple and a true kinsman of the wits of the
age of Queen Anne; yet he might easily have written every
word of his own allegory, without ever having read any
word of Arbuthnot's.

By this neat and telling bit of work, Hopkinson took his
true place as one of the three leading satirists on the Whig
side of the American Revolution,—the other two being
John Trumbull and Philip Freneau. In the long and passionate controversy in which these three satirists bore so
effective a part, each is distinguishable by his own peculiar
note. The political satire of Freneau and of Trumbull is,
in general, grim, bitter, vehement, unrelenting. Hopkinson's satire is as keen as theirs, but its characteristic note is
one of playfulness. They stood forth the wrathful critics

and assailants of the enemy, confronting him with a hot and an honest hatred, and ready to overwhelm him with an acerbity that was fell and pitiless.   Hopkinson, on the other hand, was too gentle, too tender-hearted—his personal tone was too full of amenity—for that sort of warfare.   A man who, in his private life, had so kindly and gracious a nature as to be able to establish intimate relations with a poor little Ishmaelite of a mouse which, on his taking his seat at table, would steal from its hiding-place and disport itself by him at his meals; or who could so prevail over the distrust and the fugaciousness of a flock of pigeons, that they would wait for him daily in his garden, would flutter around him as he approached, and contend for places on his person, crowding upon his head and shoulders, and even clinging to the slopes of his arms,—such a man was not the one to make use, even against his worst political enemies, of the rancorous and acrid methods of literary strife.   As a satirist, therefore, Hopkinson accomplished his effects without bitterness or violence.   No one saw more vividly than he what was weak, or despicable, or cruel, in the position and conduct of the enemy; but in exhibiting it, his method was that of good-humored ridicule.   Never losing his temper, almost never extreme in emotion or in expression, with an urbanity which kept unfailingly upon his side the sympathies of his readers, he knew how to dash and discomfit the foe with a raillery that was all the more effective because it seemed to spring from the very absurdity of the case, and to be, as Ben Jonson required, " without malice or heat."

CHAPTER XIII.

THE PARTY OF THE LOYALISTS AND THEIR LITERATURE.

I.—The slight development of Loyalist literature prior to 1774—The rapid
   crystallization of political ideas occasioned by the first Continental Congress—In argumentative literature the period of chief Loyalist activity, from
   1774 to 1776.
II.—The survival among us of the partisan ideas and prejudices of the Revolutionary controversy—The proper historic attitude toward the problems and
   parties of any Revolution.
III.—The Loyalist party judged with respect to its size—The Loyalist claim
   that the promoters of the Revolution were a minority—Opinion of John
   Adams and Thomas McKean.
IV.—The Loyalists judged with respect to personal value—In general composed
   of the more conservative section of American society—The proportion of
   college-bred men among them—Opinion of Anne Grant of Laggan.
V.—The Loyalists judged with respect to the value of their logical position—
   Complexity and difficulty of the questions involved in the dispute—The old
   maxim, " No taxation without representation," not necessarily in conflict
   with the tax claim of parliament—The maxim applauded by George Grenville—According to the historic meaning of the word, the commons of
   America were represented in the popular branch of the imperial parliament—That this representation was imperfect and unsatisfactory, was not
   denied—The true remedy was reform of the representation, and not nullification of the laws of parliament, nor secession from the empire—Opinions
   of experts in constitutional law—The Loyalist reply to the argument of
   danger from moderate parliamentary taxation.
VI.—The question of Independence kept in abeyance till 1776—Three prevalent errors as to the character and attitude of the Loyalists.

I.

THERE cannot be a more authentic introduction to the
Loyalists of our Revolution, than is to be had through an
acquaintance with their literature. As we turn over the
pages of that literature,—political essays, pamphlets, sermons, songs, satires, epigrams, burlesques, lampoons,—a

literature now having an almost pathetic insignificance as it slumbers under a hundred years of dust and contempt,— perhaps the first notable fact that calls for attention is, that, in point of time, its development lags somewhat behind that of the Revolutionist party, and does not become of much value until within the twelvemonth preceding the Lexington and Concord skirmishes—that is, until about the time of the Congress of 1774.

Of course, from the very beginning of the dispute there had been American writers who, while doubting the wisdom of the colonial policy of the English ministry, likewise doubted the soundness of the constitutional claim set up in opposition to it by many of their American brethren; and, at any rate, deprecated all violent or extreme measures in the assertion of that claim.   Nevertheless, during the eight or ten years prior to 1774, it might fairly have been assumed that this Anglo-American dispute was but one of a long series of political disagreements that had broken out, at various times, in John Bull's large and vivacious family, and that this particular dispute would probably run its natural course and come to an end, just as its predecessors had done, without any permanent rupture of the interior relations of the family, and, indeed, to the great advantage of all its members through a clearer definition of those constitutional principles which had enabled them all to live together so long under the same enormous and kindly roof. Not until after the failure of Lord North's clever device for inducing the Americans to take the taxation which they liked so little, along with that cheering beverage which they liked so much, was it necessary for any person to regard the dispute as one of peculiarly deep and tragical import.   It was, perhaps, on account of this confidence of theirs in the natural limitations of the problem then vexing the colonies and the mother country, that so many of the ablest conservative writers in America refrained, in that stage of affairs, from engaging very actively in the discussion.   Thus it is that we may in a measure explain why, in this controversy, so little part was taken prior to 1774 by the most powerful of all the Loyalist writers,—Daniel Leonard, Joseph Galloway, Samuel Seabury, Jonathan Boucher, and Jonathan Odell.

But with the events of the years 1773 and 1774 came a total change in the situation, and in the attitude of all parties toward it: first, the repulsion of the gentle tea ships by several American communities, and the destruction of valuable property belonging to liegemen of the king; then the series of stern retaliatory measures to which parliament was thereby drawn; finally, by a large portion of the colonists, the fearless summons for a great council of their own delegates, solemnly to determine and to proclaim some common plan of action. With the gathering of this celebrated council—the first Continental Congress—the wayfaring American though a fool could not err in reading, in very crimson letters painted on the air in front of him, the tidings of the arrival of a race-crisis altogether transcending those ordinary political altercations which had from time to time disturbed, and likewise quickened and clarified, the minds of his English ancestors.

Naturally, therefore, from about this time the process of political crystallization among the colonists went on with extraordinary rapidity. Then, every man had to define both to himself and to his neighbor, what he thought, how he felt, what he meant to do. Then, too, the party of insubordination in these thirteen agitated communities had, for the first time, a common and a permanent organ for the formulation of the political doctrine and purpose which should sway them all. Finally, around this official and authoritative statement of doctrine and purpose, the opposing tendencies of thought could clash and do intelligent battle,—having a set of precise propositions to fight for or to fight against, and having, likewise, the grim consciousness that such fight was no longer a merely academic one.

In a valid sense, therefore, it may be said that the formation of the great Loyalist party of the American Revolution dates from about the time of the Congress of 1774. Moreover, its period of greatest activity in argumentative literature is from that time until the early summer of 1776, when nearly all further use for argumentative literature on that particular subject was brought to an end by the Declaration of Independence. The writings of the Loyalists, from the middle of 1776 down to 1783, form no longer a literature of argumentative discussion, but rather a literature of emotional appeal, exultant, hortatory, derisive, denunciatory, —a literature chiefly lyrical and satirical.

II.

Even yet, in this last decade of the nineteenth century, it is by no means easy for Americans—especially if, as is the case with the present writer, they be descended from men who thought and fought on behalf of the Revolution—to take a disinterested attitude, that is, an historical one, toward those Americans who thought and fought against the Revolution. Both as to the men and as to the questions involved in that controversy, the rehearsal of the claims of the victorious side has been going on among us, now for a hundred years or more, in tradition, in history, in oration, in song, in ceremony. Hardly have we known, seldom have we been reminded, that the side of the Loyalists, as they called themselves, of the Tories, as they were scornfully nicknamed by their opponents, was even in argument not a weak one, and in motive and sentiment not a base one, and in devotion and self-sacrifice not an unheroic one. While the war was going forward, of course the animosities aroused by it were too hot and too fierce, especially between the two opposing groups of Americans, to permit either party in the controversy to do justice to the logical or to the personal merit of the other. When at last the war came to an end, and the champions of the Revolution were in absolute triumph, then the more prominent Tories had to flee for their lives; they had to flee from the wrath that had come, and to bury themselves, either in other lands or in obscure places of this land. Then, of course, they and all their detested notions and emotions and deeds, whether grand or petty or base, went down out of sight, submerged beneath the abhorrence of the victorious Revolutionists, and doomed, as it appears, to at least one solid century of oratorical and poetical infamy, which has found its natural and organized expression in each recurring Fourth of July, and in each reappearance of the birthday of Washington. May it not, however, at last be assumed that a solid century should be, even under such conditions, a sufficient refrigerator for overheated political emotion? May we not now hope that it will not any longer cost us too great an effort to look calmly, even considerately, at least fairly, upon what, in the words and acts of the Tories, our fathers and grandfathers could hardly endure to look at all? And, surely, our willingness to do all this can hardly be lessened by the consideration that, " in dealing with an enemy, not only dead, but dead in exile and in defeat, candor prescribes the fullest measure of generous treatment." [1] At any rate, the American Revolution affords no exemption from the general law of historic investigation,—that the truth is to be found only by him who searches for it with an unbiased mind. Until we shall be able to take, respecting the problems and the parties of our own Revolution, the same attitude which we freely and easily take respecting the problems and parties of other revolutions—that is, the attitude, not of hereditary partisans, **but of** scientific investigators—will it be forbidden us to acquire a thoroughly discriminating and just acquaintance with that prodigious epoch in our history.

III.

As preliminary to some examination of the argumentative value of the position taken by the Loyalist party, let us

---

[1] Winthrop Sargent, Preface to " The Loyalist Poetry," etc., vi.

inquire, for a moment, what recognition may be due to them
simply as persons.   Who and what were the Tories of the
American Revolution ?   As to their actual number, there is
some difficulty in framing even a rough estimate.   No
attempt at a census of political opinions was ever made
during that period; and no popular vote was ever taken
of a nature to indicate, even approximately, the numerical
strength of the two opposing schools of political thought.
Of course, in every community there were Tories who were
Tories in secret.   These could not be counted, for the good
reason that they could not be known.   Then, again, the
number of openly avowed Tories varied somewhat with
variations in the prosperity of the Revolution.   Still further, their number varied with variations of locality.
Throughout the entire struggle, by far the largest number
of Tories was to be found in the colony of New York, particularly in the neighborhood of its chief city.   Of the other
middle colonies, while there were many Tories in New Jersey, in Delaware, and in Maryland, probably the largest
number lived in Pennsylvania,—a number so great that a
prominent officer [1] in the Revolutionary army described it
as the " enemies' country."   Indeed, respecting the actual
preponderance of the Tory party in these two central colonies, an eminent champion of the Revolution bore this
startling testimony: " New York and Pennsylvania were so
nearly divided—if their propensity was not against us—that
if New England on one side and Virginia on the other had
not kept them in awe, they would have joined the British." [2]   Of the New England colonies, Connecticut had the
greatest number of Tories; and next, in proportion to
population, was the district which was afterwards known as
the State of Vermont.   Proceeding to the colonies south of
the Potomac, we find that in Virginia, especially after hostilities began, the Tories were decidedly less in number than
the Whigs.   In North Carolina, the two parties were about

[1] Timothy Pickering.
[2] " The Works of John Adams," x. 63.

evenly divided. In South Carolina, the Tories were the more numerous party; while in Georgia their majority was so great that, in 1781, they were preparing to detach that colony from the general movement of the rebellion, and probably would have done so, had it not been for the embarrassing accident which happened to Cornwallis at York-town in the latter part of that year.

If we may accept these results as giving us a fair, even though crude, estimate concerning the local distribution of the Tories, we have still to come back to the question which deals with their probable number in the aggregate. Naturally, on such a problem, the conclusions reached by the opposing parties would greatly differ. Thus, the Tories themselves always affirmed that could there have been a true and an unterrified vote, they would have had a great majority; and that the several measures of the Revolution had not only never been submitted to such a test, but had been resolved upon and forced into effect by a few resolute leaders who, under the names of committees of correspond-ence, committees of observation, committees of safety, conventions, and congresses, had assumed unconstitutional authority, and had pretended, without valid credentials, to speak and to act for the whole population of their towns, or counties, or provinces. To translate the Tory explanation into the language of the present day, it may be said that, in their belief, the several measures of the Revolution were the work of a well-constructed and powerful political machine, set up in each colony, in each county, in each town, and operated with as much skill and will and unscrupulousness as go into the operation of such machines in our time. This opinion, which, in its substance, was most ably presented in those days by the Tory writers, has been adopted by a very candid English historian now living, who says of the American Revolution that, like most other revolutions, it " was the work of an energetic minority, who succeeded in committing an undecided and fluctuating majority to courses for which they had little love, and leading them step by step to a position from which it was impossible to recede."[1]

Certainly, with such an estimate as to the superior numbers of the Tories, their own opponents did not agree; but they did admit that the Tory party was at any rate a very large one. Perhaps no statesman on the Whig side was better informed on such a subject than John Adams, or was less inclined to make an undue concession to the enemy; and he gave it as his opinion that about one-third of the people of the thirteen States had been opposed to the measures of the Revolution in all its stages.[2] This opinion of John Adams, which he affirmed more than once in the latter part of his life, was on one occasion mentioned by him in a letter to his old compatriot, Thomas McKean, chief-justice of Pennsylvania, a signer of the Declaration of Independence, and a member of every American Congress from that of 1765 to the close of the Revolution. "You say," wrote McKean in reply, "that . . . about a third of the people of the colonies were against the Revolution. It required much reflection before I could fix my opinion on this subject; but on mature deliberation I conclude you are right, and that more than a third of influential characters were against it."[3]

Out of three millions of people, then, at least one million did not approve of the policy of carrying their political opposition to the point of rebellion and separation. According to John Adams and Thomas McKean, every third American whom we could have encountered in this part of the world between 1765 and 1783 was a Loyalist. Surely, an idea—a cause—that was cherished and clung to, amid almost every form of obloquy and disaster, by so vast a section of American society, can hardly deserve any longer to be turned out of court in so summary and contemptuous a fashion as that with which it has been commonly disposed of by American writers.

---

[1] Lecky, " A History of England in the Eighteenth Century," new ed., iv. 224.
[2] " The Works of John Adams," x. 63, 110.   [3] Ibid. 87.

IV.

After the question of number, very properly comes that of quality. What kind of people were these Tories, as regards intelligence, character, and standing in their several communities ?

And here, brushing aside, as unworthy of historical investigators, the partisan and vindictive epithets of the controversy,—many of which, however, still survive even in the historical writings of our own time,—we shall find that the Loyalists were, as might be expected, of all grades of personal worth and worthlessness; and that, while there was among them, no doubt, the usual proportion of human selfishness, malice, and rascality, as a class they were not bad people, much less were they execrable people—as their opponents at the time commonly declared them to be.

In the first place, there was, prior to 1776, the official class; that is, the men holding various positions in the civil and military and naval services of the government, their immediate families, and their social connections. All such persons may be described as inclining to the Loyalist view in consequence of official bias.

Next were certain colonial politicians who, it may be admitted, took a rather selfish and an unprincipled view of the whole dispute, and who, counting on the probable, if not inevitable, success of the British arms in such a conflict, adopted the Loyalist side, not for conscience' sake but for profit's sake, and in the expectation of being rewarded for their fidelity by offices and titles, and especially by the confiscated estates of the rebels, after the rebels themselves should have been defeated, and their leaders hanged or sent into exile.

As composing still another class of Tories, may be mentioned probably a vast majority of those who stood for the commercial interests, for the capital and the tangible property of the country, and who, with the instincts natural to persons who have something considerable to lose, disapproved of all measures for pushing the dispute to the point of disorder, riot, and civil war.

Still another class of Loyalists was made up of people of professional training and occupation,—clergymen, physicians, lawyers, teachers,—a clear majority of whom seem to have been set against the ultimate measures of the Revolution.

Finally, and in general, it may be said that a majority of those who, of whatever occupation, of whatever grade of culture or of wealth, would now be described as conservative people, were Loyalists during the American Revolution. And by way of concession to the authority and force of truth, what has to be said respecting the personal quality commonly attaching to those who, in any age or country, are liable to be classed as conservative people ? Will it be denied that within that order of persons, one may usually find at least a fair portion of the cultivation, of the moral thoughtfulness, of the personal purity and honor, existing in the entire community to which they happen to belong ?

Precisely this description, at any rate, applies to the conservative class in the American colonies during that epoch, —a majority of whom dissented from those extreme measures which at last transformed into a revolution a political movement which began with the avowed purpose of confining itself to a struggle for redress of grievances, and within the limits of constitutional opposition. If, for example, we consider the point with reference to cultivation and moral refinement, it may seem to us a significant fact that among the members of the Loyalist party are to be found the names of a great multitude of the graduates of our colonial colleges—especially of Harvard, William and Mary, Yale, Princeton, and Pennsylvania. Thus, in an act of banishment passed by Massachusetts, in September, 1778, against the most prominent of the Tory leaders in that State, one may now read the names of three hundred and ten of her citizens. And who were they ? Let us go over their names.

Are these the names of profligates and desperadoes, or even of men of slight and equivocal consideration ? To any one at all familiar with the history of colonial New England, that list of men, denounced to exile and loss of property on account of their opinions, will read almost like the beadroll of the oldest and noblest families concerned in the founding and upbuilding of New England civilization. Moreover, of that catalogue of three hundred and ten men of Massachusetts, banished for an offence to which the most of them appear to have been driven by conscientious convictions, more than sixty [1] were graduates of Harvard. This fact is probably a typical one; and of the whole body of the Loyalists throughout the thirteen colonies, it must be said that it contained, as one of its ablest antagonists long after admitted, " more than a third of influential characters,"—that is, a very considerable portion of the customary chiefs and representatives of conservatism in each community.

By any standard of judgment, therefore, according to which we usually determine the personal quality of any party of men and women in this world—whether the standard be intellectual, or moral, or social, or merely conventional—the Tories of the Revolution seem to have been not a profligate party, nor an unprincipled one, nor a reckless or even a light-minded one, but, on the contrary, to have had among them a very considerable portion of the most refined, thoughtful, and conscientious people in the colonies. So true is this, that in 1807 a noble-minded Scottish woman, Mistress Anne Grant of Laggan, who in her early life had been familiar with American colonial society, compared the loss which America suffered in consequence of the expatriation of the Loyalists by the Revolution, to the loss which France suffered in consequence of the expatriation of so many of her Protestants by the revocation of the Edict of Nantes.[2]

So much, then, must be said on behalf of the Tories of

---

[1] George E. Ellis, in " Narr. and Crit. Hist. Am.," vii. 195.
[2] Mrs. Anne Grant, " Memoirs of an American Lady," etc., 353.

the Revolution,—in point of numbers, they were far from
inconsiderable, and in point of character, they were far from
despicable.   On the one hand, they formed no mere rump
party.   If they were not actually a majority of the American people,—as they themselves always claimed to be, and
as some careful scholars now think they were,—they did at
least constitute a huge minority of the American people:
they formed a section of colonial society too important on
the score of mere numbers to be set down as a paltry hand-
ful of obstructives; while in any rightful estimate of personal value, quite aside from mere numbers, they seem to
deserve the consideration which conscientious and cultivated
people of one party never ask in vain of conscientious and
cultivated people of the opposite party,—at least after the
issues of the controversy are closed.

V.

Pressing forward, then, with our investigation, we proceed to apply to the American Loyalists that test by which
we must judge any party of men who have taken one side,
and have borne an important share in any great historical
controversy.   This is the test of argumentative value.   It
asks whether the logical position of the party was or was
not a strong one.

Even yet it is not quite needless to remind ourselves that
the American Revolution was a war of argument long before
it became a war of physical force; and that, in this war of
argument, were involved a multitude of difficult questions,
—constitutional, legal, political, ethical,—with respect to
which honest and thoughtful people were compelled to
differ.   All these questions, however, may, for our purposes, be reduced to just two: first, the question of what
was lawful under the existing constitution of the British
empire; and secondly, the question of what was expedient
under the existing circumstances of the colonies.   Now,
paradoxical as it may seem to many of the American de-

scendants of the victorious party, each of those questions had
two very real and quite opposite sides; much was to be said
for each side; and for the Tory side so much was to be said
in the way of solid fact and of valid reasoning, that an intelligent and a noble-minded American might have taken that
side, and might have stuck to it, and might have gone into
battle for it, and might have imperiled all the interests of
his life in defense of it, without any just impeachment of
his reason or of his integrity—without deserving to be
called, then or since then, either a weak man or a bad one.

That we may develop before our eyes something of the
argumentative strength of the Loyalist position, in the
appeal which it actually made to honest men at that time,
let us take up for a moment the first of the two questions
to which, as has just been said, the whole dispute may be
reduced,—the question of what was lawful under the existing constitution of the British empire. Let us strike into
the very heart of that question. It was the contention of
the American Whigs that the British parliament could not
lawfully tax us, because by so doing it would be violating
an ancient maxim of the British constitution: '' No taxation
without representation.'' Have we not all been taught
from our childhood that the citation of that old maxim
simply settled the constitutional merits of the whole controversy, and settled it absolutely in favor of the Whigs? But
did it so settle it? Have we not been accustomed to think
that the refusal of the American Tories to give way before
the citation of that maxim was merely a case of criminal
stupidity or of criminal perversity on their part? But was
it so?

On the contrary, many of the profoundest constitutional
lawyers in America, as well as in England, both rejected
the foregoing Whig contention, and at the same time
admitted the soundness and the force of the venerable
maxim upon which that contention was alleged to rest.
Thus the leading English jurists, who supported the parliamentary taxation of the colonies, did not dispute that

20

maxim. Even George Grenville, the author and champion of the Stamp Act, did not dispute it. " The colonies claim, it is true," said he, " the privilege which is common to all British subjects, of being taxed only with their own consent, given by their representatives. And may they ever enjoy the privilege in all its extent; may this sacred pledge of liberty be preserved inviolate to the utmost verge of our dominions, and to the latest pages of our history! I would never lend my hand toward forging chains for America, lest, in so doing, I should forge them for myself. But the remonstrances of the Americans fail in the great point of the colonies not being represented in parliament, which is the common council of the whole empire, and as such is as capable of imposing internal taxes as impost duties, or taxes on intercolonial trade, or laws of navigation." [1]

These words of Grenville may help us to understand the position of the American Loyalists. They frankly admitted the maxim of " No taxation without representation "; but the most of them denied that the maxim was violated by the acts of parliament laying taxation upon the colonies. Here everything depends, they argued, on the meaning to be attached to the word representation; and that meaning is to be ascertained by ascertaining what was understood by the word in England at the time when this old maxim originated, and in the subsequent ages during which it had been quoted and applied. Now, the meaning then attached to the word in actual constitutional experience in England is one which shows that the commons of America, like the commons of England, are alike represented in that great branch of the British parliament which proclaims its representative character in its very name,—the house of commons. During the whole period in which the maxim under

---

[1] Given in George Bancroft, " History of the United States," last revision, iii. 98. These sentences of Grenville, which are not to be found in Hansard, seem to have been compiled by Bancroft from several contemporary reports to be met with in private letters from persons who heard Grenville. Compare 18th ed. of Bancroft, v. 237 n.

consideration had been acquiring authority, the idea was
that representation in parliament was constituted, not
through any uniform distribution, among individual persons,
of the privilege of voting for members, but rather through
a distribution of such privilege among certain organized
communities, as counties, cities, boroughs, and universities,
to which at an early day this function had been assigned
according to a method then deemed equable and just.
Furthermore, as it has been from the beginning, so is it
still a principle of parliamentary representation, that from
the moment a member is thus chosen to sit in parliament,
he is the representative of the whole empire and not of
his particular constituency. He " is under no obligation,
therefore, to follow instructions from the voters or the inhabitants of the district from which he is chosen. They
have no legal means of enforcing any instructions. They
cannot demand his resignation. In fact, a member cannot
resign." Moreover, the members of the house of lords
" represent, in principle, the interests of the whole empire,
and of all classes, as truly as the commons." [1] Therefore,
the historic meaning of the word representation, as the word
has always been used in English constitutional experience,
seemed fairly to justify the Loyalist contention, that the
several organized British communities in America, as an
integral part of the British empire, were to all intents and
purposes represented in the British parliament, which sat at
the capital as the supreme council of the whole empire,
and exercised legislative authority coextensive with the
boundaries of that empire.

It was no sufficient reply to this statement to say, as
some did say, that such representation as has just been
described was a very imperfect kind of representation. Of
course it was an imperfect kind of representation; but, what-

---

[1] John W. Burgess, " Political Science and Comparative Constitutional Law,"
ii. 67, 68. The reader should examine the whole of Professor Burgess's section
on " The Principle of Representation in the Parliament," 65–69.

ever it was, it was exactly the kind of representation that
was meant by the old constitutional maxim thus cited; for
it was the only kind of representation practised, or known,
or perhaps even conceived of in England during all those
ages which had witnessed the birth and the growth of this
old formula. The truth is that representation, as a political
fact in this world, has thus far been a thing of degrees—a
thing of less and of more; that perfect representation has
even yet not been anywhere attained in this world; that in
the last century representation in England was very much
less perfect than it has since become; and, finally, that, in
the period now dealt with, what had always been meant
by the word representation in the British empire was
satisfied by such a composition of the house of commons
as that, while its members were voted for by very few
even of the common people in England, yet, the moment
that its members were elected, they became, in the eye of
the constitution and in the spirit of this old formula, the
actual representatives of all the commoners of the whole
empire, in all its extent, in all its dominions and dependencies.

Accordingly, when certain English commoners in America
at last rose up and put forward the claim that, merely
because they had no votes for members of the house of
commons, therefore that house did not represent them, and
therefore they could not lawfully be taxed by parliament, it
was very naturally said, in reply, that these English commoners in America were demanding for themselves a new
and a peculiar definition of the word representation; a definition never up to that time given to it in England, and
never of course up to that time claimed or enjoyed by English commoners in England. For, how was it at that time
in England with respect to the electoral privilege? Indeed,
very few people in England then had votes for members of
the house of commons,—only one-tenth of the entire population of the realm. How about the other nine-tenths of
the population of the realm? Had not those British sub-

jects in England as good a right as these British subjects in America to deny that they were represented in parliament, and that they could be lawfully taxed by parliament ? Nay, such was the state of the electoral system that entire communities of British subjects in England, composing such cities as Leeds, Halifax, Birmingham, Manchester, and Liverpool,—communities as populous and as rich as entire provinces in America,—had no votes whatever for members of parliament. Yet, did the people of these several communities in England refuse to pay taxes levied by act of parliament—that is, did they, for that reason, proclaim the nullification of a law of the general government ? " We admit," continued the American Loyalists, " that for all these communities of British subjects—for those in England, as well as for these in America—the existing representation is very imperfect; that it should be reformed and made larger and more uniform than it now is; and we are ready and anxious to join in all forms of constitutional agitation, under the leadership of such men as Chatham, and Camden, and Burke, and Barré, and Fox, and Pownall, to secure such reform; and yet it remains true that the present state of representation throughout the British empire, imperfect as it is, is representation in the very sense understood and practised by the English race whenever hitherto they have alleged the maxim,—' No taxation without representation.' That old maxim, therefore, can hardly be said to be violated by the present imperfect state of our representative system. The true remedy for the defects of which we complain is reform—reform of the entire representative system both in England and in America—reform by means of vigorous political agitation—reform, then, and not a rejection of the authority of the general government; reform, and not nullification; reform, and not a disruption of the empire."

Such is a rough statement, and, as I think, a fair one, of the leading argument of the American Loyalists with respect to the first of the two great questions then dividing the American people, namely, the question of what was lawful under the existing constitution of the British empire. Certainly, the position thus taken by the Loyalists was a very strong one,—so strong, in fact, that honest and reasonable Americans could take it, and stand upon it, and even offer up their lives in defense of it, without being justly liable to the charge that they were either peculiarly base, or peculiarly stupid.

Indeed, under this aspect of legality, the concession just made by us does scant justice to the Tories—or to the truth. The dispute, it must be remembered, had arisen among a people who were then subjects of the British empire, and were proud of the fact; who exulted in the blessings of the British constitution; and who, upon the matter at issue, began by confidently appealing to that constitution for support. The contention of the Tories was that, under the constitution, the authority of the imperial parliament was, even for purposes of revenue legislation, binding in America, as in all other parts of the empire, and even though America should have no members in the house of commons. This the Whigs denied. It was, then, a question of British constitutional law. Upon that question, which of the two parties was in the right ? Is it now possible to doubt that it was the Tories ? A learned American writer upon the law, now one of the justices of the Supreme Court of the United States, in referring to the decision of Mr. Chief-Justice Hutchinson sustaining the legality of writs of assistance, has given this opinion: " A careful examination of the question compels the conclusion . . . that there was at least reasonable ground for holding, as a matter of mere law, that the British parliament had power to bind the colonies." [1]   This view, of course, has been sustained by the highest English authorities upon British constitutional law, from the time of Lord Mansfield to the present. " As a matter of abstract right," says Sir Vernon Harcourt,[2] " the

---

[1] Horace Gray, " Quincy's Mass. Reports, 1761–1762," Appendix I., page 540.

[2] Writing as " Historicus," in " The Times," for June 1, 1876, and cited in A. Todd, " Parliamentary Gov. in the Brit. Col.," 27.

mother country has never parted with the claim of ultimate supreme authority for the imperial legislature. If it did so, it would dissolve the imperial tie, and convert the colonies into foreign and independent states." "The constitutional supremacy of the imperial parliament over all the colonial possessions of the crown," says another eminent English writer, "was formally reasserted in 1865, by an act passed to remove certain doubts respecting the powers of colonial legislatures. . . . It is clear that imperial acts are binding upon the colonial subjects of the crown, as much as upon all other British subjects, whenever, by express provision or by necessary intendment, they relate to or concern the colonies."[1]

But after the question as to what was lawful under the existing constitution of the British empire, came the question as to what was expedient under the existing circumstances of the American colonies. Now, as it happened, this latter question had two aspects, one of which pointed toward the expediency of rejecting the taxing power of parliament, even though such power did exist under the constitution; the other pointed toward the expediency of separation from the empire.

Having in view, at present, the former aspect of this question, the American Whigs went forward and took the ground that, if the claim of parliament to tax them was indeed justified by the constitution, then so much the worse for the constitution,—since it was a claim too full of political danger to be any longer submitted to: "If parliament, to which we send no members, may tax us three pence on a pound of tea, it may, if it pleases, tax us a shilling, or a guinea. Once concede to it this right to tax us at all, and what security have we against its taxing us excessively ?— what security have we for our freedom or our property against any enormity of oppression ?" And what was the answer of the American Tories to this argument ? "Yes,"

---

[1] A. Todd, "Parl. Gov.," etc., 189. The act of parliament above referred to, is 28 & 29 Vict. (1865), cap. lxiii. secs. 1, 2.

said the Tories, " you allege a grave political danger. But
does it really exist ? Is it likely ever to exist ? Are you
not guilty of the fallacy of arguing against the use of a
power, simply from the possibility of its abuse ? In this
world every alleged danger must be estimated in the light
of common sense and of reasonable probability. In that
light, what ground have we for alarm ? The line drawn by
the supreme legislature itself for the exercise of its own
power, is a perfectly distinct one,—that it should tax no
part of the empire to a greater amount than its just and
equitable proportion. As respects America, the supreme
legislature has not yet overstepped that line; it has shown
no disposition to overstep that line ; we have not the
slightest reason to suppose that it ever will overstep that
line. Moreover, all the instincts of the English race are
for fair play, and would be overwhelmingly against such
an injustice, were parliament to attempt it. It is thought
in England that as we, British subjects in America, receive
our share of the benefits of membership of the empire, so
we ought to pay our share toward the cost of those benefits.
In apportioning our share of the cost, they have not fixed
upon an amount which anybody, even here, calls excessive; indeed, it is rather below than above the amount that
might justly be named. Now, in this world, affairs cannot
be conducted—civilization cannot go on—without confidence in somebody. And in this matter, we deem it reasonable and prudent to have confidence in the good sense and
in the justice of the English race, and especially of the house
of commons, which is the great council of the commoners of
the English race. True, we do not at present send members
to that great council, any more than do certain great tax-
paying communities in England; but, then, no community
even in England has, in reality, so many representatives in
parliament—so many powerful friends and champions in
both houses of parliament—as we American communities
have: not only a great minority of silent voters, but many
of the ablest debaters and party leaders there,—Barré, and

Pownall, and Conway, and Fox, and Edmund Burke in the lower house, and in the upper house Lord Camden, and, above all, the great Earl of Chatham himself. Surely, with such men as these to speak for us, and to represent our interests in parliament and before the English people, no ministry could long stand, which should propose any measure liable to be condemned as grossly beyond the line of equity and fair play.''

The Americans who took this line of reasoning in those days were called Tories. And what is to be thought of this line of reasoning to-day ? Is it not at least rational and fair ? Even though not irresistible, has it not a great deal of strength in it ? Even though we, perhaps, should have declined to adopt it, are we not obliged to say that it might have been adopted by Americans who were both clear-headed and honest-minded ?

VI.

And thus we are brought to the second aspect of the question of expediency,—the great and ultimate issue of the whole controversy,—that of Independence, which, however, need not be dealt with by us till, in the course of this history, we reach the year wherein that doctrine suddenly leaped into the arena and demanded recognition. In the meantime, for a clearer understanding of the Loyalist attitude toward all matters in dispute prior to that of Independence, it will be profitable for us here to note three grave errors closely connected with the whole subject, and still prevalent in popular American expositions of it.

First, it is an error to represent the Tories of the American Revolution as a party of mere negation and obstruction. They did deny, they did attempt to obstruct; but they also had positive political ideas, as well as precise measures in creative statesmanship to offer in the place of those ideas and measures to which they made objection, and which they would have kept from prevailing if they could.

Secondly, it is an error to represent the Tories of the American Revolution as a party opposed either to any reform in the relations of the colonists with the mother country, or to the extension of human rights and liberties here or elsewhere. From the beginning of the agitation, they clearly saw, they strongly felt, they frankly declared, that the constitutional relations of the colonies with the mother country were in a crude state, were unsatisfactory, were in need of being carefully revised and reconstructed. This admission of theirs, they never recalled. Quite aside from the question of its legality, they doubted the expediency, under modern conditions, of such an exertion of parliamentary authority as the ministry had forced into life. Upon these points, there was substantial agreement between all Americans; namely, that there was a wrong, that there was a danger, that there should be a reform. It was chiefly as to the method and the process and the scope of this needed reform, that Americans broke asunder into two great opposing parties. The exact line of cleavage between these two parties, together with the tone and the spirit characteristic of each party, may now be traced with precision in the history of the Congress of 1774. Within that body, the Tory party, both as regards its political ideas and its conscientiousness, was represented by Joseph Galloway, who then and there tried, but tried in vain, to induce the Congress to adopt such measures as would commit the American people to reform through reconciliation, rather than to reform through separation.

Thirdly, it is an error to represent the Tories of our Revolution as composed of Americans lacking in love for their native country, or in zeal for its liberty, or in willingness to labor, or fight, or even to die, for what they conceived to be its interests. As was most natural, the party which succeeded in carrying through the Congress of 1774 such measures and methods of political reform as, in fact, led to civil war, and, finally, to American Independence, took for itself the name of the patriotic party, its members being com-

monly called patriots. Beyond question, the Whig party
was a patriotic party; but it is not now apparent that
those Americans who failed in their honest and sacrificial
championship of measures which would have given us political reform and political safety, but without civil war and
without an angry disruption of the English-speaking race,
can justly be regarded as having been, either in doctrine, or
in purpose, or in act, an unpatriotic party.

CHAPTER XIV.

LOYALIST SERMON WRITERS: JONATHAN BOUCHER.

I.

WHILE almost every aspect of the Revolutionary movement may be illustrated from the published sermons of the preachers who supported that movement, the opposite is the case respecting the preachers who were in antagonism to it: their sermons having seldom found their way into print,—nay, the privilege of preaching them having been early taken away.

One of the most impressive examples of high principle and

of courageous conduct on the part of these Loyalist clergymen, is furnished by the career of Jonathan Boucher, who was born in England in 1738; removed to America in 1759; was ordained priest by the Bishop of London in 1762; served as rector in Virginia and Maryland until September, 1775; and being then " outlawed and driven away "[1] on account of his opposition to the Revolution, went back to England and was made vicar of Epsom, where he died in 1804.

He had come to America, in the first instance, as a tutor to the sons of a Virginia planter; and his taking holy orders was the result of an appeal made to him by a neighboring parish that had lost its minister. Although he performed the duties of his sacred office with great sincerity, devotion, and dignity, he never ceased to be a man of affairs, even a man of the world. He owned a large plantation, with many slaves; he conducted a boarding school for thirty or forty boys; he was active and influential in colonial politics. While in charge of the parish at Annapolis, he managed the assembly on behalf of the government, he drew up or revised nearly all the bills that passed, he wrote the speeches and messages of the governor and the most important papers of the council. He had, moreover, many a revel in newspaper controversy over affairs of church and state; he published political essays, songs, and epigrams; being a patron of the theatre, he promoted its interests by a prologue or two, and even by some lines addressed to one of the actresses.[2]

His great frankness, both in the pulpit and out of it, in opposition to the measures of the Revolutionist party, drew upon him, as was to be expected, the fiercest enmity; and in dealing with the personal attacks which, at such a time, such a man was sure to incur, he deliberately acted upon the theory, " that the true way to escape a danger is fairly

---

[1] Boucher, " A View of the Revolution," etc., 594.

[2] Passages from Boucher's " Autobiography " as contributed by his grandson, Jonathan Bouchier, to " Notes and Queries," 5th Ser. vi. 21–22.

to meet it. I have, I believe, a tolerably vigorous and resolute mind; but as to fighting, in every mode of it, there is nothing I so much dread and detest. Everything, therefore, that I did in that way was really and truly to preserve me from fighting. And it appears that I succeeded.''[1] Thus, having knocked down a burly blacksmith who had been set upon him, he acquired in all that region by that act of prowess greater honor, as he says, than would have been accorded to him there for the brains of Newton, if he had possessed them;[2] and thenceforward no man thought it prudent to provoke a personal issue with him on the supposition that he would not meet it like a gentleman.

It was, therefore, chiefly in his public capacity as a preacher that his courage was most commonly put to the test. '' I endeavored in my sermons, and in various pieces published in the gazettes of the country, to check the immense mischief that was impending, but I endeavored in vain. I was soon restrained from preaching, and the press was no longer open to me. The first open and avowed violence I met with was on account of my expressly declining, when applied to by some noisy patriots heretofore of no great note, to preach a sermon to recommend the suffering people of Boston to the charity of my parish. Their port was shut up by act of parliament; and as it was alleged that they suffered thus in the common cause, contributions were collected for them all over the continent: the true motive was by these means to raise a sum sufficient to purchase arms and ammunition. I also refused to set my hand to various associations and resolves, all, in my estimation, very unnecessary and unjust; in consequence of which I soon became a marked man, and, though I endeavored to conduct myself with all possible temper and even caution, I daily met with insults, indignities, and injuries.''[3] '' I

---

[1] Passages from Boucher's '' Autobiography '' as contributed by his grandson, Jonathan Bouchier, to '' Notes and Queries,'' 5th Ser. vi. 142.

[2] Ibid. 141.

[3] Ibid. 82.

received letters threatening me with the most dreadful consequences if I did not desist from preaching at all. All the answers I gave to these threats were in my sermons, in which I declared I could never suffer any human authority to intimidate me from doing what I believed to be my duty to God and his church; and for more than six months I preached, when I did preach, with a pair of loaded pistols lying on the cushion; having given notice that if any one attempted, what had long been threatened, to drag me out of the pulpit, I should think myself justified in repelling violence by violence. Some time after, a public fast was ordained; and on this occasion my curate, who was a strong republican, had prepared a sermon for the occasion, and supported by a set of factious men, was determined to oppose my entering my own pulpit. When the day came, I was at my church at least a quarter of an hour before the time of beginning; but, behold, Mr. Harrison was in the desk, and was expected, I was soon told, to preach. In addition to this, I saw my church filled with not less than two hundred armed men under the command of Mr. Osborne Sprigg, who soon told me I was not to preach. I returned for answer that there was but one way by which they could keep me out of it, and that was by taking away my life. At the proper time, with my sermon in one hand and a loaded pistol in the other, like Nehemiah I prepared to ascend my pulpit, when one of my friends, Mr. David Cranford, having got behind me, threw his arms round me and held me fast. He assured me that he had heard the most positive orders given to twenty men picked out for the purpose, to fire on me the moment I got into the pulpit, which therefore he never would permit me to do, unless I was stronger than himself and some others who stood close to him. I maintained that, once to flinch was forever to invite danger; but my well-wishers prevailed, and, when I was down, it is horrid to recollect what a scene of confusion ensued. Sprigg and his company contrived to surround me and to exclude every moderate man. Seeing myself thus circumstanced, it occurred to me that there was but one way to save my life,—this was by seizing Sprigg, as I immediately did, by the collar, and with my cocked pistol in the other hand, assuring him that if any violence were offered to me, I would instantly blow his brains out. I then told him he might conduct me to my house, and I would leave them. This he did, and we marched together upwards of a hundred yards, guarded by his whole company—whom he had the meanness to order to play the rogues' march all the way we went. Thus ended this dreadful day, which was a Thursday. On the following Sunday, I again went to the same church, and was again opposed, but more feebly than before. I preached the sermon I should have preached on the Thursday, with some comments on the transactions of the day." [1]

II.

Though none of Boucher's sermons were printed during the Revolution, long afterward, in 1797, he published in London a series of thirteen discourses having reference to public events in America between 1763 and 1775, and actually preached by him to various congregations in the two colonies with which he had been connected. Dealing, thus, with the chief topics that employed and agitated the minds of the American people, from the time of the English acquisition of Canada to that of the battle of Bunker Hill and the assumption by Washington of the command of the American forces, it was not unsuitable that the volume containing these remarkable sermons should be entitled " A View of the Causes and Consequences of the American Revolution." Nowhere else, probably, can be found so comprehensive, so able, and so authentic a presentation of the deeper principles and motives of the American Loyalists, particularly from the standpoint of a high-church clergyman of great purity and steadiness of character, of great moral courage,

---

[1] " Notes and Queries," 5th Ser. i. 103–104.

of great learning, finally, of great love for the country thus torn and distracted by fratricidal disagreements. " The unpopularity of my principles," said he more than thirty years after these discourses were written, " cannot, I should hope, be fairly objected to by any man who really loves truth; because it is at least some proof that my intentions are sincere, and that I am in earnest. And though it be true that there is nothing particularly attractive or alluring in the composition of these discourses, yet, as that may in some degree, perhaps, arise from their so often adverting to minute and ordinary facts and circumstances not likely to be noticed by other writers, even this defect may be pardoned by those who are less solicitous to be amused than edified, and are desirous thoroughly to understand the subject." [1]

Perhaps the deepest impression now to be made by these writings, is that of the intellectual sincerity of their author; the independence and purity of his quest for the truth; the thoroughness, refinement, and nobility of his usual method in dealing with the preplexing subjects discussed by him; his absolute fidelity to his own opinions in total disregard of their opposition to those then stormily in vogue about him.

Thus, in 1763, at a time of passionate and clamorous enthusiasm over military success and military glory, he calmly deprecates both, as products of " a perversion and misapplication of fine talents "; he contrasts the great generals of history—" the butchers and destroyers of their kind " — with men like Socrates, Fénelon, and William Penn, the true guardians and benefactors of the human family. " True greatness," he tells a people then electrified by a splendid embodiment of military genius last seen on the heights of Quebec, " deserves all the honor that the world can pay it; but fields dyed with blood are not the scenes in which true greatness is most likely to be found. He who simplifies a mechanical process, who supplies us with a new convenience or comfort, or even he who con-

---

[1] " A View," etc., Pref. xxiii.–xxiv.

trives an elegant superfluity, is, in every proper sense of the phrase, a more useful man than any of those masters in the art of destruction, who, to the shame of the world, have hitherto monopolized almost all its honors.''[1] Among a people accustomed to regard the American Indians as noxious vermin to be exterminated as fast as possible, he declares that the habitual treatment of these people by English Christians from the beginning, had been '' equally unsuitable to the genius of our government and the mild spirit of our religion.''[2] Among a people accustomed for more than a hundred years to be supported by the labor of slaves, he asserts that if ever the American colonies are to '' be improved to their utmost capacity, an essential part of the improvement must be the abolition of slavery.''[3] '' I believe it is capable of demonstration that, except the immediate interest which every man has in the property of his slaves, it would be for every man's interest that there were no slaves; and for this plain reason, because the free labor of a free man, who is regularly hired and paid for the work which he does, and only for what he does, is, in the end, cheaper than the extorted eye-service of a slave.''[4]

III.

With the same independence of mind, with the same indisposition to purchase popularity by adapting his doctrines to its demands, he dealt from the pulpit with the several topics which, during the subsequent twelve years, came into the dispute between the colonies and the English ministry.   The spirit in which he approached all these

---

[1] '' A View,'' etc., 10–11.   [2] Ibid. 29.   [3] Ibid. 40.

[4] Ibid. 39.   Like many other Americans at that time who disapproved of slavery, Boucher himself kept slaves ; but he was noted for the enlightenment and humanity of his treatment of them.   Long afterward, he wrote in his '' Autobiography '' that no compliment was ever paid him which went so near his heart as that which was bestowed by a negro, who, when asked to whom he belonged, replied, '' To Parson Boucher, thank God ! '' '' Notes and Queries,' 5th Ser. vi. 23.   When, in 1775, he and his family were compelled to flee from the country, they left their house amidst the tears and cries of their slaves. Ibid. 5th Ser. i. 104.

troublesome matters was, without variation, that of an old-fashioned believer in church and king,—in the divine origin and the divine authority of government, consequently, in obedience to government as a religious as well as a civil duty: " Of all the theories respecting the origin of government, with which the world has been either puzzled, amused, or instructed, that of the Scriptures alone is accompanied by no insuperable difficulties. It was not to be expected from an all-wise and all-merciful Creator, that, having formed creatures capable of order and rule, he should turn them loose into the world under the guidance only of their own unruly wills,—that, like so many wild beasts, they might tear and worry one another in their mad contests for preëminence. . . . We are, indeed, so disorderly and unmanageable, that were it not for the restraints and the terrors of human laws, it would not be possible for us to dwell together. But as men were clearly formed for society and to dwell together, which yet they cannot do without the restraints of law, or, in other words, without government, it is fair to infer that government was also the original intention of God, who never decrees the end, without also decreeing the means. Accordingly, when man was made . . . as soon as there were some to be governed, there were also some to govern. . . . Copying after the fair model of heaven itself, wherein there was government even among the angels, the families of the earth were subjected to rulers, at first set over them by God. ' For there is no power, but of God: the powers that be are ordained of God.' · The first father, was the first king. . . . Hence it is, that our church, in perfect conformity with the doctrine here inculcated, in her explication of the fifth commandment, from the obedience due to parents, wisely derives the congenial duty of ' honoring the king, and all that are put in authority under him.' '' [1]

Nor was he content with merely putting forward his own doctrine of the divine origin and authority of government:

---

[1] " A View," etc., 523–530.

he boldly denounced as false and disastrous the opposite doctrine then commonly held and loudly advocated by most people about him. " Government being assumed to be a mere human ordinance, it is thence inferred that ' rulers are the servants of the public '; and, if they be, no doubt it necessarily follows, that they may—in the coarse phrase of the times—be ' cashiered ' or continued in pay, be reverenced or resisted, according to the mere whim or caprice of those over whom they are appointed to rule."[1] " This low opinion of government naturally produces another false and dangerous estimate of things: in proportion as government is degraded, those who depress it exalt themselves. Hence, to be a friend of government, subjects a man to the mortifying suspicion of being of an abject and servile mind; whilst popularity is sure to attach to those who oppose government, or rather perhaps the ministers of government. And hence, too, as flimsy oratory is always most in vogue when sound principles and sound learning are least so, our forest committees, aping the members of our conventions and congresses in their volubility of speech, as well as in their patriotism, harangue not less vehemently on those unvarying topics—the abuses of government, the vileness of those whom they call the tools of government, the disinterestedness of opposition, and the genuine love of liberty which actuates those who conduct opposition. . . . This is not all. As though there were some irresistible charm in extemporaneous speaking, however rude, the orators of our committees and sub-committees, like those in higher spheres, ' prevail with their tongues.' To public speakers alone is the government of our country now completely committed. It is cantoned out into new districts, and subjected to the jurisdiction of these committees, who, not only without any known law, but directly in the teeth of all law whatever, issue citations, sit in judgment, and inflict pains and penalties on all whom they are pleased to consider as delinquents. Not only new crimes have been

---

[1] " A View," etc., 544.

thus created, but also new punishments, in comparison with which even the interdiction from fire and water among the Romans was mild and merciful." [1]

Of course, to this writer there could have been nothing but pestilent folly in the notion, then becoming popular, " that the whole human race is born equal; and that no man is naturally inferior or in any respect subjected to another; and that he can be made subject to another only by his own consent. The position is equally ill-founded and false, both in its premises and conclusions. In hardly any sense that can be imagined, is the position strictly true; but, as applied to the case under consideration, it is demonstrably not true. Man differs from man in everything that can be supposed to lead to supremacy and subjection. . . . Without government, there can be no society; nor, without some relative inferiority and superiority, can there be any government." [2]

IV.

With these as his fundamental principles concerning man and society, it is easy to infer what must have been his attitude toward the entire movement of thought and sentiment which constituted the American Revolution: he deplored and opposed it, but always like a gentleman, a scholar, and a Christian. " Many old men among us," said he, in 1771, in a sermon at St. Mary's Church, Caroline County, Virginia, " who had the happiness to be established in their principles in other times than these, see and lament that a great change has taken place . . . in Virginia. . . . Loyalty, in its excesses, may have been absurd, but it never was servile. Even in those days of exuberant loyalty, our people were capable of thinking for themselves, and what they thought, they were not afraid to assert. Virginia was the last of the British dominions that submitted to Cromwell's usurpation, and the first that proclaimed Charles the Second king. But now, taking our cue from popular

---

[1] " A View," etc., 319-321.   [2] Ibid. 514-515.

declaimers and popular writers in the parent state, we are as forward as the boldest to reprobate all those high notions of loyalty which so honorably distinguished us in the best periods of our history. On the principles of an equal zeal for the prerogatives of the crown, and for the just liberties of the people, our constitution was founded; and on these alone it can now be maintained,—though every pert smatterer in politics has the hardiness and irreverence to attack all those its strong points, which our ancestors reverenced as its chief excellence and support. It surely was something more than ridiculous, when, not long since, a popular candidate at one of our elections solicited your suffrages in his favor, on the plea of his being as to his political tenets a Whig and the advocate of Revolution principles, and in religion a low churchman. If folly can ever excuse audacity, this man's utter ignorance of the terms he used, may be admitted as some apology for his presumption. There is, no doubt, a sober sense to which these now fashionable terms may be restricted, so as not to be inconsistent with the duties which every wise and good man owes to his country; but, it is with sorrow I declare, this is not the sense in which I have of late generally heard them used, or in which they were used by the popular candidate in question. The conduct of those among us who are most forward to assume these titles, affords but too frequent proofs that to be a Whig, consists in being haughty and overbearing in domestic life, in being insolent to inferiors and tyrannical to slaves; that to support Revolution principles, is in everything to oppose and thwart the executive power; and that to be a low churchman, is to entertain and avow a low opinion of religion in general, and especially of established religion,—manifested by never going to church. That so total and important a change in the public mind cannot fail to have a mighty influence on the whole of our colonial system, is evident.'' [1]

Perhaps on no other portion of the field of Revolutionary thought is the light thrown by this writer more powerful

---

[1] '' A View,'' etc., 97–99.

than on that relating to the stormy controversy concerning
the American episcopate,—a controversy not less vital in
the development of the Revolution, than that earlier one
over the Stamp Act, or than that later one over the tea
tax.   The ability and the vigor with which Boucher maintained the proposition that the Anglican Church in America
had the right, by the introduction of bishops, to complete
its own necessary organization there, and that this involved
no menace to the religious or the civil liberties of the
American people, may be seen in his discourses '' On
Schisms and Sects,'' [1] and ''On the American Episcopate.'' [2]

Finally, concerning the secular dispute between the colonies and the British ministry from 1767 to 1774, Boucher,
like nearly all other American Loyalists, evidently thought
that the course of the ministry was a blunder; that the
colonies had serious grievances to be redressed; and that
these grievances would be fairly redressed, if the colonies,
trusting to the resistless though slow operation of moral
forces, should make their petitions and remonstrances in the
right way.   And what was the right way ?   It was that of
colonial action through their regular legislatures, and not
through irregular and lawless committees, conventions, and
congresses.   '' It is your duty,'' said he, '' to instruct your
members to take all the constitutional means in their power
to obtain redress.   If those means fail of success, you cannot but be sorry and grieved; but you will better bear your
disappointment, by being able to reflect that it was not
owing to any misconduct of your own.   .   .   .   Those
persons are as little acquainted with general history, as they
are with the particular doctrines of Christianity, who represent such submission as abject and servile.   I affirm, with
great authority, that there can be no better way of asserting the people's lawful rights, than the disowning unlawful
commands, by thus patiently suffering.   When this doctrine was more generally embraced, our holy religion gained
as much by submission, as it is now in a fair way of losing
for want of it.   Having, then, my brethren, thus long been

---

[1] '' A View,'' etc., 46–88.   [2] Ibid. 89–151.

tossed to and fro in a wearisome circle of uncertain traditions, or in speculations and projects still more uncertain,
concerning government, what better can you do than, following the apostle's advice, ' to submit yourselves to every
ordinance of man, for the Lord's sake; whether it be to the
king as supreme, or unto governors, as unto them that are
sent by him for the punishment of evil-doers, and for the
praise of them that do well ? For, so is the will of God,
that with well-doing ye may put to silence the ignorance of
foolish men; as free, and not using your liberty for a cloak
of maliciousness, but as the servants of God. Honor all
men : love the brotherhood : fear God : honor the king.' " [1]

It was for the crime of giving such instruction as this to
his congregation, in the parish of Queen Anne in Prince
George's County, Maryland, that he was at last forcibly
prevented from entering his own pulpit, and was treated, as
he himself declared, " with such unmerited insult and indig-
nity as, I believe, has seldom been experienced by persons
of my calling in any civilized and Christian country." [2]

---

[1] "A View," etc., 559–560.

[2] Ibid. 562. These words are from his " Farewell Sermon," preached in
1775. Of this noble-minded and very able man, there are two sketches by
Francis L. Hawks, one being in his "Contributions to the Ecclesiastical
History of the United States," ii. 269–278, the other in Sprague, "Annals,"
etc., v. 211–214. A good short account of Boucher by W. P. Courtney is to be
found in the " Dictionary of National Biography," sub. nom. Much valuable
material relating to Boucher has been published in "Notes and Queries," contributed by Walter Thornbury, by a writer under the signature of " Thrax,"
by Joseph Lemuel Chester, and by Jonathan Bouchier, a grandson of the old
Loyalist : 3d Ser. ix. 75–76, 282–284 ; 5th Ser. i. 102–104 ; v. 501–503 ; vi.
21–23, 81–83, 141–143, 161–162 ; ix. 50, 68, 89, 311, 371. A very important
topic connected with Boucher, is that of his relations with Washington, which
were for many years very intimate and cordial, though roughly disturbed by the
Revolution ; and besides the material in " Notes and Queries," the subject is
illustrated by a paper from Moncure Daniel Conway, in " Lippincott's Magazine," for May, 1889, containing many letters which had passed between
Boucher and Washington. These letters were placed in Mr. Conway's hands
by a grandson of Boucher, Mr. Lampson-Locker of London, known in literature as Frederick Locker, who mentions that Thackeray had had the reading of
them when he was writing " The Virginians." Among the studies which occupied Boucher after his return to England was one which led him to compile a
" Glossary of Archaic and Provincial Words," published in London in 1832–1833.

CHAPTER XV.

THE LOYALISTS IN ARGUMENT AGAINST THE MEASURES
OF THE FIRST CONGRESS—THE " WESTCHESTER
FARMER": NOVEMBER, 1774–APRIL, 1775.

I.—The papers of the first Continental Congress—The great impression made
by them in Great Britain—Lord Chatham's tribute—Testimony of British
newspapers.

II.—The two rival methods for American opposition—The bolder method
decided on by the Congress—A commercial war against England—" The
Association."

III.—Attack on the measures of the Congress by a " Westchester Farmer "—His
" Free Thoughts "—Tone and style of this powerful writer—Sounds an
alarm to the agricultural class as to the odious and dangerous features of
" The Association "—Great excitement caused by this pamphlet.

IV.—The " Westchester Farmer's " second pamphlet, " The Congress Canvassed "—An alarmist appeal to the merchants of New York—The wider
range and more elaborate character of this discussion—Constitutional and
economic aspects of the question.

V.—The " Westchester Farmer's " third pamphlet, " A View of the Controversy," in reply to Alexander Hamilton's " Full Vindication of the Measures of the Congress "—A broad treatment of the most important questions
involved—The Farmer's fourth pamphlet, "An Alarm to the Legislature of
the Province of New York"—His fifth pamphlet advertised April 20,
1775, but never published.

VI.—The " Westchester Farmer's " gifts for controversial authorship—His extraordinary literary power—The delight and the anger produced by his
pamphlets.

VII.—The " Westchester Farmer" was Samuel Seabury, rector of St. Peter's,
Westchester—His early history—Personal traits—The dangers incurred by
him on account of these pamphlets—His abduction by a mob—His imprisonment in New Haven—Subsequent persecutions—His flight within
the British lines—His work as clergyman and physician till the close of the
war—First bishop of the American Episcopal Church.

I.

THE first Continental Congress, being in secret session
at Philadelphia from the fifth of September till the twenty-

sixth of October, 1774, took final resolution as to the course of action then to be pursued by the " United Colonies of America," in opposition to the offensive measures of the ministry. In order to win for this course of action, as far as possible, the moral support of mankind, the Congress sent forth a series of state papers, which proved to be writings of extraordinary dignity, nobility, and force:—" A Declaration of Rights and Grievances," [1] an " Address to the People of Great Britain," [2] a " Memorial to the Inhabitants of the British Colonies," [3] an " Address to the Inhabitants of Quebec," [4] and a " Petition to the King's Most Excellent Majesty." [5]

These were the state papers which, being laid on the table of the house of lords, became, on the twentieth of January, 1775, the subject of a memorable discussion in that body. " When your lordships look at the papers transmitted us from America," said Lord Chatham on that occasion; " when you consider their decency, firmness and wisdom, you cannot but respect their cause, and wish to make it your own. For myself, I must declare and avow, that in all my reading and observation—and it has been my favorite study—I have read Thucydides, and have studied and admired the master-states of the world—for solidity of reasoning, force of sagacity, and wisdom of conclusion, under such a complication of difficult circumstances, no nation or body of men can stand in preference to the General Congress at Philadelphia. I trust it is obvious to your lordships, that all attempts to impose servitude upon such men, to establish despotism over such a mighty continental nation, must be vain, must be fatal." [6]

---

[1] " Journals of the American Congress," i. 19–22. This paper was prepared by a committee consisting of twenty-five members.

[2] Ibid. 26–31. This paper was written by John Jay.

[3] Ibid. 31–38. This paper was written by Richard Henry Lee.

[4] Ibid. 40–45. This paper was written by John Dickinson.

[5] Ibid. i. 46–49. This paper, in its original form, was written by Richard Henry Lee; in the form as adopted, it was written by John Dickinson.

[6] Hansard, " Parlimentary History of England," xviii. 155–156 n.

That the impression produced on Lord Chatham by these celebrated papers was not exceptional, might be shown from other contemporaneous European testimony. Thus, immediately after their arrival in Great Britain, the " Edinburgh Advertiser " for December 23, 1774, printed them in a supplement, and at the same time declared that, being " written with so much spirit, sound reason, and true knowledge of the constitution," they " have given more real uneasiness than all the other proceedings of the Congress."

A writer in the " London Public Ledger," for about the same date, bore this testimony as to the effect of these papers upon himself: " I look on the dignity of the American Congress as equal to any assembly on earth, and their deliberations and resolutions more important in their nature and consequences than any which were ever before agitated in council." As to the estimate placed on these papers in the immediate vicinity of the court, a letter written from London, and printed in the " Boston Morning Post " for March 27, 1775, said: " It is impossible that any production could have done more honor to America, or gained more universal approbation." [1]

II.

Within the seven weeks of its session, and behind those closed doors which so well protected the privacy of the Congress, was fought out, among the political chiefs of America, the final issue between the advocates of the two rival methods for conducting American opposition to a ministerial policy which was disliked by all Americans—by Tories as well as by Whigs. Either method of opposition, it was affirmed by its supporters, would be effectual in ultimately relieving us of the offensive policy; but, while the moderate method would be likely to accomplish this result without violence, and perhaps without bitterness, the extreme method could not fail, under existing circumstances,

---

[1] R. Frothingham, " Rise of the Republic," 408–409 n.

to lead to still greater exasperation between the contending parties, to civil war, and to revolution. Then and there, however, was defeated the plan for a constitutional and a peaceful solution of the problems in dispute,—defeated, it should be remembered, by a majority of only one vote.

The method of opposition thus officially chosen, was primarily that of a commercial war with Great Britain, to be brought on by means of a universal stoppage in America of every kind of trade with her,—this to be enforced throughout the colonies by agencies of terrific energy penetrating not only every community, but every household, not to say the private habits and the private opinions of every man and woman in the land. Moreover, the declaration of this commercial war with Great Britain was accompanied by the grim hint that a war other than a merely commercial one was not unlikely to ensue upon this, and, hence, that all good Americans should extend their " views to mournful events, and be, in all respects, prepared for every contingency." [1]

Finally, for a proper appreciation of the robust character and unflinching purpose of the method of procedure which the Congress thus adopted, and which it virtually enforced upon the American people, no secondary description can compare in value with the very text of the document itself —" The Association "—which was subscribed by the fifty-two members then present in that assemblage, and which was then distributed among the people for a similar endorsement by them. After recounting the grievances resulting from the " ruinous system of colony-administration, adopted by the British ministry about the year 1763, evidently calculated for enslaving these colonies, and, with them, the British empire," the paper at once proceeds to the tremendous topic of remedy: " To obtain redress for these grievances, which threaten destruction to the lives, liberty, and property of his majesty's subjects in North America, we are of opinion, that a non-importation, non-consumption, and

---

[1] " Journals of the American Congress," i. 38.

non-exportation agreement, faithfully adhered to, will prove the most speedy, effectual, and peaceable measure; and, therefore, we do for ourselves and the inhabitants of the several colonies whom we represent, firmly agree and associate, under the sacred ties of virtue, honor, and love of our country, as follows:

" 1. That from and after the first day of December next, we will not import into British America, from Great Britain or Ireland, any goods, wares, or merchandise whatsoever, or from any other place any such goods, wares, or merchandise as shall have been exported from Great Britain or Ireland; nor will we, after that day, import any East India tea from any part of the world, nor any molasses, syrups, paneles, coffee, or pimento from the British plantations or from Dominica, nor wines from Madeira or the Western Islands, nor foreign indigo.

. . . .

" 3. As a non-consumption agreement, strictly adhered to, will be an effectual security for the observation of the non-importation, we, as above, solemnly agree and associate, that from this day we will not purchase or use any tea imported on account of the East India Company, or any on which a duty hath been or shall be paid; and from and after the first day of March next, we will not purchase or use any East India tea whatever, nor will we, nor shall any person for or under us, purchase or use any of those goods, wares, or merchandise, we have agreed not to import, which we shall know, or have cause to suspect, were imported after the first day of December.

" 4. The earnest desire we have not to injure our fellow-subjects in Great Britain, Ireland, or the West Indies, induces us to suspend a non-exportation, until the tenth day of September, 1775; at which time, if the said acts and parts of acts of the British parliament hereinafter mentioned, are not repealed, we will not directly or indirectly export any merchandise or commodity whatsoever to Great Britain, Ireland, or the West Indies, except rice to Europe.

. . . .

" 11. That a committee be chosen in every county, city, and town, by those who are qualified to vote for representatives in the legislature, whose business it shall be attentively to observe the conduct of all persons touching this Association; and when it shall be made to appear, to the satisfaction of a majority of any such committee, that any person within the limits of their appointment has violated this Association, that such majority do forthwith cause the truth of the case to be published in the gazette; to the end, that all such foes of the rights of British America may be publicly known and universally contemned as the enemies of American liberty; and thenceforth we respectively will break off all dealings with him or her.

. . . .

" 14. And we do further agree and resolve, that we will have no trade, commerce, dealings, or intercourse whatsoever, with any colony or province in North America, which shall not accede to, or which shall hereafter violate, this Association, but will hold them as unworthy of the rights of freemen, and as inimical to the liberties of their country." [1]

III.

Within two or three weeks from the day on which the Congress announced its grand scheme for an agreement among the American colonists not to import or to consume the chief materials of the English carrying-trade, nor to export the chief products of their own farms, there came from the press of New York a pamphlet, ostensibly written by a farmer, and addressed to farmers, and from the level of their particular interests subjecting the proposal of Congress to a sort of criticism that was well fitted to arouse against it the bitterest and most unrelenting opposition of the great agricultural class. This is its title: " Free Thoughts on the Proceedings of the Continental Congress, held at Philadel-

---

[1] " Journals of the American Congress," i. 23–26.

phia September 5, 1774: Wherein their Errors are exhibited, their Reasonings confuted, and the Fatal Tendency of their Non-Importation, Non-Exportation, and Non-Consumption Measures are laid open to the plainest Understandings, and the Only Means pointed out for preserving and securing our present happy Constitution.''

The writer of this pamphlet professed to be a '' Westchester Farmer,''—a signature which at once became the target for vast applause and for vast execration. Entering the great debate not as a lawyer, nor as a politician, nor as a merchant, but only as a farmer—an educated farmer, certainly, but a blunt and a sturdy one—the tremendous impression produced by him was partly due to his dramatic identification of himself with the character he had assumed —expertly adopting the Doric phrases, the rustic prejudices, even the bucolic jests natural to a brawny and manly yeoman who has read and thought much on the laws of the land, who knows his rights as an English American, who loves his country, who hates needless change and every disturbance of industry, and is indignant at seeing the prosperity, even the rights and the liberties of the people, especially those of his own class, uptorn and set in peril by the unwise and audacious interference of political adventurers. Here, accordingly, the reader need look for nothing recondite, or high-flown, or fine-spun, no over-strained sentimentality, no rapture of idealized opinion, but a simple, practical, pedestrian view of the situation, such as any stalwart farmer might present to his brother farmers. Here, also, may the Son of Sirach encounter a surprise, in the discovery that even wisdom is to be had from one that holdeth the plough and that glorieth in the goad, that driveth oxen, and is occupied in their labors, and whose talk is of bullocks.

'' My first business,'' says this stout-hearted farmer to his brethren, '' shall be to point out to you some of the consequences that will probably follow from the non-importation, non-exportation, and non-consumption agreements which '' the late Congress '' have adopted, and which they have ordered to be enforced in the most arbitrary manner, and under the severest penalties. On this subject, I choose to address myself to you, the farmers of the province of New York, because I am most nearly connected with you, being one of your number, and having no interest in the country but in common with you; and also because the interest of the farmers in general will be more sensibly affected and more deeply injured by these agreements, than the interest of any other body of people on the continent."[1]

Of these agreements, probably one consequence will be a great disturbance of business in Great Britain, Ireland, and the West Indies, accompanied by wide-spread distress in all those countries,—by discord, confusion, mobs, riots, insurrections, rebellions. True, this consequence may not at first affect us; but even if it do not, where is the justice, where is the policy, in our taking measures which are likely to bring such misfortune upon others ? " The manufacturers of Great Britain, the inhabitants of Ireland and of the West Indies have done us no injury. They have been no ways instrumental in bringing our distresses upon us. Shall we then revenge ourselves upon them ?"[2] Of course, instead of conciliating them, we shall only alienate them : of friends, we shall make them enemies. " The passions of human nature are much the same in all countries. If they find us disposed wantonly to distress them, to serve our own purposes, will they not look out for some method to do without us ? Will they not seek elsewhere for a supply of those articles which they used to take from us ? They would deserve to be despised for their meanness, did they not." Thus, this proposed measure of the Congress will seriously damage our interests as farmers,—for example, it will ruin our market for flaxseed, for which our best customers have always been the Irish. " You know, my friends, that the sale of your seed not only pays your taxes, but furnishes you with many of the little conveniences and

---

[1] " Free Thoughts," etc., 4. I use the first edition, " Printed in the Year M.DCC.LXXIV."
[2] " Free Thoughts," etc., 5.

comforts of life. The loss of it for one year would be of
more damage to you, than paying the three-penny duty on
tea for twenty. Let us compare matters a little. It was
inconvenient for me this year to sow more than one bushel
of seed. I have threshed and cleaned up eleven bushels.
The common price now is at least ten shillings. My seed,
then, will fetch me five pounds ten shillings. But I will
throw in the ten shillings for expenses. There remain five
pounds: in five pounds, are four hundred three-pences.
Four hundred three-pences, currency, will pay the duty
upon two hundred pounds of tea,—even reckoning the
exchange with London at 200 per cent., that is, reckoning
100*l.* sterling to be equal to 200*l.* currency; whereas, in
fact, it is only equal to 175*l* or 180*l.* at the most. I use in
my family about six pounds of tea. Few farmers in my
neighborhood use so much; but I hate to stint my wife and
daughters, or my friendly neighbors when they come to see
me. Besides, I like a dish of tea too, especially after a
little more than ordinary fatigue in hot weather. Now,
200 pounds of tea, at six pounds a year, will last just 33
years and eight months. So that, in order to pay this
monstrous duty on tea, which has raised all this confounded
combustion in the country, I have only to sell the produce of a bushel of flaxseed once in thirty-three years.
Ridiculous!

" But, to leave jesting. The loss of the sale of your seed
only for one year, would be a considerable damage to you.
And yet the Congress have been so inattentive to your
interests, that they have laid you under almost an absolute
necessity of losing it the next year. They have decreed
and proclaimed a non-exportation, to commence in September next. The Irish will be alarmed: they will look out
somewhere else. Or, should they determine to send their
ships the earlier, we cannot, without the utmost inconven-
ience, get our seed to market by that time,—especially not
from the remoter parts of the province. The consequence
will be, that we must sell our seed at the oil mills in New

22

York, just at the price the manufacturers shall please to give us.

" Upon the whole, then, it is highly improbable that we shall succeed in distressing the people of Great Britain, Ireland, and the West Indies, so far as to oblige them to join with us in getting the acts of parliament, which we complain of, repealed. The first distress will fall on ourselves: it will be more severely felt by us, than by any part of all his majesty's dominions; and it will affect us the longest." [1]

But this is only the beginning of the misfortunes which are coming upon us should the scheme of the Congress go into effect. Not only will it lower the market for the things we have to sell, but it will raise it for the things we have to buy. Even now, " many of you find it difficult at the year's end to pay the shopkeeper for what the necessities of your families have obliged you to take up. What will you do when the prices of goods are advanced a quarter, for instance, or a half ? " Moreover, what will happen next ? Why, that this scheme of the Congress, after throwing us into all these embarrassments, will put the finishing touch to them, by provoking the home government to block up our ports. Of course, this means the cessation of all our trade. And even if the home government should not do this, the Congress will—only in a different way; for they have decreed that within the next ten months all our trade is to be stopped anyhow. In either case, then, the result of this Congressional interference will be the same. " Should the government interpose, we shall have no trade at all, and consequently no vent for the produce of our farms. Such part of our wheat, flaxseed, corn, beef, pork, butter, cheese, as was not consumed in the province, must be left to rot and stink upon our hands. Should the government leave us to ourselves, the little trade that would be open, would never keep these articles at such a price as to make it worth while to raise more of them than we want for our own consumption." Therefore, " look well to your-

---

[1] " Free Thoughts," etc., 7–8.

selves, I beseech you. From the day that the exports from this province are stopped, the farmers may date the commencement of their ruin. Can you live without money ? Will the shopkeeper give you his goods ? Will the weaver, shoemaker, blacksmith, carpenter, work for you without pay ? If they will, it is more than they will do for me. And unless you can sell your produce, how are you to get money ? Nor will the case be better if you are obliged to sell your produce at an under-rate; for then it will not pay you for the labor and expense of raising it. But this is the least part of the distress that will come upon you.

" Unhappily, many of you are in debt, and obliged to pay the enormous interest of seven pounds on the hundred, for considerable sums. It matters not whether your debts have been contracted through necessity or carelessness : you must pay them, at least the interest, punctually. The usurer will not wait long; indeed, you cannot expect he should. You have had his money, and are obliged in justice to pay him the principal and interest according to agreement. But without selling your produce, you can neither pay the one nor the other. The consequence will be that after a while a process of law will be commenced against you, and your farms must be sold by execution; and then you will have to pay not only principal and interest, but sheriff's fees, lawyer's fees, and a long list of et cæteras. Nor, under these circumstances, will your farms fetch half what they cost you. What is a farm good for, the produce of which cannot be sold ? . . . Your creditor, then, or some rich merchant, or usurer, must take it at their own price. To you it is of no consequence who takes it—for you are ruined, stripped of your farm, and very probably of the means of subsistence for yourself and family. Glorious effect of non-exportation! Think a little, and then tell me —when the Congress adopted this cursed scheme, did they in the least consider your interest ? No, impossible! They ignorantly misunderstood, carelessly neglected, or basely betrayed you! . . . Blessed fruits of non-importation and non-exportation ! The farmer that is in debt will be ruined. The farmer that is clear in the world, will be obliged to run in debt, to support his family; and while the proud merchant, and the forsworn smuggler, riot in their ill-gotten wealth, the laborious farmers, the grand support of every well-regulated country, must all go to the dogs together. Vile, shameful, diabolical device!"[1]

Not even yet is the case complete, as against the scheme of the Congress. All these disasters are to follow from only one part of that scheme. Let us now attend to another part of it, namely, that relating to non-consumption. "After the first of March, we are not to purchase or use any East India tea whatsoever, nor any goods, wares, or merchandise from Great Britain or Ireland . . . nor any molasses, syrups, etc., from the British plantations in the West Indies, or from Dominica, nor wine from Madeira or the Western Islands, nor foreign indigo.

"Will you submit to this slavish regulation ? You must: our sovereign lords and masters, the high and mighty delegates, in grand Continental Congress assembled, have ordered and directed it! They have directed the committees in the respective colonies to establish such further regulations as they may think proper for carrying their association . . . into execution. . . . Will you be instrumental in bringing the most abject slavery on yourselves ? Will you choose such committees ? Will you submit to them, should they be chosen by the weak, foolish, turbulent part of the country people ? Do as you please; but, by Him that made me, I will not! No, if I must be enslaved, let it be by a KING at least, and not by a parcel of upstart, lawless committeemen. If I must be devoured, let me be devoured by the jaws of a lion, and not gnawed to death by rats and vermin! . . . If you like it better, choose your committee, or suffer it to be chosen by half a dozen fools in your neighborhood: open your doors to them—let them examine your tea canisters, and molasses jugs, and your wives' and

[1] "Free Thoughts," etc., 9–17.

daughters' petticoats—bow, and cringe, and tremble, and quake—fall down and worship our sovereign Lord, the Mob! But, I repeat it, by Heaven I will not! No, my house is my castle: as such I will consider it, as such I will defend it, while I have breath. No king's officer shall enter it without my permission, unless supported by a warrant from a magistrate. And shall my house be entered, and my mode of living enquired into, by a domineering committee-man? Before I submit, I will die: live you, and be slaves.

" Do, I say, as you please; but should any pragmatical committee-gentleman come to my house, and give himself airs, I shall shew him the door, and if he does not soon take himself away, a good hickory cudgel shall teach him better manners." [1]

" But perhaps you will say that these men are contending for our rights; that they are defending our liberties; and though they act against law, yet that the necessity of the time will justify them. . . . These men defend our rights and liberties? . . . No, they are making us the most abject slaves that ever existed. The necessity of the times justify them in violating the first principles of civil society? Who induced this necessity? Who involved the province in discord, anarchy, and confusion? They created that necessity, which they now plead in their own justification.

" Let me entreat you, my friends, to have nothing to do with these men, or with any of the same stamp. Peace and quietness suit you best. Confusion, and discord, and violence, and war, are sure destruction to the farmer. . . . Peace, indeed, is departed from us for the present, and the protection of the laws has ceased. But, I trust in God, there is yet one method left, which by prudent management will free us from all our difficulties, restore peace again to our dwellings, and give us the firm security of the laws for our protection. Renounce all dependence on congresses and committees. They have neglected or betrayed your interests. Turn, then, your eyes to your constitu-

---

[1] " Free Thoughts," etc., 13-19.

tional representatives. They are the true, and legal, and
have been hitherto the faithful, defenders of your rights and
liberties; and you have no reason to think but that they will
ever be so. They will probably soon meet in general assembly. Address yourselves to them. They are the proper
persons to obtain redress for any grievances that you
can justly complain of. You can trust their wisdom and
prudence, that they will use the most reasonable, constitutional, and effectual methods of restoring that peace and
harmony between Great Britain and this province, which is
so earnestly wished for by all good men, and which is so
absolutely necessary for the happiness of all.'' [1]

Thus, then, into the arena of the great debate leaped this
fearless intellectual gladiator. To right and to left were
dealt his tremendous blows—to the ground tumbled many
an antagonist—far and fierce rang shouts of exultation, or
howls of anger and hate. Can he hold his own at this great
pace ? Can he keep up for long this superb fighting ?

IV.

The first pamphlet of the '' Westchester Farmer '' was
dated November 16, 1774. Twelve days from that date
came his second one—as keen, as fiery, as powerful as the
first: '' The Congress Canvassed [2]; or, An Examination into
the Conduct of the Delegates at their Grand Convention,
held in Philadelphia, September 1, 1774.'' Addressing now
the merchants of New York, even as in his first pamphlet he
had addressed its farmers, he declines to offer any apology
for laying his opinions before them: '' You must be content
with plain English, from a plain countryman: I must have
the privilege of calling a fig—a fig, an egg—an egg.'' [3]

---

[1] '' Free Thoughts,'' etc., 22–23.

[2] In a list of the pamphlets of the '' Westchester Farmer,'' as given by the
author of them, probably from memory, in 1783, he mentions one as being ''An
Address to the Merchants of New York.'' I have not met with any pamphlet
of his having that for its chief title ; while the pamphlet above cited is declared,
on its title-page, to be '' Addressed to the Merchants of New York.'' I think
that this, therefore, is the pamphlet intended.

[3] ''The Congress Canvassed,'' 3.

From first to last, then, he preserves the tone and bearing of a blunt, unterrified farmer, but with a mastery of eloquent statement, and of philosophy, history, politics, and constitutional law, not commonly to be met with in men of his class—or of any class. Launching out into a wider range of discussion than he had previously taken, he yet holds himself steady to his main purpose of exposing what he regards as the imposture, the assumption, the tyranny, and the folly of the late Congress. It was a law-making body unknown to the law or to the constitution of the country; its members had no real claim to represent the government or the people of their several provinces; in many cases their election was a sham, in all cases invalid; the doctrines they have put forth are unsound, misleading, dangerous; from beginning to end, the measures they have undertaken to force upon the people, are without authority, are tyrannical, will bring on unspeakable calamity.

As to their doctrines, all run back to this new and shallow heresy, that the allegiance of the American colonies is due to the king alone, and not to the parliament. " It is a distinction made by the American republicans to serve their own rebellious purposes,—a gilding with which they have enclosed the pill of sedition, to entice the unwary colonists to swallow it the more readily down. The king of Great Britain was placed on the throne by virtue of an act of parliament; and he is king of America by virtue of being king of Great Britain. He is, therefore, king of America by act of parliament. And if we disclaim that authority of parliament which made him our king, we, in fact, reject him from being our king,—for we disclaim that authority by which he is king at all.

" Let us not, gentlemen, be led away from our duty and allegiance by such fantastical distinctions. They are too nice and subtile for practice, and fit only for Utopian schemes of government. We have so long paid attention to sophistical declamations about liberty and property, the power of government and the rights of the people, the force of laws and the benefit of the constitution, that we have very little of any of them left among us; and if we continue to support and imitate the mad schemes of our Eastern neighbors, in the manner we have done, in a very short time we shall have none at all." [1]

Indeed, it would be most fortunate if the doctrines promulgated by the Congress were merely false in theory: for they will surely prove most disastrous in practice. "We have hitherto proceeded from bad to worse. It is time to consider and correct our conduct. As yet, it has done us no good: if persisted in too far, it will bring ruin upon us. It is our duty to make some proposals of accommodation with our parent country. And they ought to be reasonable ones,—such as might be made with safety on our part, and accepted with dignity on hers. But if we expect to oblige her to propose a reconciliation, to ask and entreat us to accept of such and such terms, to force her to concede everything, while we will concede nothing,—if we are determined to proceed as we have done, continually rising in our demands and increasing our opposition,—I dread to think of the consequence. The authority of Great Britain over the colonies must cease, or the force of arms must finally decide the dispute. Many Americans are hardy enough to suppose that, in such a contest, we should come off victorious. But horrid indeed would be the consequence of our success! We should presently turn our arms on one another, province against province, and destruction and carnage would desolate the land. Probably it would cost the blood of a great part of the inhabitants of America to determine what kind of a government we should have, whether a monarchy or a republic. Another effusion of blood would be necessary to fix a monarch, or to establish the commonwealth. But it is much more probable, that the power of the British arms would prevail; and then, after the most dreadful scenes of violence and slaughter, confiscations and executions must close the horrid tragedy." [2]

---

[1] "The Congress Canvassed," 26.   [2] Ibid. 26–27.

V.

Such was the second pamphlet of the " Westchester Farmer." In the meantime, his first pamphlet had already caused great commotion in the camp of the radical party. It could not be suffered to go unanswered. Answers, accordingly, sprang up on every hand,—the most notable one being "A Full Vindication of the Measures of the Congress, from the Calumnies of their Enemies," by a writer whose name was then concealed, but who is now known to have been Alexander Hamilton—" the marvellous boy "— then but seventeen years of age and an undergraduate of King's College. On the twenty-fourth of December, 1774, in less than four weeks from the day of his second pamphlet, the undaunted farmer was ready with a third one, —this being in reply to Hamilton's attack, and entitled " A View of the Controversy between Great Britain and her Colonies: Including a Mode of determining their present Disputes finally and effectually, and preventing all future Contentions." The method of this pamphlet is that of a strong fighter conscious of having come into close quarters with an antagonist worthy of him: he is self-possessed, wary, expert, full of resource, aroused, determined, watching to give the thrust which shall kill. Here, again, the range of the discussion is still further widened; and, indeed, the whole vast question then at issue between England and America, in its every aspect of constitutional law, of equity, of general expediency, is here discussed by this masterful farmer, and discussed with learning, acuteness, lucidity, with occasional bursts of stormy eloquence, with no little cleverness of humorous and sarcastic phrase. Here, likewise, as in every other pamphlet by the same writer, care is taken to keep prominent the fact that the American opponents of revolutionary measures are themselves dissatisfied with the existing relations of America toward the parent state; and that, while they reject the disloyal and exasperating remedy proposed by the Congress, they are not without a remedy of their own, namely, " the settlement of an

American constitution "[1] providing for colonial home-rule under the sovereign authority of the imperial parliament. "This is a scheme which we shall probably succeed in, if we attempt it with proper prudence and temper."[2] "If we grasp at too much, we shall lose everything."[3] "This scheme will secure us from slavery, and too abject a dependence on our fellow-subjects in England."[4] At the same time, "the dependence of the colonies on the mother country, will be fixed on a firm foundation; the sovereign authority of parliament over all the dominions of the empire, will be established; and the mother country and all her colonies will be knit together in one grand, firm, and compact body."[5] "You, sir, may, if you please, pride yourself in this suspicious, jealous, parsimonious, stingy, contracted, disposition of the Congress; you may call it 'equity,' 'wisdom,' 'dignity.' Be it my glory to have contributed, even in the smallest degree, to the honor, splendor, and majesty of the British empire. My ancestors were among the first Englishmen who settled in America. I have no interest but in America. I have not a relation out of it that I know of. Yet, let me die! but I had rather be reduced to the last shilling, than that the imperial dignity of Great Britain should sink, or be controlled by any people or power on earth."[6]

No sooner was this pamphlet off his hands, and a stunning blow thus given to his chief assailant, than the "Westchester Farmer" seems to have set to work upon his fourth pamphlet, wherein, turning away from all unauthorized political bodies—congresses, committees, associations, and the like—he addresses himself most solemnly to the one political body in the province which had any legal character, and was competent, besides, to interpose in that frightful emergency, and to lead all good citizens into a line of action certain to result in a manly, free, and loyal solution of their

---

[1] "A View of the Controversy," etc., 23.
[2] Ibid. 21.
[3] Ibid. 22.
[4] Ibid.
[5] Ibid. 21.
[6] Ibid. 23

difficulties. The pamphlet thus sent forth to the world had this title: " An Alarm to the Legislature of the Province of New York, occasioned by the present political Disturbances in North America: addressed to the honorable Representatives in General Assembly convened." [1]

Although they are, as he tells them, the only legal representatives of the people of the province, yet they have of late been utterly disregarded, their dignity trampled on, their authority contravened. " A committee, chosen in a tumultuous, illegal manner, usurped the most despotic authority over the province. They entered into contracts, compacts, combinations, treaties of alliance, with the other colonies, without any power from the legislature of this province." [2] " A foreign power is brought in to govern this province. Laws made at Philadelphia, by factious men from New England, New Jersey, Pennyslvania, Maryland, Virginia, and the Carolinas, are imposed upon us by the most imperious menaces. Money is levied upon us without the consent of our representatives,—which very money, under color of relieving the poor of Boston, it is too probable, will be employed to raise an army against the king. Mobs and riots are encouraged, in order to force submission to the tyranny of the Congress." [3] " To you, gentlemen, the good people of this province look for relief: on you they have fixed their hopes; from you they expect deliverance from this intolerable state of slavery. . . . If you assert your own dignity, if you maintain your own rights and privileges, we shall again be a free and happy, and, I trust, not an ungrateful people. . . . If laws made and decrees passed at Philadelphia, by the enthusiastic republicans of New England and Virginia, are to bind the people of this province, and extort money from them, why, gentlemen, do you meet ? Is it barely to register their edicts, and to rivet the fetters of their tyranny on your constituents ?

[1] This pamphlet was not signed ; but it has all the characteristic traits of the " Westchester Farmer," and was afterward avowed by him as his.

[2] " An Alarm," etc., 4–5.   [3] Ibid. 7.

. . . Your duty requires you to interpose your authority, and to break up this horrid combination of seditious men, which has already enslaved this province, and which was intended to draw the faithful subjects of our most gracious sovereign into rebellion and civil war." [1]

The date of this fourth pamphlet is January 17, 1775. On the twentieth of the following April,—only one day after the ghastly business at Lexington and Concord, but several days before the story of it could have reached New York,—there appeared in the " New York Gazetteer " the advertisement of still another pamphlet by a " Westchester Farmer," as " speedily to be published." This pamphlet was to have had for its title," The Republican Dissected; or, The Anatomy of an American Whig." It is not unlikely that the events of the nineteenth of April, as the tidings of them flew across the land, may have seemed to the public to be so literal and realistic a presentation of the very theme undertaken by this intended pamphlet, that its publication was prudently withheld.[2] At any rate, no copy of it is known to exist.

VI.

Without doubt, the pamphlets of the " Westchester Farmer " which thus came from the press in swift succession, reveal in their writer extraordinary gifts for authorship— particularly for popular controversial authorship. In the course of that long and savage debate, some pamphlets were written even on the same side, more learned than these, more elaborate and more deliberate in their treatment of constitutional law, more conciliatory in tone, more elegant in style; but no other pamphlets on the Loyalist side, and

---

[1] " An Alarm," etc., 7–8.

[2] In a note by Dr. T. B. Chandler written in a copy of " The Farmer Refuted," it is stated that " The Republican Dissected " was a rejoinder to that pamphlet, but was not published because, " by a sudden and unexpected revolution, the liberty of the press was totally destroyed, and nothing could be printed on the side of government." Paul Leicester Ford, " Bibliotheca Hamiltoniana," 5.

perhaps the pamphlets of but one writer [1] on the side of
the Revolutionists, were a match for these writings of the
" Westchester Farmer" for immediate effect upon the
mass of readers in a time of violent stir and commotion.
Indeed, the purely literary merits of these essays are such as
to entitle them to a high and a permanent reputation in the
literature of the American Revolution.   Even now, no one
can fail to find pleasure in them, who delights in genuine
English — pure, Saxon, sinewy ; in a style that moves
straight to the mark, every epithet a flash of fire, every sentence a spear-point; in pages all alive, and charged to the
full with force or humor or satire, with telling illustration,
with picturesqueness, with repartee, with outbursts of eloquent indignation, with bravuras of patriotic enthusiasm or
scorn.   Probably no pamphlets more readable, none more
witty and brilliant, none argumentatively more effective,
were called forth on either side of the question during the
whole controversy.   Even after the lapse of a hundred
years, and after the facts of history have set at naught the
dire prophecies of the " Westchester Farmer," and have
made void his logic, and have covered his political philosophy with the contempt commonly given to futile things,
any person properly acquainted with the historic situation
out of which these pamphlets sprang into life, may still find
for himself the secret of their original power, may still feel
in his own soul something of the enormous effects they
wrought, as they first swept through the country, and overpowered every reader, and carried him along in a mighty
flood of sympathetic argument and passion, or else set him
awrithing with intellectual anguish—disconcerted him, mad-
dened him—by their magnificent championship of political
doctrines which he loathed.

VII.

As to the authorship of these celebrated pamphlets, the
popular suspicion almost immediately fastened upon Samuel

---

[1] I refer to Thomas Paine.

Seabury, at that time rector of the parish of St. Peter, in Westchester; forty-five years of age, a native of Connecticut, a graduate of Yale College, himself descended from some of the earliest settlers in New England—including John Alden; after the Revolution, renowned as the first bishop of the American Episcopal Church. Although in the present century and by many American scholars, the glory or the shame of having written the essays of the " Westchester Farmer " has been awarded to others—to Chandler, to Inglis, to Myles Cooper, and particularly to Isaac Wilkins—it has at last been placed beyond dispute that the contemporaneous popular instinct, which attributed these essays to Samuel Seabury, was correct.[1]

As the actual cultivator of the glebe attached to his benefice, Seabury had a literal claim to his assumed title of " Westchester Farmer." He was a man builded after an heroic pattern: a man of powerful frame, of robust health, of tremendous energy—physical, mental, moral; of great and varied experience in the affairs of life; a physician, a theologian, a scholar; a terse and vigorous writer ; an orator of impassioned and commanding speech; his mind firmly made up to clear and reverent conclusions on all

---

[1] In the first place, it is not true, as is sometimes said, that Seabury himself ever denied that he was the author of the "Westchester Farmer" pamphlets. While in peril of his life at New Haven in 1775, he did plead " not guilty " to the charge of having written "pamphlets and newspapers against the liberties of America "; but that description did not, in his opinion, apply to the pamphlets of the " Westchester Farmer," which, as he always insisted, were on behalf of " the liberties of America," and not against them. Seabury's "Memorial," in Beardsley, 38–39. During the same imprisonment, when the authorship of those particular pamphlets was by name charged upon him, he refused to disavow them, although, as he wrote soon afterward, such disavowal would have occasioned his speedy release. Letter by Seabury, in Beardsley, 45–46. In the second place, while Seabury never denied their authorship, he did expressly lay claim to it, and that under circumstances of great seriousness. In the year 1783, being then in London seeking consecration as bishop, he submitted a memorial to the commissioners appointed by the British government to consider the claims of the American Loyalists ; and in that memorial he declares himself to be the author of the pamphlets of the " Westchester Farmer," the titles of which he gives. I have had in my hands Seabury's manuscript first

the great subjects that man, either alone or in society, has to deal with. Moreover, there were in Seabury a singular courage of opinion, a downrightness of utterance, a necessity for the frank and emphatic expression of whatsoever convictions were within him, an inability to dodge important issues, or to shuffle off responsibility, or to shirk a painful duty; with all this, too, a grave and manly prudence, entire freedom from frothy zeal, or from light-headed impetuosity, or from ambition for social martyrdom.

Almost at once after the appearance of his first pamphlet, the " Westchester Farmer " began to be threatened with dire vengeance. Not being able to lay their hands upon his person, some of those who were incensed at him gathered up copies of his pamphlets, and burned them at the stake; or, covering them with a coat of tar and feathers, they nailed them to a whipping-post,—all as a dramatic intimation of the sort of treatment which he himself might expect, should he fall into their hands.[1]

Within a year from the date of the first of his pamphlets, the public anger against Seabury, especially in the colony of Connecticut, had risen to such a pitch as to lead to a bold and a perfectly lawless plan for suppressing him by force—possibly, even for putting him to death. On Wed-

---

draft of this memorial, still in the possession of the Reverend Professor W. J. Seabury, of the General Theological Seminary in New York ; and it has since been printed in full in " The Magazine of American History," viii. 119–121. In the third place, in the year 1797, one year after Seabury's death, his authorship of these pamphlets was expressly re-affirmed by one of his most intimate and most confidential friends, the Reverend Jonathan Boucher, in " A View of the Causes and Consequences of the American Revolution," 556–557 n. Finally, the only person who, besides Seabury, has been in our time regarded as having any serious claim to this authorship, is Isaac Wilkins ; but in his memorial, entitled " My Services and Losses," etc., edited by Paul Leicester Ford, Brooklyn, 1890, while stating freely what he had done " in aid of the king's cause during the American Revolution," he makes no mention of having been even in part the author of the " Westchester Farmer " pamphlets. I think it may fairly be said that, among persons who have seen all the evidence, the question as to the authorship of these pamphlets is no longer an open one.

[1] " What Think Ye of the Congress Now?" 4–5 ; E. E. Beardsley, " Life of Seabury," 28–29.

nesday, the 22d of November, 1775, while engaged in the beneficent duties of his calling, he was suddenly seized, like a malefactor, by a band of armed men acting without any color of authority—excepting that of mob-law. The place of his arrest was at some distance from his home,—at a little school-house, where he was just then at work among his pupils. As he was being dragged away from it, towards the rectory, he was met by one of his daughters, who, in great terror, with hat torn from her head and hair hanging disheveled over her shoulders, had fled to him from their home. A dreadful story she had to relate to her father, of an experience unexampled, we may be well assured, in that orderly community, in that virtuous and honored household. These armed men, it seems,—mostly strangers in the village and even in the colony,—had at first gone straight to the rectory, which they had rudely entered—demanding the person of its master. Not finding him there, they had insulted and terrified his daughters, in the effort to compel them to say where their father could be found,—thrusting a bayonet through the cap of one of them, piercing with a bayonet the handkerchief about her neck, and pushing a bayonet against her bosom, with a threat to kill her; the men likewise amusing themselves by tossing and tearing with their bayonets the needlework on which the young ladies had been engaged. From this scene of outrage, one of the daughters had escaped, and had fled for help in the direction of her father,—but only to find him overpowered and a prisoner in the hands of about forty of the same band of men who had taken possession of his house.

And now hurried thither by these men, he was given merely time to send for his horse; and this interval his captors used in compelling his wife to open his desk, which they ransacked at will—peering into his most private papers, carrying off the money which they found there—besides pillaging the house of silver spoons, and such other valuable articles as these sons of liberty were able to lay their hands on. As soon as his horse was brought to him, the reverend prisoner was forced to mount, and to go off with his captors; and, in gross violation of every legal right, he was conducted across the borders of his own colony into Connecticut, and taken to New Haven. Through the streets of that city he was borne in insulting triumph, by a large number of men on horseback and in carriages; and after much shouting, and firing of cannon, he was committed as a close prisoner to the care of four or five guards; he was denied all visits from friends except in the presence of his guards; he was deprived the use of pen, ink, and paper, except for the purpose of writing to his family, and then only under the inspection of his captors; he was refused the sight of all letters from his family, excepting in one instance, where, however, the letter had been already broken open and read before it was handed to him.[1]

The principal charge against Seabury was, that he had written the pamphlets of the "Westchester Farmer." After more than a month's imprisonment, and in default of evidence to prove that charge, his guards were taken off, and he was allowed to return to his home. Thenceforward, as much as possible he had to avoid appearing upon the streets, always to sleep elsewhere than in his own house, never to be at home even by day for more than an hour or two at a time, and to have faithful friends constantly on the watch to warn him of approaching danger. At one time, under stress of extraordinary danger, he and his friends, Chandler of New Jersey, and Myles Cooper, the president of King's College, were forced to flee for their lives; and, for several days and nights, they lay in the old Wilkins mansion on Castle Hill Neck, where they were hidden in a secret room, in the upper part of the house, behind a chimney—their food and drink being conveyed to them from time to time through a trap-door in the floor.[2]   In the

[1] My account of Seabury's arrest and imprisonment is based chiefly on his own testimony, as given in his memorial to the general assembly of Connecticut. Beardsley, "Life of Seabury," 36–42.

[2] R. Bolton, Jr., "Hist. of the P. E. Church in the County of Westchester," 86.

32

spring of 1776, when the American soldiers began moving from the neighborhood of Boston towards New York, " bodies of them," as Seabury then wrote, " consisting of twenty or thirty men, would, every day or two, sometimes two or three times a day, come through Westchester, though five miles out of their way, and never failed to stop at my house, I believe only for the malicious pleasure of insulting me by reviling the king, the parliament, Lord North, the church, the bishops, the clergy, and the society, and, above all, that vilest of all miscreants, a ' Westchester Farmer.' One would give one hundred dollars to know who he was, that he might plunge his bayonet into his heart; another would crawl fifty miles to see him roasted." [1]

Of course, no human strength could bear a pressure like this for very long. After the battle of Long Island, and the occupation of his neighborhood by soldiers, it became necessary for Seabury to flee for his life into the British lines. Then complete wreck and desolation fell upon his parish. A troop of cavalry were quartered in the rectory, and " consumed all the produce of his glebe"; the pews of the church were wrenched out and burned for firewood; the church itself was turned into a hospital; and " the whole region for thirty miles around was pillaged and laid waste by the marches and depredations, sometimes of one army and sometimes of the other." [2] Once within the British lines, Seabury was, of course, safe from physical outrage —from the insults of armed partisans, from the menaces of mobs; and at headquarters, as was to be expected, he was admitted into confidence and honor. In New York he remained till the close of hostilities, practising his profession as a physician to men's bodies, and losing no opportunity to serve them, also, in his higher capacity as a physician to sick and troubled souls. In 1778, by Sir Henry Clinton he was made a chaplain in the army, and assigned to a regiment of American Loyalists. [3] Finally, in the spring of the

---

[1] Letter by Seabury, 29 December, 1776, in Beardsley, 45–47.
[2] Beardsley, 49–50.   [3] Ibid. 53–54.

year 1783—a year so exhilarating to a majority of the
American people, so sad and so fatal to a minority of them,
but a minority in part composed of men as noble as ever
manned a forlorn hope or went down for a sacred idea—a
little company of clergymen, assembled in a lonely parson-
age at Woodbury, Connecticut, solemnly designated Samuel
Seabury as the first bishop of the American Episcopal
Church, and requested him to go to England for consecration.[1]   At that time, and to the mass of the American people, the man thus chosen for bishop was probably the most
obnoxious clergyman of any religious denomination, to be
found in all the thirteen States.   But the great trust thus
laid upon him, Seabury accepted; the burdens of it he bore
for many years with singular wisdom, energy, patience,
fidelity, success; and when, in the latter part of Washington's second term in the presidency, Seabury laid down his
office with his life, a multitude of persons who formerly hated
him, had come to pay him honor, as one of a sort of men
always likely to be much needed in this part of the world—
men who, for a cause they believe to be right, are capable of
sacrificing public favor, private comfort, even life itself.

---

[1] Beardsley, 76–79.

CHAPTER XVI.

THE LOYALISTS IN ARGUMENT AGAINST THE MEASURES OF THE FIRST CONGRESS: " MASSACHUSETTENSIS."

I.—The letters of " Massachusettensis, ' December, 1774–April, 1775—John Adams's high estimate of their literary power—Previous career of their author, Daniel Leonard—Satirized by Mercy Warren as " Beau Trumps " —John Adams suggests a corrupt motive in his politics.

II.—The intellectual and moral notes in " Massachusettensis "—The writer's avowal of the purity and patriotism of his motives—His denunciation of the arts of demagogues.

III.—The tone and method of " Massachusettensis" suited to the argumentative and law-respecting character of the people addressed by him—His denial that the British government had overstepped its constitutional limits —The several topics discussed by him.

IV.—Examples of his acuteness and literary skill in controversy—The groundlessness of the prevailing political complaints—Committees on grievances our worst grievance—Where are the traces of our political servitude?—The tyranny of the champions of American liberty—The inevitable approach of war—The inevitable triumph of the British in such a conflict.

V.—The author of the letters of " Massachusettensis " a victim of popular violence—Personal outrages upon him and his family—His banishment— His property confiscated—His later career in Bermuda and England.

I.

NOT many weeks after the " Westchester Farmer " had, in one of the principal towns of the Middle Colonies, opened fire on the measures promulgated by the first Continental Congress, a series of attacks upon them, somewhat different in method but almost equally powerful, was begun in the chief city of New England by a writer who became famous under the name of " Massachusettensis." His papers, seventeen in number, were in the form of letters addressed " To the Inhabitants of the Province of the Massachusetts-Bay," and first appeared in a Boston newspaper [1] between

---

[1] " The Massachusetts Gazette and Post Boy," then conducted for the Loyalist side by Nathaniel Mills and John Hicks.

the middle of December, 1774, and the middle of April, 1775.[1] More than forty years afterward, John Adams bore witness to the impression which these essays originally made upon him, by saying that, on his return from the first Continental Congress late in the year 1774, he had found the letters of " Massachusettensis " " shining " among the Tory writings of that neighborhood " like the moon among the lesser stars."[2] A more discriminating, even if less picturesque, indication of their effectiveness was given by the same vigorous writer in a memorandum attached to his " Diary " for the year 1774: " These papers were well written, abounded with wit, discovered good information, and were conducted with a subtlety of art and address wonderfully calculated to keep up the spirits of their party, to depress ours, to spread intimidation, and to make proselytes among those whose principles and judgment give way to their fears,—and these compose at least one-third of mankind."[3]

The literary champion who, concealing his identity[4]

---

[1] The importance of these essays was immediately recognized by friends and foes. They were reprinted in a large pamphlet in Boston, in 1775 ; also in New York, in the same year ; and both in Boston and in London, in 1776. My citations are from this London reprint, which has a preface of its own, and a title-page also well adapted to its place and time: " Massachusettensis, or, a Series of Letters, containing a faithful State of many important and striking Facts, which laid the Foundation of the present Troubles in the Province of the Massachusetts-Bay ; interspersed with Animadversions and Reflections, originally addressed to the People of that Province, and worthy the Consideration of the true Patriots of this Country. By a Person of Honor upon the Spot."

[2] " Novanglus and Massachusettensis," Pref. vi. John Adams here fixes the time at which he found the letters of " Massachusettensis " thus " shining," as on " his return from Congress in the month of November, 1774 " ; but those letters did not begin to " shine " until after the 12th of December.

[3] " The Works of John Adams," ii. 405.

[4] So well, in fact, did he conceal his identity, that John Adams, who was an intimate friend of Leonard and who became the chief public enemy of " Massachusettensis," seems not to have supposed that the two were one : at least, with his usual emphasis he says that, as soon as he saw the letters of " Massachusettensis," he " knew " them to be by his friend Jonathan Sewall. " Novanglus and Massachusettensis," Pref. vi. In this state of blissful knowledge he re-

behind the visor of " Massachusettensis," dashed thus gallantly into the lists of political controversy,—unseating many a burly antagonist, and with his mighty lance bringing rescue and courage to many a dismounted and disheartened friend,—was Daniel Leonard, then thirty-four years of age, a graduate of Harvard, scion of an old and opulent family in the province, as lawyer and politician noted for the acuteness, energy, and eloquence with which he was accustomed to contend for his own view of things. At that period of his life, also, he seems to have had an extraordinary fondness for finery in dress and for social display,—a trait in him which was set forth by Mercy Warren in her comedy of " The Group," wherein Leonard figures under the name of " Beau Trumps." Indeed, according to the never-hesitant and ever-gossiping John Adams, it was through this very love of splendor and of the wealth needful to support it, that Leonard was gradually seduced from his original sympathy with the politics of the Revolution: " He wore a broad gold lace round the rim of his hat, he made his cloak glitter with laces still broader, he had set up his chariot and pair and constantly traveled in it from Taunton to Boston. This made the world stare—it was a novelty. Not another lawyer in the province, attorney or barrister, of whatever age, reputation, rank, or station, presumed to ride in a coach or a chariot. The discerning ones soon perceived that wealth and power must have charms to a heart that delighted in so much finery, and indulged in such unusual expense. Such marks could not escape the vigilant eyes of the two arch-tempters, Hutchinson and Sewall, who had more art, insinuation, and address than all the rest of their party." [1]

---

mained for nearly fifty years—until, in the year 1821, he was confronted by evidence which compelled him to admit that his great foeman was not Jonathan Sewall after all, but Daniel Leonard. " Works of John Adams," iv. 10. Of course, from the start he had been aware that some people attributed the letters to Leonard. Ibid. ii. 405.

[1] Ibid. x. 194-195.

II.

Whatever may be thought of this imputation of vanity and greed, as explaining Daniel Leonard's divergence from the political course taken by John Adams, certain it is that the letters of " Massachusettensis " bear no traces either of a shallow or of a sordid nature: a disinterested reader of them would be likely to say that they express high cultivation, strong judgment, and courageous moral thoughtfulness. As some offset to John Adams's disparaging account of Leonard's motives, it is only fair to note his own declaration upon that subject. In the third number of " Massachusettensis," he alludes to the curiosity which even then was asking who the writer of those essays might be: " I will tell you: it is a native of this province, that knew it before many, that are now basking in the rays of political sunshine, had a being. He was favored, not by Whigs or Tories but by the people, with such a stand in the community, as that he could distinctly see all the political manœuvres of the province. He saw some with pleasure, others with pain. If he condemns the conduct of the Whigs, he does not always approve of the conduct of the Tories. . . . He is now repaying your favors, if he knows his own heart, from the purest gratitude and the most undissembled patriotism—which will one day be acknowledged. I saw the small seed of sedition, when it was implanted: it was as a grain of mustard. I have watched the plant until it has become a great tree: the vilest reptiles that crawl upon the earth, are concealed at the root; the foulest birds of the air rest upon its branches. I now would induce you to go to work immediately with axes and hatchets, and cut it down, for a two-fold reason,—because it is a pest to society, and lest it be felled suddenly by a stronger arm, and crush its thousands in the fall." [1]

Indeed, it was not at all necessary—even if it were courteous and fair—to suggest a corrupt consideration on Leon-

---

[1] " Massachusettensis," 25–26.

ard's part, in order to explain a course of political conduct
which logically followed from his point of view—a point of
view in itself quite as rational and as honorable as that very
opposite one which was then held by his literary assailant.
As John Adams's writings down to the close of the Revolution breathe the spirit of political radicalism and of a somewhat extreme democracy, so these writings of Leonard's—
like those of John Adams himself after the Revolution—
breathe the spirit of political conservatism, together with a
contempt and an abhorrence for the arts by which the
people are often led astray into folly and crime. " Popular
demagogues," says Leonard, " always call themselves ' the
people,' and when their own measures are censured, cry out,
—' The people, the people are abused and insulted.' " [1]
" There is a propensity in men to believe themselves injured
and oppressed, whenever they are told so." [2]   " Great
allowances are to be made for the crossings, windings, and
tergiversations of a politician: he is a cunning animal." [3]
" We often read resolves denying the authority of parliament, . . . gilded over with professions of loyalty to
the king; but the golden leaf is too thin to conceal the
treason." [4]   " He that would excite a rebellion, whatever
professions of philanthropy he may make when he is insinuating and worming himself into the good graces of the people, is at heart as great a tyrant as ever wielded the iron rod
of oppression." [5]

III.

The handling of the argument in these essays was exactly
suited to the people addressed, and to the alarming condition of their affairs.   They were a law-abiding people: they
were also an argumentative people.   They had inherited, and
they still cherished, the great English traditions concerning
authority—as a thing very necessary and sacred, but as a

[1] " Massachusettensis," 114.   [2] Ibid. 12–13.   [3] Ibid. 38.
[4] Ibid. 56.   [5] Ibid. 17.

thing limited: authority itself being subject to authority, namely, the authority of those constitutional barriers which define its operation. To them it seemed as needful for government to yield obedience to the law over it, as to require obedience to the law under it. They were good subjects, therefore, so long as they were convinced that government was setting them an example of obedience by wielding its power within those barriers which reason and justice had prescribed: when not so convinced, these good subjects were apt to become good rebels. The success of the Revolutionary agitators thus far, had been largely due to their skill in convincing the people that government had lost its claims by overstepping its limits.

It was this state of the case that Leonard perfectly understood: his countrymen were on the verge of rebellion—nay, they were actually in rebellion—but it was upon a theory which, in their eyes, took from rebellion all its criminality. Their rebellion was justifiable, because, as they thought, the acts of the government were unjustifiable. The great business of Leonard, therefore, was to convince them that they had been misinformed, that they were misled; that they were rushing onward under a frightful error and delusion; that the government had not overstepped its limits; that though some of its recent acts may have been bad in policy, not one of them was unconstitutional; that these acts contained no menace to the political safety, dignity, or happiness of the American colonists; that everything of value to them in character, duty, property, and life itself, was involved in their speedily discovering their mistake, casting off the sophists and demagogues who had beguiled them, and becoming once more good subjects of the just and splendid empire within which lay all their hopes for prosperity and happiness. Accordingly, so distributing these various topics as to mingle history, anecdote, warning, sympathy, sarcasm, invective, with acute discussions of constitutional law, of equity, of the higher aspects of policy, he shows great skill in knocking away, or in seeming to knock away, piece by piece, the argumentative structure under cover of which the Revolutionary agitators had succeeded in drawing a loyal and a logical people into courses of action both disloyal and dangerous. That the authority of the imperial parliament is and must be coextensive with the empire itself [1]; that its authority in the American colonies is not invalidated by the circumstance that distance from the capital renders it impracticable for them to send members to parliament [2]; that no recent assertion of the taxing power of parliament is new—is, in fact, anything but what has been peacefully exercised and safely granted from the beginning [3]; that such taxation is contained in the very terms of the original settlement of the colonies [4]; that in the doctrine of the supremacy of parliament, according to the British constitution, is wrapped up our priceless claim to all the great rights and privileges of British subjects under that constitution—the rejection of the former carrying with it the destruction of the latter [5]; that no American petitions to the imperial government have ever yet been rejected, excepting such as were so framed as to compel their rejection on the part of any government that had the least respect either for the constitution or for itself [6]; that what are called American grievances are largely imaginary [7]—are charges trumped up by demagogues and conspirators [8] as their stock in trade while fattening upon the generous confidence of a people noble-minded but misinformed, and rushing toward misery and ruin,—such are the matters principally dealt with by this consummate debater.

Of course, the real weight and worth of his arguments in support of these several propositions, can be judged only after a thorough reading of them. Meantime, even from snatches and fragments of the discussion, we may form some notion of the literary power with which he states them, of

---

[1] " Massachusettensis," 39, 40–45.   [2] Ibid. 43–44.
[3] Ibid. 9–10, 40, 82–83.   [4] Ibid. 40–41.   [5] Ibid. 41–43.
[6] Ibid. 104–5.   [7] Ibid. 70, 74–75, 102–103.
[8] Ibid. 8–15, 17, 20, 21, 24, 76, 105–7.

the epigrammatic point, the wit, the dash, the shrewdness with which he presses them home.

IV.

Thus, the real goundlessness of the prevailing political complaints, is an essential part of his view of the whole case, and one of his strong contentions. " Perhaps the whole story of empire does not furnish another instance of a forcible opposition to government, with so much specious and so little real cause." [1] " Is it not a most astonishing instance of caprice or infatuation, that a province, torn from its foundations, should be precipitating itself into a war with Great Britain, because the British parliament asserts its right of raising a revenue in America,—inasmuch as the claim of that right is as ancient as the colonies themselves ? The parliament's refusing to repeal the tea act is the ostensible foundation of our quarrel.   If we ask the Whigs, whether the pitiful three-penny duty upon a luxurious, unwholesome, foreign commodity gives just occasion for the opposition, they tell us, ' it is the precedent they are contending about '—insinuating that it is an innovation.   But this ground is not tenable ; for a total repeal of the tea act would not serve us upon the score of precedents.   They are numerous without this.   The Whigs have been extremely partial respecting tea.   Poor tea has been made the shibboleth of party, while molasses, wine, coffee, indigo, etc., etc., have been unmolested.   A person that drinks New England rum distilled from molasses subject to a like duty, is equally deserving of a coat of tar and feathers with him that drinks tea.   A coffee-drinker is as culpable as either, viewed in a political light.   ' But,' say our patriots, ' if the British parliament may take a penny from us without our consent, they may a pound, and so on, till they have filched away all our property.'   This incessant incantation operates like a spell or a charm, and checks the efforts of loyalty in many

---

[1] " Massachusettensis," 39.

an honest breast. Let us give it its full weight. Do they mean that if the parliament has a right to raise a revenue of one penny on the colonies, they must therefore have a right to wrest from us all our property ? If this be their meaning, I deny their deduction; for the supreme legislature can have no right to tax any part of the empire to a greater amount than its just and equitable proportion of the necessary national expense. This is a line drawn by the constitution itself. Do they mean that, if we admit that the parliament may constitutionally raise one penny upon us for the purposes of revenue, they will proceed from light to heavy taxes, till their impositions become grievous and intolerable ? This amounts to no more than a denial of the right, lest it should be abused. But an argument drawn from the actual abuse of power, will not conclude to the illegality of such power; much less will an argument drawn from the capability of its being abused. I will admit that a power of taxation is more liable to abuse than legislation separately considered; and it would give me pleasure to see some other line drawn, some other barrier erected, than what the constitution has already done—if it be possible— whereby the constitutional authority of the supreme legislature might be preserved entire, and America be guaranteed in every right and exemption, consistent with her subordination and dependence. But this can only be done by parliament."[1] " It would be an endless task to remark minutely upon each of the fancied grievances that swarm and cluster, fill and deform, the American chronicles. An adeptness at discovering grievances has lately been one of the principal recommendations to public notice and popular applause. . . . We have had geniuses selected for that purpose, called ' committees upon grievances ': a sagacious set they were, and discovered a multitude, before it was known that they themselves were the greatest grievances that the country was infested with."[2] " Where are the traces of slavery that our patriots would terrify us with ?

---

[1] " Massachusettensis," 82–84.   [2] Ibid. 74–75.

The effects of slavery are as glaring and obvious in those countries that are cursed with its abode, as the effects of war, pestilence, or famine. Our land is not disgraced by the wooden shoes of France, or the uncombed hair of Poland. We have neither racks nor inquisitions, tortures nor assassinations. The mildness of our criminal jurisprudence is proverbial: ' A man must have many friends, to get hanged in New England.' Who has been arbitrarily imprisoned, disseized of his freehold, or despoiled of his goods ? . . . My dear friends, let me ask each one, whether he has not enjoyed every blessing that is in the power of civil government to bestow ? And yet the parliament has, from the earliest days of the colonies, claimed the lately controverted right both of legislation and taxation, and for more than a century has been in the exercise of it. There is no grievous exercise of that right at this day— unless the measures taken to prevent our revolting may be called grievances. Are we then to rebel lest there should be grievances ? Are we to take up arms and make war against our parent, lest that parent, contrary to the experience of a century and a half, contrary to her own genius, inclination, affection, and interest, should treat us or our posterity as bastards, and not as sons, and instead of protecting, should enslave us ? The annals of the world have not yet been deformed with a single instance of so unnatural, so causeless, so wanton, so wicked, a rebellion.'' [1]

As might be expected, this writer is too alert in the discovery of logical, and even sentimental, advantages to fail to turn against his antagonists the charge, that they, the champions of liberty, are themselves perpetrators of the grossest tyranny, in not allowing any but their own side of the controversy to have an open and a safe hearing; " that so many respectable persons have been abused, and forced to sign recantations and resignations; that so many persons, to avoid such reiterated insults as are more to be deprecated by a man of sentiment than death itself, have been obliged to

---

[1] " Massachusettensis," 102–103.

quit their houses, families, and business, and fly to the army
for protection; that husband has been separated from wife,
father from son, brother from brother, the sweet intercourse
of conjugal and natural affection interrupted, and the unfortunate refugee forced to abandon all the comforts of
domestic life. My countrymen, I beg you to pause and
reflect on this conduct. Have not these people, that are
thus insulted, as good a right to think and act for themselves in matters of the last importance, as the Whigs ?
Are they not as closely connected with the interest of their
country, as the Whigs ? Do not their former lives and
conversations appear to have been regulated by principle, as
much as those of the Whigs ? You must answer—yes!
Why, then, do you suffer them to be cruelly treated, for
differing in sentiment from you ? Is it consistent with that
liberty you profess ? . . . Do you expect to make
converts by it ? Persecution has the same effects in politics,
that it has in religion : it confirms the sectary. Do you
wish to silence them, that the inhabitants of the province
may appear unanimous ? The maltreatment they have
received for differing from you, is an undeniable evidence
that we are not unanimous. . . . It is astonishing, my
friends, that those who are in pursuit of liberty, should ever
suffer arbitrary power, in such an hideous form and squalid
hue, to get a footing among them.'' [1]

In his last letter, which was finished sixteen days before
the clash of arms at Lexington and Concord, the writer
seems burdened, even as he had been in his first letter,
written four months earlier, by a clear prescience of that
tragic event which, as John Adams said, changed '' the
instruments of warfare from the pen to the sword.'' [2]
'' The English nation will bear much from its friends; but
whoever has read its history must know, that there is a line
that cannot be passed with impunity. It is not the fault of
our patriots, if that line be not already passed. They have

---

[1] '' Massachusettensis,'' 35–36.
[2] '' The Works of John Adams,'' ii. 405.

demanded of Great Britain more than she can grant consistent with her honor, her interest, or our own, and are now brandishing the sword of defiance. Do you expect to conquer in war ? ''[1] '' Can any of you that think soberly upon the matter, be so deluded as to believe that Great Britain, who so lately carried her arms with success to every part of the globe, triumphed over the united powers of France and Spain, and whose fleets give law to the ocean, is unable to conquer us ? ''[2] '' Those that unsheath the sword of rebellion may throw away the scabbard. . . . The conquered in other wars do not forfeit the rights of men, nor all the rights of citizens; even their bravery is rewarded by a generous victor. Far different is the case of a routed rebel host.''[3]

V.

Although, at the time of their first publication, Daniel Leonard was only suspected to be the author of these terrible letters of '' Massachusettensis,'' he had otherwise done enough to entitle himself to the distinction of suffering that personal violence which, as he himself charged, was then inflicted by the champions of liberty upon those who took the liberty to differ from them in opinion. His own house in the little town of Taunton proved to be no longer his castle: bullets were fired into it by a mob of his political enemies. With his family, consisting of eight persons, he then fled for safety to Boston, and there he remained till its evacuation by the British army in March, 1776. He was among the refugees who accompanied the army to Halifax. In the lists of citizens whom the State of Massachusetts denounced to banishment[4] in September, 1778, and to confiscation of property[5] in April, 1779, his name was

---

[1] '' Massachusettensis,'' 116.   [2] Ibid. 5.   [3] Ibid. 117.

[4] The act is given entire in the appendix to Curwen's '' Journal and Letters,'' 438–443.

[5] The confiscation act is given in Curwen, 434–436.

included.   From Halifax he went to England, where he was rewarded with the office of chief-justice of Bermuda.   In London he died in 1829, at the age of eighty-nine.[1]

---

[1] Sabine, " Loyalists of the Am. Rev.," ii. 10–12 ; " Appleton's Cycl. of Am. Biog.," sub. nom. ; Curwen's " Journal and Letters, 548.

CHAPTER XVII.

THE LOYALISTS IN ARGUMENT AGAINST THE MEASURES OF THE FIRST CONGRESS: JOSEPH GALLOWAY.

I.—Joseph Galloway's preëminence as a Loyalist writer and statesman—His early activity in the politics of Pennsylvania—Associated in personal and political friendship with Franklin—His enmity to John Dickinson and the proprietary government of Pennsylvania—His "Speech" in 1764 ridiculed by Dickinson.

II.—Galloway comes into general prominence at the time of the first Continental Congress—Represents in that body the Americans who desired to secure American rights but without revolutionary violence—His "Plan of a Proposed Union between Great Britain and the Colonies"—Fragments of his speeches in Congress in support thereof.

III.—The rejection by Congress of Galloway's "Plan" marks the parting of the ways between the conservative and the revolutionary opponents of parliamentary taxation—Galloway declines a reëlection to Congress—Appeals from the adverse decision of the Congress to the higher tribunal of public opinion—Publishes early in 1775 "A Candid Examination of the Mutual Claims of Great Britain and the Colonies"—The shocking violations of American liberty by the champions of American liberty—The controversy a dispute between the supreme authority of the state and some of its members—Outline of his argument touching the rights of America and the best way to secure them.

IV.—Great immediate influence of Galloway's pamphlet—Whatever its merits, it comes too late—His noble appeals swept out of sight by Lexington, Concord, and Bunker Hill—Galloway, following his convictions, enters the British lines in the autumn of 1776—His important services therein—Seeks refuge in England in the autumn of 1778—His death there in 1803.

V.—Galloway's activity as a writer on American affairs not diminished by his residence in England—His pamphlets, there produced, fall into three groups—First, the constitutional and political issues of the controversy—Secondly, the American Revolution as a physical conflict—Thirdly, the motives, services, and sacrifices of the American Loyalists.

I.

A LOYALIST writer of less vigor than Seabury, of less agility and sparkle than Daniel Leonard, but probably of greater practical effect than either, was Joseph Galloway,[1] who shared with Thomas Hutchinson the supreme place among American statesmen opposed to the Revolution, and who persisted in his literary activity against that movement until its success was beyond the possibility of doubt. Indeed, by a recent American critic[2] Galloway has been characterized as " the giant and corypheus of the Loyalist pamphleteers."

He was born in Kent County,[3] Maryland, in 1731, of a family settled in that province in the early part of the reign of Charles the First, and possessed of large landed property there. Having established himself in Philadelphia for the practice of the law, he attained while still a young man considerable distinction both as a barrister and as a politician. From 1757 until 1774, he was, almost without interruption, a member of the assembly of Pennsylvania, and during the last nine years of that period he was its speaker. In the embittered conflicts then raging in the colony between the friends and enemies of the proprietary government, Galloway stood among its enemies—striving in close union with Franklin to bring about a transfer of the province from the control of the Penn family to that of the crown.

---

[1] An adequate biography of Galloway is much to be desired : it would be invaluable for the removal of much obscurity and injustice still prevailing in the popular conception of the American Revolution.   The sketch of him in Sabine's " Loyalists of the American Revolution," i. 453–457, is exceptionally weak, inaccurate, and unfair.   For the chief events of his life, the best materials now available are Galloway's own answers to certain personal questions put to him during his celebrated " Examination " by a committee of the house of commons in 1779 ; the notes inserted by Thomas Balch in a reprint of this " Examination," Philadelphia, 1855 ; a note by J. Francis Fisher in " The Works of Benjamin Franklin," Sparks's ed., vii. 276–277 ; and the published correspondence of Galloway's contemporaries, especially of Franklin, Dickinson, John Adams, and Joseph Reed.

[2] The late George Henry Moore, in a letter to the author.

[3] With respect to the place and date of Galloway's birth, the mistakes made by J. Francis Fisher in his note to the seventh volume of Franklin's " Works," published in 1838, were pointed out by Thomas Balch in 1855, in a note to page 43 of Galloway's " Examination."   The author of the sketch of Galloway in " Appleton's Dictionary of American Biography," ii. 581–582, seems to have trusted to Fisher's note, without taking account of Balch's corrections of it.

It was in connection with this movement—probably the only popular movement on behalf of which he was ever engaged—that he first came into public notice as a writer, publishing at Philadelphia in 1764 a " Speech " made by him in the assembly, in support of a resolution asking " his majesty to resume the powers of government into his own hands." [1] This publication is of some interest still, not only for its evidence as to Galloway's intellectual quality at that period of his career, but as a symptom of the early and sharp divergence between him and John Dickinson. His " Speech " appears to have been printed without much revision, possibly from the rough notes jotted down by him as an aid in the delivery of it,—a fact which gave occasion for Dickinson's gibe at his " continual breaches of the rules of grammar, his utter ignorance of the English language, the pompous obscurity and sputtering prolixity reigning through every part of his piece, and his innumerable and feeble tautologies." [2] Certainly, these memoranda are clumsy enough in form, but they are not otherwise weak; indeed, they indicate genuine argumentative power, solidity, sobriety, statesmanlike breadth and grasp of reasoning.

II.

Not until the time of the first Continental Congress, did Galloway come into prominence beyond the limits of his own colony. Like all of the American Loyalists, he had deprecated the unwise course of the English ministry in their treatment of the American colonies, from the time of the act for laying stamp duties, onward to that for shutting up the port of Boston. Nevertheless, Galloway held that

---

[1] " The Speech of Joseph Galloway," etc., 3. It is characteristic of the place and the time that, in order to reach a portion of the inhabitants of Pennsylvania too important to be disregarded, this " Speech " was circulated in German also: " Die Rede Herrn Joseph Galloways, eines der Mitglieder des Hauses," u. s. w. " Aus dem Englischen übersetzt. Philadelphia, gedruckt und zu finden bey Heinrich Miller, in der Zweiten-strasse."

[2] " A Reply to a Piece called a Speech of Joseph Galloway, Esq.," Appendix, 49–50.

all these bitter incidents were an inevitable result of the lack
of a proper constitutional organization of the American colonies within the general system of the British empire.   In
order to suppy this lack in a statesmanlike manner,— that
is, in order to frame a permanent constitution for the
American colonies, under which all disagreements between
them and the parent state could be quietly and wisely dealt
with,—he introduced into the Continental Congress, on the
twenty-eighth of September, 1774, his famous " Plan of a
Proposed Union between Great Britain and the Colonies."

This was simply a scheme for American home rule, on a
basis of colonial confederation, with an American parliament
to be elected every three years by the legislatures of the
several colonies, and with a governor general to be appointed by the crown.   Galloway's spirit in bringing forward
this plan may partly be inferred from some fragments of his
remarks in support of it, as preserved in notes taken on the
spot by John Adams:—" I am as much a friend of liberty
as exists ; and no man shall go further in point of fortune, or
in point of blood, than the man who now addresses you."
" We want the aid and assistance and protection of the arm
of our mother country.   Protection and allegiance are
reciprocal duties.   Can we lay claim to the money and protection of Great Britain upon any principles of honor or conscience ?   Can we wish to become aliens to the mother
state ?"   " We must come upon terms with Great Britain.
Some gentlemen are not for negotiation.   I wish I could
hear some reason against it."   " In every government—patri-
archal, monarchical, aristocratical, or democratical—there
must be a supreme legislature."   " I know of no American
constitution : a Virginia constitution, a Pennyslvania constitution, we have ;— we are totally independent of each
other."   " Is it not necessary that the trade of the empire
should be regulated by some power or other ?   Can the
empire hold together without it ?   No.   Who shall regulate
it ?   Shall the legislature of Nova Scotia or Georgia regulate it ?   Massachusetts, or Virginia ?   Pennsylvania or New

York? It can't be pretended. Our legislative powers extend no further than the limits of our governments. Where then shall it be placed? There is a necessity that an American legislature should be set up, or else that we should give the power to parliament or king."[1]

This sagacious scheme of Galloway's, which virtually anticipated the British statesmanship of the subsequent century in the solution of the British colonial problem, came very near to adoption. It was strongly supported in Congress by James Duane and John Jay; it was pronounced by Edward Rutledge to be " almost a perfect plan "; in the final trial, it was lost only by a vote of six colonies to five. Had it been adopted, the disruption of the British empire by an American schism would certainly have been averted for that epoch, and, as an act of violence and of hereditary unkindness, would perhaps have been averted forever; while the English colonies in America would have remained English colonies, without ceasing to be free.[2]

III.

The rejection by the first Continental Congress of this noble-minded measure for a practicable and permanent union between the American colonies and the mother country, seemed to Galloway to denote a final parting of the ways between himself and many of his old political colleagues; to be an indication, also, that the American politicians who had thus succeeded in carrying the vote of

---

[1] " The Works of John Adams," ii. 388–391.

[2] In giving an account of Galloway's scheme I have used, with some modifications, a few sentences from my book on " Patrick Henry," 102. No copy of Galloway's " Plan," nor any allusion to it, was allowed to appear in the " Journals " of Congress. The text of it was published at the time in newspapers ; it is to be found stitched in with some pamphlets of the time, as the one entitled " What think ye of the Congress Now? " ; it was reproduced entire in Galloway's pamphlet called " A Candid Examination," etc., 53–54, as well as in another famous pamphlet, called " Observations on the Reconciliation of Great Britain and the Colonies " ; and it is now easily accessible in 4 " Am. Arch.," i. 905–906.

Congress against him would be likely to impress upon that body a course of action which, as he thought, was intended to lead to a violent rupture with England, and to an effort at separation. Declining an election to the second Continental Congress, where his presence would have been of little avail, and would even have involved him in serious misconstruction, he thenceforward devoted himself in an independent position to the effort to avert, if possible, the final adoption by his fellow-colonists of a policy having in his eyes every aspect of illegality, of unwisdom, of public and private misfortune.

Under these circumstances it was that, early in the year 1775, he published his first notable piece of work as a pamphleteer,[1]—" A Candid Examination of the Mutual Claims of Great Britain and the Colonies: With a Plan of Accommodation on Constitutional Principles."[2]   It is probable that he had set to work on this pamphlet shortly after the rejection of his " Plan " by the first Continental Congress. At any rate, it is an avowed appeal from the adverse decision of that body to the higher tribunal of public opinion. After an impressive preamble, in which he depicts a condition of affairs in America, not only anomalous but shocking

[1] Besides his "Speech," in 1764, and his "Plan," in 1774, his hand may be traced in two slight publications prior to the serious one now referred to—" To the Public," 1764 ; "Advertisement . . . To the Public," 1765. Each of these was printed on a single leaf, in Philadelphia, and each relates to his personal concern with current political controversies. In 1765, he dealt with the questions raised by the Stamp Act, doing so in a " piece " published over the signature of " Americanus." " The Works of Benjamin Franklin," Sparks's ed., vii. 304. In January, 1766, he wrote to Franklin, with whom he was then on terms not only confidential but affectionate, that he had nearly finished a pamphlet entitled " Political Reflections on the Dispute between Great Britain and her Colonies respecting her Right of imposing Taxes on them without their Assent."   Ibid. I have found no evidence that he ever published this pamphlet. Possibly it was the basis for the one published by him in London in 1780, entitled " Historical and Political Reflections on the Rise and Progress of the American Rebellion."

[2] It is a sign of the great effect of this pamphlet, that it was reprinted in many forms both in America and in England. I here use the first edition printed by Rivington in New York in 1775.

in any community pretending to be controlled by law,—
" freedom of speech suppressed, the liberty and secrecy of
the press destroyed, the voice of truth silenced, a lawless
power established throughout the colonies . . . depriv-
ing men of their natural rights and inflicting penalties more
severe than death itself,"—he avows his determination then
and there to lay before his countrymen a faithful and fearless review of " the most important controversy that ever
was agitated between a state and its members." [1] What is
the standard by which such a controversy can be decided ?
Surely, that standard is not found by those who have undertaken to deduce the political rights of America from " the
laws of God and nature," from " the common rights of
mankind," or from the " American charters." Neither is
it to be discovered by exploring those ingenious and fanci-
ful distinctions which have been made between " a right in
parliament to legislate for the colonies and a right to tax
them, between internal and external taxation, and between
taxes laid for the regulation of trade and for the purpose of
revenue." [2] All these attempts to find the true standard
by which to decide the controversy have been futile, for the
reason that they have been sought in disregard of the true
nature of that controversy. What, then, is its nature ? " It
is a dispute between the supreme authority of the state and
a number of its members," [3] as to the limits of authority on
the part of the former and of obedience on the part of the
latter. The very nature of the dispute, therefore, shows
that the true standard for its settlement is to be sought in
the principles of government in general and of the British
constitution in particular. Well, then, in every state there
must be " a supreme legislative authority, universal in
extent," and affecting every member of the state. [4] Within
the British empire, such authority resides in parliament.
Are the American colonies members of the British empire,
or are they not ? After a long and learned presentation of

---

[1] " A Candid Examination," etc., 1, 2.   [2] Ibid. 2-3.
[3] Ibid. 3.   [4] Ibid. 4.

the evidence for and against the proposition, he concludes
that they are.[1]   With this conclusion, however, it is impossible to reconcile the claim of the Congress that in all cases
of taxation and of internal police, the colonies have exclusive control, subject only to the negative of the sovereign.[2]
That this is so, he argues at great length and with great
force.   Congress, therefore, was wrong in having rejected
the " Plan " which was submitted to it, for so organizing
the constitution of the colonies as to open a path " to a
lasting and happy reconciliation."   Instead of this beneficent result, " nothing has been the production of their two
months' labor, but the ill-shapen, diminutive brat—Independency! "   But Independency means ruin.   If England
refuses it, she will ruin us: if she grants it, we shall ruin ourselves.[3]

Having thus set forth the rights of parliament, and the
fatal consequences that must result from our refusal to
recognize them, he next turns to consider the rights of
America,—a task which he performs " with ineffable pleasure, as he is pleading a cause founded on the immutable
principles of reason and justice—the cause of his country
and the latest posterity."[4]   What are the rights of
America ?—whence derived ?—how has their exercise been
lost ?—how can they be recovered ?   The rights of America
are derived from the British constitution.   They include
those of protection, not only from foreign powers, but from
domestic injustice as well—especially from " the arbitrary
and lawless power of the state, and of every subordinate
authority."[5]   Furthermore, it is of the essence of the British constitution that from the earliest times the government
has derived " its power from the landed interest," and that
the proprietors of the land have " shared the power of making their laws,"[6] a principle which, for convenience, has
been developed into the representative system.[7]   But, with
respect to this ancient English right, how stands the case

---

[1] " A Candid Examination," etc., 24.   [2] Ibid. 30.   [3] Ibid. 31–32.
[4] Ibid. 33.   [5] Ibid. 34.   [6] Ibid. 35–36.   [7] Ibid. 39.

on behalf of the English proprietors of land in America ?
Certainly, they do not enjoy it; they have never enjoyed
it; but they ought to enjoy it,—they ought to enjoy it " in
such manner as their circumstances admit of, whenever it
shall be decently and respectfully asked for." [1] " The subjects of a free state, in every part of its dominions, ought in
good policy to enjoy the same fundamental rights and privileges. Every distinction between them must be offensive
and odious, and cannot fail to create uneasiness and jeal-
ousies which will ever weaken the government, and frequently terminate in insurrections,—which, in every society,
ought to be particularly guarded against. If the British
state, therefore, means to retain the colonies in a due obedience on her government, it will be wisdom in her to
restore to her American subjects the enjoyment of the right
of assenting to and dissenting from such bills as shall be
proposed to regulate their conduct. Laws thus made will
ever be obeyed, because by their assent they become their
own acts. It will place them in the same condition with
their brethren in Britain, and remove all cause of complaint;
or if they should conceive any regulations inconvenient or
unjust, they will petition, not rebel. Without this, it is
easy to perceive that the union and harmony, which is peculiarly essential to a free society whose members are resident
in regions so very remote from each other, cannot long subsist. The genius, temper, and circumstances of the Americans should be also duly attended to. No people in the
world have higher notions of liberty. It would be impossible ever to eradicate them,—should an attempt so unjust
be ever made. Their late spirit and conduct fully prove this
assertion, and will serve as a clue to that policy by which
they ought to be governed. The distance of America from
Britain, her vast extent of territory, her numerous ports and
conveniences of commerce, her various productions, her
increasing numbers, and consequently her growing strength
and power, when duly considered, all point out the policy

---

[1] " A Candid Examination," etc., 41.

of uniting the two countries together upon principles of English liberty. Should this be omitted, the colonies will infallibly throw off their connection with the mother country. Their distance will encourage the attempt; their discontent will give them spirit; and their numbers, wealth, and power, at some future time, will enable them to effect it." [1]

What, then, is to be done? Undoubtedly, the Americans are laboring under grievances which ought to have redress; but Congress is wrong in the mode it has proposed for obtaining such redress. There is a right mode—it is that of redress through a liberal constitutional union with the mother state.[2] "Had this measure been adopted in the year 1766, in all probability the rights of America would have been restored, and the most perfect harmony would have this day subsisted between the two countries." [3] "Great pains have been taken by the American demagogues to delude the unhappy people whom they have doomed to be the dupes of their ambition, into a belief that no justice was to be obtained of his majesty and his houses of parliament, and that they had refused to hear our most reasonable petitions. . . . It is high time that this fatal delusion should be exposed, and the good people of America disabused. It is true that his majesty and the two houses of parliament have treated petitions from the colonies with neglect; but what were those petitions? Did they rest on a denial of the essential rights of parliament, or did they ask for the rights of the subject in America? . . . They disowned the power of the supreme legislature, to which as subjects they owe obedience." [4] "Is it too late to recover from our madness, and to pursue the dictates of reason and duty? By no means. But it is high time we had changed our measures, and retreated from the dangers with which we are threatened. Let us, like men who love order and government, boldly oppose the illegal edicts of the Congress, before it is too late,—pull down the licentious tyranny they

---

[1] "A Candid Examination," etc., 42–43.   [2] Ibid. 48–49.
[3] Ibid. 49.   [4] Ibid. 49–50.

have established, and dissolve their inferior committees—their instruments to trample on the sacred laws of your country, and your invaluable rights. This done, and peace and order restored within your several provinces, apply to your assemblies, who are your constitutional guardians and can alone procure a redress of your grievances. Entreat them, in a respectful and dutiful manner to petition his majesty and his two houses of parliament, and in their petitions to assure them—' That you are sensible of the necessity of a supreme legislature over every member of the state; that you acknowledge yourselves subjects of the British government; that you have, through innumerable difficulties and perils, settled and improved a wilderness, extended the territories, and greatly increased the wealth and power of the nation; that by such settlement you have lost the enjoyment of, though not the right to, some of the first and most excellent of the privileges of Englishmen; . . . that no part of the lands in America . . . enjoy their ancient right of participating in the authority of parliament; . . . and therefore pray, that you may not only be restored to this capacity, but to all the rights of Englishmen, upon such principles of liberty and policy as shall best suit your local circumstances.'

" A petition of this kind, so reasonable and just, and so well founded and established on the principles of their own government, attended with such a plan of union as may be wisely digested by your several assemblies, there is no reason to doubt, will be graciously received and duly attended to by his majesty and his two houses of parliament, and finally terminate in a full redress of your grievances, and a permanent system of union and harmony, upon principles of liberty and safety." [1]

IV.

For the champions of extreme measures, Galloway's pamphlet became a somewhat troublesome document. More-

---

[1] " A Candid Examination," etc., 59–61.

over, with people of moderate and conservative tendencies, it was singularly persuasive by reason of the fact that it seemed to be something more than an academic and irresponsible discussion of its tremendous theme; and that, besides administering a dose of destructive criticism to the radical plans of the Revolutionary party, it was ready with a practical and statesmanlike plan as a substitute for them. Finally, an infallible token of its effectiveness was to be seen in the fact that it was accorded repeated rounds of literary abuse and refutation.   Of only one of these, however, did Galloway take particular notice,—doing so in a tract, published in New York in the spring of 1775, called " Reply to an Address to the Author of a Pamphlet entitled A Candid Examination.''

Whatever may have been the merits of Galloway's pamphlet, it had one fatal defect,—it was a good argument delivered at a bad time: in short, it was a brave attempt by words to stop and turn back the current of destiny.   No spoken or written commentary upon his presentation of the case was so unanswerable as was that furnished by actual events soon after its publication,—more particularly those of Lexington, Concord, and Bunker Hill.   After the flash and uproar of those three displays of the motherly solicitude of England, it became plain that fewer people, and still fewer, were left in the mood to attend to an examination, whether candid or otherwise, of the mutual claims of Great Britain and the colonies.   Finding, therefore, that an irresistible tide was sweeping against him and all his views of things, Galloway wisely withdrew from Philadelphia to his country seat in Bucks County, where, according to his own statement, '' he remained several months in the utmost danger from mobs raised by Mr. Adams to hang him at his own door.'' [1]

In the autumn of 1776, shortly after the surrender of

---

[1] '' The Examination of Joseph Galloway," etc., Balch ed., 51 n.   The '' Mr. Adams '' above referred to, is probably the one who rejoiced in the baptismal name of Samuel.

Fort Lee, he entered the British lines, and, joining the army, accompanied it on its march through New Jersey. With that army he remained in all its subsequent marchings and countermarchings until, in the autumn of 1777, it took possession of Philadelphia. During the British occupation of that city, he held the important offices of superintendent of the police, of the port, and of the prohibited articles; he was much relied on for information and advice by the chief officers of the army; he was himself ingenious and enterprising in the enlistment and employment of Loyalist troops. In June, 1778, upon the British evacuation of Philadelphia, he accompanied the army on its somewhat embarrassed journey back to New York.[1] A few months afterward, in the society of his only daughter, he sailed for England, where he remained until his death in 1803.

V.

His arrival in England was by no means the signal for any diminution of activity on his part in the affairs of his country and of his countrymen. He and Thomas Hutchinson, being then both in England and both alike in American unpopularity, were also both alike in the confidence of the king and ministry, and of the party which favored a vigorous prosecution of the American war. To them Galloway was as valuable for information respecting the middle colonies, as was Hutchinson for information respecting those of New England. Then it was, likewise, that he did his largest and most effective work as a pamphleteer upon topics connected with the Revolution.

The pamphlets which he thus produced may be said to fall into three principal groups. Of these, the first group, dealing with the general issues of the American Revolution as a constitutional question, as a political question, and as a question of general expediency, is made up of the following pamphlets:—" Historical and Political Reflections

---

[1] " The Examination of Joseph Galloway," etc., Balch ed.. 72–73 n.

on the Rise and Progress of the American Rebellion ";
" Plain Truth, or, A Letter to the Author of ' Dispassion-
ate Thoughts on the American War ' " ; " Cool Thoughts
on the Consequences to Great Britain of American Independence, on the Expense of Great Britain in the Settlement and Defense of the American Colonies, on the Value
and Importance of the American Colonies and the West
Indies to the British Empire " ; " Political Reflections on
the late Colonial Governments, in which their original Constitutional Defects are pointed out, and shewn to have
naturally produced the Rebellion which has unfortunately
terminated in the Dismemberment of the British Empire."
The second group, dealing with the American Revolution as a physical conflict, exposes with terrific force of
evidence and with great bitterness of expression, the
laxness, the stupendous mismanagement, and even the
probable disloyalty, of leading British officers in the conduct of the war; pointing out, likewise, the practicability
of complete and speedy success for the British arms in
America—if only directed by able leaders determined to
succeed.   This group is composed of the following pamphlets:—" Letters to a Nobleman on the Conduct of the
War in the Middle Colonies " ; " A Letter to the Right
Honorable Lord Viscount Howe, on his Naval Conduct of
the American War " ; " Observations upon the Conduct of
Sir William Howe at the White Plains, as related in the
Gazette of December 30th, 1776 " ; " The Examination of
Joseph Galloway, Esquire . . . before the House of
Commons, in a Committee on the American Papers.   With
Explanatory Notes " ; " A Reply to the Observations of
Lieutenant-General Sir William Howe on a Pamphlet enti-
tled ' Letters to a Nobleman '—in which his Misrepresenta-
tions are detected, and those ' Letters ' are supported by a
Variety of New Matter and Argument " ; " An Account of
the Conduct of the War in the Middle Colonies.   Extracted
from a late Author " ; " A Letter from Cicero to the Right
Honorable Lord Viscount Howe, occasioned by his late

Speech in the House of Commons "; " Letters from Cicero
to Catiline the Second, with Corrections and Explanatory
Notes "; " Fabricius, or, Letters to the People of Great
Britain, on the Absurdity and Mischiefs of Defensive Operations only in the American War, and on the Causes of the
Failure in the Southern Operations." The pamphlets
forming the third group seem not to have been begun till
even from the stern heart of Galloway had died away the
last hope for the further and more competent prosecution of
the war. With great ability, and at times with much pathos,
he then set forth the motives, the services, and the sacrifices
of the American Loyalists, and their claims for considerate
treatment at the hands of the British government, in support
of which they had risked and lost their all. These pamphlets,
but two in number, bear the following titles:—" Observations
on the Fifth Article of the Treaty with America, and on the
Necessity of appointing a Judicial Enquiry into the Merits
and Losses of the American Loyalists "; and " The Claim
of the American Loyalists Reviewed and Maintained upon
incontrovertible Principles of Law and Justice."

CHAPTER XVIII.

THE WHIG PAMPHLETEERS IN REPLY TO LOYALIST ATTACKS: NOVEMBER, 1774–APRIL, 1775.

I.—The two chief replies to the " Westchester Farmer " were " A Full Vindication of the Measures of the Congress," and " The Farmer Refuted "—Both by Alexander Hamilton, then an undergraduate in King's College—The extraordinary intellectual ability herein displayed.

II.—The leading points of Hamilton's argument both aggressive and defensive—The alleged lack of legality in the Congress—The essential rights of mankind not derived from parchments—The purpose of despotism not to be frustrated by the force of entreaty—Civil liberty is natural liberty.

III.—Hamilton's anticipation of the military strategy most suitable for the Americans in the war then imminent—His own confession of political faith—A monarchist and a believer in the rights of man—The vast range of thought displayed in his writings during the Revolution.

IV.—The letters of " Massachusettensis" replied to by John Adams in the essays of "Novanglus"—Great reputation of these essays—Their merits and defects.

V.—The Loyalist writer, Myles Cooper—He is assailed by a New York mob in August, 1775—His escape to England and his rewards there—His " American Querist "—His " Friendly Address to all Reasonable Americans."

VI.—Cooper's " Friendly Address " replied to in an unfriendly manner by General Charles Lee—The latter's " Strictures "—His insults to Cooper as a clergyman—Lee's droll discussion of American military competence in the impending conflict with Great Britain.

I.

AMONG the throng of replies which burst forth from the press in opposition to the tremendous pamphlets of the " Westchester Farmer "—first published between the middle of November, 1774, and the latter part of January, 1775, —were two which immediately towered into chief prominence: " A Full Vindication of the Measures of the Congress from the Calumnies of their Enemies," and " The

Farmer Refuted." The extraordinary ability of these two pamphlets—their fullness in constitutional learning, their acumen, their affluence in statement, their cleverness in controversial repartee, their apparent wealth in the fruits of an actual acquaintance with public business—led both the " Westchester Farmer " and the public in general to attribute them to some American writer of mature years and of ripe experience—to some member of the late Congress, for example—particularly to John Jay or to William Livingston.[1]

It is not easy to overstate the astonishment and the incredulity with which the public soon heard the rumor, that these elaborate and shattering literary assaults on the argumentative position of the Loyalists were, in reality, the work of a writer who was then both a stripling in years and a stranger in the country—one Alexander Hamilton, a West Indian by birth, a Franco-Scotsman by parentage, an undergraduate of King's College by occupation, a resident within the Thirteen Colonies but little more than two years, and at the time of the publication of his first pamphlet only seventeen years of age. Even the modern reader of these essays does not need to have an enthusiastic temper in order to be able to agree with the latest editor of Hamilton that, in view of the age of the writer, these essays are " little short of wonderful."[2] " There are displayed in these papers," says, also, George Ticknor Curtis, " a power of reasoning and sarcasm, a knowledge of the principles of government and of the English constitution, and a grasp of the merits of the whole controversy, that would have done honor to any man, at any age. . . . To say that they evince precocity of intellect gives no idea of their main characteristics. They show great maturity—a more remarkable maturity than has ever been exhibited by any other person, at so early an age, in the same department of thought."[3]

---

[1] John T. Morse, Jr., " The Life of Alexander Hamilton," i. 13–15 ; Henry Cabot Lodge, " Alexander Hamilton," 8–9.

[2] Henry Cabot Lodge, " The Works of Alexander Hamilton," i. 3.

[3] " Constitutional History of the United States," i. 274.

25

II.

Of these two pamphlets by Hamilton, the central doctrine is the ultimate one into which American political thinking had then developed, perhaps in half-conscious preparation for the still suppressed and repudiated doctrine of Independence, namely, that the American colonies owed allegiance to the king only, and not to parliament at all [1]; in short, that parliament had no right whatsoever to legislate for America.[2]   Moreover, in Hamilton's pamphlets, and mustered about this central doctrine, there stand in battle array those other propositions, both positive and negative, which logically attend it: especially, that every attempt at a constitutional readjustment not based on this doctrine, would be dangerous and futile [3]; that this doctine was entirely consistent with colonial fealty to the empire [4]; that in the assertion and defense of this doctrine, the American people may properly resort to every means that shall be needful—whether provided by existing laws or not, and whether pacific or otherwise.[5]

For example, the "Westchester Farmer" had made much of the supposed lack of legality attaching to the Continental Congress.   "Granting your supposition were true," retorts Hamilton, "it would be a matter of no real importance.   When the first principles of civil society are violated, and the rights of a whole people are invaded, the common forms of municipal law are not to be regarded. Men may then betake themselves to the law of nature; and, if they but conform their actions to that standard, all cavils against them betray either ignorance or dishonesty.   There are some events in society to which human laws cannot extend, but when applied to them lose all their force and efficacy.   In short, when human laws contradict or discoun-

---

[1] " The Farmer Refuted," 25–38.   [2] Ibid. 5–15, 49–50.
[3] " A Full Vindication," etc., 23–24, 33.   " The Farmer Refuted," 24–25.
[4] " The Farmer Refuted," 15–17, 21.
[5] " A Full Vindication," etc., 4, 8, 10–12, 20–21.   "The Farmer Refuted," 50–53, 55, 58, 65–66, 70, 75.

tenance the means which are necessary to preserve the essential rights of any society, they defeat the proper end of all laws, and so become null and void.

" But you have barely asserted, not proved, this illegality. If by the term, you mean contrariety to law, I desire you to produce the law against it, and maintain there is none in being. If you mean that there is no law the intention of which may authorize such a contention, I deny this also. It has always been a principle of the law, that subjects have a right to state their grievances, and petition the king for redress. . . . If so, it cannot be doubted that when a people are aggrieved, and their circumstances will not allow them unitedly to petition in their own persons, they may appoint representatives to do it for them." [1]

So, too, after he has argued at great length and with great power, that the exemption of the American colonies from parliamentary control is provided for in their charters, he shrewdly anticipates the objection that New York, at least, is an American colony which has no charter, and has never had one. To this objection he replies with unruffled composure: " It is true, that New York has no charter. But, if it could support its claim to liberty in no other way, it might with justice plead the common principles of colonization; for it would be unreasonable to seclude one colony from the enjoyment of the most important privileges of the rest. There is no need, however, of this plea. The sacred rights of mankind are not to be rummaged for among old parchments, or musty records. They are written as with a sunbeam, in the whole volume of human nature, by the hand of the Divinity itself, and can never be erased or obscured by mortal power." [2]

The " Westchester Farmer " had produced a profound effect by his contention that, while the Americans no doubt had serious grievances to be redressed, they had gone about the business in the wrong way; that, instead of such disorderly and irritating measures as they had resorted to, they

---

[1] " The Farmer Refuted," 52–53, both text and note.   [2] Ibid. 38.

should have approached the throne with loyal and respectful petitions; and that loyal and respectful petitions would have been listened to. " It betrays," says Hamilton, " an ignorance of human nature to suppose, that a design formed and ripening for several years, against the liberties of any people, might be frustrated by the mere force of entreaty. Men must cease to be as fond of power as they are, before this can be the case." [1]

Thus, at every turn in a debate which needed to be in part a technical one, this marvelous youth, while quick and expert in the use of technical arguments, never fails by the assertion of some broad, noble, and illuminating principle, to lift the controversy above the pettiness and the aridity natural to all discussion confined to the mere letter of the legal text. Here in America he finds some millions of men and women fretting themselves over nice questions touching the basis and the scope of civil liberty; when straightway he expels all pedantry and all political pharisaism from the discussion by the sweet breath of such quiet and sane words as these: " Civil liberty is only natural liberty, modified and secured by the sanctions of civil society. It is not a thing in its own nature precarious and dependent on human will and caprice; but is conformable to the constitution of man, as well as necessary to the well-being of society." [2]

III.

Even more astonishing, perhaps, is the evidence here given of military as well as of political genius on the part of this juvenile pamphleteer. He shows clear and complete foresight of the exact conditions of the stupendous physical conflict which was approaching; of the precise way in which it was to be met on behalf of the Americans; and of the attitude toward us and toward England, which would inevitably be taken by the nations of Europe—particularly by France, Spain, and Holland. [3] Thus, within the compass of

---

[1] " The Farmer Refuted," 58.　　[2] Ibid. 22.　　[3] Ibid. 70–75.

two or three pages, printed several months before there was an American army in existence, and before Washington had been appointed to take command of it, one may read a distinct delineation of the strategy which in our circumstances would be necessary for success—the very strategy, in fact, which was adopted and put into force by Washington, and through which the American cause won its weary way to victory during the subsequent eight years.[1]

Finally, near the close of his second pamphlet, this writer —still unknown to the public—has a noble passage of self-reference, in reply to certain personal allusions which his antagonist had made to him—to his supposed connection with Revolutionary measures then in progress, to his supposed motives for the part he was taking in the troubles of the time: " Whatever opinion may be entertained of my sentiments and intentions, I attest that Being whose all-seeing eye penetrates the inmost recesses of the heart, that I am not influenced, in the part I take, by any unworthy motive; that if I am in an error, it is my judgment, not my heart, that errs; that I earnestly lament the unnatural quarrel between the parent state and the colonies, and most ardently wish for a speedy reconciliation—a perpetual and mutually beneficial union; that I am a warm advocate for limited monarchy, and an unfeigned well-wisher to the present royal family. But, on the other hand, I am inviolably attached to the essential rights of mankind, and the true interests of society. I consider civil liberty, in a genuine unadulterated sense, as the greatest of terrestrial blessings. I am convinced that the whole human race is entitled to it, and that it can be wrested from no part of them, without the blackest and most aggravated guilt. I verily believe, also, that the best way to secure a permanent and happy union between Great Britain and the colonies is to permit the latter to be as free as they desire. To abridge their liberties, or to exercise any power over them which they are unwilling to submit to, would be a perpetual source

---

[1] " The Farmer Refuted," 72–73.

of discontent and animosity. A continual jealousy would exist on both sides. This would lead to tyranny on the one hand, and to sedition and rebellion on the other. Impositions not really grievous in themselves, would be thought so; and the murmurs arising from thence would be considered as the effect of a turbulent ungovernable spirit. These jarring principles would at length throw all things into disorder, and be productive of an irreparable breach, and a total disunion. That harmony and mutual confidence may speedily be restored between all parts of the British empire, is the favorite wish of one who feels the warmest sentiments of good will to mankind, who bears no enmity to you, and who is—A sincere Friend of America.'' [1]

In the exposition of his views touching the several vast fields of thought here brought under consideration,—constitutional law, municipal law, the long line of colonial charters, colonial laws and precedents, international polity as affecting the chief nations of Christendom, justice in the abstract and justice in the concrete, human rights both natural and conventional, the physical and metaphysical conditions underlying the great conflict then impending,—it must be confessed, that this beardless philosopher, this statesman not yet out of school, this military strategist scarcely rid of his roundabout, exhibits a range and precision of knowledge, a ripeness of judgment, a serenity, a justice, a massiveness both of thought and of style, which would perhaps make incredible the theory of his authorship of these pamphlets, were not this theory confirmed by his undoubted exhibition in other ways, at about the same period of his life, of the same astonishing qualities: as in his '' Remarks on the Quebec Bill,'' [2] published in 1775; in his letters under the signature of '' Publius,'' [3] published in 1778; in his essays over the signature of '' The Continent-

---

[1] '' The Farmer Refuted,'' 77–78.

[2] Consisting of two articles, first printed in '' The New York Journal,'' and reprinted in '' The Works of Hamilton,'' Lodge's ed., i. 171–178.

[3] Ibid. 189–200.

alist," [1] published in 1781; above all, in his personal letter to James Duane [2] written in 1780, and containing a powerful statement of the defects of the articles of confederation, and an almost miraculous forecast of the very incidents and sequences of the process by which, some seven or eight years afterward, the articles of confederation were actually developed into the constitution of the United States.

IV.

Not long after his return home from the first Continental Congress, John Adams seems to have been startled by the argumentative ability and the brilliance of certain essays then appearing in a Boston newspaper over the signature of " Massachusettensis," and well calculated, as he thought, to turn away popular support from that plan of American opposition which the Congress had just promulgated. These essays at once called forth many replies,—none more notable than those which were written by John Adams himself, and which, over the signature of " Novanglus," were published in the " Boston Gazette " between the twenty-third of January and the seventeenth of April, 1775. Although the series was then abruptly closed by the outbreak of hostilities,—an event which had the added effect of diminishing to some extent the pertinence of any further verbal discussion of American rights,—these papers were, even after that event, widely read on this side of the Atlantic, and were repeatedly published on the other side; as in London by Almon in the " Remembrancer " for 1775; in Amsterdam, in a Dutch version, in 1782; and again in London by John Stockdale in 1784. Even so late as the year 1819, they were once more published in this country,—bound up in the same volume with the essays to which they were originally a reply. [3]

---

[1] Originally published in " The New York Packet," and reprinted complete for the first time in the " Works of Hamilton," Lodge's ed., i. 229–273.

[2] " The Works of Hamilton," Lodge's ed., i. 203–228.

[3] The most accessible edition of " Novanglus " is that included in " The Works of John Adams," iv. 3–177.

Probably no reader of these essays can now avoid the impression that the celebrity still attaching to them is due to the celebrity achieved by their author in other fields, rather than to any unusual literary merit in the essays themselves. Trenchant, pungent, able, and indeed powerful, they are, as statements of the radical and aggressive side of the great controversy. They contain, also, single passages of passionate and energetic eloquence, snatches of caustic humor, clever strokes of retaliatory fencing and of logical word-play, occasional sentences which flash light far down into the crevices of the great problem in dispute. Above all, for a lawyer-like presentation of the later American doctrine of the allegiance of the colonies to the person of the king only, and of their total exemption from the authority of parliament, they are certainly learned, ingenious, and masterful— even if at times inaccurate and unsound. Nevertheless, as examples of literary statement they have many defects: they set out with the blustering proclamation of a large purpose, which they speedily forget and abandon; they abound in whim and extravagance; they are disjointed, rambling, disproportioned; before they have proceeded far, they plunge into a vast morass of technical discussion, into which, perhaps, no living reader will ever follow the writer, from which, in fact, the writer himself never emerges alive.

V.

Every student of the political writings produced among us in the years 1774 and 1775 will come upon many passages of satire and invective which can be understood only through some acquaintance with the person and the career of Myles Cooper, then president of King's College, New York,—an Anglican clergyman of high cultivation, of wit, and of somewhat versatile literary gifts,—closely associated with Seabury, Wilkins, Chandler, Inglis, and other Loyalist writers of the neighborhood, in the effort to enlighten their fellow-colonists respecting their political duty in those troublous times. For his own part in this campaign of

education, President Cooper became extremely odious to
the advocates of radical measures,—a fact of which he was
made painfully aware by many noisy and violent demonstrations. Finally, on a certain night in August, 1775, while in
his rooms in the college, he received notice of the approach
of a considerable body of liberty-loving gentlemen who,
being bent on " seizing him in his bed, shaving his head,
cutting off his ears, slitting his nose, stripping him naked,
and setting him adrift," had merely paused by the way to
strengthen themselves for their noble task by " a proper
dose of Madeira." [1] Making his escape through a back window, Cooper was piloted by one of his pupils to a place of
refuge for the night, and on the morrow was taken on board
an English ship-of-war, wherein he soon sailed for England.
In July, of the following year, he published in " The Gentleman's Magazine " [2] a poem, as " By an Exile from
America," giving in sixteen six-lined stanzas a narrative of
the attack of the mob upon him and of his own difficult
escape from its clutches,—a poem somewhat whimpering in
tone, and somewhat too suggestive of a martyr advertising
his own martyrdom in blissful expectation of immediate
ecclesiastical rewards. And, indeed, in this expectation
Cooper was not disappointed. For all his sufferings, he
was duly consoled by two good livings in the church. In
December, 1776, he preached at Oxford a sermon on " The
Causes of the American Rebellion," which was published
there in the following year. Dying at Edinburgh in 1785,
he was buried, according to his own wish, in a small and a
very exclusive cemetery in the neighborhood, and thus, as
his epitaph, written by himself, expressed it :

" unobscured by crowds, withdrew
To rest among a chosen few."

In consideration of his painful experience at the hand of
crowds in New York, it will perhaps be conceded that this

---

[1] " Appleton's Cyclopædia of Am. Biog.," i. 730.   [2] Pages 326–327.

preference of his for a posthumous avoidance of them, even in Edinburgh, was not unnatural.

There can be no doubt that, during portions of the years 1774 and 1775, the uncommon literary gifts of Myles Cooper were freely at the service of the Loyalist cause, and that from his pen came some of the wittiest and most stinging jeux-d'esprit in the Loyalist newspapers of that period. To him, also, by common consent, were attributed two famous political pamphlets, both published in 1774, and both dealing with the controversy precipitated by the first Continental Congress. Of these, the first was " The American Querist, or, Some Questions Proposed relative to the present Disputes between Great Britain and her American Colonies," signed by " A North American." It consists of a hundred questions, all having to do with the matters then at issue. Nothing is asserted; but the questions are so asked as to indicate how every man of sense and of right feeling is expected to answer them,—a mode of discussion whereby the author can vibrate at pleasure between conciliation and satire, and can be very dogmatic without seeming to be so. The second pamphlet, " A Friendly Address to all Reasonable Americans," was still more celebrated,— becoming, indeed, a sort of standard for the Loyalists of the time to rally to, and a favorite target for the shots of their opponents. Taking up the leading arguments urged on behalf of the radical measures then in progress, it replies to them in a fair and considerate tone, but with great acuteness and force, and thus clears the ground for the development of the conservative American position, namely, an assertion of their constitutional rights within the empire, doing this with courage and firmness, yet with decency, moderation, and good humor, and the rejection of every act or aspect of disloyalty. " The great object in view should be a general American constitution on a free and generous plan, worthy of Great Britain to give and of the colonies to receive. This is now become necessary to the mutual interest **and** honor both of the parent kingdom and of its American offspring. Such an establishment is only to be obtained by decent, candid, and respectful application, and not by compulsion or threatening. To think of succeeding by force of arms, or by starving the nation into compliance, is a proof of shameful ignorance, pride, and stupidity." [1]

VI.

Of the many replies [2] which Cooper's second pamphlet called forth, probably none was more talked about and laughed over, and none was more effective, than a certain sprightly brochure, bearing the date of February 3, 1775, [3] and styling itself, " Strictures on a Pamphlet entitled 'A Friendly Address to all Reasonable Americans.' " [4] From the first, it was attributed to the pen of General Charles Lee, and undoubtedly with truth; for it has all the notes of that brilliant and Mephistophelean personage—eccentricity, fluency, smartness, tartness, a mocking tone, a cosmopolitan air, unusual information, an easy assumption of authority on all subjects—particularly on those appertaining to military history and to military criticism. [5]

That the " Friendly Address," though an anonymous publication, was really the work of an Anglican clergyman of high position, was a fact too useful for purposes of controversy to be neglected by a debater like Charles Lee, and he does not fail to develop it in his very first paragraph; and

---

[1] " A Friendly Address," etc., 47.

[2] Among these replies, a very striking one is entitled " The Other Side of the Question," by " A Citizen," and published in New York in 1774. I used the rare copy belonging to George Bancroft, now in the Lenox Library. It is in a tone of irony and banter, and its thrusts are not less keen than those of Lee.

[3] This date stands at the head of the reprint given in " Mem. of the Life of the Late Charles Lee," etc., 136.

[4] My quotations are from an edition published in Boston, 1775.

[5] That Lee was the author of the pamphlet is further certified by its inclusion among his " Miscellaneous Pieces," as published in his " Memoirs," London, 1792, pages 136–155. For an account of the origin of this book and of its value, the reader should look at " The Writings of George Washington," Sparks's edition, ix. 108 n.

thenceforward it recurs, as an almost constant refrain of derision, in the several passes and pauses of his argument: " I know not whether the author is a layman or ecclesiastic, but he bears strongiy the characters of the latter. He has the want of candor and truth, the apparent spirit of perse- cution, the unforgivingness, the deadly hatred to dissenters, and the zeal for arbitrary power, which has distinguished churchmen in all ages, and more particularly the high part of the Church of England. I cannot help considering him as one of this order." [1]

For the convenience of his readers, he then gives a curt and well-phrased outline of the pamphlet he is to deal with: whereupon he thus disposes of it by wholesale: " Now I challenge the world to produce so many wicked sentiments, stupid principles, audaciously false assertions, and mon- strous absurdities, crowded together into so small a com- pass." [2] Notwithstanding this, and at the risk of offering " an insult to American understandings," he proceeds to pick out and to reply to some of these preposterous argu- ments; as, for instance, that the duty on tea is no tax, because " unless we consent to the tax, we are not to pay the duty—we may refuse purchasing it if we please. The same logic would demonstrate that a duty on beer, candles, or soap, would be no tax: as we are not absolutely obliged to drink beer—we may drink water; we may go to bed before it is dark; and we are not forced to wash our shirts." [3]

Hastening from the political aspect of the dispute, the writer then turns to that which was of far greater interest to him—its military aspect. If the Americans keep up their controversy with England until the appeal shall pass from arguments to arms, what reasonable hope for success can they have ? None, none whatsoever, in the opinion of the author of the " Friendly Address." " Regular armies from

---

[1] " Strictures," etc., 2.   [2] Ibid. 3–4.
[3] Ibid. 4. The inalienable right last mentioned by General Lee in the above sentence, is one which he is said to have habitually exemplified in his own toilet.

Great Britain, Hessians, Hanoverians, royal standards erected, skillful generals, legions of Canadians, and unnumbered tribes of savages, swords flaming in front and rear, pestilence, desolation, and famine, are all marshaled in a most dreadful order by this church-militant author."[1] Moreover, to the royal standard, as soon as it shall be erected, will resort " all who have the courage to declare themselves now friends to government "; and these, " in a good cause, will be of themselves formidable to their opposers. Dreadfully formidable they must be indeed ! There would resort to it—let me see—. . . there would resort to it, Mr. Justice Sewall, the Honorable Mr. Paxton, Brigadier Ruggles, and about eight or ten more mandamus councilmen, with perhaps twice their number of expectants, and not less than twenty of the unrecanted Hutchinsonian addressers: these the four provinces of New England alone would send forth. New York would furnish six, seven, or probably eight volunteers, from a certain knot who are in possession or expectation of contracts, and the fourth part of a dozen of high-flying Church-of-England Romanized priests. I represent to myself the formidable countenance they will make, when arranged under the royal or ministerial standard; but what will add to the terror of the appearance, will be their Reverend Pontifex himself, whom I conceive marching in the front, an inquisitorial frown upon his brow, his bands and canonicals floating to the air, bearing a cross in his hands, with the tremendous motto—' in hoc signo vinces '—flaming upon it in capital letters of blood, leading them on and exciting them to victory. It is impossible that men who are not under an infatuation by the judgment of Heaven, should flatter themselves that forty-thousand American yeomanry . . . should stand the shock of this dreadful phalanx.

" But I should beg pardon for attempting to be ludicrous upon a subject which demands our utmost indignation. I shall now, therefore, on the presumption that the people of

---

[1] " Strictures," etc., 4–5.

England should be so lost to sense, virtue, and spirit, as to suffer their profligate mis-rulers to persevere in their present measures, endeavor to state to you what is their force, and what is yours. I shall endeavor to remove the false terrors which this writer would hold out, in order to intimidate you from the defense of your liberties and those of posterity—that he and his similars may wallow in sinecures and benefices heaped up from the fruits of your labor and industry. Great Britain has, I believe, of infantry at home, comprehending Ireland, and exclusive of the guards, fifteen thousand men. They find the greatest difficulty in keeping the regiments up to anything near their establishment: what they are able to procure are of the worst sort. They are composed of the most debauched weavers, apprentices, the scum of the Irish Roman Catholics who desert upon every occasion, and a very few Scotch who are not strong enough to carry packs. This is no exaggeration: those who have lately been at Boston represent the soldiers there, one or two regiments excepted, as very defective in size, and apparently in strength. But we shall be told they are still regulars, and regulars have an irresistible advantage. There is, perhaps, more imposition in the term regular troops, than in any of the jargon which issues from the mouth of a quack doctor. I do not mean to insinuate, that a disorderly mob are equal to a trained, disciplined body of men; but I mean, that all the essentials necessary to form infantry for real service, may be acquired in a few months. I mean that it is very possible for men to be clothed in red, to be expert in all the tricks of the parade, to call themselves regular troops, and yet, by attaching themselves principally or solely to the tinsel and show of war, be totally unfit for real service. This, I am told, is a good deal the case of the present British army. If they can acquit themselves tolerably in the puerile reviews exhibited for the amusement of royal masters and misses in Hyde Park or Wimbledon Common, it is sufficient. In the beginning of the late war, some of the most esteemed regular regiments were sent over to this country: they were well dressed, they were well powdered, they were perfect masters of their manual exercise, they fired together in platoons,—but fatal experience taught us, that they knew not how to fight. While your militia were frequently crowned with success, these regulars were defeated or baffled for three years successively in every part of the continent. At length, indeed, after repeated losses and disgraces, they became excellent troops, but not until they had absolutely forgotten everything which, we are assured, must render regulars quite irresistible. . . . Upon the whole, it is most certain that men may be smartly dressed, keep their arms bright, be called regulars, be expert in all the antics of a review, and yet be very unfit for real action. It is equally certain, that a militia, by confining themselves to essentials, by a simplification of the neces- sary manœuvres, may become in a very few months a most formidable infantry. The yeomanry of America have, besides, infinite advantages over the peasantry of other countries: they are accustomed from their infancy to fire- arms, they are expert in the use of them; whereas the lower and middle people of England are, by the tyranny of certain laws, almost as ignorant in the use of a musket, as they are of the ancient catapulta. The Americans are, likewise, to a man, skillful in the management of the instruments necessary for all military works, such as spades, pickaxes, hatchets, etc. Taking, therefore, all circumstances into consideration, there will be no rashness in affirming that this continent may have, formed for action, in three or four months, an hundred thousand infantry.'' [1]

Finally, is it to be inferred from all this, that the writer of '' Strictures '' is desirous of precipitating a civil war? Nay, he declares, that would be to do him '' great injus- tice.'' Nevertheless, '' he is convinced that being pre- pared for a civil war, is the surest means of preventing

---

[1] '' Strictures,'' etc., 7–9.

it; that to keep the swords of your enemies in their scab-
bards, you must whet your own." [1]

---

[1] "Strictures," etc., 11.   Other examples of Charles Lee's work as a lively writer
on American affairs during the Revolution are, "A Breakfast for Rivington," in
" Memoirs" of Lee, 130–135 ; " To the Gentlemen of the Provincial Congress
of Virginia," ibid. 156–164 ; " A Short History of the Treatment of Major
General Conway, Late in the Service of America," ibid. 173–182 ; and " Some
Queries, Political and Military, Humbly offered to the Consideration of the
Public," 183–188.   The last two pieces are fine specimens of his capacity in
malice toward Washington.   Perhaps nothing that he ever wrote gives us a better idea of his wit, his eccentricity both in loving and in loathing, and his mockery of things sacred, than his " Last Will and Testament," ibid. 189–183.   Of
course, the question of his political character is not now before us ; but in dismissing him from further consideration in this place, it may be remarked that
Charles Lee's treason to the American government was perhaps more profligate,
and certainly more damaging, than that of Benedict Arnold ; but that Lee had
the singular luck to escape public exposure, and therefore the extreme infamy he
deserved, until after he had been in his grave for three quarters of a century.
He died in 1782 ; and not until 1858 was George Henry Moore's monograph
on " The Treason of Charles Lee, Major General, Second in Command of the
Army of the Revolution," first given to the world.

CHAPTER XIX.

THE ENTRANCE OF SATIRE INTO THE REVOLUTIONARY CONTROVERSY: PHILIP FRENEAU, 1775.

I.—The transition from political debate to civil war, April 19, 1775, as described by two British officers—The military incidents of the year—The new world of ideas opened to the Americans by this change in the sphere of the controversy.

II.—Contemporary comments on these events as made by Franklin in letters to Priestley and other friends in England.

III.—The change in American literary expression caused by the transfer of the issue from reason to force—The development of satire as a prominent form of literature in the Revolution.

IV.—The materials for satire furnished by the character and results of the earliest collisions between the British regulars and the American militia—British opinion as to the lack of military courage and of military discipline among the Americans—The first experience of the regulars with the militia at Lexington and Concord—The military anti-climax presented by the British retreat—The ironical ballad of " The King's Own Regulars, and their Triumph over the Irregulars."

V.—The Hibernian-Yankee's epistle, " To the Troops in Boston "—The scornful tone of " A New Song to the Tune of ' The British Grenadiers ' "—The materials for ridicule furnished by the military situation in 1775, call into the service of the Revolution two great artists in satire, Philip Freneau and John Trumbull.

VI.—Freneau's abandonment of higher poetic work for the service of satire—His fierceness as a satirist—Lines of self-description—His careful training for this work.

VII.—Freneau begins his work as a Revolutionary satirist in 1775—Five satirical poems produced by him in the latter half of that year—His response to General Gage's salutation of the Americans as rebels—" On the Conqueror of America Shut up in Boston."

VIII.—Freneau's satire, " The Midnight Consultations, or, a Trip to Boston " —Declares for American Independence nearly a year before its official proclamation—He predicts American national greatness—He relents in favor of reconciliation with England.

IX.—Freneau renews more fiercely than ever his demand for a total separation from the country that was so injuring us—His " Libera Nos, Domine."

I.

" AFTER a variety of commotions, all of which portended bloodshed, a rebellious war broke out on the nineteenth of this month. On that day, our troops were attacked at Lexington and Concord, the whole country rising upon them; and a straggling encounter ensued from these towns to this place." [1] Such is the euphemistic version of the leading events of an unforgetable day, as given by a British officer in a letter written from Boston on the 25th of April, 1775. " From Concord back to Lexington," wrote another British officer, with less disposition to smooth the rough edges of history, " we sustained a constant fire from every fence, house, hollow way, and height, as we passed along. Here Lord Percy joined us with the first brigade: he had left Boston at nine o'clock that morning. It was a necessary reinforcement, for the whole country were in arms, and all the picked men for forty miles around. We got back to Boston with the loss of upwards of fifty men, and many more wounded. This finished our excursions against rebel magazines. I cannot tell the rebel loss." [2]

Perhaps the first visible result of this " straggling encounter " was that, on the following morning, the British army awoke to find itself closely shut up within the town of Boston, and its curiosity to become better acquainted with the interior of New England thereafter effectually restrained by a motley rabble of armed peasants encamped in its neighborhood. Moreover, it should be here noted that, for the remainder of this year 1775, among the direct consequences of what happened on the nineteenth of April, were the American capture of Ticonderoga and Crown Point, on the 10th of May; the battle of Bunker Hill, on the 17th of June; the appointment of Washington as commander-in-chief, on the 19th of June; the capture of Montreal by an

---

[1] " The Detail and Conduct of the American War, under Generals Gage, Howe, and Burgoyne, and Vice Admiral Lord Howe," 5.

[2] Ibid. 9–10.

American force under Montgomery, on the 12th of November; and, finally, the disastrous failure of the American attack on Quebec, on the 31st of December.

So ended the year in which the physical conflict of the Revolution began. And, thus, all tokens point to that day of evil, April the nineteenth, 1775, as the one by which the entire period of the Revolution is cut into two nearly equal but sharply contrasted sections. After ten years of words, the disputants come at last to blows. Prior to this day, the Revolutionary controversy was a political debate: after that, it was a civil war. Of the immense transformation then and there made in the very character and atmosphere of the struggle—in its ideas, its purposes, its spirit, its tone—no modern person can in any other way procure for himself so just and so vivid a picture as by studying the writings produced among us immediately before and immediately after that fatal day. Of the former, we have just inspected the most characteristic examples. It remains for us now to look at the chief representatives of the latter.

II.

There was then at Philadelphia, watching all these dreadful developments, a very wise old man, who loathed war, not merely as a brutal way of solving practical difficulties among men, but as a singularly inapt, clumsy, and inconclusive way; a man who, having been resident in England during the previous ten years, had there put all his genius, all the energy of his heart and will, all his tact and shrewdness, all his powers of fascination, into the effort to keep the peace between these two kindred peoples, to save from disruption their glorious and already planetary empire, and especially to avert the very appeal to force which had at last been made. By a glance at the comments upon the new situation, which Benjamin Franklin then made from day to day, chiefly in the form of letters to a few distinguished friends in England, as Joseph Priestley and William Strahan,

we may now most surely introduce ourselves to the very
thoughts and passions of the noblest Americans in that
sorrowful time, and may perceive both the prodigious transformation in the nature of the controversy wrought through
this change in its method, and also by how impassable a
gulf the America subsequent to April nineteenth, 1775, is
separated from the America prior to that fatal day.

Thus, on the sixteenth of May, Franklin writes to
Priestley: " You will have heard, before this reaches you,
of a march stolen by the regulars into the country by night,
and of their expedition back again.   They retreated twenty
miles in six hours.   The governor had called the assembly
to propose Lord North's pacific plan, but, before the time
of their meeting, began cutting their throats.   You know it
was said he carried the sword in one hand and the olive
branch in the other; and it seems he chose to give them a
taste of the sword first.   .   .   .   All America is exasperated by his conduct, and more firmly united than ever.
The breach between the two countries is grown wider
and in danger of becoming irreparable." [1]   On the fifth of
July, he writes to Strahan: " You have begun to burn our
towns, and murder our people.   Look upon your hands—
they are stained with the blood of your relations!   You and
I were long friends; you are now my enemy, and I am,
Yours, B. Franklin." [2]   On the seventh of July, to Priestley he writes: " The Congress met at a time when all minds
were so exasperated by the perfidy of General Gage, and his
attack on the country people, that propositions for attempting an accommodation were not much relished; and it has
been with difficulty that we have carried another humble
petition to the crown, to give Britain one more chance, one
opportunity more, of recovering the friendship of the colonies; which, however, I think she has not sense enough to
embrace, and so I conclude she has lost them forever.   She
has begun to burn our seaport towns.   .   .   .   She may
doubtless destroy them; but, if she wishes to recover our

[1] " Works of Franklin," Bigelow ed., v. 532–533.   [2] Ibid. 534.

commerce, are these the probable means ? . . . If she wishes to have us subjects, and that we should submit to her as our compound sovereign, she is now giving us such miserable specimens of her government, that we shall detest and avoid it, as a complication of robbery, murder, famine, fire, and pestilence." [1]

On the third of October, Franklin again writes to Priestley: " Tell our dear good friend, Dr. Price, who sometimes has his doubts and despondencies about our firmness, that America is determined and unanimous,—a very few Tories and placemen excepted, who will probably soon export themselves. Britain, at the expense of three millions, has killed one hundred and fifty Yankees this campaign—which is twenty thousand pounds a head; and at Bunker's Hill she gained a mile of ground, half of which she lost again by our taking post on Ploughed Hill. During the same time sixty thousand children have been born in America. From these data, his mathematical head will easily calculate the time and expense necessary to kill us all, and conquer our whole territory." [2]

On the same date, to another friend in England, he writes: " I wish as ardently as you can do for peace, and should rejoice exceedingly in coöperating with you to that end. But every ship from Britain brings some intelligence of new measures that tend more and more to exasperate; and it seems to me that until you have found by dear experience the reducing us by force impracticable, you will think of nothing fair and reasonable. . . . If you would recall your forces and stay at home, we should meditate nothing to injure you. A little time so given for cooling on both sides, would have excellent effects. But you will goad and provoke us. You despise us too much; and you are insensible of the Italian adage, that ' there is no little enemy.' I am persuaded that the body of the British people are our friends; but they are changeable, and by your lying gazettes may soon be made our enemies. Our respect

---

[1] " Works of Franklin," Bigelow ed., v. 534–535. [2] Ibid. 539–540.

for them will proportionably diminish, and I see clearly we are on the highroad to mutual enmity, hatred, and detestation. A separation of course will be inevitable. It is a million of pities, so fair a plan as we have hitherto been engaged in for increasing strength and empire with public felicity, should be destroyed by the mangling hands of a few blundering ministers. . . . We hear that more ships and troops are coming out. We know that you may do us a great deal of mischief; . . . but if you flatter yourselves with beating us into submission, you know neither the people nor the country." [1]

III.

Of course, a swift change in the literary expression of the controversy resulted from this change in its sphere and its weapons,—this transition from reason to force, this abandonment of arguments for arms.

The deep, true love of Americans for the mother country, their pride in the British empire, their sincerity in the belief that all their political demands were compatible with their own loyalty and with the honor of England, their desire that the solution of every vexing problem should be reached in peace,—all these were realities, realities as genuine as they were pathetic. In the transactions of the nineteenth of April, 1775, at the hands of official representatives of the mother country, all these sacred realities were foully dealt with,—they were stamped upon, were spit upon, they were stabbed and shot at and covered with blood and cast into the mire. Accordingly, reaching this fatal point in his journey across the period of the Revolution, the student of its literature becomes then and there conscious of crossing a great spiritual chasm—of moving from one world of ideas and sentiments to a world of ideas and sentiments quite other and very different. As the news of the transactions of that day travels from man to man, upon white lips, up and down the country, all at once with each group of listen-

[1] " Works of Franklin," Bigelow ed., v. 540–541.

ers there seems to come a spiritual revolution: in place of
what was before in their hearts, are now mute astonishment
as of persons stunned, a shock of horror and pain, the
anguish born of affection spurned with insult and of patriotic devotion crushed under outrage; next, a consciousness
of the futility of all further appeals to reason, to tradition,
to law, to right; then, the conviction that henceforward all
these wonderful questions about stamps and paints and glass
and tea, about the right of representation and the right of
petition, about the British parliament and the British crown,
are simply things of a very dead past, mere antiquarian
trinkets and gew-gaws, themes for human discourse as obso-
lete as the gossip of that polite society that went down
under the Deluge. Moreover, instead of all these politico-
metaphysical conundrums, Americans find staring them in
the face this altogether serious and not at all metaphysical question,—whether their homes are to be forcibly entered
by red-coated ruffians, their property to be seized, their
wives and daughters to be outraged, and themselves to be
shot down on their own doorsills for making objection.
Certainly, the thing next to be done by them, is to fight;
but for what? For the privilege of resuming, on better
terms, their old place in the British empire? Away with
the British empire on any terms! For the red flag of their
king? What care they any more for the red flag of a king
who has made that flag redder yet in the blood of subjects
who loved him and who never meant to be disloyal to him?

As to American literature, from this day forward it can
only be in the moods and forms of the new situation: for
the enemy, words of loathing, of scorn, of defiance, gibes,
scoffings, mockings, taunts; for friends, words of faith,
words of deathless resolution, words of indomitable cheer,
with songs that may move men to fight in the cause of the
new fatherland and gaily to die for it. As it proved, the
most prominent and the most characteristic form of literature developed under the conditions of American society
after the nineteenth of April, 1775, was Satire.

IV.

A most enticing opportunity for satire was furnished, during the year 1775, by the character and results of these first collisions between the British troops and the poor, ill-equipped, and ill-disciplined provincials, who, as had been frankly promised, were to be scared or beaten into submission at a single display of imperial force.

If we would now perceive the point and edge of this earliest development of regular satire during the Revolutionary controversy, we must remember that, as was not at all strange, the British entered upon the war with no expectation that it was to be a long and a desperate one, and especially with extreme contempt for the military resources and for the military qualities of their insubordinate colonists, basing their judgment, apparently, upon two supposed facts : first, that the Americans were a people lacking in warlike courage, and, secondly, that being quite without military discipline, and quite without the willingness to submit themselves to it, their volunteer troops could never stand up against British regulars. Moreover, as it happened, in the months immediately before the opening of hostilities, this strong Britannic contempt was again and again flung into speech by indiscreet representatives of it, and in a way admirably calculated to give it the widest celebrity and the sharpest sting. Thus, in the house of lords, the Earl of Sandwich, a member of the ministry, had declared that as soldiers the Americans were " raw, undisciplined, and cowardly " ; that they could never " look British regulars in the face "; that " the very sound of a cannon would send them off as fast as their feet could carry them." [1] So, also, Major Pitcairn, who was shot dead while gallantly entering the American redoubt at Bunker Hill, had boasted, on embarking at Portsmouth for America, that " if he drew his sword but half out of the scabbard, the

---

[1] Geo. Bancroft, " Hist. U. S.," last rev., iv. 137–138 ; F. Moore, " Diary of the Am. Rev.," i. 344.

whole banditti of Massachusetts Bay would flee from him." [1]
Sir Jeffrey Amherst, likewise, was reported to have said
that " with five thousand English regulars he would engage
to march from one end to the other of the continent of
North America." [2]

When, accordingly, early one morning in the spring of
1775, on Lexington common, a considerable force of these
invincible British regulars first saw in front of them a little
group of undisciplined and cowardly yeomen, they very
promptly fired upon them; and having thus killed eight,
and wounded nine, they burst into a laugh, and with a few
good round British oaths they swore that, of course, the
Yankees could never bear the smell of gunpowder. Nevertheless, on that same day, and even before many hours had
passed by, these same British regulars, having ceased to
laugh, and having found rather urgent occasion to return
speedily to Boston, were so chased, and fired upon, and
otherwise harassed, by the cowardly provincials, that they
themselves were thought to have manifested some anti-
pathy to gunpowder, and even to have illustrated their
martial prowess chiefly by the quality of speed in making a
retreat. Certainly, the despicable Yankees must have been
superhuman beings to have foreborne from the uproar of
loud derision in the presence of this grotesque example of
the military anti-climax, in which, indeed, were materials
for satire too choice to be disregarded by our young brood
of American versifiers then and there looking on.

A rough specimen of such satirical work as they then did,
may be seen in an anonymous ballad soon afterward scattered broadside over the land, and entitled " The King's
Own Regulars, and their Triumph over the Irregulars; a
New Song, to the Tune of 'An Old Courtier of the Queen's,
and the Queen's Old Courtier.' " Thus adopting for his

---

[1] F. Moore, " Diary of the Am. Rev.," i. 344.

[2] This was stated in a London paper for April 15, 1775, and reprinted in the
" Pennsylvania Packet " for June 12th of the same year. F. Moore, " Diary of
the Am. Rev.," i. 96.

ballad the long, rambling, ludicrous verse then familiar to all
in the famous English ballad bearing the first part of the
same title, the poet represents one of these British regulars
in America as giving a blunt, soldierly account of the
achievements of the force to which he belonged, and especially of the little incident of their retreat from Concord,
palliating the disgrace of it by ironical excuses which really
cut the other way and made the disgrace more obvious:

" Since you all will have singing, and won't be said nay,
    I cannot refuse, when you so beg and pray ;
    So I 'll sing you a song, as a body may say,—
    'T is of the King's Regulars, who ne'er ran away.
    O ! the Old Soldiers of the King, and the King's Own
    Regulars.

        .   .   .   .

" No troops perform better than we' at reviews,—
    We march, and we wheel, and whatever you choose ;
    George would see how we fight, and we never refuse ;
    There we all fight with courage—you may see 't in the news.

        .   .   .   .

" Grown proud at reviews, great George had no rest ;
    Each grandsire, he had heard, a rebellion suppressed ;
    He wished a rebellion—looked round, and saw none—
    So resolved a rebellion to make—of his own.

" The Yankees he bravely pitched on, because he thought they
        would n't fight,
    And so he sent us over to take away their right ;
    But lest they should spoil our review clothes, he cried braver
        and louder,
    For God's sake, brother kings, don't sell the cowards any
        powder.

" Our General with his council of war did advise,
    How at Lexington we might the Yankees surprise ;
    We marched—and re-marched—all surprised at being beat,
    And so our wise General's plan of surprise was complete.

" For fifteen miles, they follow'd and pelted us—we scarce had
　　time to draw a trigger ;
But did you ever know a retreat performed with more vigor ?
For we did it in two hours, which saved us from perdition ;
'T was not in going out, but in returning, consisted our ex-
　　pedition.

　　·　　　·　　　·　　　·　　　·　　　·　　　·　　　·

" Of their firing from behind fences, he makes a great pother :
Every fence has two sides, they made use of one, and we only
　　forgot to use the other ;
That we turned our backs and ran away so fast,—don't let
　　that disgrace us,—
'T was only to make good what Sandwich said, that the Yankees
　　could not face us !

" As they could not get before us, how could they look us in the
　　face ?
We took good care they should n't—by scampering away
　　apace ;
That they had not much to brag of, is a very plain case—
For if they beat us in the fight, we beat them in the race !
O ! the Old Soldiers of the King, and the King's Own
　　Regulars." [1]

V.

Another satirical versifier, dwelling upon the comic aspects
of the retreat of the British regulars from Concord, conceived the idea of adding to the general mirth and of still
further making light of these light-footed gentlemen, by
means of a pretended epistle, as from the pen of a shrewd
and grinning Irishman on the Yankee side of the line, and
addressed

　　　" To the Troops in Boston.

" By me faith, but I think ye 're all makers of bulls,
　　Wid your brains in your breeches, your guts in your skulls !

---

[1] This ballad, which was circulated during the Revolution in many forms, is
given in full by F. Moore, " Diary of the Am. Rev.," i. 214–216, as from the
" Pennsylvania Evening Post," for March 30, 1776.

Get home wid your muskets, and put up your swords,
And look in your books for the maneing of words :
Ye see now, me honeys, how much ye 're mistaken,—
For Concord by discord can never be baten !

" How brave ye wint out wid your muskets all bright,
And thought to befrighten the folks wid the sight ;
But whin ye got there, how they powder'd your pums,
And all the way home how they pepper'd your —— ;
And is it not, honeys, a comical crack,
To be proud in the face, and be shot in the back !

" How came ye to think, now, they did not know how
To be afther their firelocks as smartly as you ?
Why, ye see now, me honeys, 't is nothing at all—
But to pull at the trigger—and pop goes the ball.

" And what have ye got now, wid all your designin',
But a town widout victals to sit down and dine in ;
And to look on the ground like a parcel of noodles,
And sing how the Yankees have conquer'd the Doodles ?
I 'm sure if ye 're wise, ye 'll make peace for a dinner,—
For fightin' and fastin' will soon make ye thinner." [1]

From mere irony, from playful ridicule to stern derision,
to proud and scoffing defiance, was for the American satirists in 1775 an easy transition, as the spring of that year
advanced into the summer and the autumn, and as the
incompetence of British generalship in America continued
to develop its almost incredible score of blunders and
disasters :

" Your dark, unfathomed councils, our weakest heads defeat,
Our children rout your armies, our boats destroy your fleet ;

---

[1] This Hibernian-Yankee ballad seems to have made a great hit, as may be
easily imagined ; and it was printed off in various versions both in the newspapers and on separate sheets.   F. Moore, who gives a version of it printed in
May, 1775, says that the trifle first appeared in the " Pennsylvania Magazine."
—" Songs and Ballads of the Am. Rev.," 92–93.

And to complete the dire disgrace, coop'd up within a town,
You live the scorn of all our host, the slaves of Washington!

" Great heaven!—is this the nation, whose thundering arms
    were hurled
Through Europe, Afric, India?—whose navy ruled the world?
The lustre of whose former deeds, whose ages of renown,
Lost in a moment, are transferred to us and Washington?"[1]

These examples of spontaneous and artless satire, from American verse-writers whose names are lost perhaps beyond recovery, may suffice to show us how the new ideas, the new hatreds, the new hopes, begotten of the first clash of arms, of the first blood and anguish of defeat or victory, found their prompt and almost unstudied utterance among us in a vast miscellany of humorous and sarcastic rhymes. It is now our pleasant duty to extend and deepen our studies in this field, and to note how the copious materials for satire furnished by this earliest chapter of military experience in the Revolution, called into the American service two great, and indeed still unrivaled, artists in satire, Philip Freneau and John Trumbull.

VI.

In a former part[2] of this work, the attempt has already been made to trace the poetic career of Freneau down to a time just prior to the events now reached by us. Though he had already given ample proof of his capacity for higher and sweeter work than that of satire, he then turned away from such work with full deliberation, as from something for

---

[1] These lines are from " A New Song to the Tune of ' The British Grenadiers,'" consisting of twelve vigorous stanzas. It seems to have escaped the researches of other explorers in this field, and was found by me among the Revolutionary broadsides belonging to the Pennsylvania Historical Society. Of course, the typographical execution of such broadsides was very careless; and in the last two lines of the portion above quoted, I have corrected two obvious errors of the press.

[2] See chapter viii.

which his own age and country did not care, and devoted his whole strength as a poet to the service of satire — of satire upon the political and military enemies of the Revolution. Whether it was by nature, whether it was by culture, Freneau succeeded in confronting the enemy, both foreign and domestic, with a visage as stern, with a scorn as bitter, with a loathing as ruthless as that required by the unamiable muse whom he had chosen for his mistress. It will scarcely be doubted by any reader of Freneau's verse, that, in the development of that awful tempest of partisan rancor and race hatred which we call the American Revolution, this man was faithful to his vocation of stimulating its violence to the utmost; or that, at its close, the thought could ever have rested as a burden upon his conscience, that any lull or pause in the ferocity of the great conflict had been due to the least self-restraint on his part in the expression of political and personal acrimony towards the armed or the unarmed foes of the Revolution. Indeed, in one of his earliest satires he acknowledges the pitiless nature of his purpose, the implacable fierceness of his method:

> "Rage gives me wings, and, fearless, prompts me on
> To conquer brutes the world should blush to own ;
> No peace, no quarter, to such imps I lend—
> Death and perdition on each line I send." [1]

In one of his latest satires, also, he causes the party-shifting printer, Hugh Gaine, in confessing the publication of some of Freneau's verses, to give a powerful and a really just description of the poet's relentless asperity in satire:

> "To gain a mere trifle, a shilling or so,
> I printed some treason for Philip Freneau,—
> Some damnable poems reflecting on Gage,
> The king, and his council, and writ with such rage,
> So full of invective and loaded with spleen,
> So pointedly sharp, and so hellishly keen,

---

[1] "The Poems of Philip Freneau," 86.

That, at least in the judgment of half our wise men,
Alecto herself made the nib to his pen." [1]

Freneau's training for the business of a satirist was thorough. From his youth up, he had been a particular student
of Latin literature—that literature, the only original and
supremely powerful element in which is satire. As could
be said of but few of his American contemporaries, he had
found his way, also, to the French poets and satirists. If
the minor English poets of his own early manhood, feeble
and even bastard as was their art,—Shenstone, Macpherson,
Mason, Akenside, Warton—seem to have had for him as a
contemporary a charm which they can never have, it may be
hoped, for any later member of the human family, it still
remains to be told that his true masters in English verse
were Churchill, Pope, and Dryden, and in their special work
as satirists.

VII.

Moreover, Freneau began his career as a satirist at a fortunate moment,—at a moment when just such a satirist was
in demand, and when the materials for just such satire—sincere, infuriate, savage, remorseless satire—were furnished to
his hand in profuse abundance by the political and the military incidents that were transacting all around him. The
first unmistakable flashes of his satiric power which can now
be recognized on themes connected with the Revolution,
belong to that pathetic and heroic year, 1775, when, at last,
after more than a decade of intellectual controversy, the
crash of the physical controversy began to be heard, reverberating all along the continent from Lexington common
and from the grim hill by the side of Charlestown. As
many as four or five poems, all elastic with vigor, and all
steeped in satiric passion and acerbity, leaped from his pen
that year:—" On the Conqueror of America Shut up in

---

[1] " The Poems of Philip Freneau," 283-284.

Boston," [1] and " General Gage's Soliloquy," [2] both published in August; " The Midnight Consultations, or, A Trip
to Boston," [3] and " Libera Nos, Domine," [4] both published
in September; and, finally, " MacSwiggen," [5] published
probably in November or December.

Thus, the first four of these poems appeared within the
two months of August and September; and the American
situation at that very time both illustrates, and is illustrated
by, them. In the last of the four the vision sweeps over the
entire scene, up and down the continent, and takes account
of all our chief assailants there. In the first three, the scene
is confined to the neighborhood of Boston, the conspicuous
person in it being General Thomas Gage, who, after two
futile and disastrous attempts at penetrating the interior of
the country, is with his half-fed army shut up in Boston
and there beleaguered by a despicable mob composed of
those American peasants whom he had just before, with
great bluster and pomp of words, denounced as rebels, and
doomed to the halter. These are the salient facts upon
which the eye of the American satirist fastens; and first
catching up the damning name which the British general
had sought to fix upon two millions of people, their poet
flings back the sombre compliment with ample reparation :

> "'Rebels you are'—the British champion cries.
> Truth, stand thou forth, and tell Tom Gage he lies !
> 'Rebels !'—and see, this mock imperial Lord
> Already threats those 'rebels' with the cord !

> "The hour draws nigh, the glass is almost run,
> When truth must shine, and scoundrels be undone,
> When this base miscreant shall forbear to sneer—
> And curse his taunts and bitter insults here." [6]

---

[1] " The Poems of Philip Freneau," 74–75.　　　　[2] Ibid. 59–63.
[3] Ibid. 63–72.　　　　[4] Ibid. 58–59.
[5] Ibid. 83–88.　　　　[6] Ibid. 74–75.

Of course, never has any man of Anglo-Saxon blood delighted, at first, in the name of rebel: the taste for it among us is an acquisition attainable only through culture. In the bestowment of that sort of culture, Freneau was quite ready to be of use to his countrymen:

> " If to control the cunning of a knave,
>   Freedom adore, and scorn the name of slave,
>   If to protest against a tyrant's laws,
>   And arm for vengeance in a righteous cause,
>   Be deemed rebellion—'t is a harmless thing,
>   This bug-bear name, like death, has lost its sting." [1]

At the same time he warns them not to forget that the mighty Power which, through its representative, now applies to Americans the word rebels, has an awful record for unshrinking thoroughness in dealing with such offenders:

> " If Britain conquers, help us, Heaven, to fly !
>   Lend me your wings, ye ravens of the sky.
>   If Britain conquers,—we exist no more :
>   These lands shall redden with their children's gore,
>   Who turned to slaves, their fruitless toils shall moan—
>   Toils in these fields that once they called their own !

> " To arms ! to arms !—and let the trusty sword
>   Decide who best deserves the hangman's cord ;
>   Nor think the hills of Canada too bleak,
>   When desperate freedom is the prize you seek.

> .   .   .   .

> " Haste ! to your tents in fetters bring
>   These slaves that serve their tyrant of a king.
>   So just, so virtuous, is your cause, I say
>   Hell must prevail—if Britain wins the day ! " [2]

---

[1] " The Poems of Philip Freneau," 75.
[2] Ibid.

VIII.

The longest and perhaps also the most powerful of these satires for the year 1775, is the one entitled " The Midnight Consultations, or, A Trip to Boston." Though not published until September, its time is a midnight in June,—the midnight following the Bunker Hill fight; and the British chiefs, again baffled by the rebels as they had been two months before, and now disheartened by the amazing power of resistance, and even of aggression, displayed by these ill-armed rustics, are represented as having come together for consultation at the house of General Gage. The poet, guided by what he calls the " glimmering beam " of the polestar, has in a vision made his journey thither at that very time, in order, as he says,—

" To view the peevish, half-starved spectres there,"

and to see for himself just how these, our lately confident assailants,

" sicken in these hostile climes,
Themes for the stage, and subjects for our rhymes." [1]

As he comes upon the scene, and remembers the sufferings which these brutal invaders have already brought, and the still greater sufferings which they are destined to bring—unless driven back—his anger breaks out in the form of an impassioned apostrophe to his imperiled country, imploring her, at last, to call forth and to use the enormous resources for destruction which nature has deposited in her forests and her mines:

" Know your own strength—in rocky deserts bred,
Shall the fierce tiger by the dog be led,
And bear all insults from that snarling race
Whose courage lies in impudence of face ? " [2]

---

[1] " The Poems of Philip Freneau," 64. [2] Ibid. 64-65.

After this gust of wrath, the poet comes into the beleaguered city, and soon finds his way

> " to the dome of state
> Where Gage resides—our western potentate,
> Chief of ten-thousand, all a race of Huns,
> Sent to be slaughtered by our rifle-guns ;
> Sent by our angry Jove—sent sword in hand
> To murder, burn, and ravage through the land." [1]

At Gage's house, he looks in upon the chiefs assembled there, — seeing, of course, Gage himself ; and Admiral Graves, commander of the British war-ships in the harbor; and General Burgoyne already known in America for his personal vanity and his windy rhetoric; and Lord Percy, who was accused of having shown rather too much agility in getting away from the scene of danger; and, finally, General Howe:

> " Twelve was the hour—congenial darkness reigned,
> And no bright star a mimic daylight feigned.
> First, Gage we saw—a crimson chair of state
> Received the honor of his Honor's weight.
> This man of straw the regal purple bound,
> But dullness, deepest dullness, hovered round.
>   Next Graves, who wields the trident of the brine,
> The tall arch-captain of the embattled line,
> All gloomy sate—mumbling of flame and fire,
> Balls, cannons, ships, and all their damned attire ;
> Well pleased to live in never-ending hum,
> But empty as the interior of his drum.
>   Hard by, Burgoyne assumes an ample space,
> And seemed to meditate with studious face,
> As if again he wished our world to see
> Long, dull, dry, letters writ to General Lee—
> Huge scrawls of words through endless circuits drawn,
> Unmeaning as the errand he 's upon.

---

[1] " The Poems of Philip Freneau," 65.

Is he to conquer—he subdue our land—
This buckram hero, with his lady's hand?
By Cæsars to be vanquished is a curse,
But by a scribbling fop—by heaven, is worse!"

"Lord Percy seemed to snore—but may the muse
This ill-timed snoring to the peer excuse :
Tired was the long boy of his toilsome day—
Full fifteen miles he fled, a tedious way.
.   .   .   .

Howe, vext to see his starving army's doom,
Once more besought the skies for ' elbow room.'
.   .   .   .

He cursed the brainless minister that planned
His bootless errand to this hostile land ;
But awed by Gage, his bursting wrath recoiled,
And in his inmost bosom doubly boiled." [1]

These, then, are the British chiefs who, occupying the
high places in the council room, are surrounded by a crowd
of inferior officers—

"a pensioned clan,
A sample of the multitudes that wait,
Pale sons of famine at Perdition's gate ;
.   .   .   .

Knights, captains, squires—a wonder-working band !
Held at small wages till they gain the land." [2]

The deliberations are opened by General Gage, who, humil-
iated and angry over the result of the war thus far, and
especially over the battle of that day, gives vent to his
spleen, and meanly trying to fasten the blame upon his
subordinates, has only courage enough to fling a taunt at
young Percy:

"Now Gage, rebounding from his cushioned seat,
Swore thrice, and cried ' 'T is nonsense to be beat !

---

[1] "The Poems of Philip Freneau," 65–67.   [2] Ibid. 66–67.

Thus to be drubbed ! Pray, warriors, let me know
Which be in fault, myself, the fates, or you !
Henceforth let Britain deem her men mere toys !
Gods ! to be frighted thus by country boys.
Why, if our army had a mind to sup,
They might have eat that schoolboy army up !
Three thousand to twelve hundred thus to yield,
And twice five hundred stretched upon the field !—
O shame to Britain, and the British name ;
Shame damps my heart, and I must die with shame,
Thus to be worsted, thus disgraced and beat !—
You have the knack, Lord Percy, to retreat ;
The death you 'scaped my warmest blood congeals,
Heaven grant me, too, so swift a pair of heels ! '

   .   .   .   .   .   .

Thus spoke the great man in disdainful tone
To the gay peer,—not meant for him alone." [1]

By this taunt roused from his slumber, Lord Percy mildly
defends himself,—arguing that, since a well-aimed ball may
hit a peer as well as a peasant, he is the wise peer who
keeps aloof from danger as much as he may ; and then he
turns upon General Howe with the insinuation that, whatever may have been his own blame that day, the disaster
on Bunker Hill was due chiefly to that officer. Of course,
to this charge General Howe makes reply ; and then, at the
close of his speech, turning from their miserable past to
their still more miserable future, he appeals to his comrades
to unite in some plan to save themselves at least from starvation. Under this appeal, Gage solemnly announces to
the council the great decision to which his mind has been
brought in consequence of their deliberations :

      " Gage smote upon his breast,
And cried, ' What fate determines must be best.

   .   .   .   .   .   .

---

[1] " The Poems of Philip Freneau," 67.

Three weeks—ye gods ! nay, three long years it seems,
Since roast beef I have touched, except in dreams.
In sleep, choice dishes to my view repair,—
Waking, I gape and champ the empty air.
Say, is it just that I, who rule these bands,
Should live on husks, like rakes in foreign lands ?—
Come, let us plan some project ere we sleep,
And drink destruction to the rebel sheep.
On neighboring isles uncounted cattle stray,
Fat beeves, and swine—an ill defended prey ;
These are fit victims for my noonday dish,
These, if my soldiers act as I would wish,
In one short week would glad your maws and mine—
On mutton we will sup, on roast beef dine ! '
  Shouts of applause reëchoed through the hall,
And what pleased one as surely pleased them all ;
Wallace was named to execute the plan,
And thus sheep-stealing pleased them to a man." [1]

Certainly, the satire in all this is genuine. The comedy of
such a situation,—the invincible troops of Great Britain discomfited by provincial militia, and, pent up in a seaboard
town, saving themselves from actual starvation by a concerted resort to sheep-stealing on the undefended islands in
Boston harbor,—not only has in it something extremely
grotesque, but has, likewise, a logical bearing on American
hopes and fears touching the issue of the contest that still
lies before them ;—and all this the poet fails not to make
use of :

  " What are these upstarts from a foreign isle,
  That we should fear their hate, or court their smile ?
  .   .   .   .
  Laughs not the soul when an imprisoned crew
  Affect to pardon those they can't subdue ;
  Though thrice repulsed, and hemmed up to their stations,
  Yet issue pardons, oaths, and proclamations ? " [2]

---

[1] " The Poems of Philip Freneau," 70.   [2] Ibid. 70–71.

And then it was—nearly a year before the project for Independence was to find official sanction—that this poet bitterly and boldly proclaimed Independence as the only sensible and adequate remedy for American wrongs:

> " Too long our patient country wears their chains,
>   Too long our wealth all-grasping Britain drains !
>   Why still a handmaid to that distant land ?
>   Why still subservient to their proud command ?
>   Britain the bold, the generous, and the brave,
>   Still treats our country like the meanest slave ;
>   Her haughty lords already share the prey,
>   Live on our labors, and with scorn repay !
>   Rise, sleeper, rise, while yet the power remains,
>   And bind their nobles and their chiefs in chains.
>   Fallen on disastrous times, they scorn our plea ;—
>   'T is our own efforts that must make us free.
>   Born to contend, our lives we place at stake,
>   And grow immortal by the stand we make." [1]

Nay, as upon their own unconquerable spirits, so upon the face of nature itself, is written the promise of a great destiny for the American people; and with the unhesitant tone and gesture of a prophet, the poet proceeds to unroll the canvas on which is painted the future of their nation, as one vast, united, free, and peaceful empire of humanity, filling all the vast domain from the Atlantic to the Mississippi:

> " The time shall come when strangers rule no more,
>   Nor cruel mandates vex from Britain's shore ;
>   When commerce shall extend her shortened wing,
>   And her rich freights from every climate bring ;
>   When mighty towns shall flourish free and great,—
>   Vast their dominion, opulent their state ;
>   When one vast cultivated region teems
>   From ocean's side to Mississippi's streams,

---

[1] " The Poems of Philip Freneau," 71.

> While each enjoys his vine tree's peaceful shade,
> And even the meanest has no foe to dread." [1]

It is a touching fact,—it tells, indeed, of the deep reluctance with which the American colonists accepted this robust remedy of national Independence, and even of their early fluctuations in mood after they had accepted it,—that at the close of this very satire, in which Freneau so early and so passionately demanded the rupture of every tie that bound us to the mother land, even he relented—he, the impersonation of Revolutionary radicalism and fierceness—and yielding, for one brief moment, to the strong plea of filial affection, himself sent forth a touching prayer for peace—for reconciliation—for a lasting union between the colonies and the mother country, such as they had enjoyed under the one English king who was ever fondly loved in America:

> " O heaven-born Peace, renew thy wonted charms ;
> Far be this rancor, and this din of arms ;
> To warring lands return, an honored guest,
> And bless our crimson shore among the rest.
> Long may Britannia rule our hearts again—
> Rule as she ruled in George the Second's reign ;
> May ages hence her growing grandeur see,
> And she be glorious—but ourselves be free ! " [2]

IX.

It must be told, however, that this sob of wounded affection—this burst of natural grief over sacred ties that were breaking—this naïve cry for an arrest of Revolutionary fury and hurly-burly, and for a return to the subordination and the quietude of the old colonial times—all this was, on Freneau's part, but a momentary relapse into political soft-heartedness. As if to proclaim his remorse for such weakness, and his full recovery from it, almost immediately afterward he sent forth his " Libera Nos, Domine,"—a

---

[1] " The Poems of Philip Freneau," 71.　　　　[2] Ibid. 72.

slashing, contemptuous, and fierce litany for total and final
deliverance from every shred of British rule and contact:

" From a junto that labor for absolute power,
  Whose schemes disappointed have made them look sour ;
  From the lords of the council, who fight against freedom,
  Who still follow on where the devil shall lead 'em ;

" From the group at St. James's, that slight our petitions,
  And fools that are waiting for further submissions ;
  From a nation whose manners are rough and abrupt,
  From scoundrels and rascals whom gold can corrupt ;

" From pirates sent out by command of the king
  To murder and plunder, but never to swing,—
  From Wallace, and Graves, and Vipers and Roses,
  Whom, if heaven pleases, we 'll give bloody noses ;

" From the valiant Dunmore, with his crew of banditti,
  Who plunder Virginians at Williamsburgh city ;
  From hot-headed Montague, mighty to swear,
  The little fat man with his pretty white hair ;

" From bishops in Britain, who butchers are grown,
  From slaves that would die for a smile from the throne ;
  From assemblies that vote against Congress proceedings—
  (Who now see the fruit of their stupid misleadings) ;

" From Tryon the mighty, who flies from our city,
  And swelled with importance, disdains the committee,—
  (But since he is pleased to proclaim us his foes,
  What the devil care we where the devil he goes) ;

" From the scoundrel, Lord North, who would bind us in chains,
  From a dunce of a king who was born without brains,
  The utmost extent of whose sense is to see
  That reigning and making of buttons agree ;

" From an island that bullies, and hectors, and swears,
  I send up to heaven my wishes and prayers
  That we, disunited, may freemen be still,
  And Britain go on—to be damned, if she will ! "[1]

---

[1] " The Poems of Philip Freneau, 58–59.

CHAPTER XX.

THE SATIRICAL MASTERPIECE OF JOHN TRUMBULL: 1775.

I.—John Trumbull in 1773 abandons letters for the law—Enters the law office of John Adams in Boston—His verses bidding farewell to verse-making—Finds himself in the vortex of Revolutionary politics.

II.—He relapses into verse-making—" The Prophecy of Balaam," " The Destruction of Babylon," " An Elegy on the Times, Composed at Boston during the Operation of the Port Bill "—His first words of harshness toward the mother country, whose ruin he predicts—His reluctance to surrender himself to the domination of politics.

III.—Trumbull returns to New Haven in November, 1774—Publishes in August, 1775, a Hudibrastic burlesque on General Gage's Proclamation—The first canto of " M'Fingal " is sent to the press before the end of 1775 —Is published in January, 1776—The action of the poem is just after the day of Lexington and Concord—The hero, Squire M'Fingal—John Adams portrayed as Honorius.

IV.—The town meeting to consider the outbreak of hostilities—Speech of Honorius against British aggressions, General Gage, and the Tories.

V.—Squire M'Fingal makes reply—Denounces the Whigs for stupidity, for lack of patriotism, for greed and cowardice—Vindicates the military proceedings of General Gage—Predicts the utter defeat of the rebellion, with titles and estates in the hands of the Tories, and the Whigs all hanged or reduced to slavery—The indignant reply of Honorius is drowned in Tory catcalls—The meeting breaks up in confusion.

VI.—Such was the plot of the poem in its original form—The poem completed in four cantos and published in 1782—Outline of the story as finished—Its adherence to the three unities.

VII.—The traditional criticism of " M'Fingal " as an imitation of " Hudibras " —Particulars of resemblance and of dissimilarity between the two poems—Trumbull's real master in satire not Butler, but Churchill.

VIII.—The breadth and variety of Trumbull's literary training shown in this poem—His delicate and effective use of parody—The essential originality of " M'Fingal "—A genuine embodiment of the spirit and life of the American people in 1775—It employs satire on behalf of lofty and humane objects—Contrast therein with " Hudibras " and " The Dunciad "—The enormous popularity and influence of " M'Fingal " during the Revolution and in several national emergencies since then.

426

I.

AFTER an early literary career altogether notable for its versatility and its brilliance, John Trumbull,[1] like so many other young Americans, before and since then, with an inward vocation for a life of letters, turned away to a calling far more likely to supply him with bread—the profession of the law. It was in November, 1773,—at the very time when the tea ships were sailing toward us with their cargoes of unimagined disquietude,—that he was admitted to the bar of Connecticut. Being then but twenty-three years of age and not desirous of settling down immediately to practice, he went to Boston with the view of spending a year of study in the law office of John Adams, having his residence during that time in the house of another political chieftain, Thomas Cushing. At this important moment in his life, as he was giving up the cloistered service of poetry and of fine letters for that of a worldly and stormy profession, he wrote in verse an eternal farewell to verse-making, and said to

"nonsense, sighs, and love, good-bye";

at the same time saluting, with a rather mocking reverence, those bewigged and august masters, in whose well-rewarded footsteps he hoped soon to tread:

"In solemn coif before my eyes,
  I see the awful Coke arise;
  There Bracton, Fleta, Blackstone, Wood,
  And fifty more, not understood,

  .   .   .   .   .   .

  Enthroned appear in awful state,
  And point and call me to their seat.
  I come, ye lawyers! oh prepare
  The wig of wide, portentous air;
  The robe of law, whose solemn grace

---

[1] A full account of Trumbull's earlier career, is given in Chapter ix. of the present work.

Gives wisdom to the important face ;
The conscience mild that sleeps at ease,
Nor trembles at the touch of fees ;
The look triumphant in the wrong,
And endless impudence of tongue." [1]

The single year which Trumbull thus passed in Boston, proved to be one of stirring and even world-famous business for that city, which was then, in fact, the very vortex of Revolutionary politics. Not long after his arrival there, he may have seen the British tea ships, as they came sailing up the harbor, and may have heard the yells of those amateur Mohawks who soon afterward rose upon the well-paved war-path, and presented in person their effectual argument against the landing of the execrated cargo. In Boston he must have been, when, a few months later, there fell upon the city the assurance of the choice and peculiar wrath of the king, and the doom of commercial annihilation at the hands of a parliament bought and owned by the king. Many weeks before Trumbull had ended his term of legal study in Boston, his illustrious preceptor had entirely ceased to receive clients, and had gone away to Philadelphia to take his seat in the first Continental Congress; while Boston itself had become inexorably committed to a huge law suit, to which the parties were two angry nations,—a bit of energetic litigation to which none of the precedents which Trumbull was then studying would apply, and in which the advocates most actively engaged on either side would be unlikely to wear wigs or silk gowns.

II.

Notwithstanding all his vows of devotion to the new mistress whom he was there to serve, Trumbull could not forget his earlier love. Even during the hurly-burly of this year in Boston, and amid his ostensible preoccupation with legal

---

[1] Trumbull MSS.

studies, he yielded his secret homage to poetry, writing, in December, 1773, " The Prophecy of Balaam " [1]; in January, 1774, " The Destruction of Babylon " [2]; and in August, 1774, " An Elegy on the Times : Composed at Boston during the operation of the Port Bill." [3] It might well be that his environment should furnish the tints and even the materials of his verse. Certain it is, that there runs through these several poems a vein of sternness, and even of melancholy: they abound in the imagery of tumult, of bloodshed, of desolated cities, of empires given over to wreck and decay. In the last of the three, the poet utters for the first time words of harshness toward the mother country; and he closes the poem with a prophetic picture in which—more than half a century before Macaulay had foreseen the arrival at London Bridge of his fatal New Zealander—Trumbull portrays England as slumbering in a desert isle " in the skirt of day," her fields thick with matted thorns, piles of ruin loading her dreary shore, her baffled genius sobbing a futile prayer to Oblivion to come and draw a veil over her latest shame—her unmotherly and unnatural treatment of her American children.

This fierce note, which one now for the first time observes in Trumbull's verses,—this strain of passionate sympathy with the direction and tone of later Revolutionary politics—marks the moment of his arrival at that culminating stage in his career as a writer, wherein he becomes an historical personage, one of the real forces to be reckoned with as we study the epoch which brought to us our national Independence. Henceforward, all his fine literary accomplishments, his subtlety, his wit, his gift for ridicule, his training in satire, are to be at the service of the popular cause, and are to produce in " M'Fingal," one of the world's masterpieces in political badinage. From such an engulfment and absorption of himself in a grim practical struggle, he seems for a time to have drawn back,—

---

[1] " Poetical Works," ii. 141–146.   [2] Ibid. 195–201.
[3] Ibid. 205–217.

moved thereto doubtless by his instincts as a man of letters, and by his love for the amenities and the gayeties of that form of literature which then took pains to define itself as polite. In the earlier part of the year 1773, for example, as he was projecting a series of entertaining literary essays, he had congratulated himself on the fact that " the ferment of politics " was, as he supposed, " pretty much subsided," and that at last the country was to enjoy a " mild interval from the struggles of patriotism and self-interest, from noise and confusion, Wilkes and liberty." [1] But, as the weeks and the months passed over him in Boston, and as he continued to view all incidents from the fiery interior of that political circle which included many of the most radical leaders in the Revolutionary movement, it is not strange that, in his mind, all merely æsthetic or dainty considerations gave way before the rugged necessities of the situation. Thenceforward, with no hesitation, with no half-heartedness, Trumbull is the scholar in politics,—the poet and the wit fighting the common enemy with an exquisite weapon which but one other American at that time could use so effectively as he.

III.

Already during this stirring year in Boston, his pen had been far busier than is indicated by the foregoing list of poems which he wrote at that time. He knew by instinct the uses to be made of anonymous journalism; and from his secret armory, he shot forth through the newspapers his own sparkling and caustic comments on the fateful events with which that year was so thickly strown, and through which the American people were hastening, half-unconsciously, toward an inappeasable revolt, and toward national autonomy. Moreover, after his return to New Haven in November, 1774, he still kept up this sort of literary-

---

[1] " The Correspondent," No. 9, in " Connecticut Journal," etc., for Feb. 12, 1773.

political warfare, becoming for the purpose a regular contributor to " The Connecticut Courant." It was in that
paper that he published on the 7th and 14th of August,
1775, a Hudibrastic burlesque of General Gage's magnilo-
quent proclamation to " the infatuated multitude,"—a
poem of some two hundred and sixteen lines, from which at
least fifty were shortly afterward reproduced in his great
satire of " M'Fingal." [1] Upon the writing of that celebrated satire he must have been engaged during the autumn
of 1775 ; for it was in January, 1776, at Philadelphia—in the
same place, and almost at the same time with Thomas
Paine's pamphlet, " Common Sense "—that the first canto
of " M'Fingal " made its appearance. [2]

The time of the poem is shortly after the 19th of April,
1775,—within those hot-footed weeks of astonishment,
grief, anger, derision, and defiance, which followed the
news of bloodshed at Lexington and Concord, and of the
scrambling retreat of the ministerial troops from those two
glorious massacres back again to Boston. The scene of the
poem is laid in a certain unnamed New England town,
apparently not far from Boston. The distinction of this
town arises from the fact that it is the home of one
Squire M'Fingal, a Scottish-American politician, who is
at once a blustering champion of the doctrine of unlimited submission to parliament, and an orator of stentorian
lungs, whose appalling volubility, when engaged in the oratorical act, is subject to an occasional reënforcement from

---

[1] This fact was first pointed out by J. Hammond Trumbull, in " The Hist.
Mag.," for Jan., 1868, in an article entitled " The Origin of M'Fingal."
Copies of this article were issued separately, to one of which my references are
made.

[2] " M'Fingal : A Modern Epic Poem. Canto First, or the Town Meeting.
Philadelphia. Printed and Sold by William and Thomas Bradford, at the
London Coffee House, 1775." Notwithstanding this date, the poem was not
published till Jan., 1776. It has 40 pages, and closes thus : " End of Canto
First." The only copy I have seen is that of the N. Y. Hist. Soc. The copy
from which I shall quote, is the London reprint of the same year, formerly belonging to Jared Sparks, and now to Cornell University.

a "Scottish gift of second-sight,"—a mysterious access of cerebral excitement under which he ascends and soars above all sublunar trammels of fact and common sense, and pours torrents of prophetic calamity upon the heads of his antagonists.   In the frequent combats which M'Fingal had in townmeeting with the champions of colonial resistance, this lucky gift of his brought him some capital advantages; for, if ever embarrassed by a dearth of information derived from the past, he was able to turn the tide in his favor by an unlimited supply of information respecting the future.   On such occasions, again and again, he

> " Made dreadful slaughter in his course,
> O'erthrew provincials, foot and horse ;
> Brought armies o'er by sudden pressings
> Of Hanoverians, Swiss, and Hessians ;
> Feasted with blood his Scottish clan,
> And hang'd all rebels, to a man ;
> Divided their estates and pelf,
> And took a goodly share himself."

This typical New England town, thus favored by the presence and the fame of so great a man, was divided with respect to the one great question of parliamentary authority, into two nearly equal factions.   Of the conservative faction, the chief, of course, was M'Fingal; while the radicals were led by an eloquent and fearless politician who bore the significant name of Honorius, and whose portrait seems to be that of Trumbull's preceptor in the law, John Adams.

IV.

And now, in the midst of all the seething and fury of passion into which the people of the several colonies are thrown by the ghastly tidings from Lexington and Concord, the people of M'Fingal's town are summoned to a meeting for the purpose of considering the dangers and duties that

lie before them, M'Fingal himself being just then absent on
a political visit to Boston. The place of assemblage was, of
course, that edifice of miscellaneous utility, then called
neither church nor chapel, but only meetinghouse,—

> " That house, which, loth a rule to break,
>   Serv'd Heaven but one day in the week ;
> Open the rest for all supplies
> Of news and politics and lies."

Within that edifice, thronging all the aisles and pews, now
stand

> " voters of all colors,
> Whigs, Tories, orators and bawlers,
> With every tongue in either faction,
> Prepared, like minute-men, for action."

High above the crowd, on the pulpit stairs, looms the
town constable, with staff in hand, himself and his staff the
embodiment and symbol of the irresistible law of Demos.
Just above him, in the pulpit itself, stands the moderator,
—his majestic head

> " In grandeur o'er the cushion bowed,
> Like Sol half-seen behind a cloud."

In the absence of Squire M'Fingal, who would himself
have had precedence in speech, the assembly is addressed
by the bold Honorius; but before he has proceeded far, in
comes the potent Squire himself, and, with many a frown
darkening his face, sits him down, while the orator, unawed
by M'Fingal's entrance, storms onward in his fiery harangue.
For many ages, says he, has Britain been a mighty power
in the world, wielding her strength, in justice and in kindness, invincible to her foes, a tower of safety and a shield to
her children; and under her benign maternal care have all
these American provinces risen and flourished. But, alas,

28

states, like persons, have their periods of old age and dotage. That period has now been reached by our poor old mother, Britain, whose dotage is shown not only by weakness in war and by folly in statesmanship, but especially by fantastic pretensions to unlimited authority over her grownup children:

> " So Britain, midst her airs so flighty,
> Now took a whim to be almighty ;
> Urged on to desperate heights of frenzy,
> Affirmed her own omnipotency ;
> Would rather ruin all her race,
> Than 'bate supremacy an ace."

In accordance with this spirit of frantic and senile arrogance, she made an idol of the Authority of Parliament, and set it up for us, her American children, to adore:

> " Proclaimed its power and right divine,
> And called for worship at its shrine,
> And for poor heretics, to burn us,
> Bade North prepare his fiery furnace."

Against all this wrong, we opposed our most earnest supplications; but disregarding us and our prayers, she proceeded to destroy our ancient guarantees of political safety:

> " Annulled our charters of releases,
> And tore our title-deeds in pieces ;
> Then signed her warrants of ejection,
> And gallows raised to stretch our necks on ;
> And on these errands sent, in rage,
> Her bailiff and her hangman, Gage ;
> And at his heels, like dogs to bait us,
> Despatched her ' posse comitatus.' "

As to General Gage—that wind-bag warrior whose professional enterprise found its most glorious vent in a crusade of thunderous proclamations—he, indeed,

" was chose to represent
The omnipotence of parliament ;
And as old heroes gained by shifts,
From gods, as poets tell, their gifts,
Our general, as his actions show,
Gained like assistance from below,—
By Satan graced with full supplies
From all his magazine of lies."

Nevertheless, though Gage be but a dunce in war—be only a rhetorical general—we must not forget that even so paltry a creature as he, is capable of causing great mischief; for

" meanest reptiles are most venomous,
And simpletons most dangerous enemies."

Then, turning full upon M'Fingal and his Tory followers, he taunts them with being the representatives of a party composed of the servile apologists for the oppression and ruin of their own country,—

" a venal band,
A dastard race who long have sold
Their souls and consciences for gold ;
Who wish to stab their country's vitals,
If they might heir surviving titles ;
. . . . .
Priests who, if Satan should sit down
To make a Bible of his own,
Would gladly, for the sake of mitres,
Turn his inspired and sacred writers ;
Lawyers who, should he wish to prove
His title t' his old seat above,
Would, if his cause he 'd give 'em fees in,
Bring writs of ' Entry sur disseisin,'
Plead for him boldly at the session,
And hope to put him in possession ;
Merchants who, for his kindly aid,

> Would make him partners in their trade ;
> And judges who would list his pages
> For proper liveries and wages,
> And who as humbly cringe and bow
> To all his mortal servants now."

For such recreant Americans, says the orator,

> "Contempts ineffable await,
> And public infamy forlorn,
> Dread hate and everlasting scorn."

V.

At the very climax of this invective, M'Fingal, stung beyond endurance, gives a signal to his followers, who instantly break forth into a tumult of yells, hisses, groans, and jeers, under which the speech of Honorius is extinguished. Then comes M'Fingal's turn.   You Whigs, he says, can only rail: you have no heads for reason.   If it were not so, you would long since have been overpowered by our arguments.   For have not our high-church clergy,—Walter, Auchmuty, Peters, Cooper, and Seabury,—proved beyond all doubt that kings and parliaments have a divine right to oppress and tease their subjects at pleasure; and hence that

> " sure perdition must await
> The man who rises 'gainst the state ? "

Has not this same noble doctrine been supported, also, by an innumerable swarm of lay scribblers, of whom are Brush, Cowper, Wilkins, Chandler, Booth ?   Has not Leonard, " our scribbler general," been able to show,

> "clear as sun in noonday heavens,
> You did not feel a single grievance ;
> Demonstrate all your opposition
> Sprung from the eggs of foul sedition ? "

Has not

> "our grave Judge Sewall hit
> The summit of newspaper wit,"

and for his great master, General Gage, drawn

> "proclamations, works of toil,
> In true sublime of scarecrow style?"

This cannonade of taunting questions, in which M'Fingal really exhibits the preposterousness of his own cause, is interrupted by a volley of sarcasms from Honorius, upon whom again M'Fingal retorts,—

> "Your boasted patriotism is scarce,
> And country's love is but a farce;
> And after all the proofs you bring,
> We Tories know there 's no such thing,—
> .   .   .   .   .   .
> That self is still, in either faction,
> The only principle of action;
> The loadstone, whose attracting tether
> Keeps the politic world together;
> And spite of all your double-dealing,
> We Tories know 't is so, by feeling."

And not only, continues M'Fingal, have you Whigs no such thing as patriotism, but you have no such thing as courage. Besides, even had you courage, what could you accomplish against the imperial strength of Great Britain?

> "'T would not, methinks, be labor lost,
> If you sit down and count the cost,
> And ere you call your Yankees out,
> First think what work you 've set about.
> Have you not roused, his force to try on,
> That grim old beast, the British lion?
> And know you not, that at a sup
> He 's large enough to eat you up?"

Then, too, have you forgotten those nimble allies of Britain, the savage Indians,

> "With each a hatchet in his hand,
> T' amuse themselves with scalping knives,
> And butcher children and your wives?"

And do you consider, also, how Britain has already

> "assayed her notes,
> To rouse your slaves to cut your throats?
> .   .   .   .   .   .
> And has not Gage, her missionary,
> Turned many an Afric slave to Tory?
> .   .   .   .   .   .
> As friends to gov'rnment, did not he
> Their slaves at Boston late set free;
> Enlist them all in black parade,
> Set off with regimental red?"

When, therefore, you remember this redoubtable Gage, with all his league of "Indians, British troops, and negroes," how can you look for any fate but discomfiture? To these vaunting questions Honorius replies, by a contemptuous review of that warrior's achievements, detailing

> "The annals of his first great year:
> While wearying out the Tories' patience,
> He spent his breath in proclamations;
> While all his mighty noise and vapor
> Was used in wrangling upon paper;
> .   .   .   .   .   .
> While strokes alternate stunned the nation,
> Protest, address, and proclamation;
> And speech met speech, fib clashed with fib,
> And Gage still answered squib for squib."

By these taunts, M'Fingal is goaded to a pretended vindication of the General's conduct of affairs,—a vindication in which the ridiculous incidents of this futile year are set forth with a mock gravity that gives to the whole an extremely absurd effect. Finally, M'Fingal, ever conscious that his real strength lies in prophecy rather than in history, passes into one of his paroxysms of vatication; and the remainder of his speech becomes a specific and confident description of the annihilating victory which the British forces are soon to gain over the rebels, and of the splendid reckoning with which the ministry are to reward the services of the faithful American Tories, when

> " The power displayed in Gage's banners
> Shall cut Amer'can lands to manors,
> And o'er our happy conquered ground
> Dispense estates and titles round !
> Behold the world will stare at new sets
> Of home-made Earls in Massachusetts ;
> Admire, arrayed in ducal tassels,
> Your Ol'vers, Hutchinsons, and Vassals ;
> See joined in ministerial work
> His Grace of Albany and York !
> What lordships from each carv'd estate,
> On our New York assembly wait !
> What titled Jauncys, Gales, and Billops,
> Lord Brush, Lord Wilkins, and Lord Phillips !
> In wide-sleeved pomp of goodly guise,
> What solemn rows of bishops rise !
> Aloft a Card'nal's hat is spread
> O'er punster Cooper's rev'rend head !
> In Vardell, that poetic zealot,
> I view a lawn-bedizened prelate !
> What mitres fall, as 't is their duty,
> On heads of Chandler and Auchmuty !
> Knights, viscounts, barons shall ye meet
> As thick as pavements in the street !
> Even I, perhaps—Heaven speed my claim—
> Shall fix a Sir before my name."

Moreover, in this paradise of triumphant American Toryism, where and what shall be the portion of the audacious men who have stirred up such treasonable commotion ?　Ah, they also will have their use; for

> " Whigs subdued, in slavish awe,
> Our wood shall hew, our water draw,
> And bless that mildness, when past hope,
> Which sav'd their necks from noose of rope.
> For since our leaders have decreed
> Their blacks who join us shall be freed,
> To hang the conquered Whigs, we all see,
> Would prove but weak and thriftless policy,—
> Except their chiefs —the vulgar knaves
> Will do more good preserved for slaves." [1]

This frank avowal of the hopes and the hatreds of the American supporters of the ministry, gives to the Whig champion an advantage which he does not fail to use. Turning away, therefore, from M'Fingal with the sneer,—

> " We can't confute your second-sight :
> We shall be slaves, and you a knight.
> These things must come, but I divine
> They 'll come not in your day, or mine !—"

he lays aside his mocking tone, and with simple and genuine passion appeals to his political friends, pointing out that now was made plain what they had to expect should their enemies triumph; and with burning words he summons them to a fearless and a determined fight for whatsoever in this world can make life honorable or home sweet. Soon, however, the Tories, unable to restrain their anger, interrupt his speech with their howls and their catcalls, with the shuffling of feet and the creaking of pew doors; and as the moderator, to quell the disorder, thumps frantically on the pulpit cushion, and adds to the noise by his cries of " silence," and as the constable increases the difficulty of

---

[1] The last six lines are cited from the edition of 1820, contained in " The Poetical Works " of Trumbull, i. 77.

hearing anybody by bawling out, "Pray hear the moderator," and as the enraged partisans on both sides are about
to come to blows,

> "on a sudden, from without,
> Arose a loud terrific shout,"

whereupon the angry partisans, with whom curiosity appears
to have been more potent than pugnacity, tear themselves
away from the fascinations of the meeting, and run out of
the house; while Squire M'Fingal, bidding the constable
attend him, sallies forth, with drawn sword and a ferocious
countenance, to disperse the mob. In the meantime, however, the wretched moderator, quite demented by fright,
has slipped down from the pulpit, and crawled under a
bench; but when, after some time, he had sufficiently rallied to be able to raise his head from under the bench, and
peeping out had discovered that all his belligerent subjects
had taken themselves off, he gravely emerged from his place
of retreat, and

> "left alone, with solemn face,
> Adjourned them without time or place."

VI.

Such was this notable poem in its original form,—a poem
of about fifteen hundred lines, and obviously broken off with
its story half told. Nevertheless, it was in this form that
"M'Fingal" did its enormous work in stimulating the
thought and passion of the American Revolution; and it
was in this form, also, that it won its first fame in the world.
Not until after the surrender of Cornwallis, in October,
1781,—when the physical struggle of the Revolution had
come to an end,—did the author set about the task of finishing the poem according to the plan which he had at the
first framed for it. Dividing the portion already published

into two cantos, and adding a third canto, and a fourth, he published the whole in the latter part of 1782.[1]

The portion thus added fits happily into what precedes; and the work, as thus made complete, bears every mark of its author's uncommon appreciation of artistic symmetry, and of the classic unities of time and place. In literary quality, also, in acuteness, in wit, in crispness of phrase, in vivacity and drollery of incident, the later portion is even stronger than the earlier; while the final development of its simple plot leads to a series of climaxes full of grotesqueness and of satiric power, and true also to the very life of that period, in which partisan emotion was inclined to express itself in certain corporeal pleasantries the humor of which was more apparent to the perpetrators than to the victims.

In the last two cantos Honorius does not appear; and the cause of the Revolution, having been thus amply vindicated by him in the sphere of reason and of wit, is thenceforward left to the rough championship of a mob of rollicking and riotous patriots, who, under the provocation of a most irritating harangue from M'Fingal, lay hands upon that obstreperous Tory, and subject him to those personal indignities which they, in the jubilance of their animal spirits, regard as comic. Finally, however, at close of day, after the mob has dispersed, contemptuously leaving M'Fingal to the new glory of his tarry and feathery costume, and glued, as it were, by the rear, to that liberty pole around which they had taken such distressing liberty with him, he succeeds after much effort in pulling himself loose. In this plight, he skulks through the village to his home, whither by secret message he summons his political allies to a clandestine meeting that very night. The place of their meeting is, perforce, the cellar. There, in that ignoble auditorium, huddled together and crouching low in their fear, they are addressed by M'Fingal, who emerges for the purpose from

---

[1] "Hartford: Printed by Hudson and Goodwin, near the Great Bridge, 1782." This editio princeps is very properly used by Benson J. Lossing for his reprint of "M'Fingal," with introduction and notes, New York, 1857.

the safe obscurity of his turnip bin. It is his last great
paroxysm of prophetic utterance. All the disaster, and
ignominy, and bitterness of the defeat which awaits them in
the war then just begun, pass before him in vision, and the
whole is reproduced by him in words for the benefit of his
miserable companions; whereupon the Whigs, who,

> "the news have found
> Of Tories must'ring under ground,"

are heard approaching the house. Loud shouts fill the air;
rough blows are rained upon the door. Escape seems impossible. The terror-stricken Tories call upon the very
cellar walls to hide them from the wrath of their implacable
pursuers. One creeps into a box; another crawls under a
tub; still another tries to obliterate his identity by placing
himself behind a row of cabbage heads. In the darkness,
however, M'Fingal, who has now had enough of the mirthful ways of the Whigs, makes his escape through a secret
window, and leaving

> "his constituents in the lurch,"

sneaks away to Boston, to return no more.

VII.

The traditional and, indeed, the stereotyped criticism
upon "M'Fingal," that it is an imitation of "Hudibras,"
is undoubtedly the judgment most naturally formed at the
first glance, and from indications apparent on the surface
of the two poems. Thus, "M'Fingal" certainly follows
"Hudibras" in its general literary type—that of the burlesque epic; and yet even here one needs to observe the
distinction that, while Butler chose the low burlesque, which
does not admit of grave or elevated passages, his follower
adopted the high burlesque, and availed himself of the

privilege it confers, by transitions that are serious and dignified.   Then, too, the verse of " M'Fingal " is obviously the verse which since Butler's time has been called Hudibrastic, that is, the rhymed iambic tetrameters of the earlier English poets, depraved to the droll uses of burlesque by the Butlerian peculiarities, to wit, the clipping of words, the suppression of syllables, colloquial jargon, a certain rapid, ridiculous jig-like movement, and the jingle of unexpected, fantastic, and often imperfect rhymes.   Furthermore, in many places Trumbull has so perfectly caught the manner of Butler, that he easily passes for him in quotation.   This is especially the case with some of those shrewd aphorismal couplets which abound in " M'Fingal " as they do in " Hudibras," and which, as taken from the former, are sometimes attributed to the latter.[1]

Beyond these aspects of resemblance, it is doubtful whether the relation of " M'Fingal " to " Hudibras " be not rather one of contrast than of imitation.   The hero of the one poem is a pedantic Puritan radical of the time of Oliver Cromwell; the hero of the other is a garrulous and preposterous high-church Scottish-American conservative of the time of George the Third.   Each poem is an attempt to exhibit, chiefly through the speeches and the ludicrous and lugubrious adventures of its hero, the questions at issue in a period of revolutionary convulsion; but the earlier poem is a satire on the ideas and methods of the party of progress, while the later one is a satire on the ideas and methods of the party of conservatism.   Moreover, in plot, in arrangement, in incident, there is in " M'Fingal " scarcely a trait that can be accounted as a reproduction of " Hudibras."

---

[1] Two notable illustrations of this remark may be cited.   One is taken from the first canto of " M'Fingal " :

> " But optics sharp it needs, I ween,
> To see what is not to be seen."

The other is from the third canto :

> " No man e'er felt the halter draw,
> With good opinion of the law."

Finally, in the essential qualities of Hudibrastic wit,—in oddity of comparison, in extravagance of fancy, and in the amusing effects produced by a sudden and grotesque assemblage of remote historical and literary allusions,—there is in "M'Fingal" little apparent effort to follow its prototype.

The truth is, that a much closer intellectual kinship existed between Trumbull and Charles Churchill, than between Trumbull and Samuel Butler; and so far as Trumbull's originality in satire was moulded and tinged by the manner of any other satirist, it was not so much by the author of "Hudibras," as it was by his own powerful contemporary, the author of the "Prophecy of Famine," and of "The Ghost." Churchill was Trumbull's true model. It is to Churchill's influence that we are to attribute peculiarities in "M'Fingal" far more fundamental and decisive than any which can be traced to the influence of any other writer. Indeed, what should perhaps be regarded as the most serious fault in "M'Fingal,"—the alien and unreal note imparted to this New England mock-epic by the prominence of the Scottish element in the satire, — can be accounted for in this way, and in this way only. Of such a poem the hero at least should have been not only a native but a typical New Englander, and thus the main force of the satire should have been made to fall, as the author undoubtedly meant that it should fall, upon that powerful class of New England conservatives who then stood forth against the politics of the Revolution. By taking for this Yankee epic a title which, owing to peculiar literary associations, was then intensely Scottish, and by concentrating the reader's derision upon its Scottish hero, and upon Malcolm, his Scottish confederate, a certain local genuineness is lost to the poem; the true direction of the satire is turned aside; and a pair of Scottish Loyalists are dragged in and thrust forward as the real objects of all this satiric venom which really belonged to Loyalists of the pure American type, like Hutchinson, and Leonard, and Oliver. By a glance at the nearly contemporary satires of Churchill, particularly at the

two that are mentioned above,—in which the leading note
is an angry and contemptuous vituperation of the Scottish
element then so prominent in English politics and in English
society,—it will be made clear that it was from Churchill
that Trumbull derived a trait which, though entirely pertinent and very effective in an English satire of that time,
had much less fitness in an American satire, and therefore
gave to it a rather pointless and weakening feature.

It would be a mistake, however, to infer that the influence of Churchill upon Trumbull is to be discovered only in
Trumbull's faults.   This is very far from being the case.   For
example, the verse of " M'Fingal " seems to have a flow
and a freedom characteristic of Churchill: this verse is
indeed Hudibrastic, but in the main it is the Hudibrastic
verse, not of " Hudibras," but of " The Ghost."   Moreover, in the sprightliness and energy of " M'Fingal," in the
robustness of its thought, in its glow of expression, and in
the special quality of its wit, which, for the most part, is
direct and spontaneous rather than artificial and subtle, one
is apt to recognize the sturdy and invigorating tone of the
later English satirist.

VIII.

We should be doing injustice, also, to the variety and the
breadth of Trumbull's literary training, if, in dealing with
the composition of " M'Fingal " as revealing the influence
of its author's literary masters, we should discover only the
influence of Churchill and of Butler.   Trumbull was, according to the best opportunity of his place and time, a catholic
student of letters; and in all his work as a satirist, particularly in this work, one finds in many quiet and indirect
ways, the evidence of his manifold contact with all the masters of his art.

As regards the literary relationships of this poem, one
notable peculiarity is its delicate and effective use of parody
as a means of humorous effect: itself a burlesque epic, it
carries the privilege of burlesque into every detail of style.
Through Trumbull's memory, which was of the miraculous

sort, there seemed to be ever floating strains and melodies borne to him from the myriad-voiced choir of English song; and continually, as he told of his droll hero, and of his hero's adventures, snatches of English classic verse became entangled in his lines, and were detained by him there, and were comically transformed into travesty. Thus, through the opening lines of " M'Fingal " one hears amusing echoes of the opening lines of " Hudibras "; and as from this beginning of the first canto, one reads on and on to the end of the last canto, the ear is continually caught, and the fancy is titillated, by playful reverberations from the ballad of " Chevy Chase," from " Paradise Lost," from the poetry of Dryden, of Swift, of Pope, of Prior, of Macpherson, of Gray.

After all that may be said of the uses which Trumbull made of his literary masters, it remains true that his poem of " M'Fingal " is a work of essential originality.[1] The form is an old one; but into that old form Trumbull put the new life of his own soul, and of his own time. He did not invent the burlesque epic; but he did invent his own treat- ment, under the form of a burlesque epic, of the social and political dispute involved in the American Revolution. In the construction of his poem, he has shown not only orig- inality, but high artistic skill. The plot has a unity, a sym- metry, a consistency which one looks for in vain in such masterpieces as " Hudibras " and " The Dunciad "; the story, though a slight one, is sufficient for the comically didactic purpose for which it is framed; in the management of this story the author avoids those bewildering digressions and those excesses of loquacity in which Butler so often loses himself and the company of his readers; finally, the story advances, by a natural and life-like progress, through a variety of ridiculous circumstances, to a conclusion where- in the ludicrous quality of the satire reaches a fitting and powerful culmination.

---

[1] This conclusion is expressed by Stedman with his usual insight and justice. Of " M'Fingal " he says that " it shows genuine originality, although written after a model." " Poets of America," 35.

No literary production was ever a more genuine embodiment of the spirit and life of a people, in the midst of a stirring and world-famous conflict, than is " M'Fingal " an embodiment of the spirit and life of the American people, in the midst of that stupendous conflict which formed our great epoch of national deliverance. Here we find presented to us, with the vividness of a contemporary experience, the very issues which then divided friends and families and neighborhoods, as they did entire colonies, and at last the empire itself; the very persons and passions of the opposing parties; the very spirit and accent and method of political controversy at that time; and at last, those riotous frolics and that hilarious lawlessness with which the Revolutionary patriots were fond of demonstrating their disapproval of the politics of their antagonists. No one can now fully understand and enjoy " M'Fingal " who is not, in a rather special sense, a student of the American Revolution; but he who is so, will find in it an authentic, a marvelously accurate, a most diverting rehearsal of the logic, the anger, and the humor of an epoch in our national experience which can never cease to have for us either a profound importance or an absorbing charm.

Satire is, of course, one of the less noble forms of literary expression; and in satire uttering itself through burlesque, there is special danger of the presence of qualities which are positively ignoble. Yet never was satire employed in a better cause, or for loftier objects, or in a more disinterested spirit. Often has satire been but the ally of partisan selfishness and malice, or of the meanness of personal spite. To add derision to defeat, to overwhelm with scoffs and with pitiless ridicule a great party which was already overwhelmed with disaster, to fling mocks and jibes at men who, never lacking ability or courage, were then crushed and powerless, and able to move neither tongue nor hand in reply—that was the object of the author of " Hudibras." To appease the stings of literary vanity, to avenge himself on his rivals, to make the world ring with his wrath at a group of paltry and obscure personal enemies—that was the object of the author of " The Dunciad." Now the author of " M'Fingal " wrote his satire under no personal or petty motive. His poem was a terrific assault on men who, in his opinion, were the public enemies of his country; and he did not delay that assault until they were unable to strike back. " M'Fingal " belongs, indeed, to a type of literature never truly lovely or truly beautiful,—a type of literature hard, bitter, vengeful, often undignified; but the hardness of " M'Fingal," its bitterness, its vengeful force are directed against persons believed by its author to be the foes —the fashionable and the powerful foes—of human liberty; if at times it surrenders its own dignity, it does so on behalf of the greater dignity of human nature.

That " M'Fingal " is, in its own sphere, a masterpiece, that it has within itself a sort of power never attaching to a mere imitation, is shown by the vast and prolonged impression it has made upon the American people. Immediately upon its first publication it perfectly seized and held the attention of the public. It was everywhere read. " Its popularity was unexampled." [1] It became " the property of newsmongers, hawkers, peddlers, and petty chapmen." [2] Probably as many as forty editions of it have been issued in this country and in England. It was one of the forces which drove forward that enormous movement of human thought and passion which we describe as the American Revolution; and in each of the great agitations of American thought and passion which have occurred since that time, occasioned by the French Revolution, by the war of 1812, and by the war which extinguished American slavery, this scorching satire against social reaction, this jeering burlesque on political obstructiveness, has been reëdited, has been republished, has been sent forth again and again into the

---

[1] J. Hammond Trumbull, " The Origin of M'Fingal," 11–12.
[2] " The Poetical Works" of Trumbull, ed. 1820, Mem., i. 19.

29

world, to renew its mirthful and scornful activity in the
ever-renewing battle for human progress.[1]

---

[1] I have had in my hands the following editions of " M'Fingal ": Philadelphia, 1775 ; London, 1776 ; Hartford, 1782 ; Boston, 1785 ; Philadelphia,
1787 ; Philadelphia, 1792 ; London, 1792 ; New York, 1795 ; Boston, 1799 ;
Baltimore, 1812 ; Hallowell, 1813 ; Hudson, 1816 ; Hartford, 1820 ; Boston,
1826 ; Philadelphia, 1839 ; Hartford, 1856 ; New York, 1864 ; New York,
1881.

CHAPTER XXI.

THOMAS PAINE AND THE OUTBREAK OF THE DOCTRINE OF INDEPENDENCE: JANUARY–JUNE, 1776.

I.—Paine's arrival in America late in the year 1774, introduced by a letter from Franklin—His previous history in England.

II.—His first employment in Philadelphia—His eagerness for information as to American politics—His gifts and limitations for political discussion.

III.—His early opinion strongly in favor of reconciliation—The events of the year 1775 changed his opinion, and prompted him to write the first open and unqualified argument for American Independence.

IV.—History of American opinion as to Independence prior to 1776—The controversy had been conducted on a perpetual disavowal of the purpose or desire for Independence.

V.—The title of Paine's pamphlet happily indicates its character—An appeal from technical law to common sense—Its argument introduced by crude and pungent affirmations as to government in general and the British government in particular—A new era in American politics created by the transfer of the dispute from argument to arms—All considerations in force prior to April 19, 1775, are like last year's almanac—Disposal of the arguments based on filial sentiment, and on our former prosperity and happiness as colonies.

VI.—The positive disadvantages of the American connection with England —Interferes with the freedom of American commerce—Involves us in European wars and quarrels—The absurdity of a great continent remaining dependent on any external power—Our business too weighty and intricate to be managed any longer by a power distant from us and ignorant of us—Reconciliation, even if now possible, would be ruinous—The American people are competent to save American society from anarchy—Solemn warning to the American opponents of Independence—Freedom, a fugitive hunted round the globe, begs for an asylum in America.

VII.—The pamphlet, even in its crudities, exactly fitted for its purpose— Effectiveness of its method of thought and statement—It uttered at the right moment what multitudes were waiting for—Numerous editions of it in America and Europe—Its authorship at first unknown, but ascribed to several eminent Americans, especially to Franklin.

VIII.—Evidence in contemporary writings of its enormous effects on public opinion between January and June, 1776.

I.

On the last day of November, 1774, there arrived at Philadelphia a solitary English pilgrim, named Thomas Paine, nearly thirty-eight years of age, having with him neither scrip, nor bread, nor money in his purse, but having nevertheless an abundant willingness to make his way in the new world by his wits, particularly " as a clerk, or assistant tutor in a school, or assistant surveyor." [1] For this rather forlorn adventurer, whose most imminent business in Philadelphia at that time was to " procure subsistence at least," the worst disadvantages of his condition were perhaps nearly balanced by a single item of good luck: he had brought with him from London a letter of introduction from Benjamin Franklin, testifying that the bearer was " an ingenious, worthy young man," and invoking on his behalf the primary and inexpensive charities of " advice and countenance."

Up to that time in his career, life had been upon the whole a somewhat baffling and unsatisfactory affair for this " ingenious, worthy young man "; and in spite of all energetic attempts on his part at climbing the steep hill, he had found himself, when well on toward middle life, still floundering and discomfited at the bottom of it.

The son of a staymaker at Thetford in Norfolk, where he was born in 1737, he had been taken from school at the age of thirteen and had been put to his father's trade. At one time, soon after the beginning of the Seven Years' War, wearied perhaps by the monotony of his too unhazardous occupation as a maker of stays, he had enlisted on board an English privateer. Very soon exhausting the charm to be found in wielding the deadly cutlass, he had returned, though with evident reluctance, to the service of the innocuous needle, which he then for several years continued to ply for a livelihood at London, Dover, Sandwich, Margate, and perhaps elsewhere. When only twenty-two years

---

[1] Franklin, " Works," Sparks ed., viii. 137.

old he had married; and when only twenty-three, he had
become a widower. In 1762, after due solicitation, he had
received an appointment in the excise, being set in the first
instance "to guage brewers' casks at Grantham," and afterward "to watch smugglers at Alford."[1] In 1765, he had
been dismissed from the excise for neglect of duty; his
offense being that of writing out his official entries at home,
without the trouble of an actual tour of his district, and of
course without an actual inspection of the excisable articles
on which he had occasion to pass,[2]—a most comfortable
way of making specific assertions, making them, it will be
observed, on purely speculative or unverified data, — a
method which might very likely stand this gentleman in
good stead in later life when he should set up for a philosopher, but which could hardly be permitted to him so long
as he was a mere exciseman. After the loss of his pittance
from the government, he had returned once more to his
trade, working for one Gudgeon, a staymaker at Diss; he
had also for some time gained his daily bread as usher in an
academy, first in Goodman's Fields, and then at Kensing-
ton; he had even earned an honest penny, at times, by
ascending the pulpit in some chapel at Moorfields or elsewhere, and preaching the gospel to such saints and sinners
as should have the grace to come and partake of his godly
ministrations.[3] In 1768, after humble petition on his part,
he had been restored to the excise and given an appointment
at Lewes, in Sussex. In 1771, being still an exciseman, he
had taken unto himself, as his second wife, a young lady
with whom he was already in partnership as grocer and
tobacconist. In 1774, he had been once more and forever

---

[1] M. D. Conway, "Life of Thomas Paine," i. 16. This chapter was written,
after independent researches of my own, several years before the publication of
Mr. Conway's book,—a book not exactly belonging to disinterested biography,
and yet by far the most valuable contribution thus far made to our materials for
a true understanding of Paine's career. In revising what I had written, I have
been greatly assisted by these labors of an old friend.

[2] The minute of the board dismissing Paine is given in Conway, "Life,"
i. 17 n.
[3] Ibid. 18–20.

dismissed from the excise,—this time for the offense of
" having quitted his business without obtaining the board's
leave for so doing, and being gone off on account of the
debts which he hath contracted." [1]   Six days after this final
dismissal from official service under the good king George
the Third, Paine's household furniture, his stock in trade,
and his other effects had been sold at auction at Lewes for
the benefit of his creditors.   Finally, two months later, he
and his wife had subscribed their names to an amicable agreement for a separation,—an incident which seems to have been
viewed by them both not as an additional misfortune to
either, but rather as a mitigation of such misfortune as
either or both may have already had in this troublous world.

It was in this doleful plight that Thomas Paine went up
to London, and laid before Franklin such credentials as induced the latter, on the thirtieth of September, 1774, to
give him an honorable passport to recognition and friendly
help in America.

II.

Reaching Philadelphia late in the year 1774, Paine soon
made his way to pleasant relations with some of the best
people in that town.   By the fourth of March, 1775, he was
able to report to his illustrious benefactor in London, that
he had already gained " many friends "; had received
from " several gentlemen " offers of profitable employment
as a tutor to their sons; and had begun to assist the book-
seller, Robert Aitkin, in the conduct of a new magazine. [2]

Not by tutorship, however, nor by surveyorship, nor

---

[1] These words are from the order for his discharge, given entire in Conway,
" Life," i. 29.

[2] Franklin, " Works," Sparks ed., viii. 138 n.   The new magazine was " The
Pennsylvania Magazine, or American Monthly Museum," begun in January,
1775.   Paine probably had nothing in the first number ; and whatever he wrote
for subsequent numbers has to be ascertained chiefly on internal evidence,
as his name is nowhere attached to any article, and in fact is nowhere mentioned, so far as I can discover, in the magazine at all.   The reader should
receive with some caution the positive statements of later writers as to Paine's
authorship of this, that, or the other article, in " The Pa. Magazine."

even by editorship, but by authorship, was this man to achieve such success in America as then lay undreamed of before him; and very likely the peculiar and the marvelous aptitude he had in him for that particular function of authorship, was still hidden even from his own eyes,— which, however, were never greatly lacking in vision of his own talents and virtues. Though in his thirty-eighth year, he had up to that time written nothing notable in all his life, and had never " published a syllable." [1] We may picture him to ourselves, during his first year in Philadelphia —the year 1775—as an alert and eager stranger, gaining his livelihood chiefly by writing for Aitkin's magazine, haunting the bookshops, pushing his way to the acquaintance of leading citizens of the town, and after the assembling of Congress, on the tenth of May, pushing his way, likewise, to the acquaintance of leading citizens from all parts of the continent. Benjamin Rush describes him as at that time visiting familiarly " in the families of Dr. Franklin, Mr. Rittenhouse, and Mr. George Clymer, where he made himself acceptable by a turn he discovered for philosophical, as well as political, subjects." [2] John Adams, who was then in Philadelphia as a member of Congress, and who at that period was accustomed to speak of Paine in a

---

[1] This is Paine's own assertion. " Political Writings," i. 97. Did he forget his memorial on the " Case of the Officers of Excise," in 1772, of which he presented a copy to Goldsmith, with the explanation that four thousand copies had been printed? Goldsmith, " Works," i. 320–321. Did he also forget his ode on " The Death of General Wolfe," written in 1759, which was published in the " Gentleman's Magazine," and was also set to music and issued as a popular song? As this chapter was written several years before the publication of Conway's admirable edition of " The Complete Works of Thomas Paine," all my citations from Paine's Revolutionary writings are either from the original tracts or from a modern reprint of them in Paine's " Political Writings," 2 volumes, Boston, 1870. In the final revision of this chapter, I have of course made careful use of Conway's edition, with the view of obtaining the latest light that has been shed on the subject.

[2] Cheetham, " Life of Thomas Paine," 39. This book is quite worthless, so far as its contents are the work of Cheetham himself, whose name, in fact, if slightly altered in the spelling, would very accurately describe the man. I have never cited the book, except for some statement resting on other testimony than his.

respectful and even in a complimentary way, long afterward said sneeringly, that Paine " got into such company as would converse with him, and ran about picking up what information he could concerning our affairs." [1]

If, indeed, Paine so employed himself, it must be confessed that he was very well employed. He could hardly have done anything more to the point. Arriving in America in the midst of a great political revolution, and casting in his lot with a kindred people over whose political wrongs he was indignant, and with whose political aspirations he was in passionate sympathy, it is hard to see what worthier course he could have taken than to try to qualify himself for the best service he might render to the great cause by studying it in its origin, its history, its methods, its aims. And how could he better do this than by applying himself diligently to the very men who were the leaders in the great enterprise ? On every hand, then, he gathered facts, opinions, impressions. He threw himself instantaneously into the American spirit; he became a naturalized American in body and soul; he caught at once the ideas that were in the air; with all his heart he responded to the immense, inarticulate impulse that was then moving a great people toward a great future. To the study, the acceptance, the advocacy of the American Revolution, Thomas Paine brought neither a wise, nor a profound, nor a cultivated mind,—not even an accurate or a temperate one; but he did bring a mind agile, alert, vivid, impressible, humane, quick to see into things and to grasp the gist of them, and marvelous in its power of stating them—stating them with lucidity, with sparkling liveliness, with rough, incisive, and captivating force.

III.

The moment of his arrival in America was one of supreme political excitement. The Congress of 1774 had but recently adjourned; and its measures for peaceful resistance to England through commercial non-intercourse had aroused the

---

[1] " Works," ii. 507.

most violent discussions throughout the colonies. Like the majority of Americans down to the nineteenth of April, 1775, Paine had at first believed in the possibility of a peaceful solution of the trouble, and had earnestly desired reconciliation between England and her colonies. What his political opinions were at the beginning of his American career, he himself explained with perfect candor some years later: " I happened to come to America a few months before the breaking out of hostilities. I found the disposition of the people such that they might have been led by a thread, and governed by a reed. Their suspicion was quick and penetrating, but their attachment to Britain was obstinate; and it was at that time a kind of treason to speak against it. They disliked the ministry, but they esteemed the nation. Their idea of grievance operated without resentment; and their single object was reconciliation. Bad as I believed the ministry to be, I never conceived them capable of a measure so rash and wicked as the commencing of hostilities; much less did I imagine the nation would encourage it. I viewed the dispute as a kind of law suit, in which, I supposed, the parties would find a way either to decide or settle it. I had no thoughts of Independence or of arms. The world could not then have persuaded me that I should be either a soldier or an author. If I had any talents for either, they were buried in me, and might ever have continued so, had not the necessity of the times dragged and driven them into action. I had formed my plan of life, and conceiving myself happy, wished everybody else so. But when the country into which I had just set my foot, was set on fire about my ears, it was time to stir. It was time for every man to stir. Those who had been long settled had something to defend; those who had just come had something to pursue; and the call and the concern was equal and universal. For in a country wherein all men were once adventurers, the difference of a few years in their arrival could make none in their right." [1]

---

[1] Paine, " Political Writings," i. 169–170.

Such, no doubt, is a true statement of Paine's opinions upon American Independence early in 1775. But, as the bitter events of that year rapidly unfolded themselves, not a few Americans became convinced that there was no true solution of the trouble except in that very Independence which they had but a short time before dreaded and denounced. Of such Americans, Thomas Paine was one; and towards the end of the year, through incessant study of passing events, and through incessant communication with the foremost minds in America, he had filled his own mind with the great decisive elements of the case, and was prepared to utter his thought thereon. Early in January, 1776, he did utter it, in the form of a pamphlet, published at Philadelphia, and entitled " Common Sense." [1]

IV.

Before entering upon a study of this epoch-making pamphlet,—the first open and unqualified argument in championship of the doctrine of American Independence,—it is important for us at least to glance at the previous history of American opinion on the subject. No one who searches the writings which have come down to us from that time, can have any doubt as to the truth of this broad statement that, for the first ten or twelve years of the Revolution, the entire Whig agitation was conducted on a perpetual disavowal of the purpose or the desire for Inde-

---

[1] In the title of his pamphlet, Paine seems not to have been original. Dr. Rush states that Paine intended to call it " Plain Truth," and that he adopted the title " Common Sense " at the suggestion of Rush himself. Cheetham, 37–38. Even Rush's title, however, had been anticipated; for, according to Thomas, " History of Printing," ii. 151 n., a political paper under the same title appeared in London in 1739. Furthermore, I have met with a pamphlet of 117 pages, published in London in the year just previous to the publication of Paine's " Common Sense," and also entitled " Common Sense: In Nine Conferences between a British Merchant and a Candid Merchant of America, in their Private Capacity as Friends." Oddly enough, " Common Sense " in 1775 viewed the questions in dispute from a side exactly opposite to that of " Common Sense " in 1776.

pendence. In every form in which a solemn affirmation could be made and reiterated, it was affirmed by the Whigs during all those years that the only object of their agitation was to obstruct and to defeat a bad ministerial policy, thereby to secure a redress of grievances; that, as for Independence, it was the thing they abhorred, and it was mere calumny to accuse them of designing or of desiring it. Nearly all the greatest Whig pamphleteers prior to 1776— James Otis, Daniel Dulany, John Dickinson, and Alexander Hamilton—abjured Independence as a measure full of calamity and crime. The Stamp Act Congress, speaking in the name of the several colonies, declared that their connection with Great Britain was their " great happiness and security," and that they " most ardently " desired its " perpetual continuance." [1] In January, 1768, the Massachusetts house of representatives sent to their agent a letter of instructions, written by James Otis, and thus defining their opposition to the renewal by parliament of its policy of taxing the colonies: " We cannot justly be suspected of the most distant thought of an Independency of Great Britain. Some, we know, have imagined this; . . . but it is so far from the truth that we apprehend the colonies would refuse it if offered to them, and would even deem it the greatest misfortune to be obliged to accept it." [2] In June, 1774, the same legislative body elected delegates to the first Continental Congress; and in their letter of instructions, signed by Samuel Adams, they declared that " the restoration of union and harmony between Great Britain and the colonists " was " most ardently desired by all good men." [3] The first Continental Congress, in its solemn petition to the king, adopted October 26, 1774, professed the most devoted loyalty: " We wish not a diminution of the prerogative. . . . Your royal authority over us and our connection with Great Britain we shall always care-

---

[1] " Prior Documents," 29, 31.
[2] Ibid. 167.
[3] " Journals of the Am. Cong.," i. 2.

fully and zealously endeavor to support and maintain."[1]
In March, 1775, Benjamin Franklin, then in London,
repeated the statement which he had made in the previous
year to Lord Chatham, that he had never heard in America
one word in favor of Independence "from any person,
drunk or sober."[2]   In May, 1775, shortly after American
blood had been shed at Lexington and Concord, George
Washington, crossing the Potomac on his way to the second Continental Congress, was met midway in the river by
a boat containing his friend, Jonathan Boucher; and while
their boats touched, Boucher kindly warned Washington
that the errand on which he was going would lead to civil
war and to an effort for Independence.   Such apprehensions
were vigorously scouted by Washington, who then added, as
Boucher says, "that if ever I heard of his joining in any such
measures, I had his leave to set him down for everything
wicked."[3]   Soon after Washington's arrival at Philadelphia,
the Continental Congress resolved upon a dutiful petition to
the king, assuring him that, although his ministry had forced
hostilities upon them, yet they most ardently wished " for
a restoration of the harmony formerly subsisting between "
the mother country and the colonies.[4]   The Americans who
had just fought at Lexington and Concord, and the Americans who, a few weeks later, were to fight at Bunker Hill,
would have spurned as a calumny the accusation that their
object in fighting was Independence.   Washington's appointment as commander-in-chief, which was made two
days before the battle of Bunker Hill, contained no intimation that he was to lead the armies in a struggle for Independence.   As soon as the news of his appointment reached
Virginia, his old military company there sent him their congratulations on the honor he had received, closing their
letter with the wish that all his " counsels and operations "

[1] "Journals of the Am. Cong.," i. 49.
[2] "The Complete Works of Benjamin Franklin," Bigelow ed., v. 446.
[3] "Notes and Queries," 5th ser., vi. 82–83.
[4] "Journals of the Am. Cong.," i. 73.

might be directed by Providence " to a happy and lasting union between us and Great Britain." [1] On the 6th of July, 1775, the Congress which had thus appointed Washington to lead their armies against the troops of the king, adopted their celebrated declaration, " setting forth the causes and necessity of their taking up arms," wherein they say: " Lest this declaration should disquiet the minds of our friends and fellow-subjects in any part of the empire, we assure them that we mean not to dissolve that union which has so long and so happily subsisted between us, and which we sincerely wish to see restored. . . . We have not raised armies with ambitious designs of separating from Great Britain, and establishing Independent States." [2] When, a few days later, that declaration was read to General Putnam's troops, parading on Prospect Hill, near Boston, they greeted, with three loud cries of " Amen," the passage in which the Almighty was implored to dispose their adversaries " to reconciliation on reasonable terms." [3] More than two months after the battle of Bunker Hill, Jefferson wrote to a kinsman of his that he was " looking with fondness towards a reconciliation with Great Britain." [4] More than three months after that battle, the committee of Chester county, Pennsylvania, with Anthony Wayne as their chairman, issued a statement denying that, in taking up arms, the people of that county intended " to overturn the constitution by declaring an Independency," and expressing their " abhorrence even of an idea so pernicious in its nature." [5] As late as the 22d of October, 1775, when Jeremy Belknap went to the American camp to officiate as chaplain, he publicly prayed for the king. [6] As late as December 25, 1775, the Revolutionary Congress of New Hampshire officially proclaimed their disavowal of any pur-

1 " Writings of Washington," Sparks ed., iii. 5 n.
2 " Journals of the Am. Cong.," i. 103.
3 D. Humphreys, " Miscellaneous Works," 271.
4 " The Writings of Thomas Jefferson," Ford ed., i. 482.
5 " Am. Archives," 4th ser., iii. 794, 795.
6 " Life of Belknap," by his granddaughter, 96, 97.

pose " aiming at Independence,"—a disavowal which they incorporated into the new constitution for New Hampshire adopted on the 5th of January, 1776.[1]

Such, then, upon the subject of Independence, was the attitude of all classes and parties in America during the first ten or twelve years of the Revolution. In just one sentiment all persons, Tories and Whigs, seemed perfectly to agree: namely, in abhorrence of the project of separation from the empire. Suddenly, however, and within a period of less than six months, the majority of the Whigs turned completely around, and openly declared for Independence, which, before that time, they had so vehemently repudiated. Among the facts necessary to enable us to account for this almost unrivaled political somersault, is that of the appearance in January, 1776, of the pamphlet entitled " Common Sense."

V.

This pamphlet was happily named: it undertook to apply common sense to a technical, complex, but most urgent and feverish, problem of constitutional law. In fact, on any other ground than that of common sense, the author of that pamphlet was incompetent to deal with the problem at all; since of law, of political science, and even of English and American history, he was ludicrously ignorant. But for the effective treatment of any question whatsoever that was capable of being dealt with under the light of the broad and rugged intellectual instincts of mankind,—man's natural sense of truth, of congruity, of fair-play,—perhaps no other man in America, excepting Franklin, was a match for this ill-taught, heady, and slashing English stranger.

From the tribunal of technical law, therefore, he carried the case to the tribunal of common sense; and in his plea before that tribunal, he never for a moment missed his point, or forgot his method. The one thing just then to

---

[1] " The Federal and State Constitutions," Poore ed., ii. 1279.

be done was to convince the average American colonist of
the period that it would be ridiculous for him any longer to
remain an American colonist; that the time had come for
him to be an American citizen; that nothing stood in the
way of his being so, but the trash of a few pedants respecting the authority of certain bedizened animals called kings;
and that whether he would or no, the alternative was at last
thrust into his face upon the point of a bayonet,—either
to declare for national Independence, and a wide-spaced
and resplendent national destiny, or to accept, along with
subservience to England, the bitterness and the infamy of
national annihilation.

The pamphlet begins with a rattling overture of pungent
but crude affirmations concerning government in general,
and concerning the English government in particular, all
intended to rid the minds of its readers of any undue reverence for organized authority, especially for monarchical
authority, and to convince a people with whom obedience
to law had long been a second nature, that the hour had
struck for them to legalize disobedience to law. Government has been often described as if it were identical with
society; whereas government and society " are not only
different, but have different origins. Society is produced
by our wants, and government by our wickedness. . . .
Society in every state is a blessing; but government, even
in its best estate, is but a necessary evil; in its worst estate,
an intolerable one. . . . Government, like dress, is the
badge of lost innocence; the palaces of kings are built upon
the ruins of the bowers of paradise." [1] Government, in
fact, is " a mode rendered necessary by the inability of
moral virtue to govern the world." Such, according to
Thomas Paine, is the origin of government; and as to its
object, he declares it to be twofold—" freedom and security." [2] And what is the true form of government ? Whatever else it may be, surely it is not monarchy. That form
of government which rests on " the distinction of men into

---

[1] " Political Writings," i. 19.   [2] Ibid. 21.

kings and subjects,'' is one for which no '' natural or religious reason can be assigned.'' '' Male and female are the
distinctions of nature; good and bad, the distinctions of
heaven; but how a race of men came into the world so
exalted above the rest, and distinguished like some new
species, is worth enquiring into, and whether they are the
means of happiness or of misery to mankind.''[1] '' The
nearer any government approaches to a republic, the less
business there is for a king. . . . In England a king
hath little more to do than to make war, and give away
places; which, in plain terms, is to impoverish the nation,
and set it together by the ears. A pretty business, indeed,
for a man to be allowed eight hundred thousand sterling
for, and worshiped into the bargain! Of more worth is
one honest man to society, and in the sight of God, than
all the crowned ruffians that ever lived.''[2]

Having thus dispatched, in a series of incisive and contemptuous propositions, the doctrine of king-craft as an
intolerable method of governing mankind,—supporting his
opinions by elaborate and reverent quotations from the
Bible,—he soon reaches the specific business he has in hand,
namely, the state of affairs in America. Here, at last, he
is on the ground of tangible facts and of their natural interpretation; and here the vigor of his mind, his shrewdness of
insight, his unhesitating confidence, the filmless lucidity of
his style, his humor, his asperity, his epigrammatic gift,
have victorious play, and give to his pages the most stimulating flavor. '' The period of debate is closed. Arms, as
the last resource, must decide the contest. . . . By
referring the matter from argument to arms, a new era for
politics is struck; a new method of thinking hath arisen.
All plans, proposals, and so forth, prior to the nineteenth of
April . . . are like the almanacs of last year.''[3]

Since the nineteenth of April, then, all talk of filial affection for England has become archaic, pointless, farcical;
and for the American who, unaware of the change that has

---

[1] '' Political Writings,'' i. 24–25.   [2] Ibid. 32.   [3] Ibid. 33–34.

come upon the earth, still pleads that England is our mother, there is but one reply: " Then the more shame upon her conduct! Even brutes do not devour their young, nor savages make war upon their families." [1]

To the objection that " as America has flourished under her former connection with Great Britain, the same connection is necessary towards her future happiness, and will always have the same effect," Paine is ready with a telling retort: " Nothing can be more fallacious than this kind of argument. We may as well assert that because a child has thrived upon milk, it is never to have meat; or that the first twenty years of our lives is to become a precedent for the next twenty. But even this is admitting more than is true; for I answer roundly that America would have flourished as much, and probably much more, had no European power had anything to do with her. The articles of commerce by which she has enriched herself, are the necessaries of life; and will always have a market while eating is the custom of Europe." [2]

VI.

Moreover, the connection of America with England brings, according to Paine, not a solitary advantage to America; nay, it brings to her disadvantages and injuries without number. The greatest of all is this: our connection with England " tends directly to involve this continent in European wars and quarrels, and sets us at variance with nations who would otherwise seek our friendship, and against whom we have neither anger nor complaint. As Europe is our market for trade, we ought to form no partial connection with any part of it. It is the true interest of America to steer clear of European contentions, which she never can do while, by her dependence on Britain, she is made the make-weight in the scale of British politics." [3]

Then, again, " it is repugnant to reason and the universal

---

[1] " Political Writings," i. 35. [2] Ibid. 34. [3] Ibid. 37.

order of things, to all examples from former ages, to suppose that this continent can longer remain subject to any external power." [1]   There is something preposterous in the mere idea of a great nation on this side of the Atlantic remaining in a state of permanent pupilage to a great nation on the other side of the Atlantic: " A greater absurdity cannot be conceived of, than three millions of people running to their seacoast every time a ship arrives from London, to know what portion of liberty they should enjoy." [2]

Furthermore, there is an obvious cosmographical argument for American Independence.   A glance at the map will show that the subordination of America to England inverts the order of nature: " Small islands, not capable of protecting themselves, are the proper objects for kingdoms to take under their care; but there is something absurd in supposing a continent to be perpetually governed by an island.   In no instance hath nature made the satellite larger than its primary planet; and as England and America, with respect to each other, reverse [3] the common order of nature, it is evident that they belong to different systems: England to Europe, America to—itself! ''

Aside from mere analogies, however, and looking directly at the welfare of America in the transaction of its own affairs, it is plain that Independence is a necessity: " As to government matters, it is not in the power of Britain to do this continent justice.   The business of it will soon be too weighty and intricate to be managed with any tolerable degree of convenience, by a power so distant from us, and so very ignorant of us. . . .   To be always running three or four thousand miles with a tale or a petition, waiting four or five months for an answer, which, when obtained, requires five or six more to explain it in, will in a few years

---

[1] " Political Writings," i. 39.

[2] According to Rush, this brilliant sentence, which does not appear in the pamphlet as printed, was in the original copy, but was stricken out apparently at the suggestion of Franklin.   Cheetham, 37.

[3] The text has " reverses."   " Political Writings," i. 40.

be looked upon as folly and childishness. There was a time when it was proper, and there is a proper time for it to cease." [1]

But if it be supposed for a moment that reconciliation were actually brought about between England and America, what would be the result ? The ruin of America. Why ? First, because England would still be the governing power. And " is the power who is jealous of our prosperity, a proper power to govern us ? . . . America is only a secondary object in the system of British politics. England consults the good of this country no further than it answers her own purpose. Wherefore, her own interest leads her to suppress the growth of ours, in every case which doth not promote her advantage, or in the least interferes with it." Secondly, because " even the best terms which we can expect to obtain can amount to no more than a temporary expedient, or a kind of government by guardianship, which can last no longer than till the colonies come of age." Thirdly, because " nothing but Independence . . . can keep the peace of the continent, and preserve it inviolate from civil wars." [2]

But there are Americans who fear that if we separate ourselves from the control of the king of England, we shall lapse into anarchy. " Where, say some, is the king of America ? I 'll tell you, friend. He reigns above, and doth not make havoc of mankind, like the royal brute of Britain. .. . . A government of our own is our natural right; and when a man seriously reflects on the precariousness of human affairs, he will become convinced that it is infinitely wiser and safer to form a constitution of our own, in a cool, deliberate manner, while we have it in our power, than to trust such an interesting event to time and chance." " Ye who oppose Independence now, ye know not what ye do: ye are opening a door to eternal tyranny, by keeping vacant the seat of government. . . . To talk of friend-

---

[1] " Political Writings," i. 40.

[2] Ibid. i. 41, 42, 43.

ship with those in whom our reason forbids us to have faith, and our affections, wounded through a thousand pores, instruct us to detest, is madness and folly. Every day wears out the little remains of kindred between us and them; and can there be any reason to hope that as the relationship expires, the affection will increase, or that we shall agree better, when we have ten times more and greater concerns to quarrel over than ever ? Ye that tell us of harmony and reconciliation, can ye restore to us the time that is past ? . . . The last cord now is broken. . . . There are injuries which nature cannot forgive; she would cease to be nature if she did. . . . O ye that love mankind! Ye that dare oppose, not only tyranny but the tyrant, stand forth! Every spot of the old world is overrun with oppression. Freedom hath been hunted round the globe. Asia and Africa have long expelled her. Europe regards her like a stranger; and England hath given her warning to depart. O! receive the fugitive; and prepare in time an asylum for mankind." [1]

VII.

With all its crudities of thought, its superficiality, and its rashness of assertion, "Common Sense" is a masterly pamphlet; for in the elements of its strength it was precisely fitted to the hour, to the spot, and to the passions of men. Even its smattering of historical lore, and its cheap display of statistics, and its clumsy attempts at some sort of political philosophy, did not diminish the homage with which it was read by the mass of the community, who were even less learned and less philosophical than Paine, and who, at any rate, cared much more just then for their imperiled rights, than they did either for philosophy or for learning.

The power of the pamphlet lay in the fitness of its method, its tone, its scope. It brushes away the tangles and cobwebs of technical debate, and flashes common sense

---

[1] " Political Writings," i. 46, 47.

upon the situation. It was meant for plain men, in desperate danger, and desperately in earnest. Its thought is homely, always blunt, occasionally humorous, rugged, palpable, overpowering; with just enough of generous and contemptuous passion,—love of freedom, hate of tyranny, and a consciousness of the latent, illimitable strength of its own cause. Its style never errs on the side of restraint; is never debilitated by any delicacy of feeling. Thomas Paine did not take up his pen in the service of the amenities. Here is no urbane concession to the foe. Here are the germs of that untempered invective which sometimes grew, at a later period of his life, into literary truculence and barbarism.

The immediate practical effects of this pamphlet in America, and the celebrity which it soon acquired in Europe as well as in America, are a significant part of its history as a potential literary document of the period. In every impassioned popular discussion there is likely to spring up a leader, who with pen or voice strikes in, at just the right moment, with just the right word, so skillfully, so powerfully, that thenceforward the intellectual battle seems to be raging and surging around him and around the fiery word which he has sent shrilling through the air. So far as the popular discussion of American Independence is concerned, precisely this was the case, between January and July, 1776, with Thomas Paine and his pamphlet "Common Sense."

It was originally published at Philadelphia on the ninth[1] of January, 1776, without the author's name. On the twentieth of that month, a second edition, with "large additions," was published by the same booksellers. On the twenty-fifth, another edition was announced by a firm of rival booksellers in Philadelphia, who state that "several hundred are already bespoke, one thousand for Virginia,"

---

[1] The date of publication often given is 10 January, 1776, on the authority of an advertisement in "The Pennsylvania Journal." Thus, Conway, "Life," i. 61. But in "The Pennsylvania Evening Post," for 9 January, 1776, there is an advertisement to the effect that the pamphlet was already out that day.

and that the work was also about to be published in German.   The edition thus announced made its appearance on the twentieth of February, being a pamphlet of fifty pages, and containing " large and interesting additions by the author."   In the enormous tide of popular interest which soon bore the pamphlet into every port and inlet of American society, were speedily drowned the competitions of the two local booksellers who had begun by trying to monopolize the profits to be got from this brain-freighted and strong-winged commodity.   In New York, Norwich, Providence, Newport, Salem, Newburyport, Charlestown, Boston, and elsewhere in America, it was soon reprinted, as well as in London,. Newcastle-upon-Tyne, Edinburgh, Rotterdam, and Paris.   Within three months from the date of its first issue, at least one hundred and twenty thousand copies of it were sold in America alone.   By that time, the pamphlet seemed to be in every one's hand and the theme of every one's talk.

In a very early edition, it was described on its title-page as " Written by an Englishman."   In later issues this description was soon omitted; and in the enlarged edition of the twentieth of February, some reference was made to the public curiosity to know the authorship of the treatise: " Who the author of this production is, is wholly unnecessary to the public, as the object of attention is the doctrine, not the man.   .   .   .   He is unconnected with any party, and under no sort of influence, public or private, but the influence of reason and principle."

Of all writers then known to the American people, probably only three were much thought of at the time as likely to have produced this pamphlet.   " ' Common Sense,' when it first appeared," wrote John Adams long afterward, with characteristic aplomb, " was generally by the public ascribed to me or to Mr. Samuel Adams." [1]   Indeed, in some parts of Europe, particularly in France, the first rumor that it was written by a great American

---

[1] " Works," ii. 507.

congressman vaguely named " Adams," seems to have remained in force for several years afterward; and in 1779, when John Adams himself arrived in France as a commissioner of Congress, he found himself welcomed as " le fameux Adams," the reputed author of " Common Sense," —a pamphlet which, as he then wrote, " was received in France and in all Europe with rapture." [1]   In America, probably, the prevailing tendency was to ascribe it to Benjamin Franklin, who, indeed, on one occasion is said to have been expostulated with by a Loyalist lady of his acquaintance, for having in that pamphlet been so discourteous as to speak of their good king as " the royal brute of Britain." "Madam," replied Franklin, " let me assure you that I did not write ' Common Sense.'   Moreover, if I had written it, I would not so have dishonored—the brute creation."   In England, where Franklin was then better known than any other American, and where he had received personal affronts which would account, it was supposed, for any asperities of style, the pamphlet was for some time commonly spoken of as his,—as in the case, for example, of an amusing story told in London in the summer of 1776, to the effect that the Prince of Wales had been discovered one day by his mother in the very act of reading, within the awful precincts of the palace, " Dr. Franklin's pamphlet ' Common Sense,' " and in response to the queen's searching questions, had refused to confess how he had come by the atrocious document.[2]

VIII.

Of all the contemporary testimonies to the immediate power of " Common Sense," one of the earliest is that of General Charles Lee, who, on the twenty-fourth of January, 1776,—fifteen days after the first issue of the pamphlet,— thus wrote to Washington : " Have you seen the pamphlet

---

[1] " Works," iii. 189.

[2] " The Pa. Evening Post," for 1 January, 1777, where the story is given as from London, 30 August, 1776.

'Common Sense'? I never saw such a masterly, irresistible performance. It will, if I mistake not, in concurrence with the transcendent folly and wickedness of the ministry, give the 'coup-de-grace' to Great Britain. In short, I own myself convinced by the arguments, of the necessity of separation."[1] On the thirty-first of January, one day after Washington had received Lee's letter, he thus wrote to Joseph Reed: "A few more of such flaming arguments as were exhibited at Falmouth and Norfolk, added to the sound doctrine and unanswerable reasoning contained in the pamphlet 'Common Sense,' will not leave numbers at a loss to decide upon the propriety of separation."[2] A few days later, on the sixth of February, in an article which was published in "The Pennsylvania Evening Post," a person in Maryland writes: "If you know the author of 'Common Sense,' tell him he has done wonders and worked miracles, —made Tories Whigs, and washed blackamores white."[3] From South Carolina, on the fourteenth of February, rises this cry of delight: "Who is the author of 'Common Sense'? I can scarce refrain from adoring him. He deserves a statue of gold."[4] On the twenty-fourth of February, a newspaper published in New York thus joins in the rising chorus of enthusiastic praise: "The pamphlet entitled 'Common Sense' is indeed a wonderful production. It is completely calculated for the meridian of North America. . . . This animated piece dispels, with irresistible energy, the prejudices of the mind against the doctrine of Independence, and pours in upon it such an inundation of light and truth, as will produce an instantaneous and marvelous change in the temper, in the views and feelings, of an American. The ineffable delight with which it is perused, and its doctrines imbibed, is a demonstration that the seeds of Independence, though imported with the troops from Britain, will grow surprisingly with proper cultivation in

[1] Sparks, "Corr. of the Am. Rev.," i. 136.
[2] Washington, "Writings," Sparks ed., iii. 276.
[3] Reprinted in Frothingham, "Rise of the Republic," 480 n.   [4] Ibid.

the fields of America." [1] On the second of March, Mistress John Adams writes from Quincy to her husband in Philadelphia: " I am charmed with the sentiments of ' Common Sense,' and wonder how an honest heart . . . can hesitate one moment at adopting them." [2] On the twelfth of March, a letter from Philadelphia says: " ' Common Sense ' . . . is read to all ranks; and as many as read, so many become converted, though perhaps the hour before [they] were most violent against the least idea of Independence." [3] A letter from Georgetown, South Carolina, on the seventeenth of March, says: " ' Common Sense ' hath made Independents of the majority of the country." [4] On the first of April, Washington, writing from Cambridge, thus speaks of the development of political thought among the people of Virginia: " My countrymen, I know, from their form of government and steady attachment heretofore to royalty, will come reluctantly into the idea of Independence, but time and persecution bring many wonderful things to pass; and by private letters which I have lately received from Virginia, I find ' Common Sense ' is working a powerful change there in the minds of men." [5] On the eighth of April, " The New York Gazette " says: " The subject of conversation throughout America for these few weeks past, hath been excited by a pamphlet called ' Common Sense.' " [6] On the twelfth of April, a news-writer in New York says: " A pamphlet entitled ' Common Sense ' has converted thousands to Independence, that could not endure the idea before." [7] On the twenty-ninth of April, " The Boston Gazette " says: " Had the spirit of prophecy directed the birth of a publication, it could not have fallen

---

[1] From the " Constitutional Gazette," reprinted in Moore, " Diary of the Am. Rev.," i. 208–209.

[2] " Letters of Mrs. Adams," i. 89.

[3] Almon, " Remembrancer" for 1776, part ii. 31.

[4] " Mass. Hist. Soc. Proc.," 1869–1870, 254.

[5] Washington, " Writings," Sparks ed., iii. 347.

[6] Quoted in Frothingham, " Rise of the Republic," 480 n.

[7] Almon, " Remembrancer " for 1776, part iii. 87.

upon a more fortunate period than the time in which ' Common Sense' made its appearance. The minds of men are now swallowed up in attention to an object the most momentous and important that ever yet employed the deliberations of a people." [1]   Finally, on the seventh of June,—the very day on which Richard Henry Lee introduced into Congress his resolutions for Independence,—William Gordon, the historian of the Revolution, sets down these words respecting the influences that had prepared the public mind for the introduction of such resolutions: " The constant publications which have appeared and been read with attention, have greatly promoted the spirit of Independency; but no one so much as the pamphlet under the signature of ' Common Sense,' written by Mr. Thomas Paine, an Englishman. . . . Nothing could have been better timed than this performance. In unison with the sentiments and feelings of the people, it has produced most astonishing effects, and been received with vast applause, read by almost every American, and recommended as a work replete with truth, and against which none but the partial and prejudiced can form any objections. It has satisfied multitudes that it is their true interest immediately to cut the Gordian knot by which the American colonies have been bound to Great Britain, and to open their commerce, as an independent people, to all the nations of the world. It has been greatly instrumental in producing a similarity of sentiment through the continent, upon the subject under the consideration of Congress." [2]

---

[1] Quoted in Frothingham, " Rise of the Republic," 480 n.

[2] " Am. Rev.," ii. 92.

CHAPTER XXII.

THE POPULAR DEBATE OVER THE PROPOSAL OF INDE-PENDENCE: JANUARY – JUNE, 1776.

I.—The proposal of Independence was the proposal of a political heresy and a crime—American Independence was American secession—Impossible for the Whigs to forget their repeated denials of any purpose or desire for Independence.

II.—Two classes of Americans opposed to Independence, the Loyalists and many Whigs who had approved even of armed opposition but drew back from national disruption—The side of the Loyalists less ably presented in this discussion than in previous controversies—" Plain Truth "—" The True Interest of America Impartially Stated."

III.—The ablest opposition to Independence came from American Whigs—Substance of their appeal to their old associates against a measure so inconsistent.

IV.—John Joachim Zubly, of Georgia, a champion of armed resistance who spurned the proposal of secession from the empire—His career and writings—The exact nature of the offense for which he was loaded with reproach.

V.—Philadelphia as the focus of the popular debate over Independence—The doctrine denounced in the " Letters of Cato " by Provost William Smith—The temper of the discussion playfully exhibited in " A Prophecy " by Francis Hopkinson.

VI.—Extraordinary influence of the advocacy of Independence by William Henry Drayton, of South Carolina—His character as a political thinker and essayist—His writings—As chief justice of South Carolina, in April, 1776, he declares the government of that colony abdicated by the king, and all obedience to him there no longer due.

I.

In tracing the history of public opinion in America as to the doctrine of American Independence, it has been convenient for us in the first place to follow by itself the story of the astonishing effects wrought by the pamphlet " Common Sense," which, having been sent forth at the very moment when the minds of the people were fully ripe for it, precipitated the popular debate upon that question. We should, however, be in danger of missing the true perspective of events, if we failed to observe some other prominent participants in this debate, particularly those who were frankly and strenuously opposed to the new doctrine.

American Independence is a fact now so long established among us, so glorious to our imaginations, so hallowed in our faith and love, that it cannot be easy for us to realize the intellectual and spiritual conditions of a time when the doctrine of American Independence was among our own ancestors a startling novelty, a dangerous political heresy, the suggestion of an appalling crime—the very crime of treason. Nevertheless, we must realize all this, if we would now appreciate, on the one hand, the sincerity of disapproval and the horror with which vast numbers of patriotic Americans then contended against a proposal so audacious, or, on the other hand, the faith in ideas, the courage, the capacity for self-sacrifice, required by those Americans who then at last rallied to the support of a proposal so perilous.

Especially do we need, by a strong effort, to view the proposal as standing in the very light, and against the very background, which the men and women of 1776 were conscious of, when they first took it into their consideration. They were then members of a great empire of which they had always been proud, to the constitutional authority of which they had always been loyal. Upon the integrity of that empire, the new proposal was a direct and a terrific assault: upon their own loyalty to the constitutional obligations incurred by membership of that empire, the new proposal offered a violent shock. Of course, no one then pretended that separation could be resorted to, except as a revolutionary measure required by some vast and commanding need in the existing circumstances of the American colonies. If, accordingly, we would now see the subject as it was seen by them, and would understand how easy it was

for one portion of the American people to oppose the plan
for separation from the empire, and how hard it was for the
rest of them to favor it, we must translate their word Independence into its modern American equivalent. For, just
as the earlier Whig doctrine for the rejection of the taxing-
power of the general government meant what in the
nineteenth century we have known under the name of Nullification, so the later Whig doctrine of separation from the
empire meant precisely what we now mean by the word
Secession. Under this aspect, the American Revolution
had just two stages: from about 1764 to 1776, its champions
were Nullifiers, without being Secessionists; from 1776 to
1783 they were also Secessionists, and, as the event proved,
successful Secessionists. The word Independence was
merely a euphemism for national disunion, for a disruption of the British empire. What the Whig leaders resolved
to do, under the name of Independence, about the middle
of the year 1776, seemed to many Americans of that time
precisely the same political crime as, to the people of the
Northern States, seemed the measure undertaken by certain
Southern leaders, in the latter part of 1860, under the name
of Secession. In short, the Loyalists of the American
Revolution took, between 1776 and 1783, constitutional
ground similar to that taken by the people of these Northern States and by the so-called Loyalists of the Southern
States between 1861 and 1865; that is, they were champions of national unity, as resting on the paramount
authority of the general government.

The proposal of American Independence had, therefore,
for all Americans in 1776, the background of this fact: it
was in reality, a revolutionary and treasonable proposal,
which might or might not be justifiable; which, if practically asserted, would involve us in almost incalculable risks
and sufferings; which, even if successfully asserted, might
prove anything but a blessing to us, and if unsuccessfully
asserted, would certainly prove a curse.

Finally, when early in 1776, the American Whigs began

openly to discuss the doctrine of Independence, they did
not and they could not dismiss from their minds the fact
that, ever since they had begun to agitate for the exclusive
right of laying taxes in America, they had been accused,
both in America and in England, of masking under that
demand the secret purpose of Independence,—an accusation which they had always repelled as both a falsehood and
a calumny.

II.

Of course, for several months before the appearance of
the pamphlet " Common Sense," and particularly in consequence of the shedding of American blood by royalist
troops at Lexington and Concord, many Americans had
come to the conclusion that, sooner or later, separation from
Great Britain was inevitable; but, excepting in satire or in
an occasional irresponsible paragraph in some newspaper, no
downright avowal of the doctrine had been made until it
was made in that pamphlet.   Of the persons who then rose
up against the new doctrine, may now be recognized two
classes: first, the old American Loyalists, who had always
objected to extreme measures even in opposition to a bad
ministerial policy; and, secondly, many of the old American Whigs, who, while they had always approved of such
opposition even when carried to the point of armed resistance, yet drew back from it when carried to the point of
treason and of national disruption.

In the heated popular debate which arose over the new
proposal, the reader cannot fail to see that the side of the
Loyalists was now sustained with far less force of argument,
with far less wit or literary cleverness than had been the case
in the controversies of the two previous years.   This diminution in the debating ability of the Loyalists may be explained
partly by the fact that their greatest writers had then been
driven out of the country or driven into silence; partly, by
the fact that most of those who were left in position to

write, realized the uselessness of further discussion,—the Revolutionary movement having at last acquired an impetus not to be checked by mere words, however logical, or eloquent, or witty.

Two pamphlets, evidently the work of steady Loyalists, may be selected by us as examples of the work capable of being done by their available writers in that final crisis of the controversy. Of these pamphlets, the one which has acquired the greater distinction but which deserves it the less, is " Plain Truth, Addressed to the Inhabitants of America, containing Remarks on a late Pamphlet entitled Common Sense: Wherein are shewn, that the scheme of Independence is ruinous, delusive, and impracticable, that were the author's asseverations respecting the power of America as real as nugatory, Reconciliation on liberal principles with Great Britain would be exalted Policy; and that, circumstanced as we are, permanent Liberty and true Happiness can only be obtained by Reconciliation with that Kingdom. Written by Candidus." The purpose of this pamphlet is well enough set forth in the copious announcement which thus confronts us upon the title-page; but a still more copious announcement would be necessary in order to set forth the intellectual poverty of its actual contents,—its lack of order, its feebleness in argument, its garrulity, its dismal attempts at humor, its bad grammar, its pitiful failure to perform what it announces as its purpose to perform.[1]

---

[1] " Plain Truth " was very caustically and justly disposed of, soon after its publication, in an essay signed " Aristides," which is one of the pseudonyms of President Witherspoon. "Works," ix. 89-92. A new and an undeserved prominence has been given to the pamphlet by attempts made within the past twenty years to ascertain who was its author. Thus, the distressing compliment has been handed round by various scholars to Joseph Galloway, to Charles Inglis, to George Chalmers, to Provost William Smith ; even as, in the last century, it was offered to William Wells, and, with immeasurable absurdity, even to Alexander Hamilton. The subject is really not worth the room it would take for a discussion of these various suggestions, the most of which, indeed, have fallen dead without anybody's help. From evidence both of substance and of form, I am confident that not one of these guesses as to the authorship of

It must be admitted that the incompetence of the first of these Loyalist pamphlets against American separation from the empire, is more than offset by the ability of the second of them: " The True Interest of America Impartially Stated, in Certain Strictures on a pamphlet intitled Common Sense. By an American."[1] The writer, whose signature as " an American " is thus placed in contrast to that of " an Englishman " on some of the earlier copies of " Common Sense," was undoubtedly Charles Inglis, then assistant rector of Trinity Church, New York, and from 1787 to his death in 1816 the bishop of Nova Scotia.[2]

As to " Common Sense," he regards it as " one of the most artful, insidious, and pernicious pamphlets " he had ever met with. In fact, he finds " no common sense " in it, " but much uncommon phrensy. It is an outrageous insult on the common sense of Americans. . . . The principles of government laid down in it, are not only false, but too absurd to have ever entered the head of a crazy politician before. Even Hobbes would blush to own the author for a disciple."[3] Dividing his little book into sections corresponding to the leading topics of Paine's pamphlet, he endeavors, tersely and sharply, to expose the falsity and shallowness of Paine's statements, whether of fact or of principle; he expresses perfect sympathy with his countrymen in their anxiety for a clearer definition and a stronger protection of their political rights within the empire; and in

---

" Plain Truth " is the true one ; and in short, that the man who wrote it, and who, doubtless, had misfortune enough in being the member of a party so routed and discredited, has had at least this felicity—he has thus far escaped detection as the author of so much stupidity and broken syntax as are to be found in that pamphlet.

[1] The first edition of this pamphlet, published in New York early in the spring of 1776, is said to have been seized and burned by the Sons of Liberty there ; but soon afterward a second and a third edition of it were printed in Philadelphia. I am using a copy of this second edition.

[2] A good sketch of Inglis is given in Sprague, " Annals," v. 186–191. Many references to him occur in " The History of the American Episcopal Church," edited by W. S. Perry.

[3] " The True Interest," etc., Preface, v.–vi.

a thoroughly manly tone, with great aptness and with great force, he tries to prove to them that all their interests are to be best served by rejecting this wicked and pestilent doctrine of Independence.

Perhaps in no other part of his argument does he show greater cleverness than in that where he deals with Paine's contention that the necessary effect of the 19th of April, 1775, was to exclude all further thought of reconciliation. "That the expedition to Lexington," says Inglis, "was rash and ill-judged—that it was risking the peace of the continent, and wantonly involving fellow-subjects in blood, for a most inconsiderable object—I shall most readily allow; and our author has my leave to load that expedition with all the reproaches he can invent. I disapprove the design of it as much as he—I lament its effects much more."[1] But, "on the very best authority," the writer adds, he is able to prove that it was opposed both to the letter and to the spirit of the king's orders to General Gage. If, then, the author of "Common Sense" can say that "no man was a warmer wisher for reconciliation than himself before the fatal 19th of April 1775," how is the case justly changed by that event? "If peace and reconciliation on constitutional grounds, and proper security for our several rights, were desirable and advantageous before the 19th of April, 1775, must they not have been equally so after the event of that unfortunate day? Let reason and common sense answer."[2]

III.

Incomparably the strongest words then uttered against the new proposal of Independence, were uttered, not by American Tories but by some of the American Whigs, who, while they had been in full accord with the rough methods of opposition thus far pursued by their party, were shocked by this project for committing them to a doctrine which from

---

[1] "The True Interest," etc., 37.

[2] Ibid. 37-38.

3¹

the first they had all rejected and condemned. These were the Whigs, till that time, held in highest honor in their party, who now made solemn appeal to their old associates against a measure so repugnant to all their professions as public men and as loyal subjects. " It cannot be," said they, in substance, to their former political comrades, " that you are thus entering upon this long repudiated measure for Independence, because you really think that the objects for which we began the agitation and have thus far conducted it, cannot be obtained within the empire. All our demands are on the point of being granted. Our great friends in parliament—Chatham, Camden, Burke, Conway, Barré, and the rest—continually send us word that complete success is in sight; that if we will but hold on to our plan of agitation for larger rights inside the empire, retaining our allegiance, they can help us; that if we run up the flag of separation, of Independence, we shall at once discredit them, and destroy all their power to be of any further use to us; that these political demands of ours have thus far been made by us after the method of our English ancestors, who, in cases of need, have roughly acquired an increase of political privilege, doing this as loyal subjects with weapons in their hands, and even enrolled as troops, never in the spirit of treason, never for the rejection of allegiance, never for the dissolution of national unity; that, even now, Lord North is quite ready to grant all our terms; that though the king still holds out against any concession, even he will have to yield to the people and to parliament; that commissioners will soon be on their way hither to negotiate with us, and to concede to us that measure of local self-government which we have hitherto proclaimed as our sole object in the controversy; that by persisting a little longer in the line of action upon which we have hitherto conducted the whole movement, we shall certainly win for ourselves every political advantage we have ever professed to desire, and shall become a group of great, free, self-governing colonies within the British empire. But as separation from the empire is not called for by any requirement of political safety, so our present resort to it would show either that we are fickle in opinion, or that we are political hypocrites—as our enemies have always charged us with being—and that, under all our disavowals of the purpose or the wish for Independence, we have been treacherously working with that very object all the time in view."

Of the American Whigs who took this stand against the project for Independence, were also two groups,—the one consisting of those who, like Zubly, a member of the Continental Congress from Georgia, never afterward yielded up their opinion on the subject; the other consisting of those who, like John Dickinson, Robert Morris, James Wilson, and William Smith, finally and reluctantly succumbed to the measure, and, in some cases, put forth great efforts and made great sacrifices in its support.

IV.

The case of John Joachim Zubly may help us to understand the attitude of the first group of Whig opponents of American Independence. Born in Switzerland in 1725, and at an early age settled as a clergyman in South Carolina and Georgia, he put at the service of the Revolution in its primary stage, his practical wisdom, his great local influence, and his uncommon ability as a writer. In 1769, under the name of " A Freeholder of South Carolina," he published a strong and temperate pamphlet entitled " An Humble Enquiry into the Nature of the Dependency of the American Colonies upon the Parliament of Great Britain and the Right of Parliament to lay Taxes on the Said Colonies." A still more striking statement of the virile claim of the American colonies was made by him in 1775, in an address to the Earl of Dartmouth, prefixed to a sermon on " The Law of Liberty,"—a sermon which he had preached at the opening of the provincial congress of Georgia. In this address, he rings the changes on that fatal phrase which had been used by parliament when it asserted its right to " bind the colonies in all cases whatsoever." "My lord, the Americans look upon this as the language of despotism in its utmost perfection. What can . . . an emperor of Morocco pretend more of his slaves, than to bind them in all cases whatsoever." [1] "My lord, the Americans are no idiots, and they appear determined not to be slaves. Oppression will make wise men mad; but oppressors, in the end, frequently find that they were not wise men. There may be resources even in despair, sufficient to render any set of men strong enough not to be bound 'in all cases whatsoever.'" [2] "The bulk of the inhabitants of a continent extending eighteen hundred miles in front of the Atlantic, and permitting an extension in breadth as far as the South Sea, look upon the claim 'to bind them in all cases whatsoever,' as unjust, illegal, and detestable. Let us suppose for a moment, that they are grossly mistaken; yet an error imbibed by millions, and in which they believe the all of the present and future generations lies at stake, may prove a very dangerous error. Destroying the Americans, will not cure them; nor will any acts that condemn them to starve or be miserable, have any tendency to persuade them that these acts were made by their friends." [3] "My lord, the violence of the present measures has almost instantaneously created a continental union, a continental currency, a continental army; and before this can reach your lordship, they will be as equal in discipline, as they are superior in cause and spirit, to any regulars. The most zealous Americans could not have effected in an age, what the cruelty and violence of administration has effectually brought to pass in a day." [4] "In this respect, as well as in the strong sense of liberty, and in the use of firearms almost from the cradle, the Americans have vastly the advantage over men of their rank almost everywhere else. From the constant topic of present conversation, every child unborn will be impressed with the notion—it is slavery

---

[1] "The Law of Liberty," etc., vi.   [2] Ibid. vi.–vii.
[3] Ibid. ix.–x.   [4] Ibid. xiii.–xiv.

to be bound at the will of another ' in all cases whatsoever.' Every mother's milk will convey a detestation of
this maxim. Were your lordship in America, you might
see little ones acquainted with the word of command before
they can distinctly speak, and shouldering the resemblance
of a gun before they are well able to walk." [1]

Such was the essence of Zubly's doctrine touching Revolutionary politics. Such, also, was its limitation. In his
opinion, the colonial policy of the British parliament constituted a set of grievances not to be borne by free men—
grievances to be thrown off by all means, even by a resort
to war—grievances to be thrown off by all means this side
of separation from the empire. That those grievances
could thus be thrown off, he doubted not. That separation
from the empire had become necessary for that purpose,
or was likely ever to become so, he did not believe. And
this opinion, which he held from the beginning, he held to
the end. In June, 1766, on the repeal of the Stamp Act,
he had said in a sermon at Savannah, with reference to any
man who would divide British America from Britain—" let
him be accursed by both." [2] And in 1775, after men's sincerity in political speculation had come to the test of blood,
in his sermon before the provincial congress of Georgia, he
reaffirmed this opposition to Independence: " The idea of
a separation between America and Great Britain is big with
so many and such horrid evils, that every friend to both
must shudder at the thought. Every man that gives the
most distant hint of such a wish, ought instantly to be suspected as a common enemy. Nothing would more effectually serve the cause of our enemies, than any proposal of
this kind. All wise men, and all good men, would instantly
speak, write, and act against it. Such a proposal, whenever
it should be made, would be an inlet to greater evils than
any we have yet suffered." [3]

---

[1] " The Law of Liberty," etc., xv.
[2] " The Stamp Act Repealed," 19.
[3] " The Law of Liberty," etc., 25.

When, however, a few months later, many of Zubly's colleagues in political action began to go over to this long repudiated doctrine of separation, he was ferociously denounced, and his character blackened, for the reason that he was unwilling to go with them. That such should have been his fate, especially at such a time, was natural. Nevertheless, the judgment of history must be, that while he and they had alike for years disclaimed and denounced every idea of Independence, they at last came to take a different view of the matter, and he did not. Having shared in the earlier stages of a great political agitation, Zubly could not admit that anything had in the meantime occurred to justify an abandonment of the limits that had been originally fixed for it. His crime was that of every man who begins as a political reformer and refuses to end as a revolutionist.

V.

For palpable reasons, both political and military, it happened that between January and July, 1776, the focal point of the debate over the proposal of Independence was Philadelphia. Shall the American Congress, which had hitherto mentioned that word only to ban it, now bestow upon it an official blessing ? Upon that question, even so early as in April, 1776, the minds of all Americans were violently stirred. At Philadelphia, among the most conspicuous of those who were ready to have Congress give its sanction to the word Independence, was Benjamin Franklin, then but a twelvemonth returned from his long sojourn in England, crowned with years and with honors, the most illustrious American at that time in the world. Among those who would refuse to have Congress give its sanction to Independence, was the Reverend William Smith, provost of the College of Philadelphia, orator, writer, a plausible, brilliant, captivating man, an active supporter of all the measures of American opposition down to that time, suspected, however, of having his eye steadfastly fixed on a mitre, suspected, also, of acting just then under the special advice and favor of the king.

On the thirteenth of March, there appeared in the " Pennsylvania Gazette " the first of a series of powerful essays, devoted, in part, to a hostile discussion of the pamphlet " Common Sense," and of the terrible political heresy to which that pamphlet had already won so many converts. These essays, eight in number, bore the title of " Letters of Cato, to the People of Pennsylvania." They were in process of publication from week to week, until the twenty-fourth of April. Partly because they were very able, and partly because they were at once suspected to be by so eminent a citizen and so eminent a Whig as Provost William Smith, they created a most violent fluttering in the highest social circles of Philadelphia, as well as among all ranks of politicians then gathered there. For a modern reader there can be no better reproduction of the very stir and tumult then agitating the capital of the new nation in the weeks immediately preceding the decision for Independence, than is to be derived from one of the replies then given to these " Letters of Cato." [1] This reply was in the form of a playful tract by Francis Hopkinson, entitled " A Prophecy," wherein some seer of an age in the remote past is represented as having a vision of the great and anxious scene then enacting in Philadelphia, in that April, 1776:

" Now it shall come to pass in the latter days, that a new people shall rise up in a far country, and they shall increase exceedingly, and many shall flock unto them; and they shall build cities in the wilderness, and cultivate their lands with the hand of industry, and the fame of them shall spread far and near.

---

[1] There need be no doubt that Provost Smith was " Cato." In a letter to his wife, written from Philadelphia April 28, 1776, John Adams mentions that it was then " so reported." Francis Hopkinson, in a publication made during Smith's lifetime, expressly declares that it was a fact. Finally the great-grandson and biographer of William Smith expressly admits the fact. " Familiar Letters of John Adams and His Wife," 167 ; Hopkinson's " Works," i. 94 ; " Life and Correspondence of William Smith," by H. W. Smith, i. 575.

" And it shall be that the king of islands shall send over and plant in the midst of them a certain tree.[1] Its blossoms shall be delightful to the eye, its fruit pleasant to the taste; and its leaves shall heal them of all manner of diseases. And the people shall cultivate this tree with all possible care; and they shall live under the shadow of its branches, and shall worship it as a god.

" But in process of time, there shall arise a North[2] wind, and shall blast the tree, so that it shall no longer yield its fruit, or afford shelter to the people, but it shall become rotten at the heart; and the North wind will break the branches thereof, and they shall fall upon the heads of the people, and wound many.

" Then a prophet[3] shall arise from amongst this people, and he shall exhort them, and instruct them in all manner of wisdom, and many shall believe in him; and he shall wear spectacles upon his nose; and reverence and esteem shall rest upon his brow. And he will cry aloud, and say: ' Seeing that this tree hath no strength in it, and that it can no longer shelter us from the winds of the North, but is become rotten in the heart, behold now let us cut it down and remove it from us. And in its place we will plant another tree,[4] young and vigorous; and we will water it, and it shall grow, and spread its branches abroad. And, moreover, we will build an high wall to defend it from the winds of the North, that it may be well with us, and our children, and our children's children.'

" And the people shall hearken to the voice of their prophet, for his sayings shall be good in their eyes. And they shall take up every man his spade and his axe,[5] and shall prepare to dig up and cut away the shattered remains

---

[1] English colonial government in America.

[2] The too obvious facilities offered by the name of George the Third's famous prime minister were a constant source of temptation to political punsters on both sides of the Atlantic.

[3] Dr. Franklin.

[4] American Independence.

[5] The military uprising of the Americans, especially on and after April 19, 1775.

of the blasted and rotten tree, according to the words of their prophet.

" Then a certain wise man [1] shall arise, and shall call himself Cato; and he shall strive to persuade the people to put their trust in the rotten tree, and not to dig it up, or remove it from its place. And he shall harangue with great vehemence, and shall tell them that a rotten tree is better than a sound one; and that it is for the benefit of the people that the North wind should blow upon it, and that the branches thereof should be broken and fall upon and crush them.

" And he shall receive from the king of the islands fetters of gold and chains of silver [2]; and he shall have hopes of great reward if he will fasten them on the necks of the people, and chain them to the trunk of the rotten tree. And this he shall strive to do by every insinuating art in his power. And he shall tell the people that they are not fetters and chains, but shall be as bracelets of gold on their wrists, and rings of silver on their necks, to ornament and decorate them and their children. And his words shall be sweet in the mouth, but very bitter in the belly.

" Moreover, he will threaten them that, if they will not obey his voice, he will whistle with his lips, and raw-head and bloody-bones shall come out of France [3] to devour them and their little one; and he will blow with his horn, and the wild bull of Spain will come and gore them with his horns, and trample upon them with his hoofs, even until they die. And he shall stand upon Mount-seir, and shall pun upon Mount-seir in the face of all the people. And all the people shall laugh him to scorn.

" And it shall come to pass that certain other wise men

---

[1] The Reverend William Smith, D.D., provost of the College of Philadelphia.

[2] Dr. Smith was accused of promising offices, titles, and other marks of royal favor as a reward for opposing American Independence.

[3] A frequent and very formidable argument against Independence was that, on losing the protection of England, America would be overrun and parcelled out between France and Spain.

shall also stand up and oppose themselves to Cato; and shall warn the people not to trust in the allurements of his voice, nor to be terrified with his threats, and to hearken to his puns no more. And they shall encourage the people to go on with the work they had taken in hand according to the words of their prophet. And they shall earnestly exhort the people to despise and reject the fetters of gold and the chains of silver, which the king of the islands would fasten upon them.

" And one of these men shall call himself Cassandra,[1] and the other shall call himself the Forester[2]: and they shall fall upon Cato, and shall strip him of every disguise, and show him naked before all the people. And Cassandra shall tie him up, and the Forester shall scourge him until he shall become exceeding sore. Nevertheless, Cato shall not repent, but shall harden his heart, and become very stubborn, and shall be vexed till he die. . . .

" And in process of time, the people shall root up the rotten tree, and in its place they shall plant a young and vigorous tree, and shall effectually defend it from the winds of the North by an high wall. And they shall dress it, and prune it, and cultivate it to their own liking. And the young tree shall grow and flourish and spread its branches far abroad; and the people shall dwell under the shadow of its branches, and shall become an exceeding great, and powerful, and happy nation. And of their increase there shall be no end. And Cato and his works shall be no more remembered amongst them. For Cato shall die, and his works shall follow him."[3]

---

[1] Said to be James Cannon, a tutor in the College of Philadelphia, who thus attacked his own official chief. " Letters of John Adams, Addressed to his Wife," i. 105.

[2] Thomas Paine who, during April and May, 1776, published in the Philadelphia newspapers four articles over that signature, the fame of which paled in the incomparable success of his pamphlet entitled " Common Sense."

[3] Hopkinson, " The Miscellaneous Essays," etc., i. 92–97.

VI.

Perhaps no other living voice then lifted up among the people in championship of the proposed assertion of complete nationality, spoke out with greater authority, than the voice of William Henry Drayton, then chief justice of South Carolina by appointment of its provincial congress, himself of an opulent and aristocratic family in that colony, educated at Westminster School and at Baliol College, Oxford, and already distinguished for his activity as a political writer,—an activity which did not cease until shortly before his death in 1779.

In politics, his master principle seems to have been individualism—personal and local; and he was, perhaps, the first citizen of South Carolina to set forth on behalf of his own neighborhood those extreme claims to political autonomy which have since had both a brilliant and a tragic connection with the history of that State. In 1769, under his favorite signature of " Freeman," he wrote against the new patriotic " associations " then pushing for adoption in the several colonies—to which he objected for the characteristic reason that, under the pretence of promoting liberty, they wrought the most brutal " encroachments on his private rights." [1] Being on this account regarded as a friend of prerogative, he enjoyed for some years the royal favor, which was shown by his appointment as privy councillor for South Carolina in 1771, and as assistant judge in 1774. Gradually, however, the ministerial policy toward the colonies aroused his jealousy on behalf of the same imperiled interest—that of individual rights; and in August, 1774, he published in Charleston a bold and powerful pamphlet, entitled " Letter from Freeman of South Carolina, to the Deputies of North America, assembled in the High Court of Congress at Philadelphia." In consequence of the antiministerial position taken by Drayton in this pamphlet, he was shortly afterward removed from his offices as assistant

---

[1] J. Drayton, " Memoirs of the American Revolution," i. xiv.

judge and privy councilor—a chastisement which had the effect of winning for him the confidence and affection of the Revolutionist party.   In 1775, he was made a member both of the council of safety and of the provincial congress in South Carolina ; in March, 1776, he was made chief justice.   In October, 1776, over the signature of " A Carolinian," Drayton published a trenchant address to Lord Howe and to General Sir William Howe, exposing the dangerous tendency of their declaration for restoring peace to the colonies.[1]   In January, 1778, he delivered before the general assembly of South Carolina a speech against the ratification by that State of the articles of confederation,[2]—the burden of his argument being one upon which the subsequent decade threw a grotesque light,—namely, that, by those articles, the States were stripped of powers that they could not safely part with, while thereby was created a central government of portentous aspect through its enormous accumulation of authority!   In September, 1778, he published " An Answer to the Letters and Addresses of the Commissioners " of the king [3]—probably Drayton's last contribution to the literary discussion of Revolutionary topics.

It was while serving in his great office as chief justice of South Carolina, and in accordance with a custom then prevalent, that he delivered from time to time a series of oratorical and politico-legal harangues to the grand jury, on the leading questions then at issue.   In one of these harangues, he virtually issued on behalf of his own colony, a declaration of independence, more than two months in advance of the more renowned Declaration made by the Continental Congress on behalf of all the colonies; for, so early as the 23d of April, 1776, acting as chief justice, he gave from the bench the opinion that, by " the law of the land," and in consequence of violence done to American rights by King George the Third, that monarch had " abdi-

---

[1] John Drayton, " Memoirs of the American Revolution," i. xvii.

[2] Niles, " Principles and Acts," etc., 98–115.

[3] " The Remembrancer," vii. 55–64.

cated the government " of South Carolina, and that, with respect to that particular colony, the throne had become vacant—the king having henceforth " no authority " there, and its people owing " no obedience to him." As this fearless and trenchant speech of the Revolutionary chief justice of South Carolina was couched in the language of judicial authority, and was delivered from the bench to the grand jury with all the ceremony of the judicial function, it deeply impressed the popular imagination, and seemed to give to a measure previously called lawless the consecration of law.[1]

---

[1] Any reader who may care to go more deeply into this curious phase of Revolutionary agitation, will find it profitable to read the three principal charges given by Mr. Chief Justice Drayton, which may be conveniently found as follows : for April 23, 1776, in Niles, " Principles and Acts," etc., 72–80 ; for October 15, 1776, ibid. 81–92 ; for October 15, 1777, ibid. 92–98.

CHAPTER XXIII.

THOMAS JEFFERSON AND THE GREAT DECLARATION.

I.

ON the twenty-first of June, 1775, Thomas Jefferson took his seat for the first time as a member of the Continental Congress, bringing with him into that famous assemblage, as we are told by an older member of it, " a reputation for literature, science, and a happy talent of composition. Writings of his were handed about, remarkable for the peculiar felicity of expression." [1] He had then but recently passed his thirty-second birthday, and was known to be the author of two or three public papers of considerable note.

Of these, the first one, written in 1769, could hardly have been among those compositions of his which were handed about for the admiration of Congress: it consisted of the " Resolutions of the Virginia House of Burgesses " in response to the speech of their new governor, Lord Botetourt, and was remarkable for nothing so much as for its obsequious tone—especially for its meek assurance on behalf of the burgesses that, in all their deliberations, it should be their " ruling principle " to consider the interests of Virginia and those of Great Britain as " inseparably the same." [2]

His second public paper, written in the early summer of 1774, indicates how perfectly, within that interval of five years, this adept at " felicity of expression " had passed from the stage of deference, to something bordering on that of truculence, as regards the official custodians of authority. The extraordinary composition now referred to, was first published at Williamsburg in the year in which it was written, and bears the following title: " A Summary View of the Rights of British America. Set Forth in Some Resolutions intended for the Inspection of the Present Delegates of the People of Virginia now in Convention." [3] Herein his majesty is informed, without the waste of a single word in mere politeness, that " he is no more than the chief officer of the people, appointed by the laws, and circumscribed with definite powers, to assist in working the great machine

---

[1] John Adams, in " The Life of Timothy Pickering," by Charles Wentworth Upham, iv. 466–467; also, in " The Works of John Adams," ii. 513–514 n.

[2] " Journal of the House of Burgesses for 1769," p. 4; reprinted in " The Writings of Jefferson," Ford ed., i. 369.

[3] Ibid. 421–447.

of government erected for their use, and consequently sub-ject to their superintendence." This, of course, might be a somewhat novel and startling view of himself for the "chief magistrate of the British empire" to take; but after he shall have got accustomed to it, he would see, doubtless, how eminently fitting it was that he should at last receive from the people of America a "joint address, penned in the language of truth, and divested of those expressions of servility which would persuade his majesty that we were asking favors, and not rights."[1] "Let those flatter who fear: it is not an American art. To give praise which is not due might be well from the venal, but would ill become those who are asserting the rights of human nature. They know, and will therefore say, that kings are the servants, not the proprietors, of the people. Open your breast, sire, to liberal and expanded thought. Let not the name of George the Third be a blot in the page of history. . . . The whole art of government consists in the art of being honest. Only aim to do your duty, and mankind will give you credit where you fail. No longer persevere in sac-rificing the rights of one part of the empire to the inordinate desires of another, but deal out to all equal and impartial right. . . . This, sire, is the advice of your great American council, on the observance of which may perhaps depend your felicity and future fame, and the preservation of that harmony which alone can continue both in Great Britain and America the reciprocal advantages of their con-nection."[2] Another notable state paper of Jefferson's, was one on which he had been engaged immediately prior to his departure from the legislature of Virginia, in order to take his seat in Congress,—an "Address of the House of Bur-gesses,"[3] adopted June 12, 1775, and having reference to Lord North's plan for conciliating the American colonies. In this paper, the burgesses of Virginia are made to review the long record of political blunders and crimes perpetrated

---

[1] "The Writings of Thomas Jefferson," Ford ed., i. 429.
[2] Ibid. 446.   [3] Ibid. 455–459.

by the British government in its relation to America, and then to declare that, for the further management of the dispute, they looked to the General Congress.

II.

Certainly, it is not strange that the more radical members of Congress welcomed among them this young man, who, being in opinion even more radical than themselves, also possessed so striking a talent for unabashed and sonorous talk to governors of royal provinces and even to kings. Moreover, he soon won the hearts of the speech makers in that body by being himself no speech maker; and while he thus avoided irritating collisions and rivalries with his associates, he commanded their further admiration by being always " prompt, frank, explicit, and decisive upon committees and in conversation,"—not even Samuel Adams himself being more so.[1] Accordingly, only three days after he had taken his seat, the great honor was paid him of being joined with the foremost political writer of the day—the author of the " Farmer's Letters "—as a special committee for preparing the declaration of the Americans on taking up arms.[2] Furthermore, in less than a month after his arrival, this novice in congressional business was given the second place on a committee, consisting of such veterans as Franklin, John Adams, and Richard Henry Lee, appointed to draft the American reply to Lord North's conciliatory propositions.[3]

Thus it came to pass, that when, early in June, 1776, Congress saw before it the probability of its soon adopting

---

[1] " The Works of John Adams," ii. 514 n.

[2] For this declaration, Jefferson prepared two drafts, both of which are given in Ford's edition of his " Writings," i. 462–476. The famous and noble declaration actually proclaimed by Congress, was wholly the work of Dickinson ; although, through an error of memory to which, in such matters, Jefferson was peculiarly liable, he himself, in his " Autobiography," laid claim to the authorship of " the last four paragraphs and the half of the preceding one." Ibid. 17.

[3] His rough draft for this important paper is given by Ford, in Jefferson's " Writings," i. 476–482.

32

the tremendous resolution,—"that these United Colonies are, and of right ought to be, free and independent States; that they are absolved from all allegiance to the British crown; and that all political connection between them and the state of Great Britain is, and ought to be, totally dissolved," [1] — then Thomas Jefferson, receiving the largest number of votes, was placed at the head of the committee of illustrious men to whom was assigned the task of preparing a suitable Declaration of Independence, and thereby he became the draftsman of the one American state paper that has reached to supreme distinction in the world, and that seems likely to last as long as American civilization lasts.

III.

It can hardly be doubted that some hindrance to a right estimate of the Declaration of Independence is occasioned by either of two opposite conditions of mind, both of which are often to be met with among us: on the one hand, a condition of hereditary, uncritical awe and worship of the American Revolution and of this state paper as its absolutely perfect and glorious expression; on the other hand, a later condition of cultivated distrust of the Declaration, as a piece of writing lifted up into inordinate renown by the passionate and heroic circumstances of its origin, and ever since then extolled beyond reason by the blind energy of patriotic enthusiasm. Turning from the former state of mind,—which obviously calls for no further comment,— we may note, as a partial illustration of the latter, that American confidence in the supreme intellectual merit of this all-famous document received a serious wound, some forty years ago, from the hand of Rufus Choate, when, with a courage greater than would now be required for such an act, he characterized it as made up of "glittering and sounding generalities of natural right." [2] What the great advocate then so unhesitantly suggested, many a thought-

[1] " Journals of the American Congress," i. 368–369.
[2] " Letter of Rufus Choate to the Whigs of Maine," 1856.

ful American since then has at least suspected,—that this famous proclamation, as a piece of political literature, cannot stand the test of modern analysis; that it belongs to the immense class of over-praised productions; that it is, in fact, a stately patchwork of sweeping propositions of somewhat doubtful validity; that it has long imposed upon mankind by the well-known effectiveness of verbal glitter and sound; that, at the best, it is an example of florid political declamation belonging to the sophomoric period of our national life—a period which, as we flatter ourselves, we have now outgrown.

Nevertheless, it is to be noted that, whatever authority the Declaration of Independence has acquired in the world, has been due to no lack of criticism, either at the time of its first appearance or since then,—a fact which seems to tell in favor of its essential worth and strength. From the date of its orginal publication down to the present moment, it has been attacked again and again, either in anger or in contempt, by friends as well as by enemies of the American Revolution, by liberals in politics as well as by conservatives. It has been censured for its substance, it has been censured for its form: for its misstatements of fact, for its fallacies in reasoning; for its audacious novelties and paradoxes, for its total lack of all novelty, for its repetition of old and threadbare statements, even for its downright plagiarisms; finally, for its grandiose and vaporing style.

IV.

One of the earliest and ablest of its assailants was Thomas Hutchinson, the last civil governor of the colony of Massachusetts, who, being stranded in London by the political storm which had blown him thither, published there, in the autumn of 1776, his " Strictures upon the Declaration of the Congress at Philadelphia " [1]; wherein, with an unsur-

---

[1] His pamphlet is dated October 15, 1776. The copy of it now before me, the property of Cornell University, is the very copy presented " To Sir Francis Bernard, Bart., From the Author."

passed knowledge of the origin of the controversy, and with an unsurpassed acumen in the discussion of it, he traverses the entire document, paragraph by paragraph, for the purpose of showing that its allegations in support of American Independence are " false and frivolous." [1]

A better written, and, upon the whole, a more effective arraignment of the great Declaration, was the celebrated pamphlet by an English barrister, John Lind, " An Answer to the Declaration of the American Congress,"—a pamphlet evidently written at the instigation of the ministry, and sent abroad under its approval. Here, again, the manifesto of Congress is subjected to a searching criticism, in order to show that the theory of government put forward in its preamble is " absurd and visionary " [2]; that its political maxims are not only " repugnant to the British constitution " but " subversive of every actual or imaginable kind of government " [3]; and that its specific charges against the king and parliament are " calumnies," [4]—since they allege as usurpations and as encroachments certain acts of government under George the Third identical in character with those which had been " constantly exercised by his predecessors and their parliaments," and which had been on many occasions recognized as constitutional by the American colonial assemblies. [5] It is doubtful if any disinterested student of history, any competent judge of reasoning, will now deny to this pamphlet the praise of making out a strong case against the historical accuracy and the logical soundness of many parts of the Declaration of Independence.

Undoubtedly, the force of such censures is for us much broken by the fact, that those censures proceeded from men who were themselves partisans in the Revolutionary controversy and bitterly hostile to the whole movement which the Declaration was intended to justify. Such is not the case, however, with the leading modern English critics of the

[1] " Strictures," etc., 3.   [2] " An Answer," etc., 119.
[3] Ibid.   [4] Ibid. 5.   [5] Ibid. 123–130.

same document, who, while blaming in severe terms the policy of the British government toward the Thirteen Colonies, have also found much to abate from the confidence due to this official announcement of the reasons for our secession from the empire. For example, Earl Russell, after frankly saying that the great disruption proclaimed by the Declaration of Independence, was a result which Great Britain had " used every means most fitted to bring about," such as " vacillation in council, harshness in language, feebleness in execution, disregard of American sympathies and affections," also pointed out that " the truth of this memorable Declaration " was " warped " by " one singular defect," namely, its exclusive and excessive arraignment of George the Third " as a single and despotic tyrant," much like Philip the Second to the people of the Netherlands.[1]

This temperate criticism from an able and a liberal English statesman of the present century, may be said to touch the very core of the problem as to the historic justice of our great indictment of the last king of America; and there is deep significance in the fact, that this is the very criticism upon the document, which, as John Adams tells us, he himself had in mind when it was first submitted to him in committee, and even when, shortly afterwards, he advocated its adoption by Congress. After mentioning certain things in it with which he was delighted, he adds: " There were other expressions which I would not have inserted if I had drawn it up,—particularly that which called the king tyrant. I thought this too personal; for I never believed George to be a tyrant in disposition and in nature. I always believed him to be deceived by his courtiers on both sides of the Atlantic, and, in his official capacity only, cruel. I thought the expression too passionate, and too much like scolding, for so grave and solemn a document; but, as Franklin and Sherman were to inspect it afterwards, I

[1] Russell, Lord John, " Memorials and Correspondence of Charles James Fox," i. 151–152.

thought it would not become me to strike it out. I consented to report it."[1]

A more minute and a more poignant criticism of the Declaration of Independence has been made in recent years by still another English writer of liberal tendencies, who, however, in his capacity as critic, seems here to labor under the disadvantage of having transferred to the document which he undertakes to judge, much of the extreme dislike which he has for the man who wrote it,—whom, indeed, he regards as a sophist, as a demagogue, as quite capable of inveracity in speech, and as bearing some resemblance to Robespierre " in his feline nature, his malignant egotism, and his intense suspiciousness, as well as in his bloody-minded, yet possibly sincere, philanthropy."[2] In the opinion of Professor Goldwin Smith, our great national manifesto is written " in a highly rhetorical strain "[3]; " it opens with sweeping aphorisms about the natural rights of man, at which political science now smiles, and which . . . might seem strange when framed for slave-holding communities by a publicist who himself held slaves "[4]; while, in its specifications of facts, it " is not more scrupulously truthful than are the general utterances "[5] of the statesman who was its scribe. Its charges that the several offensive acts of the king, besides " evincing a design to

[1] " The Works of John Adams," ii. 514 n. The distinction here made by John Adams between the personal and the official character of George III., is quite pointless in its application to the Declaration of Independence ; since it is of the King's official character only that the Declaration speaks. Moreover, John Adams's testimony in 1822 that he " never believed George to be a tyrant in disposition and in nature," is completely destroyed by John Adams's own testimony on that subject as recorded at an earlier period of his life. For example, in 1780, in a letter to M. Dumas, he thus speaks of George III.— " Europe, in general, is much mistaken in that character ; it is a pity that he should be believed to be so amiable ; the truth is far otherwise. *Nerone neronior* is nearer the truth." Ibid. vii. 327.

[2] Goldwin Smith, in " The Nineteenth Century," No. 131, January, 1888, p. 109.

[3] " The United States. An Outline of Political History," 88.

[4] Ibid. 87–88.

[5] " The Nineteenth Century," No. 131, p. 111.

reduce the colonists under absolute despotism," " all had as
their direct object the establishment of an absolute tyranny," are simply " propositions which history cannot accept." [1] Moreover, the Declaration " blinks the fact that
many of the acts, styled steps of usurpation, were measures
of repression which, however unwise or excessive, had been
provoked by popular outrage." [2] " No government could
allow its officers to be assaulted and their houses sacked, its
loyal lieges to be tarred and feathered, or the property of
merchants sailing under its flag to be thrown by lawless
hands into the sea." [3] Even " the preposterous violence
and the manifest insincerity of the suppressed clause"
against slavery and the slave-trade, " are enough to create
suspicion as to the spirit in which the whole document was
framed."

V.

Finally, as has been already intimated, not even among
Americans themselves has the Declaration of Independence
been permitted to pass on into the enjoyment of its superb
renown, without much critical disparagement at the hands
of statesmen and historians.   No doubt Calhoun had its
preamble in mind, when he delcared that " nothing can be
more unfounded and false " than " the prevalent opinion
that all men are born free and equal "; for " it rests upon
the assumption of a fact which is contrary to universal
observation." [5] Of course, all Americans who have shared
to any extent in Calhoun's doctrines respecting human society, could hardly fail to agree with him in regarding as
fallacious and worthless those general propositions in the
Declaration which seem to constitute its logical starting
point, as well as its ultimate defense.

---

[1] " The United States," etc., 88.   [2] Ibid.
[3] " The Nineteenth Century," No. 131, p. 111.   [4] Ibid.
[5] " A Disquisition on Government," in " The Works of John C. Calhoun,"
i. 57.

Perhaps, however, the most frequent form of disparagement to which Jefferson's great state paper has been subjected among us, is that which would minimize his merit in composing it, by denying to it the merit of originality. For example, Richard Henry Lee sneered at it as a thing " copied from Locke's treatise on government." [1] The author of a life of Jefferson, published in the year of Jefferson's retirement from the presidency, suggests that the credit of having composed the Declaration of Independence " has been perhaps more generally, than truly, given by the public " to that great man. [2] Charles Campbell, the historian of Virginia, intimates that some expressions in the document were taken without acknowledgment from Aphra Behn's tragi-comedy, " The Widow Ranter, or, The History of Bacon in Virginia." [3] John Stockton Littell describes the Declaration of Independence as " that enduring monument at once of patriotism, and of genius and skill in the art of appropriation,"—asserting that " for the sentiments and much of the language " of it, Jefferson was indebted to Chief Justice Drayton's charge to the grand jury of Charleston delivered in April, 1776, as well as to the declaration of independence said to have been adopted by some citizens of Mecklenburg County, North Carolina, in May, 1775. Even the latest and most critical editor of the writings of Jefferson calls attention to the fact, that a glance at the declaration of rights, as adopted by Virginia on the 12th of June, 1776, " would seem to indicate the source from which Jefferson derived a most important and popular part " of his famous production. [5] By no one, however, has the charge of a lack of originality been pressed with so much decisiveness as by John Adams, who took evident pleasure in speaking of it as a document in which were merely " reca-

---

[1] " The Writings of Thomas Jefferson," H. A. Washington ed., vii. 305.
[2] Stephen Cullen Carpenter, " Memoirs of Thomas Jefferson," i. 11.
[3] " History of Virginia," 317.
[4] " Graydon's Men and Times of the American Revolution," 323 n.
[5] Paul Leicester Ford, " The Writings of Thomas Jefferson," i. Introd. xxvi.

pitulated " previous and well-known statements of American rights and wrongs,[1] and who, as late as in the year 1822, deliberately wrote that " there is not an idea in it but what had been hackneyed in Congress for two years before. The substance of it is contained in the declaration of rights and the violation of those rights, in the journals of Congress, in 1774. Indeed, the essence of it is contained in a pamphlet, voted and printed by the town of Boston, before the first Congress met, composed by James Otis, as I suppose, in one of his lucid intervals, and pruned and polished by Samuel Adams."[2]

VI.

Perhaps nowhere in our literature would it be possible to find a criticism brought forward by a really able man against any piece of writing, less applicable to the case, and of less force or value, than is this particular criticism by John Adams and others, as to the lack of originality in the Declaration of Independence. Indeed, for such a paper as Jefferson was commissioned to write, the one quality which it could not properly have had—the one quality which would have been fatal to its acceptance either by the American Congress or by the American people—is originality. They were then at the culmination of a tremendous controversy over alleged grievances of the most serious kind—a controversy that had been fiercely raging for at least twelve years. In the course of that long dispute, every phase of it, whether as to abstract right or constitutional privilege or personal procedure, had been presented in almost every conceivable form of speech. At last, they had resolved, in view of all this experience, no longer to prosecute the controversy as

---

[1] " The Works of John Adams," ii. 377.

[2] Ibid. 514 n. Thus, the ingenuous reader has the happiness of seeing the eternal fitness of things complied with, and the chief intellectual merit of the Declaration of Independence brought back to the place where it belongs, and there divided between the town of Boston, James Otis, and the Adams family.

members of the empire: they had resolved to revolt, and
casting off forever their ancient fealty to the British crown,
to separate from the empire, and to establish themselves as
a new nation among the nations of the earth. In this emergency, as it happened, Jefferson was called upon to put into
form a suitable statement of the chief considerations which
prompted them to this great act of revolution, and which,
as they believed, justified it. What, then, was Jefferson to
do ? Was he to regard himself as a mere literary essayist,
set to produce before the world a sort of prize dissertation,
—a calm, analytic, judicial treatise on history and politics
with a particular application to Anglo-American affairs,—
one essential merit of which would be its originality as a
contribution to historical and political literature ? Was he
not, rather, to regard himself as, for the time being, the
very mouthpiece and prophet of the people whom he represented, and as such required to bring together and to set in
order, in their name, not what was new, but what was old;
to gather up into his own soul, as much as possible, whatever was then also in their souls—their very thoughts and
passions, their ideas of constitutional law, their interpretations of fact, their opinions as to men and as to events in all
that ugly quarrel; their notions of justice, of civic dignity,
of human rights; finally, their memories of wrongs which
seemed to them intolerable, especially of wrongs inflicted
upon them during those twelve years by the hands of insolent and brutal men, in the name of the king, and by his
apparent command ?

Moreover, as the nature of the task laid upon him made
it necessary that he should thus state, as the reasons for
their intended act, those very considerations both as to fact
and as to opinion which had actually operated upon their
minds, so did it require him to do so, to some extent, in
the very language which the people themselves, in their
more formal and deliberate utterances, had all along been
using. In the development of political life in England and
America, there had already been created a vast literature of

constitutional progress,—a literature common to both portions of the English race, pervaded by its own stately traditions, and reverberating certain great phrases which formed,
as one may say, almost the vernacular of English justice,
and of English aspiration for a free, manly, and orderly
political life. In this vernacular the Declaration of Independence was written. The phraseology thus characteristic
of it, is the very phraseology of the champions of constitutional expansion, of civic dignity and of progress, within the
English race ever since Magna Charta; of the great state
papers of English freedom in the seventeenth century, particularly the Petition of Right in 1629, and the Bill of
Rights in 1689; of the great English charters for colonization in America; of the great English exponents of legal
and political progress,—Sir Edward Coke, John Milton,
Algernon Sidney, John Locke; finally, of the great American
exponents of political liberty and of the chief representative
bodies, whether local or general, which had convened in
America from the time of the Stamp Act Congress until
that of the Congress which resolved upon our Independence.
To say, therefore, that the official Declaration of that resolve
is a paper made up of the very opinions, beliefs, unbeliefs,
the very sentiments, prejudices, passions, even the errors in
judgment and the personal misconstructions—if they were
such—which then actually impelled the American people to
that mighty act, and that all these are expressed in the very
phrases which they had been accustomed to use, is to pay
to that state paper the highest tribute as to its fitness for
the purpose for which it was framed.

Of much of this, also, Jefferson himself seems to have been
conscious; and perhaps never does he rise before us with more
dignity, with more truth, than when, late in his lifetime,
hurt by the captious and jangling words of disparagement
then recently put into writing by his old comrade, to the
effect that the Declaration of Independence " contained no
new ideas, that it is a commonplace compilation, its sentiments hackneyed in Congress for two years before, and its

essence contained in Otis's pamphlet," Jefferson quietly replied that perhaps these statements might " all be true: of that I am not to be the judge. . . . Whether I had gathered my ideas from reading or reflection, I do not know. I know only that I turned to neither book nor pamphlet while writing it. I did not consider it as any part of my charge to invent new ideas altogether, and to offer no sentiment which had ever been expressed before." [1]

Before passing from this phase of the subject, however, it should be added that, while the Declaration of Independence lacks originality in the sense just indicated, in another and perhaps in a higher sense, it possesses originality—it is individualized by the character and the genius of its author. Jefferson gathered up the thoughts and emotions and even the characteristic phrases of the people for whom he wrote, and these he perfectly incorporated with what was already in his own mind, and then to the music of his own keen, rich, passionate, and enkindling style, he mustered them into that stately and triumphant procession wherein, as some of us still think, they will go marching on to the world's end.

There were then in Congress several other men who could have written the Declaration of Independence, and written it well—notably, Franklin, either of the two Adamses, Richard Henry Lee, William Livingston, and, best of all— but for his own opposition to the measure—John Dickinson; but had any one of these other men written the Declaration of Independence, while it would have contained, doubtless, nearly the same topics and nearly the same great formulas of political statement, it would yet have been a wholly different composition from this of Jefferson's. No one at all familiar with his other writings as well as with the writings of his chief contemporaries, could ever have a moment's doubt, even if the fact were not already notorious,

[1] " The Writings of Thomas Jefferson," H. A. Washington ed., vii. 305. This was written to Madison, 30 August, 1823, and should be compared with Madison's letter in reply, 6 September, 1823 : " Letters and Other Writings of James Madison," iii. 336–337.

that this document was by Jefferson. He put into it something that was his own, and that no one else could have put there. He put himself into it,—his own genius, his own moral force, his faith in God, his faith in ideas, his love of innovation, his passion for progress, his invincible enthusiasm, his intolerance of prescription, of injustice, of cruelty, his sympathy, his clarity of vision, his affluence of diction, his power to fling out great phrases which will long fire and cheer the souls of men struggling against political unrighteousness. And herein lies its essential originality, perhaps the most precious, and indeed almost the only, originality ever attaching to any great literary product that is representative of its time. He made for himself no improper claim, therefore, when he directed that upon the granite obelisk at his grave should be carved the words,—" Here was buried Thomas Jefferson, author of the Declaration of Independence." [1]

VII.

If the Declaration of Independence is now to be fairly judged by us, it must be judged with reference to what it was intended to be—namely, an impassioned manifesto of one party, and that the weaker party, in a violent race quarrel; of a party resolved, at last, upon the extremity of revolution, and already menaced by the inconceivable disaster of being defeated in the very act of armed rebellion against the mightiest military power on earth. This manifesto, then, is not to be censured because, being avowedly a statement of its own side of the quarrel, it does not also contain a moderate and judicial statement of the opposite side; or because, being necessarily partisan in method, it is likewise both partisan and vehement in tone; or because it bristles with accusations against the enemy so fierce and so unqualified as now to seem in some respects overdrawn; or because it resounds with certain great aphorisms about the

---

[1] Randall, " The Life of Thomas Jefferson," iii. 563.

natural rights of man, at which, indeed, political science cannot now smile except to its own discomfiture and shame —aphorisms which are likely to abide in this world as the chief source and inspiration of heroic enterprises among men for self-deliverance from oppression.

Taking into account, therefore, as we are bound to do, the circumstances of its origin, and especially its purpose as a solemn and piercing appeal to mankind, on behalf of a small and weak nation against the alleged injustice and cruelty of a great and powerful one, it still remains our duty to enquire whether, as has been asserted in our time, history must set aside either of the two central charges embodied in the Declaration of Independence.

The first of these charges affirms that the several acts complained of by the colonists, evinced " a design to reduce them under absolute despotism," and had as their " direct object the establishment of an absolute tyranny " over the American people. Was this, indeed, a groundless charge, in the sense intended by the words " despotism " and " tyranny,"—that is, in the sense commonly given to those words in the usage of the English-speaking race ? According to that usage, it was not an oriental despotism that was meant, nor a Greek tyranny, nor a Roman, nor a Spanish. The sort of despot, the sort of tyrant, whom the English people, ever since the time of King John and especially during the period of the Stuarts, had been accustomed to look for and to guard against, was the sort of tyrant or despot that could be evolved out of the conditions of English political life. Furthermore, he was not by them expected to appear among them at the outset in the fully developed shape of a Philip or an Alva in the Netherlands. They were able to recognize him, they were prepared to resist him, in the earliest and most incipient stage of his being— at the moment, in fact, when he should make his first attempt to gain all power over his people by assuming the single power to take their property without their consent. Hence is was, as Edmund Burke pointed out in the house of commons only a few weeks before the American Revolution entered upon its military phase, that in England " the great contests for freedom . . . were from the earliest times chiefly upon the question of taxing. Most of the contests in the ancient commonwealths turned primarily on the right of election of magistrates, or on the balance among the several orders of the state. The question of money was not with them so immediate. But in England it was otherwise. On this point of taxes the ablest pens and most eloquent tongues have been exercised, the greatest spirits have acted and suffered. . . . They took infinite pains to inculcate, as a fundamental principle, that in all monarchies the people must in effect themselves, mediately or immediately, possess the power of granting their own money, or no shadow of liberty could subsist. The colonies draw from you, as with their life-blood, these ideas and principles. Their love of liberty, as with you, fixed and attached on this specific point of taxing. Liberty might be safe or might be endangered in twenty other particulars without their being much pleased or alarmed. Here they felt its pulse; and as they found that beat, they thought themselves sick or sound." [1]

Accordingly, the meaning which the English race on both sides of the Atlantic were accustomed to attach to the words " tyranny " and " despotism," was a meaning to some degree ideal: it was a meaning drawn from the extraordinary political sagacity with which that race is endowed, from their extraordinary sensitiveness as to the use of the taxing-power in government, from their instinctive perception of the commanding place of the taxing-power among all the other forms of power in the state, from their perfect assurance that he who holds the purse with the power to fill it and to empty it, holds the key of the situation,—can maintain an army of his own, can rule without consulting parliament, can silence criticism, can crush opposition, can

---

[1] Speech on moving his " Resolutions for Conciliation with the Colonies," March 22, 1775. " The Works of Edmund Burke," ii. 120–121.

strip his subjects of every vestige of political life; in other words, he can make slaves of them, he can make a despot and a tyrant of himself. Therefore, the system which in the end might develop into results so palpably tyrannic and despotic, they bluntly called a tyranny and a despotism in the beginning. To say, therefore, that the Declaration of Independence did the same, is to say that it spoke good English. Of course, history will be ready to set aside the charge thus made in language not at all liable to be misunderstood, just so soon as history is ready to set aside the common opinion that the several acts of the British government, from 1763 to 1776, for laying and enforcing taxation in America, did evince a somewhat particular and systematic design to take away some portion of the property of the American people without their consent.

The second of the two great charges contained in the Declaration of Independence, while intimating that some share in the blame is due to the British parliament and to the British people, yet fastens upon the king himself as the one person chiefly responsible for the scheme of American tyranny therein set forth, and culminates in the frank description of him as " a prince whose character is thus marked by every act which may define a tyrant." Is this accusation of George the Third now to be set aside as unhistoric ? Was that king, or was he not, chiefly responsible for the American policy of the British government between the years 1763 and 1776 ? If he was so, then the historic soundness of the most important portion of the Declaration of Independence is vindicated.

Fortunately, this question can be answered without hesitation, and in few words; and for these few words, an American writer of to-day, conscious of his own bias of nationality, will rightly prefer to cite such as have been uttered by the ablest English historians of our time, who have dealt with the subject. Upon their statements alone it must be concluded, that George the Third ascended his throne with the fixed purpose of resuming to the crown many of those powers which by the constitution of England did not then belong to it, and that in this purpose, at least during the first twenty-five years of his reign, he substantially succeeded,—himself determining what should be the policy of each administration, what opinions his ministers should advocate in parliament, and what measures parliament itself should adopt. " The king desired," says Sir Erskine May, " to undertake personally the chief administration of public affairs, to direct the policy of his ministers, and himself to distribute the patronage of the crown. He was ambitious not only to reign, but to govern." " Strong as were the ministers, the king was resolved to wrest all power from their hands, and to exercise it himself." " But what was this, in effect, but to assert that the king should be his own minister ? . . . The king's tactics were fraught with danger, as well to the crown itself, as to the constitutional liberties of the people." [1]

Already, prior to the year 1778, according to Lecky, the king had " laboriously built up " in England a " system of personal government "; and it was because he was unwilling to have this system disturbed, that he then refused, " in defiance of the most earnest representations of his own minister and of the most eminent politicians of every party . . . to send for the greatest of living statesmen at the moment when the empire appeared to be in the very agonies of dissolution. . . . Either Chatham or Rockingham would have insisted that the policy of the country should be directed by its responsible ministers, and not dictated by an irresponsible sovereign." This refusal of the king to adopt the course which was called for by the constitution, and which would have taken the control of the policy of the government out of his hands, was, according to the same great historian, an act " the most criminal in the whole reign of George the Third, . . . as criminal as

---

[1] These sentences occur in the chapter on " The Influence of the Crown during the Reign of George III.," in Sir Erskine May's " Constitutional History of England," i. 11, 12, 14–15.

33

any of those acts which led Charles the First to the scaffold."[1]

Even so early as the year 1768, according to John Richard Green, " George the Third had at last reached his aim." In the early days of the ministry which began in that year, " his influence was felt to be predominant. In its later and more disastrous days it was supreme; for Lord North, who became the head of the ministry on Grafton's retirement in 1770, was the mere mouthpiece of the king. ' Not only did he direct the minister,' a careful observer tells us, ' in all important matters of foreign and domestic policy, but he instructed him as to the management of debates in parliament, suggested what motions should be made or opposed, and how measures should be carried. He reserved for himself all the patronage, he arranged the whole cast of the administration, settled the relative place and pretensions of ministers of state, law officers, and members of the household, nominated and promoted the English and Scotch judges, appointed and translated bishops and deans, and dispensed other preferments in the church. He disposed of military governments, regiments, and commissions, and himself ordered the marching of troops. He gave and refused titles, honors, and pensions.' All this immense patronage was steadily used for the creation and maintenance of a party in both houses of parliament attached to the king himself. . . . George was, in fact, sole minister during the fifteen years which followed; and the shame of the darkest hour of English history lies wholly at his door."[2]

Surely, until these tremendous verdicts of English history shall be set aside, there need be no anxiety in any quarter as to the historic soundness of the two great accusations which together make up the principal portion of the Declaration of Independence. In the presence of these verdicts, also, even the passion, the intensity of language, in

---

[1] " A History of England in the Eighteenth Century," iv. 457–458.
[2] " A Short History of the English People," 736–737.

which those accusations are uttered, seem to find a perfect justification. Indeed, in the light of the most recent and most unprejudiced expert testimony, the whole document, both in its substance and in its form, seems to have been the logical response of a nation of brave men to the great words of the greatest of English statesmen, as spoken in the house of commons precisely ten years before: " This kingdom has no right to lay a tax on the colonies.[1] . . . Sir, I rejoice that America has resisted. Three millions of people so dead to all the feelings of liberty as voluntarily to submit to be slaves, would have been fit instruments to have made slaves of the rest." [2]

VIII.

It is proper for us to remember that what we call criticism, is not the only valid test of the genuineness and worth of any piece of writing of great practical interest to mankind: there is, also, the test of actual use and service in the world, in direct contact with the common sense and the moral sense of large masses of men, under various conditions, and for a long period. Probably no writing which is not essentially sound and true has ever survived this test.

Neither from this test has the great Declaration any need to shrink. Probably no public paper ever more perfectly satisfied the immediate purposes for which it was sent forth. From one end of the country to the other, and as fast as it could be spread among the people, it was greeted in public and in private with every demonstration of approval and delight.[3] To a marvelous degree, it quickened the friends of the Revolution for their great task. " This Declaration," wrote one of its signers but a few days after it had been

---

[1] " The Celebrated Speech of a Celebrated Commoner," London, 1766, p. 5.
[2] Ibid. 12.
[3] Frank Moore, in his " Diary of the American Revolution," i. 269–285, has given extracts from the American newspapers for July and August, 1776, describing the official and popular demonstrations in many of the States at the first reading of the Declaration.

proclaimed, " has had a glorious effect—has made these colonies all alive." [1] " With the Independency of the American States," said another political leader a few weeks later, " a new era in politics has commenced. Every consideration respecting the propriety or impropriety of a separation from Britain is now entirely out of the question. . . . Our future happiness or misery, therefore, as a people, will depend entirely upon ourselves." [2]   Six years afterward, in a review of the whole struggle, a great American scholar expressed his sense of the relation of this document to it, by saying, that " into the monumental act of Independence," Jefferson had " poured the soul of the continent." [3]

Moreover, during the century and a quarter since the close of the Revolution, the influence of this state paper on the political character and the political conduct of the American people has been great beyond all calculation. For example, after we had achieved our own national deliverance, and had advanced into that enormous and somewhat corrupting material prosperity which followed the adoption of the constitution, the development of the cotton interest, and the expansion of the republic into a trans-continental power, we fell, as is now most apparent, under an appalling national temptation,—the temptation to forget, or to repudiate, or to refuse to apply to the case of our human brethren in bondage, the very principles which we ourselves had once proclaimed as the basis of every rightful government, and as the ultimate source of our own claim to an untrammeled national life. The prodigious service rendered to us in this awful moral emergency by the Declaration of Independence was, that its public repetition, at least once every year, in the hearing of vast throngs of the American

---

[1] William Whipple, of New Hampshire, in Force, "American Archives," 6th series, i. 368.

[2] Jonathan Elmer, of New Jersey, given in Moore, " Diary of the American Revolution," i. 279–280.

[3] Ezra Stiles, president of Yale College, in Connecticut election sermon, for 1783, p. 46.

people, in every portion of the republic, kept constantly before our minds, in a form of almost religious sanctity, those few great ideas as to the dignity of human nature, and the sacredness of personality, and the indestructible rights of man as mere man, with which we had so gloriously identified the beginnings of our national existence, and upon which we had proceeded to erect all our political institutions both for the nation and for the States. It did, indeed, at last become very hard for us to listen each year to the preamble of the Declaration of Independence, and still to remain the owners and users and catchers of slaves; still harder, to accept the doctrine that the righteousness and prosperity of slavery was to be taken as the dominant policy of the nation. The logic of Calhoun was as flawless as usual, when he concluded that the chief obstruction in the way of his system, was the preamble of the Declaration of Independence. Had it not been for the inviolable sacredness given by it to those sweeping aphorisms about the natural rights of man, it may be doubted whether, under the vast practical inducements involved, Calhoun might not have succeeded in winning over an immense majority of the American people to the support of his compact and plausible scheme for making slavery the basis of the republic. It was the preamble of the Declaration of Independence which elected Lincoln, which sent forth the Emancipation Proclamation, which gave victory to Grant, which ratified the Thirteenth Amendment.

Moreover, we cannot doubt that the permanent effects of the great Declaration on the political and even the ethical ideals of the American people are wider and deeper than can be measured by our experience in grappling with any single political problem; for they touch all the spiritual springs of American national character, and they create, for us and for all human beings, a new standard of political justice and a new principle in the science of government. " Much ridicule, a little of it not altogether undeserved," says a brilliant English scholar of our time, who is also

nobly distinguished in the sphere of English statesmanship, "has been thrown upon the opening clause of the
Declaration of Independence, which asserts the inherent
natural right of man to enjoy life and liberty, with the
means of acquiring and possessing property, and pursuing
and obtaining happiness and safety. Yet there is an implied corollary in this which enjoins the highest morality
that in our present state we are able to think of as possible.
If happiness is the right of our neighbor, then not to hinder
him but to help him in its pursuit, must plainly be our
duty. If all men have a claim, then each man is under an
obligation. The corollary thus involved is the corner-stone
of morality. It was an act of good augury thus to inscribe
happiness as entering at once into the right of all, and
into the duty of all, in the very head and front of the new
charter, as the base of a national existence, and the first
principle of a national government. The omen has not been
falsified. The Americans have been true to their first doctrine. They have never swerved aside to set up caste and
privilege, to lay down the doctrine that one man's happiness ought to be an object of greater solicitude to society
than any other man's, or that one order should be encouraged to seek its prosperity through the depression of
any other order. Their example proved infectious. The
assertion in the New World, that men have a right to happiness and an obligation to promote the happiness of one
another, struck a spark in the Old World. Political construction in America immediately preceded the last violent
stage of demolition in Europe."[1]

We shall not here attempt to delineate the influence of
this state paper upon mankind in general. Of course, the
emergence of the American Republic as an imposing world-
power is a phenomenon which has now for many years
attracted the attention of the human race. Surely, no slight
effect must have resulted from the fact that, among all civilized peoples, the one American document best known, is

[1] John Morley, "Edmund Burke : A Historical Study," 161–162.

the Declaration of Independence,[1] and that thus the spectacle of so vast and beneficent a political success has been everywhere associated with the assertion of the natural rights of man. " The doctrines it contained," says Buckle, " were not merely welcomed by a majority of the French nation, but even the government itself was unable to withstand the general feeling."[2] " Its effect in hastening the approach of the French Revolution . . . was indeed most remarkable."[3] Elsewhere, also, in many lands, among many peoples, it has been appealed to again and again as an inspiration for political courage, as a model for political conduct; and if, as the brilliant English historian just cited has affirmed, " that noble Declaration . . . ought to be hung up in the nursery of every king, and blazoned on the porch of every royal palace,"[4] it is because it has become the classic statement of political truths which must at last abolish kings altogether, or else teach them to identify their existence with the dignity and happiness of human nature.

IX.

It would be unfitting, in a work like the present, to treat of the Declaration of Independence without making more than an incidental reference to its purely literary character.

Very likely, most writings—even most writings of genuine and high quality—have had the misfortune of being read too little. There is, however, a misfortune—perhaps, a greater misfortune—which has overtaken some literary compositions, and these not necessarily the noblest and the best,—the misfortune of being read too much. At any rate, the writer of a piece of literature which has been neglected, need not be refused the consolation he may get from reflecting that he is, at least, not the writer of a piece of literature which has become hackneyed. Just this is the

---

[1] The editor of the latest edition of " The Writings of Thomas Jefferson," i. Introd. xxv., does not shrink from calling it " the paper which is probably the best known that ever came from the pen of an individual."

[2] " History of Civilization in England," 846.   [3] Ibid. 847.   [4] Ibid. 846.

sort of calamity which seems to have befallen the Declaration of Independence. Is it, indeed, possible for us Americans, near the close of the nineteenth century, to be entirely just to the literary quality of this most monumental document—this much belauded, much bespouted, much beflouted document ?—since, in order to be so, we need to rid ourselves, if we can, of the obstreperous memories of a lifetime of Independence Days, and to unlink and disperse the associations which have somehow confounded Jefferson's masterpiece with the rattle of fire-crackers, with the flash and the splutter of burning tar-barrels, and with that unreserved, that gyratory and perspiratory, eloquence now for more than a hundred years consecrated to the return of our fateful Fourth of July.

Had the Declaration of Independence been, what many a revolutionary state paper is, a clumsy, verbose, and vaporing production, not even the robust literary taste and the all-forgiving patriotism of the American people could have endured the weariness, the nausea, of hearing its repetition, in ten thousand different places, at least once every year, for so long a period. Nothing which has not supreme literary merit has ever triumphantly endured such an ordeal, or ever been subjected to it. No man can adequately explain the persistent fascination which this state-paper has had, and which it still has, for the American people, or for its undiminished power over them, without taking into account its extraordinary literary merits—its possession of the witchery of true substance wedded to perfect form :—its massiveness and incisiveness of thought, its art in the marshaling of the topics with which it deals, its symmetry, its energy, the definiteness and limpidity of its statements,[1] its exqui-

---

[1] Much has been said of the generalities, whether glittering or otherwise, of the Declaration ; yet they who have most objected to its teachings seem to have found them sufficiently specific and distinct. Its famous assertion that "all men are created equal," has been complained of as liable to be misconstrued ; "but," as a recent biographer of Jefferson cleverly says, "no intelligent man has ever misconstrued it, except intentionally." John T. Morse, Jr., "Thomas Jefferson," 40.

site diction—at once terse, musical, and electrical; and, as an essential part of this literary outfit, many of those spiritual notes which can attract and enthrall our hearts,—veneration for God, veneration for man, veneration for principle, respect for public opinion, moral earnestness, moral courage, optimism, a stately and noble pathos, finally, self-sacrificing devotion to a cause so great as to be herein identified with the happiness, not of one people only, or of one race only, but of human nature itself.

Upon the whole, this is the most commanding and the most pathetic utterance, in any age, in any language, of national grievances and of national purposes; having a Demosthenic momentum of thought, and a fervor of emotional appeal such as Tyrtæus might have put into his war-songs. Indeed, the Declaration of Independence is a kind of war-song; it is a stately and a passionate chant of human freedom; it is a prose lyric of civil and military heroism. We may be altogether sure that no genuine development of literary taste among the American people in any period of our future history can result in serious misfortune to this particular specimen of American literature.

END OF VOLUME I.